# NEW INTERNATIONAL
# BIBLICAL COMMENTARY

*Old Testament Editors,*
Robert L. Hubbard Jr.
Robert K. Johnston

# MINOR PROPHETS I

*Old Testament Series*

# NEW INTERNATIONAL BIBLICAL COMMENTARY

# MINOR PROPHETS I

# ELIZABETH ACHTEMEIER

Based on the New International Version

© 1996 by Hendrickson Publishers, Inc.
P. O. Box 3473
Peabody, Massachusetts 01961–3473

First published jointly, 1996, in the United States by Hendrickson Publishers
and in the United Kingdom by the Paternoster Press, P. O. Box 300, Carlisle,
Cumbria CA3 0QS.

*Printed in the United States of America*

*Second printing — November 1999*

### Library of Congress Cataloging-in-Publication Data

Achtemeier, Elizabeth Rice, 1926–
    Minor Prophets I  /  Elizabeth Achtemeier.
      (New International biblical commentary; 17)
      Includes bibliographical references and indexes.
      1. Bible.  O.T.  Minor Prophets—Commentaries.  I. Title.  II. Series:
New International biblical commentary.  Old Testament series; 17.
BS1560.A58   1996
224′.907—dc20                                            96–31321
                                                             CIP

ISBN 0–943575–05–2 (U.S. softcover)
ISBN 1–56563–534–5 (U.S. hardcover)

### British Library Cataloguing in Publication Data

Minor prophets I.—(New International biblical commentary; 17)
    1. Bible.   O.T. Minor Prophets. English. New International — Criticism,
interpretation, etc.
    I. Title
    224.9′06

ISBN 0–85364–809–3 (U.K. softcover)

To Bud
Committed Christian
Beloved Husband
Caring Father
Renowned Scholar
Dearest Friend

# Table of Contents

## *Joel*

## *Amos*

*Foreword*
*New International Biblical Commentary*

As an ancient document, the Old Testament often seems something quite foreign to modern men and women. Opening its pages may feel, to the modern reader, like traversing a kind of literary time warp into a whole other world. In that world sisters and brothers marry, long hair mysteriously makes men superhuman, and temple altars daily smell of savory burning flesh and sweet incense. There, desert bushes burn but leave no ashes, water gushes from rocks, and cities fall because people march around them. A different world, indeed!

Even God, the Old Testament's main character, seems a stranger compared to his more familiar New Testament counterpart. Sometimes the divine is portrayed as a loving father and faithful friend, someone who rescues people from their greatest dangers or generously rewards them for heroic deeds. At other times, however, God resembles more a cruel despot, one furious at human failures, raving against enemies and bloodthirsty for revenge. Thus, skittish about the Old Testament's diverse portrayal of God, some readers carefully select which portions of the text to study, or they avoid the Old Testament altogether.

The purpose of this commentary series is to help readers navigate this strange and sometimes forbidding literary and spiritual terrain. Its goal is to break down the barriers between the ancient and modern worlds so that the power and meaning of these biblical texts become transparent to contemporary readers. How is this to be done? And what sets this series apart from others currently on the market?

This commentary series will bypass several popular approaches to biblical interpretation. It will not follow a *precritical* approach that interprets the text without reference to recent scholarly conversations. Such a commentary contents itself with offering little more than a paraphrase of the text with occasional supplements from archaeology, word studies, and classical theology. It mistakenly believes that there have been few insights into the Bible since Calvin or Luther. Nor will this series pursue an *anticritical* approach whose preoccupation is to defend the Bible against its detractors, especially scholarly ones. Such a commentary has little space left to move beyond showing why the Bible's critics are wrong to explaining what the biblical text means. The result is a paucity of vibrant biblical theology. Again, this series finds inadequate a *critical* approach that seeks to understand the text apart from belief in the meaning it conveys. Though modern readers have been taught to be discerning, they do not want to live in the "desert of criticism" either.

Instead, as its editors, we have sought to align this series with what has been labeled *believing criticism*. This approach marries probing, reflective interpretation of the text to loyal biblical devotion and warm Christian affection. Our contributors tackle the task of interpretation using the full range of critical methodologies and practices. Yet they do so as people of faith who hold the text in the highest regard. The commentators in this series use criticism to bring the message of the biblical texts vividly to life so the minds of modern readers may be illumined and their faith deepened.

The authors in this series combine a firm commitment to modern scholarship with a similar commitment to the Bible's full authority for Christians. They bring to the task the highest technical skills, warm theological commitment, and rich insight from their various communities. In so doing, they hope to enrich the life of the academy as well as the life of the church.

Part of the richness of this commentary series derives from its authors' breadth of experience and ecclesial background. As editors, we have consciously brought together a diverse group of scholars in terms of age, gender, denominational affiliation, and race. We make no claim that they represent the full expression of the people of God, but they do bring fresh, broad perspectives to the interpretive task. But though this series has sought out diversity among its contributors, they also reflect a commitment to a common center. These commentators write as "believing critics"—scholars who desire to speak for church and academy, for academy and church. As editors, we offer this series in devotion to God and for the enrichment of God's people.

ROBERT L. HUBBARD JR.
ROBERT K. JOHNSTON
Editors

## Abbreviations

| | |
|---|---|
| *Adv. Marcion* | *Against Marcion* |
| *Ant.* | *Antiquities* |
| *ANET* | J. B. Pritchard, ed., *Ancient Near Eastern Texts* |
| cf. | compare |
| ch(s). | chapter(s) |
| Hb. | Hebrew |
| *IDB* | *The Interpreter's Dictionary of the Bible* |
| L | Leningrad Codex |
| LXX | Septuagint |
| MT | Masoretic Text |
| NIV | New International Version |
| NRSV | New Revised Standard Version |
| OTL | Old Testament Library |
| pl. | plural |
| RSV | Revised Standard Version |
| sing. | singular |
| Syr. | Syriac version |
| Tg. | Targums |
| Vg. | Vulgate |
| v(v). | verse(s) |
| *War* | *The Jewish War* |
| WBC | Word Biblical Commentary |

# Hosea

# Introduction: Hosea

## The Message of the Book

The central announcement of the prophet Hosea can be summarized in one short sentence: God promises to do what human beings ought to do but cannot. The God of Israel, Yahweh, who is revealed to us through the prophecies of Hosea, has an ongoing love story with the people of the covenant. The story started when Yahweh delivered the Israelites out of Egyptian slavery (12:13; 13:4; 11:1; 2:15), took them into the wilderness, wooed and took them as his bride (13:5; 2:14–15), and then gave them the promised land with all its gifts (2:8, 15).

Yahweh became like a husband to his beloved Israel, like a father to this infant people (11:1, 3). This relationship of inner love and devotion was beyond all concepts of legalism and overbearing domination. God desired above all else to enter into a communion with his people in which they trusted and faithfully loved God, and thus reaped the abundant life that harmony with God's will could produce.

But Israel had a rebellious spirit (12:3); as soon as she entered the promised land she turned to other lovers, the detestable baals of Canaanite fertility religion (9:10). The more the Father called to his child, the more Israel ran away like a disobedient son (11:2). Israel established a kingship under Saul that rejected Yahweh's rule (9:15), relied for security on foreign alliances instead of on Yahweh (5:13; 7:8–9, 11; 8:9–10), and set up idols to Baal throughout the land (8:4–6; 13:2). Thus, the covenant people's spirit of rebellion against God was present from the first but reaches its climax in the lack of faithfulness, covenant love, and knowledge of God in Hosea's time (4:1).

Hosea most often describes this sin in terms of Israel's "harlotry" against her divine husband. He holds the priests and the political leaders primarily responsible. The priests have led the people to look to Baal for the gifts that sustain their inner life (4:4–6). The political leaders have taught the people to trust in military strength (8:14; 10:13) and foreign alliances (7:8–11) for their external security.

Gone from Israel is the knowledge of Yahweh as the source of life and security (2:8; 4:6; 8:12). The Israelites "do not know" God. They have forgotten their God (2:13; 4:6; 8:14; 13:6). They are a people "without understanding" (4:14). Because they have abandoned the intimate communion with the Lord that is the source of all life, Israel cannot repent and return to God (5:4). Israel's destruction is therefore inevitable (5:14; 13:7–8, 9) and will take two forms, corresponding to the two primary forms of Israel's sin. First, both nature and human life will become infertile (2:9, 11–12; 9:11–14); Israel will lose the sustenance of its internal life. Second, Israel will fall victim to foreign conquerors and will cease to exist as a nation (9:3, 6, 17; 11:5). According to Hosea, the death of Israel, the rebellious son, is sure (this punishment was later codified in Deuteronomic law: Deut. 21:18–21). Israel cannot return to her divine husband (cf. Deut. 24:1–4). Israel is doomed.

Nevertheless, Hosea's promise for the future is that God will save Israel (2:14–23; 3:1–5; 11:8–11; 14:4–8). This future salvation will be totally God's act. Israel will know no savior besides Yahweh (13:4), who will heal her faithlessness and love her freely (14:4).

The salvation of the covenant people can take place, however, only if Yahweh removes from his people's lives all that would draw them away from him (2:16–17; 3:4), takes them back to Egypt (8:13; 9:3), and then from there once again leads them into the wilderness, to be wooed anew (2:14). In short, to save his people Yahweh must begin his salvation history of love with Israel all over again. This is exactly what Yahweh, through Hosea, promises he will do.

The interpreter of Hosea should ask how that promise was fulfilled. Hosea is an open-ended book, straining toward the future in God's love story with his people. We shall further discuss that future in the commentary.


### The Prophet

All we know about the prophet who delivered this remarkable message is that his father was named Beeri. From the superscription of 1:1 and the contents of his book, we can surmise that Hosea's ministry began about 750 BC and ended about 723 BC, shortly before the northern kingdom of Israel's fall to Assyria, since Hosea never mentions that final fall. We are certain that Hosea was a resident of northern Israel. He makes frequent reference to the northern cities of Gilgal, Bethel, and the capital Samaria, and he knows the political and religious situation obtaining in the North. Linguistic experts tell us that his Hebrew is marked by northern dialectic peculiarities. The northern forebear, Jacob, is the only patriarch named (12:12), and Hosea understands himself to stand in the northern line of the prophets reaching back to Moses (12:13).

It is therefore highly probable that Hosea had connections with that northern levitical reform movement which hearkened back to Mosaic pre-monarchical tribal league covenant theology, worshiped Yahweh as King, and is typified by the book of Deuteronomy. Such a reform movement probably included the prophet Jeremiah and gave form to Isaiah 56–66.[1]

No prophet, including Jeremiah, experiences a more intimate connection with his God than does Hosea, and the fact that Hosea repeatedly characterizes communion with God in terms of ʾāhab, love, and yādaʿ, intimate knowledge, testifies to the depths of that relationship. Often in the book, the prophet himself drops out of view and God speaks directly to the people through him in first person address.

Those closest to the Lord, however, often seem the ones to whom the Lord assigns the most severe trials in his service. Therefore, while Hosea is still a young man of marriageable age—perhaps in his late teens—he is commanded by Yahweh to marry a "wife of harlotry" (RSV; 1:2). That is, the woman named Gomer is already known to be given to whoredom and is neither a virgin nor inclined to faithfulness when Hosea marries her. Very likely she had succumbed to the false religion of the baal cult and had participated, perhaps sporadically, in the fertility rites involving sexual intercourse ("sacred marriage"). Baalistic religion held that by sympathetic magic, these rites would coerce Baal into granting fertility to land and humans. Hosea knows from the first what Gomer is, and he suffers for it. But by such a deed, he thereby becomes the prophetic "sign" that Yahweh too is married to the unfaithful harlot, Israel.

It is a mistake to believe that Hosea's experiences with unfaithful Gomer were the trigger that led him to see that Israel too was unfaithful to her divine husband. Hosea's marriage was the *result* of the divine word given to him; the word was not the result of the marriage. God's word precedes human action; human action does not produce the word. As Hosea lived with Gomer, his actions toward her then became what are known as "prophetic symbolic actions." That is, they became prophecies of what Yahweh would do to Israel.

It is characteristic of many of the prophets of the OT that they become suffering mediators of the word of God to their people. When they pronounce God's judgment on Israel or Judah, they must first suffer within their own lives and bodies the effects of that judgment. They bear the action of the word first! For example, Jeremiah is forbidden to marry, to go to a party, and even to attend a funeral, because God is withdrawing all grace and mercy from Judah (Jer. 16:1–9; 15:17). Similarly, Ezekiel must eat unclean food and ration his water as signs of the coming siege of Jerusalem (Ezek. 4:9–17). These prophetic symbolic actions take on the character of prophecy, and they begin the action of judgment that Yahweh will then bring to fulfillment. But the prophet does not escape the judgment. On the contrary, he experiences it first, just as the servant of Isaiah 52:13–53:12 suffers and, in final fulfillment, just as our Lord Jesus Christ dies for the sin of the nations. The word of judgment is proleptically incarnated in the prophets' lives; and finally in the NT the word of judgment becomes flesh. So Hosea bears within his life with Gomer the judgment coming upon the northern kingdom of Israel.

Over at least five years of marriage with Hosea, Gomer bears three children, only one of whom is specifically said to be Hosea's (1:3). It is very difficult to reconstruct the course of Hosea's marriage from chapters 1–3 of his book, however, because the chapters are intended to be not biography but the word of God, and there is no scholarly consensus concerning the course of the marriage. Apparently chapter 2 indicates that Hosea divorced Gomer, but then we do not know if the woman whom he buys back in chapter 3 is Gomer or another. Often the interpretation given to chapter 3 depends on whether or not the interpreter thinks the hopeful passages in the book are genuine to the prophet. Because I believe they are, I affirm that the "woman" in 3:1 is indeed Gomer.

The person who lives in intimate communion with God is often also the one who can creatively and yet authoritatively describe the character of the Lord through metaphors and similes. No one betters Hosea in such description. Throughout his book, we shall encounter startling language used to describe the

Lord that will cast new light on the character of the God of the Bible and that is to be taken with utmost seriousness as revelation of God's nature.

Like all of the prophets, Hosea met opposition in his ministry and was called a "maniac" by some of his contemporaries (9:7)—a title given as well to Elisha (2 Kgs. 9:11), Jeremiah (Jer. 29:26), Jesus (John 10:20), and Paul (Acts 26:25). The wisdom of this world does not readily accept the wisdom of God.

### The Time

The superscription (1:1) indicates that Hosea began his ministry during the last years of the reign of Jeroboam II (786–746 BC), a member of the Jehu dynasty (cf. 1:4). It was a time of stable government and economic prosperity, although, as Hosea's contemporary Amos also shows, Israel's society was sharply divided between the prosperous and the desperately poor, had corruption in law court and cult, and exhibited a general breakdown of public morality. Hosea's words in chapters 1–4 reflect a thoroughgoing syncretism with baalistic fertility religion and a loss of all covenant responsibility toward Yahweh (4:1–10).

The chapters that follow then mirror, in rough chronological order, the dissolution of the political life of the nation, which was shot through with intrigue and anarchy (cf. 2 Kgs. 15–17). Jeroboam's son, Zechariah, ruled only six months before he was assassinated by the usurper Shallum, who was in turn murdered one month later by Menahem (745–736 BC). At the same time, the great emperor of Assyria, Tiglath-pileser III (745–727 BC), ascended to that throne and led his armies in an invasion of the small states of the West. In order to survive, Menahem was forced to pay a large tribute (2 Kgs. 15:19–20). Menahem's son, Pekahiah, ruled for only two years (737–736 BC) before the anti-Assyrian party, led by Pekah ben Remaliah, assassinated him and put Pekah on the throne (cf. Hos. 7:6–7).

In 735 BC, Pekah attempted to put together a Syro-Ephraimitic alliance that would turn back Assyrian aggression, and he hoped to enlist Ahaz of Judah in such cause. When Ahaz refused he was attacked by the armies of Syria and Israel (2 Kgs. 15:37; 16:5–9; Isa. 7:1–17). This Syro-Ephraimitic war is reflected in Hosea 5:8–15. Ahaz summoned Assyria to his aid, and the result was that Assyria subjugated Israel in 733 BC, reduced its land-holdings to the capital city of Samaria and the hill country, and deported much of its population (2 Kgs. 15:29). The remnant of the country was saved only by Hoshea ben Elah's (732–724 BC) assassination of Pekah and submission as a vassal to Assyria (Hos. 8:9–10).

Some portions of Hosea 9–12 reflect the relatively quiet time under the rule of Assyria before Shalmaneser V took the throne of that empire (726–722 BC). However, the small states of the ancient Near Eastern world vacillated constantly between alliance to one or another empire of Mesopotamia and of Egypt, and Israel was never an exception (cf. Hos. 7:11). Hosea 11:5 and 12:1 probably reflect the fact that when Shalmaneser took the throne, King Hoshea sent a mission to Egypt in the hope that the Pharaoh would support him in a rebellion against Assyria (2 Kgs. 17:4). As a result, Shalmaneser invaded Palestine in 724 BC, imprisoned Hoshea (Hos. 13:10), and laid siege to Samaria, which then fell to his successor, Sargon II (721–705 BC). In 721 BC Israel's remaining population was deported and replaced with aliens, and the ten northern tribes of Israel disappeared from history (2 Kgs. 17:24). Hosea does not record the final fall, but one of his latest texts, 13:16, reflects Samaria under siege.

## Form and Transmission

The book of Hosea divides into two broad sections, chapters 1–3 and 4–14, with the former providing something of a summary of the message of the whole. Chapters 1–3 have five distinct passages that alternate between messages of doom and of hope for the future—an arrangement that is probably the work of a disciple of Hosea. That a hand besides that of the prophet himself has worked on the book is clear from the biographical accounts in 1:2–6, 8–9.

The division of chapters 4–14 into separate oracles is not so clear, however. Typical beginning and ending prophetic formulae, "Thus says the LORD" and "oracle of Yahweh," are often missing, and the oracles alternate constantly between the first person speech of Yahweh and the third person speech of the prophet, sometimes even within the same oracle. Nor is there an overarching structure or progression of thought in the section. Themes and thoughts are often repeated, albeit in different words, and it appears that separate oracles have been loosely joined together by catchwords or common themes. Thus, the way this commentary divides chapters 4–14 into separate oracles may sometimes be open to question.

The preservation of Hosea's book after the fall of the northern kingdom shows that it was carried to the southern kingdom of Judah either by the prophet himself or by his disciples. We have no evidence of Hosea's final fate; he could have been exiled with his compatriots, or he might have escaped to the south. There are a number of references to Judah in the book, some judgmental, some promissory, and each must be assessed as to whether it was part of Hosea's original preaching or was added later by a Judean hand. These questions will be dealt with in the commentary, but certainly most of the book originated with the prophet himself, though 1:1a and 14:9 are most likely added by a later editor.

Hosea was a master of language, and the Hebrew of the book exhibits frequent use of repetition, assonance, and alliteration; sadly, these are largely lost in translation into English.

## The Text

The Hebrew text of Hosea is unfortunately one of the worst-preserved texts in the Scriptures. Some scholars suggest that it was damaged when it was carried to the South after the fall of the northern kingdom, a suggestion that implies that Hosea himself did not escape southward. Other scholars point to peculiar northern dialectic difficulties that make the text hard to read. Reconstruction of difficult passages often requires reference to the Greek Septuagint or, less frequently, to the Syriac, Latin, and Aramaic versions. These instances will be noted in the commentary. However, it is my practice to emend the Hebrew Scriptures only when absolutely necessary in order to garner any sense whatsoever from the MT, and thus my emendations may be fewer than those of many other commentators.

Though we are dealing with the NIV in this commentary series, frequent reference will be made to the RSV translations, which are often closer to the original Hebrew than are either the NIV or, for that matter, the NRSV. The RSV translation has largely disappeared from bookstore shelves and catalogues, in order that publishers may sell the NRSV. But the RSV is a treasure not to be lost, and this commentary will frequently refer to its readings.

## Note

1. See E. Achtemeier, *The Community and Message of Isaiah 56–66* (Minneapolis: Augsburg, 1982), and *Jeremiah,* Knox Preaching Guides (Atlanta: John Knox, 1987). Paul Hanson, *The Dawn of Apocalyptic: The Historical and Sociological Roots of Jewish Apocalyptic Eschatology,* revised edition (Philadelphia: Fortress, 1979). Gerhard von Rad, *Deuteronomy,* OTL (Philadelphia: Westminster, 1966).

## §1 The Superscription (Hosea 1:1)

In a sense, chapters 1 through 3 in Hosea's book serve as a summary of his entire message. Centered around the "sign" of Hosea's marriage to Gomer, they prepare for and condense all that follows after in the story of God's poignant love affair with the people of Israel in the eighth century BC. Perhaps they originally circulated in Judean circles independently of chapters 4–14. But whoever placed them in their present position intended to help us understand the oracles of chapters 4–14 in their proper context by first having us read chapters 1–3.

**1:1** / The superscription now functions as the title for the entire book of Hosea, although in its original form, which did not include the names of Judean kings, it probably was the heading for only the collection of chapters 1–3, which most likely date from the last years of the reign of Jeroboam II. Now, however, **the word of the LORD** refers not only to the following words spoken by the prophet and by Yahweh but also to the biographical material, the quotations from the people, and all other material found in Hosea's book. The phrase encompasses the entire event of God's act toward his people Israel in the time of Hosea, and indeed, also God's words that portray the future. God's word in the Scriptures is not only speech but also action and happening—all that is revelatory of God's character.

The fact that the word **came to Hosea** emphasizes that his prophecy was not the result of his own convictions or experience, not even of his experience with Gomer, but rather that the word was given to him from outside of himself, by God. The word of God is always a transcendent, revelatory word, that breaks into human life and history from the divine sphere, and until God reveals this word, it cannot be known by human beings (cf. 1 Cor. 2:6–11).

The word is spoken, however, into particular times in history, and it first of all concerns those specific times. Thus the Bible

always gives us datelines, timelines: "In the year that King Uzziah died" (Isa. 6:1); "In those days Caesar Augustus issued a
decree that a census should be taken. . . . This was the first census
that took place while Quirinius was governor of Syria" (Luke
2:1–2). The word of God is not a timeless "spiritual truth" or
"eternal principle," but an action of God concerned with concrete
times, places, and happenings in human life. It comes because
God the sovereign constantly watches over human life, governs
it, interacts with it, and speaks the word into it to change it.

We are therefore told that the word came to Hosea during
the reign of Jeroboam II, son of Joash (distinguishing him from
Jeroboam I, son of Nebat), who was king of the northern state of
Israel from 786 to 746 BC. The book of Hosea is thus primarily
concerned with that specific time and must be read in that context.

As we have seen in the introduction, Hosea's ministry
lasted well beyond the reign of Jeroboam, until about 723 BC. But
the editors of the book of Hosea, who appended the rest of this
superscription to Hosea's prophecies, dated the rest of his ministry not in terms of the reigns of northern kings but rather in terms
of the reigns of the kings of the southern state of Judah, covering
the period from the accession of Uzziah (783–742 BC) to the death
of Hezekiah (687 BC?). That is evidence of two facts. One, the
editors were Judean, very likely the Deuteronomic editors during
the period of the exile who edited all of the preexilic prophetic
books. Two, they realized that the word of God spoken to Hosea
applied not only to the time of Hosea's ministry, about 750–723
BC, but also to the time in which they were living. As the great
preacher Paul Scherer once remarked, "God did not stop speaking when his book went to press." The word of God, once spoken
into a specific time in history, continues to act in human life in
each subsequent generation. And so we, who stand in continuity
with that sacred history through Christ, find the word of God as
spoken to Hosea acting in the specificity of our lives also. The
word is never to be understood apart from history—it always
applies to particular times and events, to the things we are
doing—but neither is its action limited by time and place. It
moves on through time, working God's will in the world, until
God's kingdom comes.

The word of God, which according to the Bible is always
an active, effective force (cf. Isa. 55:10–11), may work independently of any human agency. For example, the word of God
sustains all the processes of nature (cf. Gen. 1; Matt. 6:25–33; Col.

1:17). But God also uses human beings as the mediators of his word, and so, the word of the Lord **came to** *Hosea* (italics added). The fact that not much is told us about Hosea—who is not called a prophet here—shows that it is not the man but the message that is important.

The name **Hosea** means "he has helped" or "he has saved," from the hiphil perfect of the Hebrew verb *yāšaʿ*. The name, which may take the form "Hoshea," is found elsewhere in the OT, as the earlier name given to Joshua (Num. 13:8), as the name of the last king of Israel (2 Kgs. 15:30, etc.), and as the appellation of two different clan chieftains (Neh. 10:23; 1 Chron. 27:20). The prophet is distinguished from these others who bear the name by being called **the son of Beeri**, which itself is a name of a Hittite in Genesis 26:34. But as we said in the introduction, we know that Hosea was a resident of the northern kingdom of Israel. The compilers of Hosea's book did not think it was important that we know anything more than that, and indeed, it is not. The book of Hosea is not biography; it is word of God, and the important thing is that we read it as such.

## §2 Prophetic Sign and Symbolism (Hosea 1:2–9)

**1:2–3** / This prose passage comes from the hand of an editor, who was probably a contemporary disciple of the prophet, and it recounts the event that led to Hosea's ministry. Thus, v. 2a in the Hebrew is a superscription: "The beginning of the speaking of Yahweh through Hosea." However, that phrase refers only to Yahweh's initial command to Hosea to "Go, take to yourself a wife of harlotry and have children of harlotry, for the land commits great harlotry by forsaking the LORD" (RSV). The births of the three children that follow occur over at least five years' time, during which Hosea was undoubtedly proclaiming some of the oracles found in chapters 4–13. So Hosea's ministry *began* with Yahweh's command to marry a harlotrous woman.

The NIV translation has obscured the Hebrew's emphasis on the obedience of the prophet. Hosea is commanded, **Go, take** . . . Verse 3 therefore reads, "And he went and he took . . ." His obedience to the command of his God is immediate, with no questions asked and with no notice given to his own personal feelings. Yahweh wants to speak *through* Hosea—not with him, not to him, but through him. Hosea is to be the living word of the Lord in the midst of his contemporaries, a "sign," a channel of God's speaking, a foreshadowing of that complete incarnation in Jesus Christ of the Word of every century.

Hosea is commanded to marry an ʾēšet zᵉnûnîm, a "woman of harlotry." What that means has been endlessly debated in scholarly circles. Was Gomer at first faithful, becoming **adulterous** after the marriage ceremony, as implied by the NIV? Was she a common or a sacred prostitute? Had she offered her virginity to a male prostitute in a baalistic ritual in order to ensure that she would bear children? Or was she simply like every other Israelite, apostate from Yahweh and therefore harlotrous toward her divine husband?

Several facts seem clear. Gomer was not faithful at the first nor was she like every other Israelite: Hosea's marriage to Gomer functioned as an obvious announcement about the "harlotrous" status of Israel in relation to God. Second, Gomer's harlotry had something to do with Israel's worship of the fertility gods and goddesses of Canaan. Thus, Gomer was one who had participated in some way, whether once or sporadically or often, in the cultic fertility rites of baalism; she was a living symbol of Israel's participation in that pagan religion, and Hosea's marriage to her was the sign that God was married to a people who had forsaken him for other deities.

In commanding such a marriage, God spoke through Hosea in the language of the time, for Canaanite religion presupposed that the mythical god of storm and rain, Hadad, upon whom all fertility depended in dry Palestine, was manifested in the form of local baals (or "owners," "masters," "lords") at cult sites (often called "high places") throughout the land. These baals "impregnated" the land, the mother goddess, with rain, causing it to bring forth produce. They were also seen as the source of fertility in human beings. Thus, by enacting the "marriage" of Baal with the land and humans, by means of sexual intercourse with male and female prostitutes at the cult sites, worshipers thought to coerce the god of fertility, through sympathetic magic, to bring forth fertility. In short, Baal was understood as the source of life, and worshiping him assured his devotees that they would have the good life.

By using the imagery of his marriage with his people Israel, Yahweh, through Hosea, preempted the language of baal religion and moved it entirely from the mythological realm into history. The giver of life was no longer a mythological nature deity but Israel's historical Lord who had in fact claimed Israel and "married" Israel in the exodus from Egypt and the covenant on Mt. Sinai. Baal religion was mythic fantasy; Yahweh's relation with his people was historical fact. Through Hosea, God was giving the people Israel an entirely new worldview—a worldview based on historical events and not on nature's cycle.

According to verse 2, the children born to the marriage of Hosea and Gomer would also be "children of harlotry" (RSV), not because they were illegitimate, but because they were born of a harlotrous mother: like mother, like children. In the verses that follow, only the first child is attributed to Hosea's fatherhood (v. 3), but the style becomes increasingly succinct in vv. 6 and 8, and that may be the reason for the omission from those verses of the Hebrew *lô,* "to him."

Hosea's marriage is a "sign." The naming of the children
that follows is prophetic "symbolic action." Throughout the prophetic literature the prophets are sometimes commanded by God
to perform particular symbolic acts instead of speaking. For example, Jeremiah is commanded to wear a wooden yoke, forecast-
ing the subjection of Judah and other nations to Babylonia (Jer.
27). Ezekiel is commanded to draw a picture of Jerusalem on a
brick and to make (clay?) siegeworks around it, foretelling the
siege of that city by Nebuchadnezzar (Ezek. 4:1–2). Bizarre in
themselves, such actions are intended, like the word, to be announcements of what God is going to do. Indeed, in prophetic
understanding, they begin that action of God. They are God's
insertions into history of his effective word that will then work to
initiate and shape events, until it is fulfilled. Thus, in commanding Hosea to give his three children such bizarre names (vv. 4, 6,
and 9), God is announcing and beginning his judging action
toward his people Israel.

**1:4–5** / The first child, born probably within a year after
the marriage, is to be named **Jezreel**, v. 4, and the **because** or "for"
(*kî* in the Hebrew) gives the reason (cf. "for" in vv. 6, 9). God will
punish the dynasty of King Jehu for the events that he instigated
in the city of Jezreel and will put an end to the kingship (instead
of the NIV's **kingdom**) in Israel. We have only to read 2 Kings 9–10
to know the massacre to which the verse refers.

The problem is that Jehu's revolution which toppled the
Omri dynasty in 844 BC was initiated by the prophet Elijah at the
command of the Lord (1 Kgs. 19:16) and was subsequently pro-
moted by Elijah's successor, Elisha (2 Kgs. 9:1–13; 10:10, 17). Why,
then, is Jehu's revolution a cause for punishment, according to
Hosea? Has Yahweh changed his mind about the event? Or is
the house of Jehu, with his great-grandson Jeroboam II on the
throne, to be punished because Jehu's wholesale slaughter of his
enemies overstepped the will of the Lord? Or has Jehu incurred
bloodguilt for his dynasty that has never been expiated? None of
those seem to be the reason for God's word in Hosea 1:4. Rather,
the reason seems to be that Jehu's dynasty, begun at Jezreel,
which initially opposed the worship of Baal (2 Kgs. 10:18–28),
over time came to foster that apostasy (cf. 2 Kgs. 10:29–31) that
reached its climax in the reign of Jeroboam. The kingship has
proved false, and Yahweh will bring it to an end. Hosea's prophecy belongs firmly in that tribal league theology of northern

Israel that had no room for a king because Yahweh was king (cf. 1 Sam. 8:4–8).

Some commentators have maintained that Hosea 1:5 is a later insertion into this pericope, perhaps from the hand of Hosea himself, and that it reflects the loss of the Valley of Jezreel, which lay between the highlands of Samaria and Galilee, to the Assyrian Tiglath-pileser III in 733 BC. Such a theory is necessary only if the interpreter believes that the prophetic word cannot precede an event. Hosea here prophesies that military defeat of Israel, which did indeed take place in the plain of Jezreel when Assyria invaded the West. Thus the naming of Hosea's first child begins the action of the Lord that will result in the loss of the kingship and in national military defeat.

**1:6–7** / The name of the second child, a daughter, furnishes a further reason for what is happening. She is called *Lō'-ruḥāmâ,* "Not pitied" (RSV)—a better translation of the Hebrew than "Not loved," which tends to confuse the verb *rāḥam* with Hosea's frequent use of the verb *'āhab,* "to love." *Reḥem* is the Hebrew word for "womb," and the verb *rāḥam* denotes the tenderness of a mother toward a child, or, generally, the love and sympathy aroused by the need and dependence of another. Thus, "Not pitied" is an outrageous name for a daughter, but it is the prophetic symbol that Yahweh will no longer be moved by the need of his people, even though they are totally dependent on Yahweh for life. From the beginning, Yahweh had such tender pity (cf. Exod. 3:7). Now that sympathy, which prompted his help for Israel throughout their history, is gone.

Verse 7 is very likely a later Judean insert into this passage. It interrupts the carefully constructed structure and in its final phrase switches from the first person speech of Yahweh to the third person. In verse 7 God **will show** mercy to Judah and **will save them** from their enemy, but not by military defeat. Many commentators have speculated that this verse was inserted into Hosea's prophecy at the time of the miraculous deliverance of Jerusalem from the forces of the Assyrian Sennacherib in 701 BC (2 Kgs. 19:32–37), but before the destruction of Jerusalem in 587 BC. Among all of the cities of Syria-Palestine, only Jerusalem did not fall in 701 BC. But of course the prophecy proved no guarantee for the time after that.

**1:8–9** / After a span of two or three years, during which Hosea was undoubtedly preaching many of the oracles found in chapters 4–13, *Lō'-ruḥāmâ* was weaned. The prophet's disciple, who wrote 1:2–9, tells us that a third child was born to Gomer and that Yahweh commanded this son to be named *Lō'-'ammî*, "Not my people," v. 9. The imagery of the naming has now reached its climax: the name embodies the negation of Yahweh's covenant with his people and foretells the final destruction of Israel.

The traditional covenant formula, which is found throughout the OT, was Yahweh's promise, "I will be your God, and you shall be my people" (Exod. 6:7; Lev. 26:12; Jer. 7:23; 11:4; et al.). By that promise, the Lord bound himself to his people. Through centuries of struggle with their disobedience and lack of faith, he nevertheless sustained his relationship with them. Now, however, God's mercy and patience and forgiveness will come to an end. He will rid himself of them and let their enemies destroy them.

The latter half of verse 9 literally reads, in the Hebrew, "for you are not my people, and I am not *'ehyeh* to you." *'Ehyeh ᵃšer 'ehyeh* is the name of God that was revealed to Moses on Mt. Sinai (according to Exod. 3:14, a northern tradition). *'Ehyeh* is the first person singular future form of the verb *hāyāh,* from which the name Yahweh, in the third person singular, is formed. In Exodus 3:14, the name *('Ehyeh ᵃšer 'ehyeh)* by which Yahweh names himself is made intensive by the phrase *ᵃšer 'ehyeh* and should be understood to be a promise: "I will indeed be with you." Thus, the latter half of Hosea 1:9 should be read, "for you are not my people, and I will not be with you." Yahweh, the God of the covenant, upon whom Israel's very life depends, is declaring his covenant bond null and void, divorcing his wife Israel, deserting his beloved people. There can be no other outcome of that word of God than the death of Israel.

Our secular age does not know or acknowledge the fact, but human beings cannot live unless God sustains their life. The word through Hosea and the subsequent fate of Israel should lead us to reassess our secular worldview in which we foolishly believe that we are self-sufficient apart from this God of the Bible.

# §3 Abundant Life Restored (Hosea 1:10–2:1)

**1:10–2:1** / Immediately following the announcement of Israel's judgment that can mean only death, in 1:2–9, we find this short passage announcing her restoration to abundant life. The promises for the future that the passage contains are very clear: (1) Israel's population will come to number as many as the sands of the sea; (2) The covenant relation with Yahweh will be restored; (3) Israel and Judah will be reunited as one people; (4) They will be ruled by one "head"; and (5) They will once again inhabit their own land. All of this will take place on the great day of Jezreel.

Thus, the passage marks a reversal of every element of the judgment that Hosea preaches. Throughout his oracles, the prophet announces: (1) the decimation of Israel's population (4:10; 9:12–14, 15); (2) the abrogation of the covenant relationship (1:9; 8:1); (3) the warfare of Israel with Judah (5:8–14) during the Syro-Ephraimitic war of 734–733 BC; (4) the rejection of the kingship (1:4; 7:7; 8:4; 10:7, 15; 13:10–11); (5) the loss of the fertility of the land and ultimate exile (2:9, 11–12; 9:3, 6, 17; 11:5). Beyond these fearful words of judgment, this pericope announces a future hope for the people of God.

The passage has undoubtedly been placed in its current position by the disciple of Hosea who gathered together and arranged the summary of Hosea's message that is constituted by chapters 1–3. In that summary, the disciple deliberately alternated oracles of salvation with those of judgment. But does the passage come from the prophet himself?

Certainly 1:10 and 2:1 reverse the judgments of 1:9 and 1:6 respectively. And **Jezreel** recalls 1:5. But the passage should be read primarily in relation to 2:21–23, and H. W. Wolff may be correct in stating that originally 1:10–2:1 followed 2:21–23. In 2:22, "Jezreel" takes on its etymological meaning of "God sows," the figure being that of God sowing fertility in the land. That is the context of **Jezreel** here in 1:11 also. The primary emphasis of

1:10–2:1 is on the restoration of life, fertile and abundant, to Israel and Judah. Both nations are seen as one here, in the one Israel of the old tribal league. As one Israel, they will become as numerous as the sands of the sea, and will be called **sons of the living God,** a phrase found only this once in the OT. God is above all **the living God,** a designation seen elsewhere only in Joshua 3:10 and Psalms 42:2 and 84:2. That is, God is the source of life. Hosea is fighting in his ministry a baal fertility religion, which claims to give life to its adherents, and so this passage emphasizes, in the strongest terms, that God is the source of life (cf. 14:5–8).

Verse 11, in the Hebrew, reads "and they shall go up from the land," contrary to the NIV reading. The reference is not to the deliverance from exile: **land** in Hosea refers always to the land of Canaan. And the phrase does not mean "they shall take posses-sion of the land," referring to a military victory. Rather, the mean-ing is that found also in 2:23: "they shall spring/sprout up from the land," referring again to the increase of the population, "for great is the day (when) God sows!" "Here is your source of life," Hosea is saying to his people, "not Baal, but the living God, who will fulfill his ancient promise to your fathers" (Gen. 22:17; 32:12; cf. 13:16; 15:5; 26:24; 28:14, etc.). When that takes place, then the members of reunited Israel will be able to say to a *multiplicity* of **brothers** and **sisters, my people** and "shown mercy," 2:1.

If the passage is not genuine to Hosea, it certainly reflects the prophet's thought and carries on the Hosianic tradition. The vision for the future is set firmly in the context of the northern tribal league. Israel is one people, with only a "head," not a king. The king of the tribal league was Yahweh (cf. Judg. 8:22–23). Doubt of the genuine nature of the passage is raised only by the reference to the promise to the patriarchs, which Hosea nowhere else mentions; indeed, he judges Jacob negatively (12:2–4). Nev-ertheless, the strong emphasis on Yahweh as the source of all vitality, and the connection with 2:21–23, affirm the place of this passage in genuine Hosianic tradition.

Beyond the inevitable judgment of Israel, Israel has, in the mercy of God, a glorious future of abundant life. According to the NT, the people of God have indeed become as many as the sands of the sea, through their entrance into the new covenant of Jesus Christ. But the fulfillment is not yet. Israel and all the nations still await the final salvation (Rom. 11:26; Rev. 7:9–10). The word of God through Hosea still strains toward his future.

## §4 The Desire of the Lord (Hosea 2:2–15)

Once again the disciple who arranged chapters 1–3 has included a passage that serves as a summary of much of Hosea's preaching (2:16–14:9). All of 2:2–15 represents genuine oracles of Hosea, but it is possible that this unit as a whole has been put together from originally independent oracles, such as 2:2–4; 2:5–7a; 2:7c–10; 2:11–13; and 2:14–15. As it now stands, however, the pericope forms a rhetorical whole.

The setting for these words is a court of law, indicated by the initial imperative verb, *rîbû*, which often has the meaning, "go to court," but which in this context means, "plead" or "accuse." (The NIV **rebuke** does not adequately convey the legal setting.) Yahweh, the aggrieved husband, has taken Israel, his unfaithful wife, to court. But this is a very unusual court case. Instead of filing for divorce from his harlotrous wife (cf. Deut. 24:1) or demanding the lawfully stipulated death penalty for unfaithfulness (cf. Gen. 38:24; Lev. 21:9; Deut. 22:23–24), Yahweh pleads with Israel to amend her ways in order that she may continue to be his wife. This is a love that will not let her go!

**2:2–4** / The plea is directed at the couple's children, meaning Israel as a whole, as much as to say that if all the individual Israelites will turn from their harlotry, then the "collective wife," Israel, whom they represent, will also turn. Yahweh pleads that Israel put away the marks of harlotry **from her face** and **from between her breasts,** verse 2, referring perhaps to makeup and jewelry worn by harlots or in the cult of Baal (cf. v. 13). If the wife Israel will not do so, then Yahweh threatens serious punishment, verse 3. It was the legal duty of a husband to clothe his wife (Exod. 21:10), but if Israel will not return in faithfulness to him, then Yahweh will leave her naked and helpless like a newborn infant (cf. Ezek. 16:4, 10), like a land upon which no rain falls (a daring contradiction of Baal's supposed fertilization of the land with rain), like a traveler who dies of thirst in the desert. Yahweh will show no pity toward any of the children of Israel in their helplessness (cf. 1:6).

**2:5–8** / The reason for this threat is stated in verse 5: Israel has believed that all of the goods that sustain its life have come from Baal—the basic necessities of bread (NIV has **food**) and **water, wool** for warm clothing, flax (so the Hebrew) from which to make cool **linen** cloth, **oil** for anointing and healing, and pleasant drinks.

Yahweh, however, has the resources to disabuse Israel of her faith in Baal. He will **block her path** to her lovers—perhaps meaning the paths to the Baal cult sites—with thorn-hedges or stone walls, so that Israel cannot run after other gods, verse 6. The image is of an animal that needs to be fenced in (cf. 4:16; 8:9; Jer. 2:23–25). Israel is like a wanton prostitute, who not only waits for her lovers to come to her (as in Gen. 38:14–18; Jer. 3:2), but who searches them out and pursues them. But her search will be fruitless. No good things—no bread and water, clothing and luxuries, fertility and vitality—will be granted by Baal. Such is the meaning of **she will look for them but not find them**, verse 7. Israel the wife will therefore decide to return to her first husband, Yahweh, who gave her food and clothing and increase in the beginning.

Israel's decision to return to Yahweh is crucial in this passage, because it shows what Israel is looking for from her God. She wants material goods, prosperity, multiplication of her population—in short, the good life. In this attitude, Israel mirrors those in our day who turn to religion to gain success or wealth, political office or social approval (cf. the same attitude in Jer. 44:15–18).

Yahweh, however, will not be satisfied with such superficial religion. He does not want Israel to return simply for what she can get out of him! That is never the purpose of the worship of God: we do not go to church for what *we* gain—though we gain much—but rather for what we give, namely, glory and adoration to the Father, Son, and Holy Spirit. Yahweh, in Hosea's time as in ours, desires a people who love him, as a faithful wife loves her husband, or as an obedient son loves and admires and adores his father. Yahweh wants communion with his people, the heartfelt, trusting, unwavering communion of persons who love one another to the deepest depths. Once the Israelites attain that communion, they will realize from whom come all the sources and sustenance of their life. But the Israelites' faith in their God is far from such communion.

**2:9–15** / Thus, according to verse 9, the Lord will deny Israel the goods for which she has returned to him. God will prevent the **grain** from ripening and the vineyards from yielding fruit. He will prevent the flocks from yielding **wool** and the flax from growing. Israel will be left naked and ashamed before the eyes of her former **lovers** (cf. Lam. 1:8; Ezek. 16:37), and the baals will be helpless to give any aid or to rescue her from Yahweh's omnipotent hand, verse 10.

As a result of such deprivation, all of the cultic festivities, the **yearly festivals**, the **New Moons**, and **Sabbath days**, which have been so shot through with syncretistic worship of Baal alongside Yahweh, will come to an end, for there will be no animals to sacrifice and no produce to offer, verse 11. **Yearly festivals** *(ḥāg)*, in verse 11 [MT v. 13], refer to the three annual pilgrimage festivals of unleavened bread, harvest, and ingathering that were coordinated with the agricultural year (Exod. 23:14–17; 34:18–23). Among these, the feast of harvest in the autumn was, in Hosea's time, the most important; it was the time when the fruit from grapes and **fig trees** was gathered. Harlotrous Israel considered such fruit the payment by the baals in return for her worship of them, verse 12, but she shall no longer enjoy such fruit. In reality Yahweh gave these and Yahweh can take them away. **New Moons**, verse 11, occurring monthly (cf. Isa. 1:13–14), may have included the sexual baal rites of *hieros gamos*, "sacred marriage," since they occurred in the same temporal pattern as that of female menstruation—a pattern that modern-day feminist celebrations of new moons and menstrual cycles resemble. **Sabbath days**, verse 11, were the weekly days of rest (cf. Amos 8:5) stipulated in the covenant law (Exod. 20:8–11; Deut. 5:12–15). In verses 11–13 Yahweh is saying that the entire cultic calendar will be canceled. Israel's worship has been used to honor the pagan baals. Therefore it will be done away.

Israel's harlotrous sin is summarized in the last line of verse 13: **but me she forgot,** says **the LORD.** "To forget" Yahweh, in the oracles of Hosea, is the opposite of knowing Yahweh (v. 8), of participating in that intimate communion of love that Yahweh so desires to have with the covenant people. "To know the LORD" is to know the sacred history and all the gracious acts that Yahweh has done for his people. As the Psalmist put it: "Bless the LORD,

O my soul, and forget not all his benefits" (Ps. 103:2 RSV). But to know the Lord is also to live in such inner, daily, heartfelt fellowship that one delights in God's presence, and sees everything in the context of God's love and will, and rejoices in obeying divine directions for one's daily life. It is that inner relationship of love and delight and obedience that Israel has rejected for the sensuous and materialistic worship of the baals.

Yahweh, however, will not forget his faithless people, and so the final two verses of this oracle, which summarize the totality of Hosea's message, tell what the Lord will do in the future, after Israel has been punished (v. 13) for her apostasy and syncretism.

In effect, the Lord will begin the sacred history with his people all over again. After bringing Israel out of the inevitable exile that will requite Israel for her sin, God will **lead her into the desert,** as he led her at the first. There in the wilderness, where there is no baal to come between them, the Lord will "woo" his young bride again. Literally, in the Hebrew, God will "speak to her heart" (cf. Gen. 34:3), for it is Israel's heart that Yahweh wants to win, verse 14.

There the Lord will give Israel gifts (cf. 2:19–20), as he leads her farther into the promised land (v. 5). The **Valley of Achor,** meaning "the valley of trouble," probably led from the plain of the Jordan River southwest of Jericho up toward the hill country. It will become for Israel **a door of hope,** leading to a new beginning and a new life. There Israel will "answer" her divine husband (the NIV incorrectly reads **sing**; see the RSV), heart to heart, love to love, in true commitment and faithfulness. Such is the future to which God through Hosea looks forward.

Perhaps, then, it is no accident that the wilderness is a significant place for Jesus of Nazareth. He begins his ministry in the wilderness, when he is baptized by John the Baptist in the River Jordan. It is in the wilderness that he faces and overcomes the temptations of Satan (Mark 1:2–15 and parallels).

## Additional Notes §4

**2:5** / **Lovers**, *me'ahªbay* [MT v. 7], is used only of adulterous lovers in the OT and especially in the oracles of Jeremiah and Ezekiel. For the payment given prostitutes, see 9:1; Mic. 1:7; cf. Gen. 38:16.

**2:13** / **Baals**, in the plural: Baal gods were thought of as diffuse numina who could be found at a multiplicity of cult sites. Thus, the OT refers to Baal of Hermon (Judg. 3:3); Baal-Berith of Shechem (Judg. 8:33; 9:4); the Baal of Samaria (1 Kgs. 16:32) and of Carmel (1 Kgs. 18:19), both of which were identified with the god Melkart of Tyre; Baal Zebul of Ekron (2 Kgs. 1:2), etc. All may have been seen mythologically as the manifestation of one high god of fertility, but the diffusion of baal numina, worshiped at "high places" throughout Canaan, led Deuteronomy and Jesus to insist that "the LORD is one" (Deut. 6:4; Mark 12:29), to be worshiped only at one place where God "put his name" (Deut. 12:5; cf. Acts 4:12).

## §5 The New Covenant in the New Age (Hosea 2:16–23)

In 2:2–15 we saw Yahweh's desire for an intimate, inner relation with his people, and from 2:15 we learned that Israel would, indeed, "answer" the Lord's desire for that relationship. This oracle, which the NIV correctly translates as poetry (contra RSV prose), now details how such a new communion between God and his people can come to be. Yahweh is the speaker throughout, and every action mentioned is the result of his initiative.

Yahweh will establish a new relation with his people **in that day,** verse 16 (cf. vv. 18, 21). The phrase most often refers to the eschatological future in the OT, to the time when the Lord sets up his rule over all the earth in the Kingdom of God, although here the reference is to his rule over only Israel. But it is an indefinite time in the future, after Israel has passed through judgment on its faithlessness toward God. And it is a time that can be ushered in not by human action, but only by God alone.

To create the new intimate relationship of love between himself and his people, Yahweh will take several actions. We saw in 2:14–15 that God will lead Israel once again into the desert, "woo" her like a lover wooing his beloved, and lead her once again into the promised land, through the Valley of Achor that has been transformed into a "door of hope." Now, as she enters the promised land, she will find all the fertility gods removed, and the cult purified of all syncretistic baal worship.

**2:16–18** / Verse 16 implies that Yahweh had been worshiped as a baal god. To call on the name of a God in the cult meant to invoke that deity's presence and aid or action (cf. 1 Kgs. 18:26), and the presence of Yahweh had been invoked with the name "My Baal" (NIV: **my master**), a practice expressly forbidden in Exodus 23:13. Now the very mention of the name of Baal will be lost to Israel's vocabulary, v. 17. Israel will call out, "my husband," using the expression of personal devotion (cf. Gen. 29:32, 34; 30:15, 20; 2 Kgs. 4:1), instead of "my baal," which means "my master" or "my owner" or "my lord." Worship will be characterized by love, instead of by duty and fear.

Second, the Lord will mediate a **covenant** between Israel and the animal kingdom so that the latter will no longer be a threat to Israel's security, verse 18a–c. The promise seems strange, because only in verse 12 has there been any previous mention of the enmity of wild **beasts**. Hosea is, however, using a promise characteristic of Israel's eschatological traditions.

The Israelites always knew, as we moderns often do not, that sin disrupted their relations not only with human beings but also with the natural world (Gen. 3:15, 17–18; 9:2; Deut. 7:22; Ps. 91:13) and that Yahweh, the Lord of nature, could use the wild beasts as instruments of judgment (Jer. 5:5–6; 8:17; 15:3; Ezek. 5:17, etc.). Here Hosea begins the prophetic tradition of Israel looking forward to a restoration of peace with the animal kingdom in the kingdom of God (Isa. 11:6–9; 35:9; Ezek. 34:25, 28).

God's promise for the future includes peace with the animal kingdom and also peace between Israel and its surrounding enemies, verse 18d. God will abolish all weapons of war from the land, because they will no longer be needed (cf. Isa. 9:5, 7). As has often been noted, however, **land** in verse 18 refers here, as elsewhere in Hosea, only to the land of Canaan, and this eschatological vision does not encompass the cosmic peace that is typical of later prophetic promises (cf. Isa. 2:4; Mic. 4:3; Ezek. 39:9; Zech. 9:10).

The emphasis in Hosea is on security for Israel—for that wayward people that has looked for life and security to Baal instead of to Yahweh. And Yahweh here affirms that he is Israel's one source of security, the one sovereign ruler who can enable Israel to **lie down in safety** and not be afraid (cf. Isa. 32:17–18; Jer. 23:6=33:16; Mic. 4:4–5).

**2:19–20** / Having reassured the Israelites of their guarantee of safety so that they have come to trust God with their lives, Yahweh will then enter into a formal betrothal with his beloved people, verse 19.

A betrothal or engagement was arranged in Israel by the future groom's payment of a brideprice to the father of the future bride. Based on Deuteronomy 22:29, the customary price was probably 50 shekels or about one and one-quarter pounds of silver, and the father's acceptance of the gift signified that he had no further objections to the marriage. Betrothal, however, signified far more than it does in our society. Legally, it was tantamount to marriage (cf. Exod. 22:16; Deut. 20:7; 2 Sam. 3:14; Matt. 1:18–20) and therefore a binding commitment. Yahweh will be betrothed to Israel **forever,** in a life-long, faithful marital covenant.

The brideprice that Yahweh will pay for Israel is not silver, however, but **righteousness** *(ṣedeq)* and **justice** *(mišpāṭ),* "covenant, steadfast love" *(ḥesed;* NIV: **love**) and "mercy" *(raḥᵃmîm;* NIV: **compassion**), and **faithfulness** *(ᵓᵉmûnâ),* verses 19–20 [MT vv. 21–22]. Those are all terms describing relationships. Throughout the Scriptures, **righteousness** is the fulfillment of the demands of a relationship, and very often Yahweh's "righteousness" consists in his salvation of his people, which fulfills the demands of his covenant relation with them. **Justice** signifies the fulfillment of those legal rights and claims appropriate to the relationship. *Ḥesed* is that steadfast love and devotion given within a covenant relation. "Mercy" is sympathy and help toward the dependent. **Faithfulness** or *ᵓᵉmûnâ* comes from the same stem as our word "amen," and is unswerving, day-by-day, step-by-step obedience, devotion, and affirmation of one's ties to another. With such gifts, Yahweh betroths Israel to himself.

There has been some confusion about the meaning of verses 19–20, however. Obviously there is no father to whom the brideprice is paid, and some commentators have maintained that these are qualities that Yahweh pledges to manifest toward Israel—that he here promises to be righteous, just, devoted, merciful, and faithful toward his "wife." But that is not correct. Yahweh already has these qualities, and it is Israel who needs them! Thus, these are the qualities that Yahweh gives, not to the father of the bride, but to the bride herself, so that henceforth the relation between God and his people Israel will be characterized by mutual righteousness, justice, devotion, mercy, and faithfulness. Here is the promise that the Israelites will be transformed in their inner selves to live with their God in that relation of intimate love and faithfulness for which God so yearns. And when the Israelites become such a people, then they will, indeed, "know" the Lord—the key word in Hosea for the intimate relation of devotion between God and his people. (The NIV translation of *yāda'* with **acknowledge** instead of "know" completely obscures the meaning of v. 20b.) In short, this is the establishment of a new, everlasting, marital covenant with Israel, like the new covenant that Jeremiah foretells in Jeremiah 31:31–34, and indeed, this is the first mention of that new covenant in the OT, although the word "covenant" itself is not used. The Israelites are here promised that they will enter into the new, eschatological age of the kingdom with their God.

**2:21–23** / Verses 21–22 might be characterized by Jesus' saying, "Seek first his kingdom and his righteousness, and all these things will be given to you as well" (Matt. 6:33). In the new age, the new Israel will lack no good thing. The Lord will **respond** to the heavens, that is, he will cause them to give rain, and they will in turn water the earth. The earth will therefore give forth its produce of grain, grapes, and olives, and will respond with the word **Jezreel,** which here means "God sows." It does not refer to the people; it is simply the celebrative cry of nature in response to its God. The natural world often celebrates the action of God, according to the OT (cf. Ps. 96:11–13; 98:7–9; Isa. 35:1, etc.)—a characteristic of the new eschatological kingdom (cf. Isa. 43:19–20; 45:8; 49:13; 55:12)—and that is the celebration here in verse 22.

That such is the meaning of verse 22 is shown by verse 23a, which reads, **And I will plant *her* for myself in the land.** Many commentators emend the text to read, "plant *him*" (so the RSV), since a masculine pronoun is required if "Jezreel" in the preceding verse refers to Israel. But it does not. It is simply the exultant cry of nature, celebrating the God who fructifies it.

Verse 23 then points back to 1:6 and 1:8–9 and corresponds to the promise of 2:1. There is no need to mention "Jezreel" from 1:4–5, because all warfare has been abolished, 2:18. Rather, the need is to reverse the rejection of Israel and the abrogation of the covenant relation, recounted in 1:6, 8–9. And that is what is said in 2:23. Yahweh will henceforth have mercy on his dependent people, and he will restore his covenant with them in the most intimate of relationships.

In that new covenant, Israel, here referred to by a masculine pronoun as in 1:9, will respond with a confession of complete trust, surrender, and love, **my God!** (cf. John 20:28). The new age of the new covenant will come, Hosea is saying, as the result of God's action alone. Israel will have done nothing to deserve it, and it is not conditional on Israel's work. By transforming the people from the inside out, and by altering their circumstances in the world, God will usher in a new age of righteousness and

justice, covenant love and mercy, in which Israel will be forever
faithful to the God who has been everlastingly faithful to her.

The new covenant is not simply a repair of the old, but
an entirely new relationship (cf. Mark 2:18–22). And yet it will
gather up all of the promises of God in the old covenant and
bring them to fulfillment. The interpreter needs to be aware,
then, that when Jesus sat at table with his disciples on the night
in which he was betrayed, he took the cup after supper and gave
it to his disciples, saying, "This cup is the new covenant in my
blood. . . . For whenever you eat this bread and drink this cup,
you proclaim the Lord's death until he comes" (1 Cor. 11:25–26).
With that act, our God began the new age, promised by Hosea,
that will be present in its fullness when the Lord returns.

---

### Additional Notes §5

**2:16**  /  The Hb. [MT v. 18] reads, "You will call, 'My husband',"
omitting "me," which has been supplied from the LXX, Syr., and Vg. The
Hb. has an air of immediacy and intimacy, which the emendation does
not fully capture.

# §6 The New Covenant Acted Out (Hosea 3:1–5)

**3:1–5** / This short prose piece, composed by Hosea himself (in contrast to 1:2–9, which comes from another hand) is really an explication, through a symbolic action on the prophet's part, of the meaning of 2:2–23. It spells out in relation to one individual wife what Yahweh will do to his wife Israel as a whole, and indeed, it initiates that action. Thus, it may have been performed at the same time that the pieces in 2:2–23 were delivered, so that word and symbolic action together began to set in motion the fulfillment of God's purpose for this people.

There is no specific mention that a divorce has taken place. Thus, Gomer's relations with her "friend," a word which may be used of a desired lover (cf. Jer. 3:1, 20 Hb.; Song Sol. 5:16), are indeed "adulterous." She is still married to the prophet, but has become the property of another man. It is therefore necessary that she be bought back from the other man, and the total price paid for her is about thirty shekels of silver (in silver and barley), which was the price paid for a slave (cf. Exod. 21:32).

Hosea buys back Gomer in obedience to the word of the Lord. Once again, as in 1:2–9, his actions are prompted entirely by God's command. Hosea shows love to Gomer because God is going to show love to Israel, not vice versa. Hosea's experience with Gomer does not teach him about God; rather, Hosea's experience with God teaches him about Gomer. Only because of the love of God for Israel does Hosea seek out and buy back his adulterous wife. His action is not the result of human compassion but of obedience to the divine will.

It is instructive to note the nature of "love" in this passage. The word *ʾahab*, love, is used four times in verse 1, and the content of Israel's love is clear. The Israelites love other gods because they think those gods bring with them the good things of life, such as the **raisin-cakes** or sweet meats of pressed grapes that were eaten in the cult (cf. Song Sol. 2:5) and such as the ecstasies of cultic prostitution. But God's love is made of sterner stuff. God's love brings deprivation. For **many days**, Gomer must live with Hosea, confined to the house apart from any other man, and sharing a purely platonic relation with the prophet, verse 3. And likewise Israel must dwell for **many days** without royal officials and cult and divination, verse 4.

"Princes" in Israel were functionaries of the king (7:3; 8:4, 10 [RSV]; 13:10), who sometimes played military roles (7:16 [RSV]), so Israel will be stripped of the entire royal institution. **Sacred stones** or pillars *(maṣṣēbôt)* were stones erected at shrines to symbolize the male deity, and they were often set beside lush trees or wooden posts, which represented the female deity. Thus they were standard features at Canaanite baal shrines, symbolizing the sexual fertility of the deities, and they are vigorously condemned throughout the OT (Exod. 23:24; Deut. 7:5; Lev. 26:1; Hos. 10:2; Amos 2:7–8; Mic. 5:13). The exact nature of the **ephod** is unknown, but it was some sort of priestly garment (Exod. 28; 39) and may have had pockets that contained divination instruments, such as the urim and thummim or sacred dice used to give answers to questions (cf. 1 Sam. 23:9–12; 30:7–8). **Idols** were statues or figurines representing household deities and could also be used for divination purposes (cf. Zech. 10:2; Hab. 2:19).

God's love will deprive the Israelites of goods and institutions that have undergirded their faithless life. God's love "takes away the sin of the world" (John 1:29). Very often that means that God removes from us those things that cause us to fall into sin (cf. Hos. 2:17) and that God hedges up our way to those loves of ours that turn us from love of him (cf. Hos. 2:6). God's is a vigorous discipline of us, all in the effort to give us abundant life, like the discipline of a loving father for his children (cf. Deut. 8:2–5). God's love is a love that wants it to go well with us and our children forever (cf. Deut. 5:29). And so the prayer of every Christian is not only thanks for what God has given us, but also thanks for what God has taken away. Through abundance or deprivation, God works for our good in love. **Afterward**, emerging from their period of disciplined training, the Israelites will **seek their God**, verse 5, that is, the covenant relation will be restored or better, be made new (cf. 2:23). And Israel will return to God in obedience, seeking only the good that God offers.

The Hebrew of the last sentence in verse 5 reads, "And they will fear Yahweh and his good in the latter days." To "fear God" can mean either trembling in awe, or obeying, and the latter is the meaning here. Israel will in the future obey the Lord. Further, in obedient faithfulness Israel will seek the good things God offers—not only "the grain, the new wine, and the oil" (2:8 RSV), all those material goods that God alone can give—but also true communion that brings with it joy and peace and the blessings of life, pressed down and running over. From God come all good things. Some day an obedient people of God will acknowledge that fact and act accordingly. Hosea gives no timelines in this prophecy, however, and we do not know if it concerns the discipline of the Assyrian exile after 721 BC or some time beyond that. Only the NT gives a further answer.

---

## Additional Notes §6

---

**3:1 / Your wife**: It is almost inevitable that the question will arise of the identification of the woman in 3:1. The NIV translation simply assumes that the woman is Gomer, when what the Hb. actually says is, "Again go, love a woman who is loved by a friend and is an adulteress, as Yahweh loves the children of Israel, though they are turning to other gods and are lovers of cakes of raisin." Thus, as it is often wont to do, the NIV has adopted one interpretation of a passage that has been almost endlessly and variously interpreted by commentators, though the NIV interpretation is probably correct. It seems impossible that the woman is anyone else than Gomer. Otherwise, she has simply been abandoned to her punishment and fate, and that is a far cry from what we read elsewhere in Hosea's oracles (cf. 2:14–20; 11:8–9; ch. 14).

**Again**: Some commentators read, "And the LORD said to me again," but the word should be connected with "go" and not with "said."

**3:2 / Fifteen shekels of silver and about a homer and a lethek**: A shekel was customarily used in trade and weighed about 11.5 grams. A homer was a dry measure of about eleven bushels, a lethek of about five and one-half bushels. Barley, which was not as valuable as wheat, was often used as fodder in plenteous times. The fact that Hosea pays for Gomer in both silver and kind indicates that he was probably not a wealthy man.

**3:3 / I will live with you**: In the Hb., the last line reads, "And even I to you." That is, just as Gomer must be celibate, so also Hosea will be to her.

**3:5 / And David their king** is probably a Judaic addition to the original, found elsewhere only in Jer. 30:9 and intended to update Hosea's prophecies after the time of the Babylonian exile.

## §7 God's Court Case with People and Priests (Hosea 4:1–10)

The redactor of Hosea's book summarized the prophet's message for us by collecting together the material in chapters 1–3 and placing it at the beginning of the work. The redactor's intention with such a collection was that we read chapters 4–14 in the light of that introductory summary.

With chapter 4, however, we begin an examination of the separate oracles delivered by the prophet. But they too have been arranged by a redactor, and that constitutes a difficulty for their interpreter, because the separate oracles have been strung together in a sequence that often defies clear division.

How, for example, can we determine the original separate units of chapter 4? Only at 4:1 and 5:1 do we have clear indications of the beginnings of oracles. No phrase such as "says the LORD" marks their endings. The speaking of the prophet alternates abruptly with that of the Lord. And the original units seem to be strung together loosely by means of catchwords and subjects.

As a result, scholars differ among themselves as to how to divide chapter 4, and yet that division is crucial for the interpretation of the prophet's message. Should we say that verses 1–3, 4–6, 7–10, 11–14, 15, and 16–19 were all originally independent sayings? Should the chapter be divided into verses 1–3 and verses 4–14, as many commentators divide it? Or should the division be verses 1–3, 4–10, 11–14, and 15–19, again as many scholars make it?

For our purposes, we will divide the chapter as follows, on the basis of rhetorical analysis: verses 1–10, whose theme is really the loss of the springs of life in the land; verses 11–19, which concerns the cultic life of the people, and which begins and ends with the thought of a "spirit of harlotry" (vv. 12 and 19 RSV; the NIV obscures the reference in v. 19).

**4:1–3** / The prophet speaks in verses 1–3 as the messenger of God, repeating the words with which he has been entrusted by his sovereign: God has a court case, a *rîb*, against the citizens of northern Israel, and as both judge and prosecutor God calls them to trial, immediately giving the indictment against them. There is no reliability (*ʾᵉmet*, NIV: **faithfulness**), no loyalty (*ḥesed*, NIV: **love**), no knowledge of God (*daʿat ʾᵉlōhîm*, NIV: **acknowledgment of God**) in the land.

The indictment concerns the relation of the Israelites to both their God and their compatriots. *ʾᵉmet* is found only here in Hosea, but it is synonymous with *ʾᵉmûnâ*, "faithfulness," found in 2:20. It indicates firmness, reliability, truth in both word and deed. *Ḥesed* is always a term of relationship, referring to absolute loyalty in the maintenance of some relationship, and so it is often used of God's covenant love for Israel (Exod. 34:6) and of Israel's for God (Mic. 6:8). *Daʿat ʾᵉlōhîm*, or the knowledge of God, is a key word in Hosea's preaching (RSV cf. 4:6; 6:6) and means much more than simply to "acknowledge" (NIV) that God exists or that one is bound to serve God. Rather, as we saw in connection with 2:20, to "know" Yahweh ( cf. 2:8, 20; 5:4; 6:3; 8:2; 11:3; 13:4) or to have knowledge of him is to know what he has done and said in the past and therefore to love him and cling to him, like a faithful wife to her husband or like an obedient son to his father, in an intimate relation of devotion and trust. We are to read this indictment of Israel in the light of chapters 1–3, and they help us define what is meant by the "knowledge of God."

Because Israel does not walk in reliability and loyalty and knowledge of God, chaos reigns in its society. Lifestyle mirrors the presence or absence of a faithful relation with God. The Israelites break the commandments of the Decalogue, and five of those commandments are mentioned. The people curse and damn one another in God's name (cf. Exod. 20:7). They lie in their relations with their neighbors and especially in their law courts (cf. Exod. 20:16). They murder one another (cf. Exod. 20:13). They steal (which, as in the Decalogue, probably originally referred to kidnapping in the slave trade, cf. Exod. 20:15; 21:16). And they commit adultery (cf. Exod. 20:14). This is one of only two places in the prophetic writings that list stipulations from the Decalogue (the other is in Jer. 7:9). The prophets rarely quoted the law because they knew that the relation with Yahweh entailed heartfelt trust and not just legalistic observance. And indeed, it is noteworthy that these violations of the law are the *result* of a lack of trust and devotion. We betray the Lord first of all in our hearts. Then our betrayal manifests itself in our outward actions toward our neighbors.

Some commentators, who believe that verses 1–3 form a separate unit in themselves, read verse 3 in the future tense, as the judgment on the faithless people, i.e., they will suffer a great drought in which the land will wither and even the sea will dry up. But the NIV is correct in reading the present tense of the verbs, and this is the word of the Lord, inserted into history in the present, that begins to work its way until it is fulfilled. Yahweh, the Lord of life, starts then and there to cut off all the springs of life in the earth. Fertility begins to shrivel away: that is the major theme of verses 1–10.

**4:4–5** / The indictment in this court case takes a sudden and surprising turn when the Lord begins to speak in verse 4. When the Israelites—and we—hear of approaching disaster, their inclination—and ours—is to blame the other fellow. That shunning of responsibility is exactly what the Lord warns the priests against in verse 4. Speaking to each priest personally, God tells him, in so many words, "You are to blame!"—an accusation that does not sit well with the clergy in any age.

The NIV has obscured this meaning by mistranslating verse 4c–d as, **for your people are like those who bring charges against a priest**. Verse 6 clearly shows that God is addressing the priests, and the lines of verse 4c–d should read, as in the RSV, "for with you is my contention *(rîb)*, O priest." The major blame for the people's sin lies with their religious leaders!

An initial sentence is pronounced on each of the priests. They shall stumble by day, along with those cultic prophets who are also leading the people astray and who will stumble by night, i.e., both priest and prophet of the cultic establishment will be punished, verse 5.

Then occurs the strange sentence in verse 5c, **So I will destroy your mother.** Understanding of this comes from remembering that this oracle deals with the sources of life and fertility, which the Lord is going to take away. Thus, the priests' mothers, who bear children, will also be destroyed. The sentence anticipates the thought of verses 7–10.

**4:6** / In verse 6, then, the indictment against each of the priests becomes very specific. Israel's society is soaked with blood (cf. v. 2) and all covenant faithfulness is lacking because the people have no **knowledge** of God. It is the priest's duty to teach such knowledge. It is the priest's responsibility to preserve all of the sacred traditions, to teach them to the people, and to spell out the covenant obligations that such traditions presupposed. All that Yahweh has said and done, all his covenant commandments, all his long history of struggle and love and forgiveness and grace toward his people—these things priests were to teach (cf. Deut. 33:10; Lev. 10:10–11; Ezek. 22:26), as clergy in our day are to teach them. But the priests had not done so. They had rejected that **knowledge,** so Yahweh would **reject** them. They had forgotten the *tôrâ* of their God, so God would "forget" them (NIV reads **ignore,** which is not strong enough) and their offspring. But of course to be forgotten by God is to be loosed from the one source of life itself.

We see here the comprehensive meaning of *tôrâ* (**law**) in the OT. It actually encompassed the whole of Israel's religious tradition—all of its "teaching" about God and what God had done. Perhaps the best illustration of *tôrâ's* full meaning is the book of Deuteronomy, which tells the history of God's loving dealings with Israel and then spells out, by means of commandments, the nature of the love Israel owes to God in return for covenant love. But that comprehensive *tôrâ* the priests of Israel had not taught their people, any more than many clergy in our day have taught it from the Scriptures.

**4:7–10** / The logic of the passage continues in verses 7–10, which further spell out the Lord's judgment on the priests. In verse 6e, God says, he will also "forget" the priests' **children.** That is, such children will no longer be born. Why? Verse 7 furnishes the answer. The more the priests have multiplied, the more of them there have been to sin against God. Rather than teaching the people the *tôrâ*, the priests have simply sought their own welfare by requiring of the people more and more sacrifices at the syncretistic cult sites. Because priests were given portions of the sacrifices and tithes for their food (Num. 18:8–32; Lev. 7:28–38), they greedily encouraged frequent offerings, leading the people to engage more and more in the worship of the fertility deities.

Yahweh the judge therefore pronounces punishment on both the priests and the people. First, in verse 7c he says, "I will change their glory into shame." The NIV has drastically emended the text at this line to make **glory** stand for Yahweh, as in Jeremiah 2:11. But that is not the meaning here. Rather the priests' "glory" in v. 7c stands for their numerous children, and it is that multiplication of their numbers that Yahweh will bring to an end. As the priests and people alike have multiplied, their sins have become more numerous. Yahweh will therefore prevent their further increase, verse 10. They will eat and never have enough. They will engage in the pagan rites of the fertility gods and goddesses, but they will have no fertility, because they have forsaken the Lord who alone is the source of all life and fertility.

This theme—that in God alone are to be found the springs of life—will be sounded again in Hosea's oracles (cf. 7:9; 9:10–14, 16; 13:15–16), as it has been sounded previously (1:10–2:1; 2:8–9). It constitutes one of the major challenges that Hosea's preaching hurls in the face of baalism's fertility cult, ripping from that cult all claims to give abundant life to worshipers. And it still challenges all those religious movements, gurus, and cults that would claim to give us vitality apart from the one Son of God who came that we might have life and have it more abundantly.

### Additional Note §7

**4:4** / The RSV translation of v. 4c–d is based on the reconstructed Hb. *we'immekâ rîbî kōhēn* instead of the MT.

## §8 Israel's Enslavement to Sin (Hosea 4:11–19)

**4:11–12** / The NIV has read all of verse 11 as a continuation of verse 10, adding the second preposition **to** in order to maintain the connection. In the Hebrew, "to harlotries" (NIV: **prostitution**) at the beginning of verse 11 belongs with verse 10. But the following line, **old wine and new,** begins a new oracle. In addition, **my people** is the subject of the first line of verse 12. Thus the whole should read:

> Old wine and new take away understanding (v. 11b).
>
> My people consult a wooden idol (v. 12).
>
> Their staff gives them oracles (reading the suffixes in the pl. instead of the Hb. sing.; cf. the RSV).

The reference to wine reads like a typical wisdom saying. "New wine" refers to grape juice freshly squeezed at the harvest; "old wine" is that which has been fermented. But Hosea is not criticizing drinking as such. Rather, his reference is to the wild bacchanalian rites that Israel is participating in at the baalistic cult sites, and the passage goes on to give us a description of those rites.

First the prophet scornfully mentions the oracles that the Israelites seek from **a wooden idol,** verse 12. The Hebrew reads "tree" and the reference can be to the wooden cultic poles or *ᵃšērôt* that were set up beside altars, to wooden images or teraphim as such, or to oracular trees, from which the people sought answers to their questions. **Stick of wood** is literally "staff" and can refer to an *ᵃšērâ*. The pagan thought that any natural object could be used by the deity to mediate a revelation; this understanding of the relation of God to the natural world is fiercely contested throughout the OT and in Israel's basic covenant law (cf. Exod. 20:4–5; Deut. 4:15–19; 5:8–9).

**4:13** / Verse 13 then gives us a description of the baalistic "high places" or worship sites. Located on high **mountaintops** or lower **hills,** they were furnished with an altar, $^{\jmath a}s\bar{e}r\hat{o}t$ (or perhaps $ma\d{s}\d{s}\bar{e}b\hat{o}t$, which were stone heaps or pillars), and one or more sacred trees. Hosea specifies three kinds of trees, all of which provide abundant shade. Thus the Deuteronomic tradition speaks repeatedly of such high places "on every high hill and under every green tree" (RSV; 1 Kgs. 14:23; 2 Kgs. 17:10, etc.). Regular sacrifices were offered at such high places; a portion of the sacrifices was eaten in the pleasant shade of the trees, while the inedible parts were burned as offerings to the gods.

Most disgusting, however, were the sexual rites carried on under the trees. There, says the prophet, the virgin **daughters** of Israel played the harlot, and brides committed adultery: such is the reading of the Hebrew of verse 13e–f. To what is Hosea referring?

Very likely the picture is of those maidens and betrothed young women who offer their bodies to strangers at the baal cult site, acting out the rite of "sacral marriage" just once, in order to ensure fertility in their subsequent marriages (cf. Jer. 2:20, 25). The women were given a gift of money at the time, a "harlot's hire" (Deut. 23:18 and Deut. 22:13–21 were probably directed at this Canaanite practice).

**4:14–16** / Surprisingly, however, the Lord says in Hosea 4:14 that he **will not punish** the women. Rather, he lays the blame on the men who go to the cult sites to ravish such young women. If the men did not participate, the women would not be violated and harlotrous! The verse forms a marvelous and early divine rejection of all sexual double standards. Indeed, Yahweh says that the men corrupt not only the young women, but also the cultic **prostitutes,** who are regular employees at the baal shrines. If the men did not seek them out, the prostitutes' trade would be eliminated. This verse is very pertinent to those still involved in "the world's oldest profession."

The origin of verse 15 has been endlessly debated. It is most likely that the mention of **Judah** is a later Judean insert into Hosea's original prophecy. We made such a judgment in connection with "the house of Judah" in 1:7. It is very unlikely that Judeans would make pilgrimages to the northern shrines of **Gilgal** and Bethel. Gilgal lay in the Jordan Valley near Jericho. Bethel, which Hosea labels **Beth Aven,** "house of wickedness," following Amos 5:5 (NIV margin), was one of the two most important cult sites founded by Jeroboam I (1 Kgs. 12:28–30) and was the location of the "king's sanctuary" (Amos 7:13). North of Jerusalem, it lay at an elevation of 2400 feet, and so pilgrims "went up" to Bethel, but we have no record of southerners making the trip. Thus, verse 15 probably originally read: "Though you are a harlot, O Israel, do not become guilty." That is, "do not give in to your harlotrous nature. Do not make pilgrimages to Gilgal and Bethel, where the baal cult has corrupted all worship, and do not there swear by Yahweh's name, taking an oath or making a vow in his name when you are really worshiping Baal. That is taking the Lord's name in vain, and 'the LORD will not hold him guiltless who takes his name in vain' " (Exod. 20:7 RSV). The verse, with its mention of guilt, is a clear reference to the third commandment of the Decalogue, Hosea having earlier mentioned five commandments from that covenant law (4:2).

**4:17–19** / What follows reads like the prophet's musing on the futility of giving Israel such commandments, however. For Israel is **joined to idols,** and the verb means Israel has entered into confederacy or covenant with them, verse 17. Israel is **stubborn** like an untamed **heifer,** fighting against Yahweh's yoking law. There is no way it can be let loose into the broad place of responsible freedom, as if it were a lamb in a roomy pasture. The word that the NIV translates with **meadow** has the meaning of a broad space, and the figure of such broadness is often used in the OT of Yahweh's salvation; that is, salvation is having room to live, being set in the wide space of responsible freedom (cf. 2 Sam. 22:20, 37; Job 36:16; Ps. 31:8; 118:5; 119:45, 96; Isa. 33:21).

Thus, Israel, here called **Ephraim,** is just to be left alone to follow its harlotry to ruin, verse 17 (cf. 14). Even after all the old and new wine are gone, at the cult sites of the baals the people and the rulers of the people continue in their sexual, shameful ways, verse 18. Why? Because a "spirit," a wind (*rûaḥ;* NIV: **whirlwind**), has wrapped them in its wings and bears them steadily toward their doom.

Israel in its worship of the fertility gods and goddesses is captive to a "spirit of harlotry" (vv. 12 RSV, 19). That is the major theme of this oracle, and it is a theme that Hosea will develop further in chapter 5. The Israelites are unable to repent and mend their ways. They can not relinquish their worship of the baals and obey the covenant commandments of their God. They are slaves of their sin (cf. Rom. 6:16–18), and unless God does away with the baals (cf. 2:17) and gives the Israelites a new nature, bestowing on them a faithfulness that they do not have in themselves (cf. 2:20), they cannot reform. What the people cannot do for themselves, God must do for them. Otherwise they are lost.

# §9 God's Absence (Hosea 5:1–7)

In this oracle, Hosea describes the deeds of his three addressees in the exact reverse of their order in verse 1a–c. First, he tells of the murderous ways of the royal house, verses 1e–2a. Then he discusses the captivity of the Israelites to a spirit of harlotry, verses 3c–5. Finally, he turns to the cult where the priests officiate, verses 6–7b. And after each description, the punishment for such ways is stated, verses 2b, 5b–c, and 7c–d. The oracle holds together in a unified form, as it stands in the MT.

**5:1–2** / The interpreter is confronted with at least two very difficult and interrelated problems in 5:1–7. The first has to do with the reading of the text in verse 2a, the second with verse 7c–d. The NIV has translated verse 2a, **The rebels are deep in slaughter.** The Hebrew reads, "and killing revolters, they have made deep," which seems to make little sense. Therefore most commentators have emended the line to read, "And a pit dug deep at Shittim," reading *wᵉšaḥat haššiṭṭîm*.

This latter translation has the advantage of continuing the metaphor of hunting, which begins in verse 1 with the mention of the fowler's snare and the hunter's net. It also yields a perfectly formed divine saying in verse 1–2, consisting of a threefold call to listen, a threefold hunting image, and a line occurring after each of the triads.

On the basis of the proposed emendation to 5:2a, some commentators have maintained that verses 1–2 form a separate and complete oracle. If that is the division made in the text, however, it means that the prophet and not Yahweh is speaking in verse 3, when he says "I know Ephraim" (RSV), and that seems highly unlikely.

Rather, the complete oracle is formed by verses 1–7, and the meaning of verse 2a must be made clear. What is being said here in verses 1–2? The prophet proclaims a threefold imperative to the **priests,** to all of the **Israelites** (not just to the elders, as some would interpret), and lastly, to the **royal house.** In short, the whole populace is called upon to hear Hosea's words. (For the form, cf. Isa. 1:2, 10; Joel 1:2; Mic. 1:2.) But the emphasis falls on the third member of the triad, as is often the case in Hebrew rhetoric—on the **royal house**—and a special admonition is given: **This judgment is against you.**

The royal house, the king and the officials of the court, have been a fowler's **snare at Mizpah** and a hunter's **net at Tabor,** catching not birds and game, but persons. And those whom they have unjustly caught and killed have been those Israelites who have opposed their rule. Contrary to the NIV's translation, royalty have not been the **rebels;** rather, the word refers to those who have opposed the unjust and syncretistic ways of royalty. And the line should be read, "killing revolters, they have made deep corruption," supplying the noun *šaḥaṭ*, "corruption," as in 9:9. Because some persons have opposed the royal house, they have been captured and killed, and the royal house has thereby corrupted itself. Commentators have long wondered what events occurred at the border town of Mizpah and at Tabor on the northeastern edge of the Jezreel Valley, but Hosea tells us what occurred there: rebels against the royal house were caught and killed.

Because of the murderous ways of the royal house, Yahweh says, "I will be a chastisement for them all," verse 2b and the pronoun "I" is emphasized, pointing to God's sovereignty over human royalty. The NIV has translated **discipline,** and that does indeed catch the meaning of the noun for "chastisement," *mûsār* (cf. Prov. 3:11; Job 5:17; Isa. 26:16). As in 3:3-4, the Lord will chastise or reprove in order to correct. The purpose of God's judgment will be salvation, as is always God's purpose, but not before Israel and its royal house have undergone the most severe judgment.

**5:3-4** / In verses 3ff., the prophet then turns to the Israelites as a body. The Hebrew of verse 3a reads, "I know Ephraim," and that means much more than simply knowing **about** them and what they have done.

The Lord speaks from a covenant relation of love with a bride, of tenderness toward a son. God knows Israel as a husband knows his wife and as a father knows his child. Nothing about Israel is hidden. And so from a relationship gone sour, Yahweh states that his bride has turned to harlotry with the fertility deities of the land and thereby corrupted herself. The niphal verb (and it is a verb and not an adjective) has the meaning of making oneself unclean, defiled (cf. 6:10; Jer. 2:23; Ezek. 20:30, etc.) and therefore of making oneself incapable of participating in worship and of approaching God (cf. Lev. 10:10).

It follows that the defiled and unclean Israelites cannot **return to their God,** verse 4, for the true God is a jealous God, who will allow no rivals to his rule (cf. Exod. 20:3–6; Josh. 24:19–20). Or, perhaps better, God is a holy God who cannot be approached in worship by sinful and therefore defiled and unholy human beings (cf. Lev. 15:31; Isa. 6:2–5; Zech. 13:1; 1 Thess. 4:7).

The Israelites, however, are unable to repent and to cleanse themselves of their sin by renouncing and turning from their harlotry with the baals, for they are captive to **a spirit of** harlotry in their midst (contra NIV: **in their heart**). As in 4:12 and 4:19, the Israelites have become enslaved to their sin and have no possibility of returning by their own power to a faithful and loving relationship with God.

Verse 4, along with 4:12, 19, is a powerful illustration of the futility of moralism, according to the biblical faith. A prophet or a preacher may admonish the people to turn from their evil ways and to do the good, in obedience to God alone. But if that people is captive to a "spirit of harlotry," they have no power to turn, and urging them to do so is like urging a prisoner in a cage to decorate his cage a bit—maybe by putting a rug on the floor or hanging a picture on the wall—when what he really needs is for someone to come and open the door. Slaves to sin must be released from their captivity by the action of God. Only then do they have the freedom to do the good. And that, of course, is the primary message of Hosea: God will do for Israel what Israel cannot do for itself. God will free Israel from captivity to Baal (see the comment at 2:16–20). Equally, that is the message of the Christian gospel—that God in Jesus Christ has opened the door of the cage. Or to use a different figure, God has broken the chains of sin that enslave us and has set us free to walk by the Spirit (Rom. 6; Gal. 5:22–24).

**5:5–7** / Before this act of salvation, God will judge Israel's faithlessness, however, verses 5–7. Though helpless in sin, Israel does not recognize its own corruption and takes great pride in its syncretistic and lavish worship (v. 5), flocking to the high places to offer multitudinous sacrifices (v. 6). That very action condemns Israel, however, testifying to its faithlessness, as in a court of law. Israel worships Baal under the guise of worshiping Yahweh and brings forth children conceived in the abhorrent sexual rites of the baal cult (v. 7). As a result, Yahweh has withdrawn himself from his faithless people and left them to their fate, abandoning them to the death that is inevitable when the God of life is absent (v. 7).

Some commentators have emended verse 7c–d to read, "Now the locusts shall devour their fields," because it is unclear how the **New Moon festivals** could **devour** the people **and their fields.** Apparently, however, the baalistic sex rites were practiced at the time of the new moon, and verse 7c–d is stating that the deathly consequences of that idolatrous worship will be allowed by God to run their course.

Both Old Testament and New include the thought of God abandoning the people and "giving them over" to the consequences of their sin (Amos 8:11–12; Rom. 1:24–32; Rev. 6:8; cf. Isa. 1:15; Jer. 14:12; Ezek. 20:3, 31). No punishment could be greater than to be entirely loosed from the hand of God, for that means that one is cut off from the very source and sustainer of life itself. Chaos and death are the inevitable consequences, as Israel in the time of Hosea will finally learn.

## §10 Yahweh's Use of the Syro-Ephraimitic War (Hosea 5:8–15)

When we moderns read the Scripture, we are tempted to divest it of its historical contexts and to turn it into timeless truths and principles. The result is that we deny the basic testimony of the Scripture and therefore its actual revelation—namely, that God has acted in human history in particular times and places, in relation to specific nations and persons.

Scripture itself repeatedly recalls us from such ahistorical piety, however, by giving us date lines and time lines. And sometimes the historical setting of a passage intrudes so prominently that it sets us running to our reference books to read up on the years to which it is related. Such is the case with Hosea 5:8–15.

This passage is set within the context of the Syro-Ephraimitic war of 735–733 BC. The quiet time of the last years of the reign of Jeroboam II is past; a time of international intrigue and conflict now ensues. We know that when Tiglath-pileser III (745–727 BC) ascended the Assyrian throne, he marched with his armies to the West to conquer the small states of the Fertile Crescent. More than a century earlier, in 853 BC, a coalition of Western states had turned back Assyrian aggression. Pekah of Israel (735–732 BC) banded together with Rezin of Aram and a number of other small kingdoms in the effort to halt the Assyrian advance once again. Ahaz of Judah (735–715 BC) refused to join the alliance, whereupon Pekah and Rezin attacked Jerusalem (Isa. 7:1–9). Judah summoned Assyria to its aid, and the allies were overwhelmed. Much of Israel's population was deported and its landholdings were reduced to the central hill country of Ephraim and Benjamin.

Judah reclaimed Gibeah and Rabah as part of its northern defense, and the rest of Israel's land was incorporated into the Assyrian provincial system. Pekah was assassinated by Hoshea ben Elah (732–724 BC), who preserved what was left of Israel only by payment of heavy tribute to Assyria (2 Kgs. 15:27–17:1). These are the events that lie behind Hosea 5:8–15.

**5:8–12** / Thus, in verse 8, the prophet, serving as a watchman would serve, calls for the sounding of horns and trumpets to warn the inhabitants of Israel, here called **Ephraim,** to flee to their fortified cities and to prepare for war against an approaching enemy (cf. Jer. 4:5; 6:1). The enemy comes from the south, and the advance of Judah to retake **Gibeah** and **Ramah,** which were respectively three and five miles north of Jerusalem, is probably in view. Bethel is eleven miles north of Jerusalem, and all three towns lay in the territory of **Benjamin.** Verse 8d reads, in the Hebrew, "after you, Benjamin," and has the meaning, "They are coming after you, Benjamin" (contra NIV).

**Ephraim will be laid waste on the day of** punishment (v. 9), referring most likely to Assyria's devastation of the country. That is the word that Hosea has heard from Yahweh, and it is a **certain** word, that is, it will come to pass. The judgment announced is not only against Ephraim, however, for **Judah** too is guilty, because as it has advanced northward into Ephraim it has removed the **boundary stones** that marked out each tribe's allotment of land from Yahweh at the time of the conquest under Joshua. The land has been Yahweh's gift to his people. He, as Lord of the earth, has fixed its tribal and familial boundaries just as he fixes the boundaries of all nations (cf. Acts 17:26). To remove those boundary stones is a sin against his lordship (Deut. 19:14; cf. Job 24:2), a rebellious deed for which the sinner is cursed (Deut. 27:17). Hosea is speaking here according to the ancient tribal traditions of Israel in the time of the Judges and early monarchy, when instead of being two nations of North and South, with many shrines, Israel was one people in a federation formed around a central shrine. Judah's sin against Ephraim, therefore, is a sin against its own countrymen, a breach of brotherly covenant, a betrayal of a family member, and for that sin, Yahweh will pour out his wrath like water upon Judah, verse 10.

Ephraim thought to protect itself from Assyria by its pact with Rezin of Aram, verse 11. But in doing so, Ephraim went after "vanity" (RSV), and it has been crushed by Assyria. The NIV has emended *ṣāw* to read **idols,** but the word is probably a synonym of *šāwᵓ*, meaning "what is worthless." Ephraim cannot protect itself from destruction, because the nations moving against it are being used by Yahweh as instruments of judgment on its sin. The Lord is eating away at the fabric of Ephraim's life, **like a moth.** God is destroying Ephraim's underpinnings like dry **rot** destroys wood, and there is no defense, verse 12. The similes that Hosea employs here for Yahweh's work apply not to his person but to his action. God is not a moth or dry rot, but God sometimes works in human life in the hidden fashion of those destroyers—as Isaiah later puts it, "Here a little, there a little; that they may go, and fall backward, and be broken, and snared, and taken" (Isa. 28:13 RSV). Silent and unseen, and sometimes gradually but also steadily, God works his judgments until disaster falls upon the rebels against his rule.

**5:13–15** / There is nothing that Ephraim and Judah can do, moreover, to turn aside God's advancing judgment upon them. They finally wake up to the fact that Assyria's military advance is destroying their life, verse 13, and Hoshea desperately seeks to preserve his kingdom by sending a tribute to Shalmaneser, son of Tiglath-pileser III (2 Kgs. 17:3). The NIV has added the words **for help** to verse 13d, but the reference is probably to Hoshea's payment of tribute. Thus, both Judah and Ephraim seek to preserve their lives by political maneuver. But those who would save their lives and who desert their God will lose their lives, for the source of Israel's downfall is not Assyria, but God, the Lord over Assyria and all nations (cf. Isa. 10:5–6), and it is in God alone that Ephraim and Judah can find any healing for their wounds.

The Hebrew of verse 14 is therefore absolutely emphatic. *I* **will be like a lion . . .;** *I* **will tear them to pieces. . . .** There is no help from anyone when God, like a hungry young lion, attacks a people. (For the same simile, cf. 13:7; Amos 1:2; 3:4, 8.) Once again the similes startle, this time to picture the ferocity of God's attack. God will **carry** this people **off**—a veiled reference to the people's exile—and there is no one who can "save" *(nṣl)* the people of God from that God-decreed fate.

Some commentators have understood the simile of the lion to continue into verse 15, so that the picture in that verse is one of the lion returning to his lair. More probably, the verse is either the prophet's or the collector's transitional device, to introduce the litany of repentance in 6:1–3. The thought that Yahweh will withdraw from the people echoes 5:6. The people's realization of their guilt before God and their turning to God recall 3:5 and anticipate 14:2–3. However, since the prophet has earlier stated that it is impossible for the people to repent and return to their God (5:4–5), verse 15 must be set in the context of the book as a whole: finally, only Yahweh will make Israel's return possible.

## §11 Israel's Hollow Repentance (Hosea 6:1–6)

Contrary to the LXX, which connects this passage with 5:15 by the addition of the word, "saying" (as in the RSV), this pericope is complete in itself as one more record of Israel's deceitful ways toward God. Overcome by Assyria's engulfment of them (see the comment on 5:8–15), the Israelites call a day of repentance in the effort to secure for themselves God's aid once again.

Such fasts of repentance are held in Israel whenever there is a calamity of any sort—defeat by enemies, pestilence among the population, plagues of locusts, drought, famine, and so forth. Summoned by the priests, the people abstain from food and drink and all normal activity, and gather at the sanctuary to offer sacrifices, to mourn their sinfulness, and to cry for God's help. Often they prostrate themselves in the dust, strike their breasts, rend their clothes, sprinkle ashes on themselves (cf. the practices of Ash Wednesday), and don sackcloth (cf. Judg. 20:26; Isa. 32:12; 58:5; Joel 1:14; 2:12–13; Amos 5:16–17; Jonah 3:5–9, etc.).

**6:1–3** / Hosea therefore quotes the words of the Israelites in 6:1–3, as they gather for a public fast of repentance. But their arrogance is vividly portrayed. They make no prayer to God for rescue. Rather, they speak only to one another, assuring themselves that the God who **has torn** them (cf. 5:14) **will heal** them, and the God who has wounded them (cf. 5:13) will bandage them up—the verbs are deliberately repeated from 5:13–14, though the NIV obscures the repetition. The Israelites still had enough faith to know that God was behind their military defeat and that Assyria was the rod of God's anger (cf. Isa. 10:5). But they did not have enough knowledge of God's character to know that they could not presume on God's love for them.

In 5:15, God announces, "I will return (NIV: "go back") to my place." But the Israelites believe that if they **return** to God (6:1) by offering sacrifices at a public fast, God will automatically appear (6:3) and come forth with aid and protection for them once more. Certainly sacrifices were sufficient to appease Baal; surely meal offerings (v. 6a) and burnt offerings (v. 6b) were sufficient for Yahweh also. Indeed, God's ways are compared in verse 3 with the ways of nature and therefore of the nature deities. **As surely as the sun** always **rises** and the **winter** and **spring rains** always come, God's return to the covenant people is also guaranteed. The verse shows how seriously Israel had confused Yahweh with Baal, a confusion comparable to our equation of the resurrection of Christ with the return of all life in the springtime—a confusion in which nature's cycle is substituted for God's historical activity.

**6:4–6** / God replies in first person speech to Israel's arrogant certainty, in verses 4–6. But surprisingly, his reply is not a blast in wrath, announcing destroying judgment, but an agonized inner searching to find some saving way to deal with his wayward people (cf. 11:8–9). In the past, God's judgments by means of the prophets have fallen **like lightning** (Hb.: "light") upon the chosen. God's word has worked its punishing effect: the word of God is understood here, as always in the Bible, as an active, objective force that works until it effects that of which it speaks. But apparently those prophetic words of judgment, though they have **killed,** have not brought the people to repentance.

God therefore gives clear instruction about just what is desired from his covenant folk, verse 6. He wants *ḥesed,* "covenant loyalty" (NIV: **mercy**) and not daily sacrifices, *daᶜat ᵓelōhîm,* "knowledge of God" (NIV: **acknowledgment of God**) and not **burnt offerings.** In short, Yahweh wants his wife Israel's heart, or his son Israel's loyalty, bound to him in trust and love and faithfulness. No sacrifice, no ritual repentance can substitute for that intimate relation of cleaving to God. And of course what God desires, and not what human beings desire, finally determines the destiny of all peoples.

The Lord is not here condemning all sacrifice per se, as if a purely spiritual religion were being substituted for a sacrificial religion. Rather, God is explaining to his people that their worship apart from the sincere engagement of their hearts in love and loyalty for their God is a worthless exercise (cf. 1 Sam. 15:22; Isa. 29:13–14). Devotion of the heart, loyal love of God for his people and of his people for God, characterizes the true nature of the biblical covenant relationship (cf. Matt. 9:13; 12:7).

## Additional Note §11

**6:5**  /  The Hb. reads "Your judgment," as in the LXX and Syr., and it really is not necessary to emend the text as the NIV, RSV, and NRSV have done.

## §12 Supporting Evidence of Sin (Hosea 6:7–11a)

It is very difficult to know whether or not these verses should be understood as a continuation of the unit in 6:1–6. Certainly they give evidence of the fact that Israel's repentance is totally hollow, and the Hebrew connects verse 7 with verse 6 by means of an adversative *waw* (omitted in the NIV): "But they like Adam . . . ." The specific sins (vv. 8–9) are bracketed by general indictments in verses 7 and 10. Thus, though verses 7–11a may originally have made up a separate unit, the assembler of Hosea's oracles has placed them here as illustrations of verses 4–6.

**6:7** / Many commentators emend verse 7 to read, "But at Adam . . . ," taking **Adam** as the name of the city mentioned in Joshua 3:16. The verses then become a "geography of sin in Israel" (Mays) that points to specific sins in the three cities of Adam, Gilead, and Shechem. What those sins were, however, is uncertain.

Rather, it seems preferable to read, with the NIV, **Like Adam**. . . . It is very possible that the tradition of Genesis 3 was known to Hosea, and that the prophet is here referring to the universal perfidy of humankind, in which Israel has implicated itself. Thus, Judah too is party to that **covenant** breaking of Adam and will consequently face the judgment, along with Israel. Verse 11a need not be regarded as a later Judean addition, despite the fact that "harvest" usually refers to a final eschatological judgment (Jer. 51:33; Joel 3:13; cf. Matt. 9:37 and parallel). By starting with Adam, Hosea speaks of Israel's history in its totality, from beginning to end.

**6:8** / In verse 8, however, Hosea leaves the general for the specific. What were Israel's sins at **Gilead** (probably referring to Ramoth-Gilead in the central highlands of Gilead, on the eastern side of the Jordan)? Two possibilities present themselves. It was at Gilead that the prophet sent by Elisha anointed Jehu king of Israel (2 Kgs. 9), and given the fact that Hosea has earlier called to mind Jehu's bloody revolution (1:4), this anointing may be the reference intended by **footprints of blood** (cf. 2 Kgs. 9:26, 33). On the other hand, according to 2 Kings 15:25, fifty men of Gilead participated in Pekah's assassination of King Pekahiah, and given the following pericope concerning the intrigues and murders connected with the kingship (7:3–7), the assassination may be the sin being specified here. Although Hosea's hearers knew to what bloody deeds Yahweh was referring in this speech, we have no way of knowing for sure. In either instance, however, it had to do with the turbulent and murderous ways of the monarchy.

**6:9–11a** / With regard to **murder on the road to Shechem,** verse 9, the verse is probably further evidence of Hosea's connection with the northern levitical and prophetic reform movement (see the introduction), that harked back to the Mosaic covenant theology of the tribal federation. The central shrine of that federation was first located at Shechem (Josh. 24:1; 8:30–35), a territory occupied peacefully by Israel at the time of the conquest. There all of the Israelite tribes, who had moved into Canaan in various ways and various times, were initiated into covenant with Yahweh and made one people. There they pledged themselves to obey the Sinai covenant (Josh. 24:24–25; Deut. 27:1–10). Thus Shechem became the symbol of loyalty to the Mosaic faith, and Hosea, with his references to the covenant commands (4:2, 15), was among those reformers who championed that faith in the eighth century.

Opposing such reformers were the Israelite monarchy and the priests of the syncretistic cult, whom Hosea so condemns (4:4–8; 5:1, 3–7). Judging from Hos. 6:9, the priests' opposition to those championing pure Mosaic religion went so far as to lead them to murder some of the reform's followers.

The sin of Israel is summed up, then, in verse 10, and it has its origin in Israel's harlotrous worship of the gods and goddesses of fertility—that **horrible thing** in which the Israelites have placed their confidence and to which they have given their lives.

## §13 God's Wistful Lament (Hosea 6:11b–7:2)

Anyone who thinks that the concerns of faith should never be mixed with the concerns of politics will have a difficult time with Hosea, chapter 7, for it is with Israel's political life that this section deals. Moreover, it is Yahweh, the Lord of history, who speaks most of the time in this section, with the prophet's voice joining that of his Lord at only two points (7:5–6, 10).

**6:11b–7:2** / God muses and sometimes seems to have internal arguments in the book of Hosea (cf. 6:4; 11:8–9). That is what we find in 6:11b–7:2, where God's musing takes on the tone of an apologetic lament. God wants to **heal** Israel, which is Hosea's way of saying that God wants to forgive the people (cf. 14:4) and return to the intimate communion that they knew in the wilderness (cf. 2:15). To **restore the fortunes,** in 6:11b, means "to return to the former state," to make Israel once more blessed. God is loathe to give up on **my people.** Always God's desire is to do good to his people (cf. Deut. 5:29; Ezek. 18:32), to love them and bless them and pour out his grace upon them.

When God's people deliberately turn away, however, he cannot fulfill these merciful desires for them. For in Israel, God sees a people whose sins encompass (literally, surround; NIV: **engulf**) them and hold them captive (cf. 5:4; 4:12). The holy one (cf. 11:9, 12) cannot dwell with sin. The Israelites think that God does not remember their evil deeds of the past, but God says, **they are always before me,** 7:2. Thus, in this short pericope, we find God regretfully lamenting the fact that Israel will not let him carry out his fond desire to forgive and restore them to his fellowship.

The **thieves** and **bandits** of verse 1 refer not to robbers of goods, but to the priests who gain their own lavish lifestyle from numerous sacrifices to Baal (4:8) and who murder those who are opposed to them—the word for "bandits" is the same as that translated "marauders" in 6:9. The thought is remarkably similar to Jeremiah 2:26, where kings, princes, priests (RSV), and prophets are also likened to thieves.

## §14 Israel's Efforts to Save Herself (Hosea 7:3–7)

**7:3–7** / These verses are an illustration from the political realm of Israel's **evil deeds** mentioned in 7:2. Indeed, the same word is repeated in 7:3a to tie the two passages together, but the NIV has obscured that fact by translating the word as **wickedness** instead of repeating "evil deeds."

The passage mirrors the turbulent state of Israel's monarchy. Between 746 and 732 BC, four of Israel's kings were assassinated by their successors (see the introduction). Hosea's specific reference in verse 3 is probably to those supporters of Hoshea ben Elah, who put Hoshea on the throne by assassinating King Pekah. But the plural reference to **kings** in verse 7 indicates that Hosea has the whole bloody history of the monarchy in mind.

In the most vivid of images, Hosea compares the plotters of royal intrigue and overthrow to the fire of an **oven** that first smolders and then bursts into flame. So hot are the murderous passions of the plotters that they burn like a fire that needs no stirring, verse 4. Ovens in Israel were made of fired clay, cylindrical in shape, with stone or earthen floors and sides that sloped upward toward an orifice at the top. Dough was kneaded with yeast and made into flat cakes that were then plastered on the sloping walls of the oven. Every household had its oven, but there were also royal and urban bakeries (cf. 1 Sam. 8:13; Jer. 37:21; Neh. 3:11), and Hosea may have drawn his figure of speech from the royal ovens of the capital city.

It is difficult to know how to interpret verse 5. Does **the festival of our king** refer to the coronation of a new king or to a festal celebration of an established king? Which king do **the princes** support? Does their drunkenness lead them to revolt against the throne or is it just a sign of their senselessness? And who are the **mockers** whom the king joins, and what are they mocking? The general meaning of the passage is clear, but we cannot be sure of specific details.

One fact stands out, however: the Israelites **devour their rulers,** like a fire burning up a loaf of bread or like a fire devouring a city (cf. 8:14; Jer. 17:27; Amos 1 passim, etc.). In the frantic effort to save its own life in the international realm of empires, Israel relies first on one king and then on another, hoping with each successive ruler that its life will be made secure. But Israel does not look to the one who rules over empires and who is the giver of all life, verse 7. Thus, Israel's political leaders are also called **adulterers** by the prophet, verse 4, for they are unfaithful to their covenant God when they rely on any power besides God. Those who would save their own lives will lose them. Life cannot be had apart from the Lord.

## §15 Israel's Loss of Identity (Hosea 7:8–12)

**7:8–12** / Hosea 7:3–7 dealt with Israel's internal politics. Hosea 7:8–12 now looks to its international relations. Israel **mixes with the nations,** verse 8. Continuing the metaphor of baking from 7:3–7, Israel's relation with other nations is compared to the mixing of oil with flour to form a flat loaf of bread (cf. Exod. 29:2; Lev. 2:5). In short, Israel has become like all the other nations.

The passage undoubtedly reflects the frantic efforts of Israel's kings to ally themselves militarily with their neighbors or with one of the great powers in order to preserve the nation. When Tiglath-pileser III of Assyria began his march to the west in 745 BC, King Menahem of Israel paid him an enormous tribute in order to prop up his shaky throne (2 Kgs. 15:19–20). However, Menahem's successor-son Pekahiah was assassinated in 737 BC by Pekah ben Remaliah, who attempted to put together an anti-Assyrian alliance formed with Aram and Philistia—an alliance that led to the Syro-Ephraimitic war when King Ahaz of Judah refused to join it. Possibly Pekah also hoped for Egyptian help. The alliance totally failed to halt the armies of Assyria, however, and the complete loss of Israelite territory to Tiglath-pileser was prevented only by the assassination of Pekah and the payment of an enormous tribute to Assyria by King Hoshea ben Elah (2 Kgs. 15:30; 17:3). However, when Tiglath-pileser was succeeded on the Assyrian throne by Shalmaneser V in 726 BC, Hoshea sent messengers to Egypt in the attempt to gain that empire's help in throwing off the Assyrian yoke (2 Kgs. 17:4–6). Egypt was too weak to lend any aid, and in 722–721 BC, the ten northern tribes were exiled to Mesopotamia and the population replaced by foreigners.

To our way of thinking, Israel's actions on the international scene might seem logical and necessary, but God compares those frantic actions to the wild flying back and forth of a silly **dove** that has no sense, verse 11. Why? Because Israel was God's elected nation, intended to be set apart and different from every other nation on the face of the earth. Israel was Yahweh's "holy nation" (Exod. 19:6), that is, Israel was a people set apart for the purposes of God, "a people who live apart and do not consider themselves one of the nations" (Num. 23:9). Israel was never to consider itself to be like other nations (Ezek. 20:32). Rather, it was God's chosen people, God's *sᵉgullâ*, God's "treasured possession" (Exod. 19:5), unlike any other people in the world.

But according to this passage in Hosea, Israel has forgotten who it is; it has lost its unique identity. Israel is, says the prophet, like a **flat cake** of bread inside of an oven, that is **not turned over** by the baker and therefore burns and becomes inedible, verse 8. Israel is like an old man, with **gray hair,** approaching death, verse 9. The remarkable fact, however, is that Israel does not realize it is dying. Twice in verse 9, the prophet repeats the phrase, "and he knows it not," a repetition obscured by the NIV translation (see the RSV). Israel is totally without understanding and sense. In pride, Israel does not turn to the Lord (**a flat cake not turned over**); Israel does not even realize her fatal condition. Because he is dealing with the issue of life and vitality, Hosea repeatedly uses figures that depict Israel's sin in terms of the loss of vitality.

The result of Israel's senselessness is the judgment pronounced by God in verse 12. Like a fowler catching birds, the Lord will pull Israel down from its frantic flight between nations and subject it to judgment.

The NIV has adopted an emendation of verse 12c that was suggested by *Das Alte Testament Deutsch.* The Hebrew of the line reads, "I will chastise them according to the report to (of?) their congregation" (cf. the NRSV). Many scholars emend the last word, so the sentence reads, "I will chastise them according to the report of their evil." The RSV reads "I will chastise them for their wicked deeds." Either of these last two emendations seems preferable to the NIV reading. Certainly, however, the verse forms God's announcement of judgment on his sinful folk.

## §16 The Fatal Contrast (Hosea 7:13–16)

The whole section of 6:11b–7:16 begins and ends with the same theme: the disappointment of God's love. God wanted to restore Israel to communion with himself (6:11b). God wants to redeem Israel from the Assyrian threat (7:13). God has always been the Israelites' stay, disciplining and strengthening them (7:15). But the Israelites will have none of God. They have strayed from God's fellowship, rebelled against God's lordship, and even spoken ill of him. Therefore, God's judgment on Israel is inevitable.

**7:13** / **Woe** in verse 13 clearly marks off verses 13–16 as a separate oracle. Woes were pronounced over those who were doomed or who were already dead, and so this oracle is an announcement from Yahweh that Israel is doomed to die. The reason for the announcement gathers up the two primary sins for which Israel is condemned throughout the book of Hosea: the sin of apostasy, in turning to worship the baals, and the sin of rebellion, in relying on politics and other nations for deliverance (see the introduction).

The depth of Israel's perfidy is emphasized by the contrasts drawn in the Hebrew:

> verse 13c: "*I* [emphasized with a separate pronoun] would redeem them, but *they* [again emphasized with a separate pronoun] spoke against me lies."

> verse 15: "And *I* [emphasized] trained them, I strengthened their arms, but me they regarded as evil."

The verb **rebelled** in verse 13b is from the Hebrew *pāšaʿ*, is frequently found in the prophetic writings, and is the strongest term used for sin in the OT. It is a political term, indicating refusal to submit to authority, e.g., rebellion against a king (cf. 1 Kgs. 12:19). Thus God here accuses Israel of denying his lordship, of being subversive in his kingdom. But the fact that God is Lord over Israel makes judgment on this rebellion necessary, for if God overlooked such revolt, he would not be Israel's Lord. God wants to **redeem** Israel. That is, he wants to buy Israel back from religious slavery to Baal and political slavery to foreign nations. Both hold Israel captive, encompassing the people with a spirit of harlotry (4:12; 5:4) and of adultery (7:4). But when God would redeem his people, **they speak lies against** God. The term "lies" probably refers to Israel's false identification of Yahweh with the fertility gods and is intended to characterize what follows in verse 14.

**7:14–16** / The Israelites cry to God for help in the face of the Assyrian onslaught, but their petitions are not **from their hearts,** that is, they are senseless (cf. 7:11), showing no understanding of God's true nature. Rather, Yahweh is worshiped as if he were Baal, with wailing and with self-torture, verse 14.

The NIV has emended verse 14b to read **they gather together . . .** , but the Hebrew literally reads, "for grain and new wine they gash themselves." The whole of verse 14 refers to Canaanite rituals, in which there was loud crying and cutting of oneself, often accompanied with dancing, in order to produce revelatory trances (cf. 1 Kgs. 18:26–29). To such depths of misunderstanding Israel's worship of Yahweh has fallen, and so it represents not a seeking of Yahweh, but a turning away from him.

Verse 15 recalls Yahweh's constant gift throughout the history of Israel of aid in times of warfare, but now Israel looks not to that aid, but to the foreign nations for help. And that, Yahweh says, is tantamount to a **plot . . . against me.**

The first line of verse 16 is corrupt, reading "They turn *lōʾ ʿāl.*" The LXX and Syriac read "They turn to nothing," i.e., "to that which does not profit" (so the NRSV; cf. Jer. 2:8, 11). The RSV reads "to Baal." Either of these emendations seems preferable to that of the NIV, but once again, we have no certainty about the precise meaning of the text. The general sense is clear, however: Israel has abandoned God. It is like a slack **bow,** i.e., like a bow that is not strung tightly enough to allow the archer to hit a target (cf. Ps. 78:57).

Thus, closing this section on Israel's political life is Yahweh's judgment on its political leaders, verse 16. They will fall by the sword before Assyria's onslaught, because of their arrogance in believing that they are equal to the threats to their life. They will become the objects of ridicule among the nations to whom they have looked for help (cf. Ps. 12:3–4; Mal. 3:13–15; Ezek. 23:32). God is the source of Israel's life, and by rebelling against him, Israel has brought on its own death.

## §17 Israel Shall Reap What She Sows (Hosea 8:1–7a)

As is frequently the case with Hosea, it is very difficult to know how to divide chapter 8 into its separate oracles. From a form-critical standpoint, verses 1–3 could form an independent unit because they include summons, accusation, and judgment. But they are intimately linked to what follows by their subject matter. Verse 4 spells out the two primary ways in which Israel has rejected what is good (v. 3). It is then connected with verse 5 by the repetition of the verb *zānaḥ*, meaning "to reject" (v. 5; NIV: **throw out**) or "to go astray" (v. 3; NIV: **rejected**), and verses 5–7 contain a further accusation and judgment.

Many commentators believe that verse 7 is made up of two independent wisdom sayings, which have been attached to the unit of verses 8–10 by the repetition of "swallow." Verse 11 then begins, in their view, a new unit of verses 10–13, and verse 14 is regarded as secondary by some.

From the standpoint of rhetorical criticism, however, I believe that the first unit comprises verses 1–7a. Neither the NIV nor the RSV indicates it, but verses 6c and 7a both begin with *kî*, "for," and they read: "*for* the calf-idol of Samaria shall become splinters; *for* they have sowed a wind, and they shall reap a whirlwind." That is the concluding judgment of the oracle.

Verses 7b–10 form the second unit, verses 11–14 (13?) the third, each ending with the judgment pronounced (v. 10b; v. 13b or 14b).

The whole chapter, however, concerns Yahweh's attitude and action toward Israel's harlotrous idolatry and political "adultery" (cf. 7:4)—the two spheres of Israel's life in which Hosea sees Israel's sin concentrated.

**8:1–3** / In the midst of the turbulent time immediately following Assyria's conquest of most of Israel's land in 733 BC, Yahweh himself interprets the meaning of that military event for his people. The swift bird of prey, the **eagle,** is hovering over the land, which is here called **the house of the** LORD (cf. the same usage in 9:15), and Yahweh calls the watchman to sound his trumpet of alarm (cf. 5:8). But that which should be announced is the reason for Israel's situation.

The God of the Bible most often reveals himself by means of his actions within human history. But that revelation remains opaque until a prophetic interpreter explains its meaning. Always God's revelatory actions must be made clear by God's word, which either precedes or follows them. For example, the Babylonian exile of Judah in 587 BC could have been understood as just one more military defeat had the prophets not proclaimed that the exile represented God's judgment on Judah's sin. And so, here too, in Hosea, the assault of Assyria against Israel could be understood as a merely secular event, but Yahweh himself, here in verse 1, points out its real meaning: The Assyrian eagle hovers over Israel **because** Israel has **broken** Yahweh's **covenant** and **rebelled** against Yahweh's *tôrâ.*

Israel has turned its back on its relationship with Yahweh and on the responsibilities inherent in that relationship. As in 4:6, *tôrâ* here refers to the entire tradition of God's relations with Israel—his actions toward Israel throughout its history, and his will disclosed to Israel through prophet and priest. *Tôrâ* is the whole story of God's dealings with his people.

To be sure, Yahweh says in verse 2, the people cry out to him in their distress, in cult and in private. The actual Hebrew reading is important here. Verse 2 reads: "To me they cry; 'My God, we, Israel, know you'!" Each individual claims that his or her relationship with Yahweh is still an intimate one of knowledge and obedience. But Yahweh knows better. Israel has **rejected** the **good,** verse 3.

That which is **good,** according to the Bible, is God (cf. Mark 10:18 and parallels). He is the possessor and source of all goodness (e.g., cf. Ps. 16:2; 25:8; 34:8; 73:28, etc.). No one can be good apart from God, and to do God's will is to do the good. Indeed, no one can have a good life except in God's company. Thus, when verse 3 states that Israel has **rejected what is good,** it means that the people have not only rejected God's covenant will for their lives, but they have also rejected the good life that is given by God's presence with them. As a result, **an enemy will pursue** them.

**8:4–7a** / The following verses then specify how the Israelites have rejected God's "good" will for their life. First, they have selected their leaders with no thought of whom Yahweh would choose to lead them, verse 4. Those put upon the throne have been singled out for the office by neither the gift of the spirit nor prophetic designation. Rather, the history of Israel's monarchy has been one of intrigue, deceit, and power-plays (cf. 7:3–7). As Paul states in Romans 13, civil authority has been instituted by God to guarantee good conduct within the body politic. But God has had nothing to do with the choice of Israel's leaders. Indeed, those leaders have been so bad that God has used them to punish the faithless people (13:10–11). Hosea here shares the ancient tribal league's assessment of the kingship, in which a king really was not necessary, because Yahweh was king (cf. 1 Sam. 8:7), but in which any king was to be subservient to the *tôrâ* (cf. Deut. 17:14–20).

Second in Israel's rejection of the "good" is the fact that they have made **idols** of **silver and gold** for themselves, verse 4b. From the very first, the covenant laws forbid Israel to make any representation of a deity (cf. Exod. 20:3–6, 23; 34:17; Lev. 19:4), for the God of Israel could not be revealed through anything "in heaven above" or "in the earth beneath" or "in the water under the earth" (Exod. 20:4 RSV). Those who broke the law were set under God's curse (Deut. 27:15). Ironically, the Israelites of Hosea's time were going to great expense—using the most precious metals—to mandate their own destruction, verse 4b.

Verse 4b not only sets forth a prohibition of idolatry, but it also assumes the manner of Yahweh's revelation: God is not revealed through anything made by human hands, and God is not revealed through the things and forces of nature, as were the baals. God gives himself to be known only through his actions, interpreted by his words, in Israel's history. Verse 5a in the Hebrew reads: "He has rejected your calf-image, O Samaria." If that is the reading accepted, then verse 5a is the one line in this oracle in which the prophet, and not Yahweh, speaks. Thus, the rendering of either the RSV ("I have spurned. . .") or of the NRSV ("Your calf is rejected. . .") is to be preferred.

To our knowledge, there was no **calf-idol** in the capital city of **Samaria**, where the king dwelt. Jeroboam I had erected golden calves, or better, golden young bulls, representing the strength of the deity, at both Bethel and Dan (1 Kgs. 12:28–29). But since this oracle probably dates immediately after 733 BC, Dan has already fallen to the army of Assyria. The "calf-idol of Samaria" therefore means, "the calf-idol of the royal house" and is another name for the idol at Bethel, which is the site of the king's sanctuary (cf. Amos 7:13).

Far from being a medium of revelation, as baal worshipers intended their idols to be, the calf-idol of Samaria is a cause of Yahweh's burning anger, verse 5. Made of wood overlaid with gold by human hands, the idol certainly cannot give aid to Israel, but instead will itself **be broken** into splinters, verse 6.

In the midst of anger, however, the God of Hosea also laments Israel's lack of purity and the pollution of its life with abominable idols. **How long** . . .? is his cry—a question only the sovereign God can answer. His anguish is deepened by knowing that Israel is his elect people: **They are from Israel!** God laments, "all of these idolaters!"—Israel, to whom God has shown grace and favor throughout all the past years of its history; Israel, who was God's faithful bride, who received lavish gifts of grain and wine and oil; Israel the beloved. This husband, the God of Hosea, suffers and weeps, because his wife Israel is unfaithful.

Nevertheless, because of her idolatry and her political rebellion from Yahweh's rule, Israel has sown for herself **wind,** i.e., vanity, illusion, nothingness (cf. Isa. 41:29; Job 7:7; 15:2; Eccl. 1:14, etc.), and that which she will reap will be the **whirlwind** of Yahweh's wrath (cf. Isa. 29:6; Amos 1:14; Zech. 7:14). God is not mocked. Despite all God's love for his covenant people, what Israel has sown, Israel shall reap (cf. Gal. 6:7).

---

### Additional Notes §17

---

**8:1** / The eagle is noted, according to the OT, for its swiftness (cf. Deut. 28:49; Jer. 4:13; 48:40; Lam. 4:19, etc.).

**8:2** / The NIV has read **our** instead of the original Hb. "my," thus turning an individual's cry into that of the people as a whole.

## §18 The Uselessness of Israel (Hosea 8:7b–10)

**8:7b–10** / The prophet used a wisdom saying to set forth the concluding announcement of judgment in the preceding oracle. Now he uses another wisdom saying to sound the theme that follows in this brief oracle: Grain that forms no **head** yields no kernels that may be ground into **flour;** it is useless. Or if it does form heads and aliens eat it, it is useless to its grower. So too is Israel (v. 8) **swallowed up** and useless to the one who has "planted" it (cf. 2:23), to Yahweh.

Verse 9 then explains the reason why Israel is useless to its grower: Israel has **gone up to Assyria** and become like every other nation (cf. 7:8; 1 Sam. 8:5; Ezek. 20:32). The reference is almost certainly to King Hoshea's payment of a huge tribute to Tiglath-pileser of Assyria, after the latter's armies had conquered the regions of Galilee and Gilead in 733 BC. Israel was supposed to be a nation set apart for God's purposes alone (Exod. 19:5–6), looking only to God for protection and sustenance (cf. 7:10; Isa. 30:1–5; 31:1). Instead, Israel had sought out Assyria's aid on its own initiative: **For they** is emphasized in the Hebrew.

Verse 9c then changes the metaphor from that of a wild ass, wandering the desert alone, to that of a harlot who is so desperate for **lovers** that she herself seeks them out and pays them. (Jer. 2:23–25 implies the same combination of metaphors, although there the reference is to foreign gods, rather than to foreign political allies.) Despite the fact that Israel pays tribute to foreigners, however, and makes itself as one of the foreign **nations,** mingling among them (cf. 7:8), Yahweh will **gather them together**—not, however, for future salvation, as in 1:11, but for judgment (cf. 9:6; cf. Zeph. 3:8; Joel 3:2).

The content of the judgment is then given in the last two lines of verse 10, but unfortunately, that verse is incomprehensibly corrupted in the Hebrew text. The NIV has read the verb as *weyeḥlû,* having the meaning of "they shall become sick" or "they shall waste away"; that is, under the oppression of the king of

Assyria, when they are exiled. Many commentators give different
vowel points to the verb, so that it reads, "They will writhe. . . ,"
also referring to the burden of foreign rule in the exile (cf. the
NRSV). The RSV follows the LXX: "And they shall cease for a little
while / from anointing king and princes," which makes a great
deal of sense in relation to 3:4. If chapters 1–3 are understood
as a summary of the message of chapters 4–14, the LXX/RSV
rendering should be preferred. But we cannot be sure. The
general thrust of the pericope, however, is that Israel, who has
looked to foreign nations rather than to Yahweh for its life, has
become totally useless to Yahweh as he works out his purpose
in the world. Therefore, Israel will soon go into exile because
of its faithlessness.

### Additional Note §18

**8:8** / According to Assyrian texts, Tiglath-pileser III boasted of
his conquest of Israel, "They overthrew their king Pekah and I placed
Hoshea as king over them. I received from them 10 talents of gold, 1,000
(?) talents of silver as their [tri]bute and brought them to Assyria" (*ANET,*
p. 284a).

## §19 The Cult, the Occasion of Sin (Hosea 8:11–14)

**8:11–14** / Having treated the political realm in the two preceding oracles, Hosea in this oracle turns to the other sphere of Israel's grievous sin—to the cult! One would tend to think that it would be an oxymoron to connect "sin" and "cult," for the worship of a people is precisely the place where deity and people are brought together in the most intimate relationship. It is through the cult that God pours out powers and vitality upon the gathered folk, and it is in the cult that the people give back to God the earned sacrifices of worship and praise. The cult is the meeting place of God and people. To call it a place of sin seems therefore out of the question.

But not for the prophets! For it is precisely in its attempts to meet with its God in its worship that the prophets find Israel's corruption. Through Hosea's contemporary, Amos, God declares hate for Israel's worship (Amos 5:21), as God still hated it a century later, according to Isaiah (Isa. 1:14). And through Jeremiah, Yahweh declared that Judah's place of worship had become a "den of robbers"—a hiding place for sinners (Jer. 7:11)—as it was again in the time of Jesus of Nazareth (Mark 11:17 and parallels). Thus, perhaps it is precisely its own corporate worship practices that the church should carefully examine as it interprets this oracle from Hosea.

Verse 11 opens with the little word *kî*, which could be translated "indeed," "because," "when," "though." The NIV has translated the verse rather loosely. The Hebrew reads "Though Ephraim has multiplied altars for sin (*ḥēṭ᾽*), they are for him altars for sin (*ḥēṭ᾽*). Thus the NIV has caught the basic meaning, even though the text is not dealing specifically with sin offerings, which are only one type of sacrifice. Rather, the meaning is that Israel has **built many altars** to offer sacrifices to atone for and cover over its sinfulness, but those very altars and sacrifices have themselves become occasions of sinning.

Verses 12 and 13 then explain why this is so. In the first place (v. 12), Israel has entirely forgotten who its God is and what it is that God requires. Verse 12 is better read, "Were I to write for him a multitude of my instructions, they would be regarded as alien." The line shows that there were already written traditions of the *tôrâ* in existence, but the line is referring to the present, not the past: Even if Yahweh *multiplied* his instructions, as Israel has *multiplied* its altars, Israel would think the instructions were alien teachings of some strange god.

Israel does not know who Yahweh is anymore! Israel has God confused with all of the fertility gods and goddesses. It does not remember what God has done in the past or the fact that at the heart of the law are the requirements of love and trust and obedience to God (cf. Deut. 10:12–13; 6:4–6).

Accordingly, verse 13, Israel's sacrificial rites have become ends in themselves, opportunities to have a party. The word used for "sacrifice" in this verse is *zebaḥ*, referring to the common, daily offering, part of which was burnt and the rest of which was eaten in a communion (communal) meal.

The third line of verse 13, which is the only line of the oracle in the third person, is a priestly declaration that Hosea has borrowed. As can be seen in Leviticus, for example, it was the role of the priest to pronounce a sacrifice acceptable or not acceptable to God (cf. Lev. 1:17; 2:14; 3:5, etc.). Here the prophet, taking the role of a priest, pronounces Israel's sacrifices unacceptable to Yahweh.

The judgment therefore will immediately follow. **Now!** Assyria hovers like an eagle over the land (v. 1). And God, the Lord over Assyria and every empire, God the final judge, in his law court, remembers Israel's offenses and will call Israel to account for its faithlessness. **They** at the beginning of the final line of verse 13 is emphasized, and the sentence reads in the Hebrew order: "*They* to Egypt shall return!"

The meaning of that judgment has been a matter of debate among commentators. Does the return to Egypt mean that Israel's only hope is to look to Egypt once more for help against the Assyrian invader (cf. 2 Kgs. 17:4)? That would scarcely be equivalent to God's judgment. Does the line mean that the Israelites' only recourse will be to flee to Egypt to escape the invading Assyrian armies, as many did before the Babylonians in Jeremiah's time (cf. Jer. 43)? Once again, that does not seem the same as Yahweh's judgment. Or does the line mean that, as Hosea has said before (cf. the comment at 2:14–15), God, giving up this sinful people to Assyria's destruction of them, will nevertheless begin his salvation-history with them all over again on the other side of the judgment? This latter seems to be the meaning, and taken by itself the statement would furnish a ray of hope for the future in an otherwise dark situation. But in its present context, the judgment that Israel will return to Egypt forms part of the threat to Israel's life: Israel *must* return to Egypt, and Yahweh *must* start his salvation-history all over again, because Israel will be destroyed by Yahweh's agent, Assyria.

The Lord will make himself a people again in the future. But first, the past must be done away. The old must be destroyed before the new can come. The new patch cannot be sewed on the old garment or the new wine poured into old wineskins (Matt. 9:16–17). The seed must fall into the ground and die before it can bring forth fruit (John 12:24). Israel must undergo its crucifixion before it can have a resurrection. Therefore, God's final word in verse 14 is of Israel's destruction in the **fire** of God's wrath.

Some commentators have regarded verse 14 as secondary. Some see it as a "floating piece" (Mays) used by the redactor of Hosea's oracles to bring the series of pronouncements in chapter 8 to a conclusion. Hosea nowhere else names Yahweh **Maker,** both **Israel** and **Judah** are judged, and the pronouncement of judgment sounds very much like the pronouncements in Amos 1. None of those arguments are decisive, however. Israel's forgetfulness of God is a familiar theme in Hosea's work (2:13; 4:6; 13:6), as is its reliance on its own strength (5:5; 7:10), here symbolized in verse 14 by the **palaces** and fortifications and **cities.** Thus it may very well be that Hosea himself ends this oracle with this word of judgment.

### Additional Notes §19

**8:12** / Read the pl. of *tôrâ* with LXX<sup>s</sup> MT: sing.

**8:13** / The first line of the verse is corrupt. Many read: "Sacrifices they love, so they sacrifice" (*zebaḥ ʾāhabû wayizbᵉḥû),* flesh (they love), so they eat." The last line of v. 13 is perhaps quoted in Jer. 14:10.

## §20 *Israel's Loss of the Stuff of Life (Hosea 9:1–4)*

Some commentators would regard 9:1–9 as the first complete unit in this chapter. Others would point to 9:1–6. Judging on the basis of rhetorical criticism, it seems best to divide the chapter into five separate oracles: verses 1–4, 5–6, 7–9, 10–14, 15–17. What we have here are several oracles, strung together by the redactor/disciple of Hosea on the basis of the common theme of the loss of vitality. In this instance, however, the beginnings and endings of the separate pieces, while not indicated by oracular formulae, are nevertheless rather clearly indicated by an imperative (v. 1), question (v. 5), or a change in subject matter (vv. 7, 10, 15), and by the pronouncement of judgment at the end of each piece.

**9:1–4** / It is possible that Hosea pronounced these words at the Feast of Tabernacles, the eight-day celebration of the ingathering of produce at the end of September or the beginning of October. It is doubtful that he was calling for an end to that feast, which had existed in Israel from the time of the Judges (cf. Judg. 21:19–21; Exod. 34:22) and which was firmly established in the Deuteronomic and later priestly law (Deut. 16:13–15; Lev. 23:33–36). Indeed, according to Deuteronomy, the feast was to highlight the covenant faithfulness of the old tribal league of all Israel to Yahweh by a covenant renewal ceremony and by the reading of the *tôrâ* to the people (cf. Deut. 31:10–13).

What Hosea inveighs against in this oracle, therefore, is the bacchanalian, baalistic nature that has invaded the feast's celebration from Canaanite fertility practices. We have both biblical and extrabiblical evidence of cultic dancing, not only in relation to the Feast of Booths (Judg. 21:21) but also in pagan worship (cf. Exod. 32:19; 1 Kgs. 18:26–29). The latter could lead to wild ecstasy, undoubtedly heightened by the sexual rites practiced in baalism, and sometimes even to states of unconsciousness. It is this wild,

baalistic celebration against which Hosea speaks the judgment
from his God. The Hebrew of verse 1 reads:

> Rejoice not, O Israel,
>     to exultation, like the peoples!
> for you have played the harlot from your God,
>     you have loved a harlot's hire
> upon every threshing floor of grain.

The Hebrew reading is a good deal stronger than that given
in the NIV.

The Israelites are not to give themselves to the wild celebration characteristic of the "heathen" around them—such is the
meaning of "peoples" in the verse. The Israelites have considered
the grain of the harvest to be their "payment" or "hire" for their
whoring worship of the fertility gods and goddesses. But the time
is soon coming when they will no longer be able to enter into
such paganism. That is the substance of the judgment uttered,
then, in verses 2–4.

God will reverse the entire history of salvation. God will
start all over again by returning the people to **Egypt**—the same
thought as seen in 8:13. But before that, the Israelites will go into
exile. They will **eat unclean food** in Assyrian exile; that is, food
that is not grown in Yahweh's land, verse 3. No longer will there
be the harvest of grain and oil and new wine, verse 2. There will
be no **wine** or animal **sacrifices** to offer to the Lord, verse 4.
Rather, any sacrifices offered will be like **bread of mourners**,
which is **unclean** and cannot be offered to God, because it has
come in contact with the dead (cf. Num. 19:11–13; 5:2; 6:6; Lev.
21:1, 11). Indeed, bread will be so scarce that there will be only
enough to feed themselves.

The last line of verse 4 has seemed puzzling, because it
makes no sense to speak of **the temple** in Jerusalem when Israel
is in Assyrian exile. Some have therefore understood the line as a
Judean addition. What it may be is a scribal insertion into the text
to explain that mourner's bread may not be offered to God. Very
probably the line should be regarded as a gloss.

## Additional Notes §20

**9:1b** / It is not necessary to adopt the reading of the LXX, as the NIV, RSV, and others have done. Hosea is telling the Israelites not to give themselves over to the wild exultation and dances of the baal cult.

**9:2** / **Winepresses** can also be read as "oil presses," which is probably intended here, since Hosea frequently mentions the triad of grain, wine, and oil (2:8). Wine and oil presses were carved basins in rock, in which the grapes or olives were trodden out. The juice then flowed out of the basin into a lower vessel.

**9:4** / Because Yahweh was the God of life, the dead were considered to lie outside of his sphere of holiness and were therefore ritually unclean. In many ways, illness and death were considered alien and evil intrusions into God's sphere of life-giving vitality.

## §21 Israel Lost to Exile (Hosea 9:5–6)

**9:5–6** / This little independent piece continues the thought of 9:1–4 by describing Israel's situation after its conquest and exile by Assyria. But the way **Egypt** is used here is very different from the way it is used in 9:3, and this is a brief oracle that has been attached to verses 1–4 by the disciple-redactor of Hosea.

The picture that the prophet paints of the northern land after its fall to Assyria is bleak. Nothing is left there but **briers** growing over Israel's abandoned idols of silver (cf. 8:4), and the **tents** of its pilgrims to its religious festivals stand empty and windblown, possessed by **thorns**, verse 6.

As for Israel's situation in Assyrian exile, her religious festivals cannot be kept, verse 5. The prophet therefore asks the people, who wildly celebrate in their homeland (cf. 9:1), what they are going to do in Assyria when the autumn Feast of Tabernacles rolls around. The NIV has the plurals **feasts** and **days** in verse 5, but the Hebrew is singular, and the reference is probably to the autumn festival, which began the New Year and which constituted Israel's principal cultic festival up until 621 BC. How, Hosea asks his compatriots, are you going to celebrate in Assyria?

The meaning of verse 6a is properly construed in the NIV. The Hebrew reads, "For behold! (though) they flee from destruction"; that is, though some Israelites escape the Assyrian onslaught by fleeing to **Egypt,** it will do them no good, for there they will die and be gathered together for burial in **Memphis**'s famous burial grounds.

Bleakness, lostness, death—such are the fates that await a faithless and idolatrous people.

## Additional Note §21

**9:6** / Memphis was located some fifteen miles above the peak of the Nile Delta and was a place of exile or retreat for many foreigners, who were settled and subsequently died there. It is noted for its huge grave sites or pyramids, built for its pharaohs during the Fourth Dynasty, ca. 2700–2200 BC.

## §22 *Israel's Rationalization (Hosea 9:7–9)*

**9:7–9** / In a deadly repetition, which the NIV translation obscures, Hosea announces Israel's inevitable punishment:

> Days of punishment have come;
> days of requital have come.
> Israel shall know it (v. 7a–c).

The drum beat of the announcement reminds one of the same deadly repetition of "come" in Ezekiel 7:5–7. God is not mocked, and what Israel has sown in faithlessness to its Lord, Israel will also reap in the form of punishment (cf. Gal. 6:7). With wrath poured out, Yahweh will be Lord over this people (cf. Ezek. 20:33). Indeed, God's wrath has already begun its work of destruction in the devastation wrought in Israel by Assyria's armies in 733 BC.

The reaction of all people everywhere to God's messengers, however, is one first of disbelief and then of hostility.

> O Jerusalem, Jerusalem, killing the prophets and stoning those who are sent to you! How often would I have gathered your children together as a hen gathers her brood under her wings, and you would not! (Luke 13:34 RSV)

In a world that has deserted God, the announcement of God's coming judgment is always first rationalized away, and the people in Hosea's Israel are no exception to the rule. Verse 7 quotes the people's words of rationalization: "A fool is the prophet; led astray is the man of spirit." Hosea is charged with being stupid and with being led to excessive and ecstatic raving, like some of the ecstatic prophets of the ninth century BC (1 Sam. 10:6, 10–11; cf. Jer. 29:26; Ezek. 13:3). The Israelites simply do not believe that what Hosea announces can be true, and they attribute his words to craziness.

But then the disbelief is deepened to hostility. The NIV has reversed the last four lines of verse 7. The lines read in the original Hebrew:

> A fool is the prophet;
> > led astray is the man of spirit.
> Because of the greatness of your iniquity,
> > (your) hostility is great.

The Israelites cannot stand the prophetic charges leveled against them, and thus they finally turn against the prophet in hatred.

Speaking of himself in the third person (like Jeremiah [cf. 6:17] and Ezekiel [3:17; 33:7] after him), Hosea calls himself **the watchman over Ephraim,** verse 8 (cf. 5:8; 8:1)—the one who warns the people from his watchtower of approaching danger (cf. 1 Sam. 14:16; 2 Kgs. 9:17–20), and therefore one who has the good of his people at heart. Moreover, he says he is a watcher **with my God;** that is, his message comes from the presence of God with him. But the Israelites respond to his care with hatred, laying fowler's **snares** in **all his paths,** as if he were some wild animal to be caught, and showing him nothing but **hostility.** The phrase, **in the house of his God** refers to the whole region of Israel (cf. 8:1; 9:15), which is Yahweh's land (cf. 9:3).

The Israelites have deeply corrupted themselves, verse 9. The prophet compares their corruption to that of the Benjamites at Gibeah, in the horrible story found in Judges 19–21. According to that story, the man whose concubine was killed was a Levite. This may be further evidence of Hosea's connection with the northern reform movement of levitical priests and prophets that influenced Jeremiah, Deuteronomy, and the authors of Third Isaiah. Similarly, it is significant in this regard that the prophet is linked, in verse 8, with the northern charismatic prophets, even by his compatriots.

Despite Israel's rejection of him and his message, despite the refusal of his compatriots to repent, Hosea nevertheless delivers the decree of God: "He will remember their iniquity; he will punish their sins" (Hb.). The NIV has substituted **God** for the pronoun, added a conjunctive *waw,* and supplied **them for.** But the oracle ends with the same staccato drumbeat that it had at the beginning, and **punishment** (v. 7) and **punish** (v. 9) form its inclusio. Israel cannot rationalize its guilt. Punishment comes.

## Additional Note §22

**9:8a** / This is very difficult in the Hb.: "A watcher of Ephraim with my God. Prophet." Presumably the verb and article should be furnished: ". . . is the prophet." The word **along** in the NIV should be omitted.

## §23 A Conversation between God and the Prophet (Hosea 9:10–14)

**9:10–14** / These words are not addressed to the Ephraimites. Those people are spoken of in the third person. Rather, the Lord speaks the words found in verses 10–12 to Hosea, and Hosea responds in verses 13–14. Thus, what we have here is a conversation between the prophet and his God, much like the conversations (laments) that we find Jeremiah later carrying on with his Lord (cf. Jer. 11:18–23; 12:1–6; 15:15–21). Form critically, the passage is not in the form of a lament, but like the Jeremiah passages, it gives a glimpse into Hosea's inner life with his God. It should not be thought that God is trying to justify his judging actions to the prophet, though there are prophetic passages that seem to do that (cf. Jer. 7:17–19; 11:14–15). But certainly God reviews the past, in verse 10, in order to make clear the reason for the punishment of his people.

The tradition that says that Yahweh **found** or **saw** (the meaning is identical here) Israel in the wilderness is one peculiar to the northern tribal league theology of Deuteronomy (32:10–11) and later expanded on in Ezekiel 16. It sets forth the fact that God has "adopted" the foundling Israel (cf. Deut. 8:5; Hos. 11:1). This is not a reference to the election of Israel in the exodus, nor does it contain the thought of Yahweh's "honeymoon" with the bride Israel during the idyllic time in the wilderness, as in 2:15 (cf. Jer. 2:2). Rather, the passage reaches back to what is apparently one of the oldest traditions concerning Yahweh's loving relation with this people. God **found** the fathers, the forebears of his people and of the prophet (**your fathers**). Finding them was as delightful to him as **finding grapes in the desert**—a fantastic possibility—or the first tender figs on a **fig tree.** Always, in Hosea's oracles, there is notice of Yahweh's love for his people, which serves to emphasize the perfidy of Israel's faithlessness.

Despite God's adoption of and love for Israel, when Israel, guided through the desert by the love of God, first encountered the fertility cult of baalism at Baal Peor, twelve miles east of the northern end of the Dead Sea, it succumbed to the lure of baalism's sexual rites of fertility and consecrated itself to "shame." The NIV has rendered the one Hebrew word, *bōšet*, with **that shameful idol**, but the reference is not to an idol, but to the sexual rites of the baal cult, as seems evident from the account in Numbers 25:1. What one worships, one becomes, however (cf. Jer. 2:5; 1 Cor. 6:16), and by joining in the vile rites of baalism, Israel became vile and has continued in her abominable behavior ever since.

Therefore, Yahweh's judgment will strike at the very thing that the Israelites have tried to foster through their baalistic worship—namely, fertility, verse 11. Israel's **glory** is here, as in 4:7, its vitality in the Lord, its ability to increase by God's blessing (cf. Gen. 1:28), in fulfillment of God's promise (cf. Gen. 22:16–17; 28:14). But that glory **will fly away** from it **like a bird.** Without God, who gives all life, the Israelites cannot conceive **children** in the womb, or carry them to term, or give birth to them. And even those children who are already alive will be taken from them, by war or exile or flight. Thus, the final word God pronounces over childless Israel is **Woe!**—that lament for one who is doomed to die. Having sought life from Baal instead of from the God of life, Israel's parents are left without a future.

In verse 13, Hosea replies to this picture of woe which his God has painted for him. Unfortunately, verse 13a is a corrupted text in the Hebrew, and every translation of it is tentative. The NIV rendering is a guess based on the actual Hebrew and is near to the reading found in the NRSV: "Once I saw Ephraim as a young palm planted in a lovely meadow." Such a reading returns to the thought, found in verse 10, of Yahweh's delight in Israel in the beginning, and is then contrasted, in verse 13c–d, with the destruction that awaits it. But we have no other such picture of Israel as a young palm plant in a lovely meadow anywhere else in the OT. Thus, it seems best to follow the suggestion of the LXX and of many commentators to read, "Ephraim's sons, as I have seen, are destined for a prey" (so the RSV), the reference being to the destruction that has already taken place in Ephraim in 733 BC. Verse 13c–d then repeats the judgment consigning Ephraim's children to destruction. Thus, in this verse, Hosea is affirming God's judgment upon his people.

But in verse 14, the prophet turns to God in prayer, and apparently begins an intercession that would ask that Ephraim be spared: **Give them, O LORD—**. Such intercessions formed part of the prophetic function (cf. Ezek. 13:5) and are frequently found in the prophetic writings (Amos 7:2, 5; Jer. 7:16; 11:14) and in the Deuteronomic traditions (Num. 14:13–19; Deut. 9:19–20, 25–29). The prayer breaks off, however, and the prophet bows to the will of his God. "Give them a miscarrying womb and dry breasts." God's judgment is affirmed. "Not my will, but thine be done" (Mark 14:36) is Hosea's assent. Israel, in order to be raised to new life, must undergo crucifixion.

## §24 God's Love Turns to Hatred (Hosea 9:15–17)

**9:15–17** / This oracle is closely connected with 9:10–14. The pronouns in verse 15 presuppose the subject "Ephraim" in 9:13, and the theme of Israel's infertility continues. It seems doubtful, however, that this is a continuation of the dialogue between Hosea and his God that we saw in verse 10–14. Rather, it is made up of a judgment speech of Yahweh in verse 15–16, followed by the affirmation of that judgment by the prophet in verse 17.

The NIV has given a somewhat loose translation of verse 15. The Hebrew reads, "All their evil (is) in Gilgal; for there I hated them," or ". . . began to hate them" (cf. RSV). The question is, however, what is intended by the mention of **Gilgal.** In 4:15 and 12:11, Gilgal is connected with idolatrous worship in the baal cult (see the comment on 4:15). Because it served for a time as the cult center of the tribal league in the time of the Judges (cf. Judg. 2:9), this verse in Hosea would then indicate that Israel began its idolatrous baal worship already at that time, and indeed it did (cf. Judg. 2:6—3:6). As a result, Yahweh began to "hate" Israel, verse 15.

On the other hand, Gilgal was the site of the anointing of Saul as the first king of Israel (1 Sam. 11:15), the place of Saul's disobedience (1 Sam. 13:1–15), and the site of his rejection as king by Yahweh (1 Sam. 15:21–26). Given Hosea's immersion in the theology of the tribal league, in which there was no place for a king because Yahweh was king, his references to the kingship as an act of apostasy (8:4; 13:10–11), and the notice in 9:15 of the obstinacy of the political "leaders," it seems more likely that the mention of **Gilgal** in verse 15 is referring to Israel's lack of trust in God, exhibited by its desire to have a king "like all the other nations" (1 Sam. 8:20).

Indeed, the punishment that Yahweh therefore decrees, according to verse 17,—the rejection of his people—echoes Israel's rejection of Yahweh in the time of Saul (cf. 1 Sam. 10:19) and Yahweh's rejection of Saul (cf. 1 Sam. 15:26). From the first, as a political entity among other nations, the Israelites spurned their God. God therefore now spurns them, and the people shall become **wanderers among the nations,** verse 17, without homeland, without God, without future.

The lack of a future for Israel is further emphasized by verse 16, which reiterates the theme of 9:11–14 (see the comment there). However, this verse is even more emphatic than that passage. Now Israel's vitality is already dried up. It is like an uprooted tree or like an unwatered tree that shrivels and dies and therefore cannot bear fruit. And the death of its children is now, not the result of war or exile or flight, but the result of the act of Yahweh himself: **I will slay their cherished offspring.** God himself will do his people to death.

God, the lover of his bride Israel (2:15), God who reared his infant son of a people (11:1–4), God who desires to heal his people (6:11–7:1) and who agonizes over losing them (11:8–9), God who finally will begin his salvation history with them all over again (2:14–23), here "hates" his covenant people. Is it possible for such a God to hate? Is it possible to turn Romans 8:31 upside down and to say that God is against us and that therefore no one can be for us? Does God hate that which he loves?

According to Hosea 9:15 and Jeremiah 12:8, the answer is "yes" (cf. Ps. 5:5; Rom. 9:13). That the God who holds the springs of our life in his hands should hate us for our faithlessness and rebellion—that possibility should cause us to tremble.

# §25 Israel's Refusal to Worship Its King Yahweh (Hosea 10:1–8)

The prophet himself speaks in this oracle, perhaps to his inner circle of disciples, perhaps in a reflective musing on the message the Lord has given him to deliver. Both Yahweh and the people are spoken of in the third person; thus, neither Yahweh himself speaks, nor are the people addressed. But the message is fully consonant with all that has gone before.

**10:1–8** / Verse 3 forms the crux for the meaning of this passage, but it has received several different interpretations from commentators and translators. Contrary to the NIV's rendering, the verse in the Hebrew reads: "For now they say, 'There is no king among us, / for we do not fear Yahweh, / and the king, what does he do for us?' "

The question is, to whom does **king** refer? The most common answer is that the word refers to the Israelite king Hoshea, who first submitted to Assyrian rule, but who then rebelled against it by sending a mission to ask for Egyptian aid (2 Kgs. 17:4). As a result, say many interpreters, the verse reflects the fact that Hoshea will be deposed when the remnant of Israel is totally overrun and destroyed by Assyrian forces, shortly before the fall of the northern kingdom to that enemy in 721 BC. At that time, the people will repent, acknowledging that they have been destroyed because they have not revered the Lord. And at that time, no human king will be able to help them. In short, this is understood as a threat against Israel's political life, and the oracle is combining the prophet's usual judgment on both the pagan worship of Israel and its political life.

I cannot agree. **King** in verse 3 refers to Yahweh, who was always understood as Israel's king in the theology of the tribal league (cf. Deut. 33:5; 1 Sam. 8:7). The people are quoted here as saying that Yahweh is not their king, that they do not fear (= obey) him, and that he does nothing for them (cf. 2:8). Instead, it is Baal who sustains their life. The entire oracle concerns the Israelites' false worship, in which they have substituted Baal for their King Yahweh, and the judgment that will therefore fall upon them.

By the same token, therefore, verse 6d reads in the Hebrew, "and Israel shall be ashamed of its counsel"; i.e., its decision to worship Baal rather than the Lord. That is what will bring ruin upon it. As for human kings, like the king of Samaria, in verse 7, they are just like helpless twigs cast upon a torrent of water in comparison with the kingship of the Lord. The whole oracle is held together by the principal word **king**, and the whole concerns Israel's desertion of its king, the Lord.

As is so often the case in Hosea, the prophet's words reflect Israel's past history with its Lord, verse 1. Israel was the **vine** planted by God—a frequent figure of speech in the OT (Ps. 80:8–11, 14–15; Isa. 5:1–7; Jer. 2:21; 12:10; Ezek. 17:6; 19:10; cf. John 15:1). Under God's care, Israel spread out luxuriantly and yielded abundant fruit and prospered—perhaps a reference to the prosperous days under Jeroboam II. But the Israelites used their abundance to build more and more altars to Baal (8:11) and to adorn their stone *maṣṣēbôt* or pillars for Baal more gloriously. Their heart, their love for their covenant God, has been entirely deceitful (cf. 6:4). Therefore God will now destroy their **altars** and their sacred *maṣṣēbôt*. The fact that verse 3 begins with "because" or "for" (*kî* in the Hebrew) gives the reason for Yahweh's destruction. They have completely rejected him as their King (see above).

Verse 4 then illustrates their rejection of Yahweh, but the NIV has obscured the meaning. The Hebrew reads: "Speak words, swear falsely, make a covenant," and the reference is to the empty words and **false oaths** and faithless loyalty that the Israelites speak to their God and with each other in God's name. As a result, justice (*mišpāṭ*, not **lawsuits** as in the NIV)—God's proper ordering of life (cf. Amos 5:7; 6:12)—seems to the Israelites like poisonous weeds infesting a plowed field.

Verse 5 goes on to picture the people's false worship. They "stand in awe of" (*gûr*, cf. Ps. 22:23; 33:8 contra NIV **fear for**) the calf-idol of Bethel (see the comment at 8:5–6), which is here called **Beth Aven**, "house of wickedness" (cf. 4:15). But they will soon **mourn** over the loss of its splendor, as will the idolatrous priests, "for it shall depart from them," verses 5f. (Hb.). The idol itself **will be carried** into exile in **Assyria** and used as part of a tribute-payment to the Assyrian king (cf. 5:13), verse 6. In exile, Israel will be **disgraced** and shamed by the course it has chosen.

The Israelite king will be carried away on the flood of destruction, and **the high places** of worship to Baal, which constitute Israel's sin, will be destroyed, verse 8. **Thorns and thistles will cover their altars,** and Israel, left desolate—without a land, without a king, without a cult, without their God—shall wish only for death.

The cry of the people in verse 8 is quoted in Luke 23:27–31 to the women of Jerusalem, by Jesus as he carries his cross to Golgotha. It is quoted again in the final vision of Revelation 6:12–17 to all who are enemies of God. The judgment of God that Hosea prophesies has yet to come fully upon the earth. That should be a sobering message for everyone who reads Hosea's words.

---

### Additional Notes §25

---

**10:1** / *Maṣṣēbôt*, or stone pillars, were originally accepted in Israel as memorials (cf. Gen. 31:13; 35:20; Josh. 24:26–27). Because they were corrupted into what were probably phallic symbols for Baal, they are prohibited in Deut. 16:22 (cf. Lev. 26:1).

**10:4** / The first verb should be read as an infinitive absolute, in accordance with the following two verbs.

**10:5** / The priests are here called *kᵉmārîm* for the first time in Hos. In 2 Kgs. 23:5 and Zeph. 1:4, the term means those priests who were committed to the idolatrous baal cult.

## §26 Israel Yoked for Destruction (Hosea 10:9–15)

**10:9–15** / Some commentators have divided this oracle into three, verse 9–10, 11–12 (or 13a), 13 (or 13b)–15. However, it is one piece, held together by the central figure of the **yoke,** verse 11. By its rearrangement of lines and mistranslation of verse 11, the NIV has considerably muddled the understanding of the whole, however. The Hebrew of verse 11 reads:

> Ephraim was a trained heifer
>> that loved to thresh,
>> and I spared her fair neck;
> but I will put Ephraim to the yoke,
>> Judah must plow,
>> Jacob must harrow for himself. (So too the RSV.)

What is the picture implied? According to verse 11, in the time of its wilderness "honeymoon" with the Lord (cf. 2:15), Ephraim was like **a trained heifer** that would willingly tread out the grain spread on the threshing floor. In the metaphor used, it was free to move as it willed and to eat as it walked (cf. Deut. 25:4; 1 Cor. 9:9; 1 Tim. 5:18). It therefore needed no guiding yoke upon it (cf. Hos. 4:16). But because Israel has refused to fulfill its covenant with its Lord and turned aside to its own willful way, it must now be put to a **yoke.** And that yoke is the disciplining war (cf. 3:3–4) that is already coming upon Israel at the hands of the Assyrians.

Two other lines in the text support such an interpretation. In verse 10c, Yahweh says that he **will put them in bonds** (Hebrew: "I will bind them"). The reference is not to bondage to the Assyrians, but to the Lord's binding yoke that will be laid on Israel's neck. Similarly, in verse 13d, the Hebrew reads, "Because you have trusted in your *way*. . . ." Israel, the heifer, has gone astray in its trust and followed its own way (cf. Jer. 50:11). Therefore, it must now be subjected to Yahweh's yoke.

As in 9:9, Israel's sin at **Gibeah** is recalled, verse 9. Once again, the incident in mind is the terrible story now preserved in

Judges 19–21, according to which the Benjamites ravished the Levite's concubine and were nearly exterminated by the other tribes of Israel. There already with the northern tribe of Benjamin, verse 9 is saying, northern Israel's sin began, and it has continued until the present day. As northern Israel, symbolized by Benjamin, was in the beginning, so it is still. **War** overtook Benjamin then. Now it will overtake all of northern Israel, but now the war will come from the **nations,** whom Yahweh himself will gather together to destroy the people, verse 10.

Israel must be put to the Lord's yoke, and Israel and Judah must plow and harrow (NIV: **break up the ground**) under God's bond. That is, they must now be subjected to divine will, verse 11. Some have thought that **Judah** is a southern insertion in this verse, but in the tradition of the tribal league, Hosea's language includes all Israel.

The will of God is set forth in verse 12. Israel, now under the figure of the farmer who turns under the seed as he plows the ground, was bidden from the first, and is still bidden, to sow the seed of **righteousness** (cf. Jer. 4:3). As in 2:19, the word stands for the proper fulfillment of the demands of a relationship. If Israel sows righteousness, it will give its Lord the love and obedience expected of it in the covenant relation with God. And by sowing righteousness, Israel will then be able to reap the fruit of its *ḥesed*—of its **unfailing** (covenant) **love** toward the Lord. Moreover, Hosea urges his people to sow such seed in **unplowed ground** (= fallow ground); that is, ground that has never been farmed or that has lain fallow for a period of time, so that it will yield especially abundant fruit (cf. Prov. 13:23).

Israel can plant such ground by seeking its God. The concept can signify turning to God through worship, but it also has the meaning in northern tradition of inquiry of the will of the Lord through the medium of a prophet (Wolff), very often before the opening of a battle or at other times of crisis (cf. 1 Kgs. 22:5; 2 Kgs. 3:11; 8:8; 22:13). Thus, Hosea is urging not only that the people truly seek their God in the cult, but also that they pay heed to God's words in this time of crisis with the armies of Assyria.

If the people will so seek the Lord, then the Lord will come to them and rain "salvation" *(ṣedeq)* upon them. The NIV has translated *ṣedeq* with **righteousness,** which is correct in so far as God's "righteousness" is often equated with the "salvation" of the people; salvation is God's fulfillment of the demands of a covenant relationship with Israel.

The salvation that God will bring to a faithful Israel should not be thought of as the reward for its righteousness, however. God's salvation is never merited, and Israel does not earn it. Rather, salvation—which in the OT designates fullness of life, prosperity, abundance, peace, security, room to live, *šālôm* in its fullest meaning—is the natural fruit of a whole relationship with God (cf. 1 Cor. 9:10–11). Like the fruits of the Spirit (Gal. 5:22–23), it flows naturally out of faithful fellowship with the God who is the source of all life and good (cf. Mal. 3:10–12; Ps. 1; 37).

Rather than sowing **righteousness** and reaping for itself its fruit, Israel has sown **wickedness,** however. Its relationship with God has been one of deception. As a result, the Israelites **have reaped evil,** verse 13. They have already **eaten** some of the **fruit** of their iniquity in 733 BC, when Assyria conquered most of their land. She has depended on her own "way" (Hebrew; NIV: **strength**); the accusation returns to the figure of the stubborn heifer, which has gone its own way, and which will now be subjected to Yahweh's yoke.

Instead of relying on God, and following God's way, Israel has gone its own way and relied on its many professional soldiers **(warriors)** for security (cf. Amos 6:13; Isa. 31:1). Now it will reap the fruits. The tumult of **battle** will assault every ear, the fortified cities will fall before the Assyrian hosts, leaving Israel defenseless. Indeed, the slaughter will be comparable to that at **Beth Arbel,** when mothers and children were dashed to pieces (cf. 13:16).

We do not know what incident at **Beth Arbel** is referred to in verse 14. Some have conjectured that **Shalman** is identical with the Moabite king Shalamanu, who is named by Tiglath-pileser III in a list of those paying tribute to him (cf. *ANET,* p. 282). We do know that the ripping open of pregnant women and the dashing of children's heads against rocks was a feature of ancient warfare (cf. 2 Kgs. 8:12; Isa. 13:16; Amos 1:13; Nah. 3:10; Ps. 137:9).

That God would bring such cruelty against the covenant people is a thought that gives us a great deal of difficulty, of course. But the OT is the most realistic of books. When God gives the people over to their own way (cf. Rom. 1:26, 28) and their fate is left to the forces of secular history, they become subject to all the cruelties and destructiveness of sinful human beings. Israel has chosen its own way and will reap the consequences. Its **king** will fall at the dawn of the battle-day, and its country will be no more.

In the midst of such a devastating picture, we would not expect to find a word of hope for the future. Yet we must consider the fact that to wear a "yoke" is to be subject to guidance by a Master who holds the reins—in short, to be the subject of discipline (cf. Matt. 11:28–30), and discipline has as its object correction for the future (cf. Hos. 3:3–5). It points forward toward a new and different life. Thus, by using the figure of the yoke, Hosea here preserves that almost unnoticeable, quiet note of hope. Beyond the disciplining and death of Israel, there is still a future in God's plan.

---

### Additional Notes §26

---

**10:9d–10a** / The Hb. reads, "In my desire (I will come) against the children of iniquity *(ʿawlâ)* / and I will chastise them." *ʿawlâ* is repeated then in v. 13b, helping to tie the whole oracle together.

**10:13e** / Instead of **own strength** (Hb.: "way"), many commentators follow the LXX and read "chariots." The emendation should not be made.

**10:15** / For **Bethel**, we should probably read "house of Israel," as in the LXX. Hosea usually calls Bethel *"Bêt ʾāwen,"* "house of wickedness," 4:15; 5:8.

## §27 The Nature of God (Hosea 11:1–11)

The almost hidden note of hope with which chapter 10 ended is here sounded at full volume: God cannot give up this people! (Cf. **my son** v. 1; **my people** v. 7.)

The principal theological question that this passage raises is, What finally will be the factor that determines the outcome of human history? And certainly the prophetic answer to that is "God." As the Lord of all history, God will make the final decision as to what the recompense of human action and attitude will be. But then the question presses deeper: What will be the nature of God's recompense? In response to the corruption and faithlessness of human beings, will God's wrath finally burn up the world? Will God abandon the goal of making the earth once again "very good," as it was in the beginning? Will God consign earth's inhabitants to the annihilation of death that their sin so richly deserves (Rom. 6:23)? Or will God, in lordship over even the worst of human evil, choose a different outcome?

Those are cosmic questions, and Hosea 11 is not dealing with the cosmos, much less the world, as a whole. Its focus is on Israel and the relation of that chosen people to their God. But the Scriptures answer universal questions by dealing in particulars—by dealing with one people or, in the case of the NT, with one Man. And the revelation given through the particular becomes assurance and pledge for the universal. Such is the case with this pivotal passage in Hosea. Here is revealed to us the nature of the Lord of the universe.

**11:1–4** / Verse 1 tells us that God adopted Israel as his **son** in the exodus from Egypt. Thus the delivery from slavery was not only a liberation, but an incorporation of the people Israel into the family of God. God *redeemed* Israel; Yahweh was the *family member* who bought his son back out of slavery (cf. Lev. 25:47–55), and from the time of the exodus onward, Israel is therefore considered to be Yahweh's *adopted* son. The same thought lies behind Exod. 4:22–23; Jer. 31:20, and perhaps Deut. 8:5 and Isa. 1:2.

It is this sonship of Israel which makes it possible for Matt. 2:15 to draw the parallel between Israel, the adopted son, and Jesus, the begotten son. And indeed, using the whole OT story, the NT continually contrasts the two: Jesus is the faithful son, who does not count equality with God a thing to be grasped in the garden (Phil. 2:6; Gen. 3:5); who does not rebel in the wilderness (cf. Num. 14; Matt. 4:1–11 and parallel); who submits to the will of God (Mark 14:32–42 and parallels), though it costs him his life on the cross. Like Jesus, Israel the adopted son is called to be God's servant in the salvation of the world (cf. Isa. 52:13–53:12), but it is finally the begotten son who must fulfill that mission. In one sense, the Bible's whole story is an accounting of this sonship. Thus, few names for Israel are more important than **my son** here in Hosea 11:1.

The adoption of Israel as a son at the time of the exodus is an act of pure grace on God's part. Israel has done nothing to deserve such status. No law has been given, no piety worked, no obedience rendered. God simply sets his love on this people and chooses them (cf. Deut. 7:6–8). The covenant relation in Hosea's thought, therefore, goes far beyond all legalistic reckoning to find its essence in the deepest devotion—as we have said before, in the love of an obedient son for his father, or in the love of a faithful wife for her husband.

Further, God's love for his people has been shown continually in God's ongoing education of them. Such is the meaning of the calling of Israel in verse 2. God's love for his people has included his nurture of them through the words of prophets and priests (cf. Isa. 1:2; 30:9; Jer. 3:14, 19, 22; 4:22). God has acted as a good Father, raising his child. God has patiently taught the infant Israel how to walk, holding the tiny hand, as each difficult new step was taken, verse 3.

The NIV follows the Hebrew of verse 4, except for reading **neck** instead of "jaws." But many have questioned whether this verse reverts to the figure of an animal, with a yoke, as in 4:16 and 10:11, or whether the Hebrew ʿōl should be read as ʿûl, "baby." The emendation would then read, "And I was to them as those who lift a baby to their cheek, and I bent down to feed him." To support such a translation, many have pointed out that 10:11 says Yahweh left Israel unyoked, and that the yoke on a heifer did not rest on the heifer's jaws, but on its neck, as the NIV has emended.

There is no way to decide definitively between these two readings, but in either case, the tenderness of Yahweh toward Israel is indicated.

Despite God's unmerited love for his son Israel, that people has continually gone away and worshiped **the Baals,** verse 2, never remembering that their redemption from slavery came from Yahweh's healing, verse 3. Given the context, this healing has the meaning of deliverance from political disaster (cf. 6:1; 7:1).

**11:5–7** / The NIV has translated verse 5 as questions. The Hebrew reads, "He shall return to the land of Egypt, but *(waw)* Assyria—he shall be his king, for they have refused to return." Because the Israelites have stubbornly rejected all invitations to return to Yahweh, they will be subjugated to Assyria's rule. The **return to Egypt** here may be a reference to King Hoshea's attempt to enlist Egyptian aid in breaking free from the Assyrian yoke after the death of Tiglath-pileser III in 727 BC (2 Kgs. 17:4), dating this passage about the middle of Hoshea's reign. Verse 6 then portrays the Assyrian sword, conquering the last of the northern kingdom and putting an end to all its **plans** to free itself. The NIV translation of verse 7 is strange. Though 7a is somewhat uncertain, the reading in the Hebrew is probably, "And my people are bent from returning to me, and to the yoke (that is, of Assyria) they shall be appointed; none will lift them up."

**11:8–9** / However, when God contemplates the destruction and captivity of his people Israel, which will historically mean the disappearance of the ten northern tribes from among the nations, he cannot stand the sight, verse 8. God breaks out in what we might almost consider to be great sobs. Wrath against his people turns to grief and weeping and lament (cf. Gen. 6:6; Luke 19:41). God cannot give up his adopted son!—the verb has the meaning of "total surrender." God cannot make Israel like **Admah** and **Zeboiim,** those cities that were totally destroyed along with Sodom and Gomorrah (Deut. 29:23).

God's refusal to surrender his people to everlasting destruction is emphasized by the repetition of "I will not," "I will not," "I will not" in verse 9a, 9b, and 9e—a repetition that the NIV translation has obscured. God says, "I will not 'do' (Hb.) my burning wrath" (cf. 8:5), "I will not again destroy Ephraim," "I will not come to burn them up *(bāʿar)*." And the reason is given by the crucial *kî* phrase in 9c: **For** (kî) **I am God, and not man—the Holy One** "in your midst."

Yahweh of Israel is the "holy" God, which means that God is more completely other than anything or anyone else—totally and qualitatively different from all human beings and from everything in all creation. God's holiness is his divinity, that which distinguishes him as God. And because he is holy he is inexhaustible love (cf. 1 John 4:8, 16). That is the nature, the divinity of God, which he cannot set aside, even in the face of Israel's total faithlessness and refusal to return his love. God will not give up his people Israel, whom he has adopted as a beloved son, precisely because he is a God who is love.

As love, God is sovereign. Israel's sinfulness cannot overcome or change this. Israel will not and does not repent, but Israel's attitude and action cannot finally dictate what God will be. He will be what he is, namely sovereign love, that will determine Israel's destiny beyond the effects of its evil, beyond the results of Assyria's imperial conquests, beyond all human will and working. God's holiness, God's divinity, God's sovereignty, God's love rules the history of the world, and nothing in all creation can overcome that divine rule.

**11:10–11** / Thus, verses 10–11 picture Israel's return to God. Verse 10, with its figure of the roaring **lion,** is alien to Hosea's language and sounds very much like Amos (cf. 1:2; 3:8). It may be a secondary insertion. But the thought is that of verse 11, which is genuine with Hosea (cf. his use of doves, 7:11, and his coupling of Egypt and Assyria, 7:11; 9:3; 12:1). After the Assyrian conquest, on the other side of judging them, God will gather his dispersed people and return them to **their homes.** God's act of salvation will arise out of love for his adopted son.

So in connection with this particular people Israel, God's elected and loved nation, we hear that no sinfulness, no apostasy, no stubborn refusal to repent, can finally overcome the love of the God who wills to save them and to give them a new life in the future. Unmerited grace rules the day.

It is with the cross and resurrection of Jesus Christ that this message of love breaks out of Israel's particularity to encompass all people on the earth. Human sin does the Son of God to death, but this God of the Bible will not surrender his world to the effects of sin and death. Instead, his sovereign love raises Christ from the grave and wins its triumph over all wrong, offering to

all persons everywhere a new life in his blessed future. Unmerited grace rules human history. The love of the holy one of
Israel will be the final word.

---

### Additional Note §27

---

**11:2** / The Hb. reads "they" for "I" and "them" for "me," giving
the meaning that it is the baals that call to Israel. The emendation
reflected in the NIV follows some manuscripts of the LXX and is almost
universally accepted.

## §28 Deceit, Grace, and Judgment (Hosea 11:12–12:14)

Originally, this passage was probably not one unit. Verses 11:12 and 12:1 both appear to be isolated accusations with no following announcement of judgment. And it could be argued that 12:2–6, 12:7–9, and 12:10–14 all form complete units in themselves. However, as the passage now stands, whether as the result of Hosea's arrangement or of a redactor/disciple's, it is a unified whole centered around the thought of the deceit of Israel (so too Wolff, *Hosea*). Punctuating the passage at three points is the recollection or reassurance of Yahweh's grace that answers that deceit (12:4c–6, 9, 13). And prominent in the passage is the role of prophets.

**11:12–12:1** / There is some debate over who speaks in 11:12. The NIV has considerably altered the Hebrew of 11:12c–d [MT 12:1c–d], which reads, "But Judah still wanders (or goes) with God (*ʾēl*), and with the holy ones (plural) is faithful." Because God is called *ʾēl*, as in 11:9, but is spoken of in the third person, it is likely that the prophet himself speaks here and that he is reflecting the opposition against him (cf. 9:7). All sorts of lying accusations are being made against him by his compatriots. Contrarily, however, Judeans are still faithful to the "holy ones," 11:12d.

Who are these holy ones? Many have read the plural as a plural of majesty, to refer to God. However, the prophet Elisha was called "holy" (2 Kgs. 4:9), as were the northern Levites (2 Chron. 35:3 RSV)—that is, they were set apart for God's service (Num. 3:12). It is very likely, therefore, that Hosea is referring here to those Levites and prophets of the North, who were the instigators of the Deuteronomic reform in Judah in 622/1 BC. Hosea numbers himself among them, and he states that though his northern compatriots persecute him, Judeans are still sympathetic to God's cause.

In contrast to the Judeans who still "wander" with God, 11:12c, Ephraim "herds" (NIV **feeds on**) **the wind** and wanders after **the east wind**—the sirocco, that hot, blasting draft that blows in from the Arabian desert, scorching everything before it, 12:1. The figure of wandering or roaming is very prominent in both verses. And Israel's wandering, then, is to **Assyria**—a reference to Hoshea's vassal treaty with Shalmaneser, son of Tiglath-pileser III, in 733 BC (2 Kgs. 17:3), which Hoshea promptly breaks by turning to **Egypt** for aid and paying it a tribute of **oil** (2 Kgs. 17:4; cf. Hos. 7:11; 8:9: "a wild ass wandering alone" RSV). Thus, this passage probably dates from early in the reign of Shalmaneser V.

**12:2–6** / The result is that God takes Israel to court, 12:2, and the deceitfulness of Ephraim is spelled out in three charges, 12:2–14. Most commentators emend **Judah,** in 12:2a, to "Ephraim," to preserve the parallelism of the verse (contra NIV).

The first charge in the court indictment is that Ephraim has been deceitful from the very first, verse 3. Its ancestor Jacob **grasped his brother** Esau's **heel** while still **in the womb** (Gen. 25:26), and so earned the name of "Jacob." The etymology of the name—"he takes by the heel," which is given in the Genesis account—is not followed. Rather, Jacob's well-earned title of "supplanter" or "deceiver," which the name can also signify, is used. Ephraim's ancestor was a deceiver even before he was born, and his descendants have continued in that role ever since.

Nevertheless, God showed grace to Jacob, as he has shown grace to Ephraim. This is affirmed by recalling Jacob's encounter with **the angel** of God at the ford of the River Jabbok (Gen. 32:24–29), when the angel blessed him, and by recalling Jacob's meeting with God at **Bethel,** in Genesis 28:10–19. There God spoke to Jacob, Hosea 12:4, as God has continued to speak to Jacob's descendants in Ephraim, 12:10. And there God instructed Jacob to keep covenant **love** *(ḥesed)* and God's order or **justice** *(mišpāṭ),* and to worship and follow God continually, 12:6. The latter verse is a quotation of what Hosea envisions God to have said to Jacob at Bethel. It is not an exhortation to Hosea's compatriots, as the NIV has rendered it. Nevertheless, Hosea intends the instructions to the forebear Jacob to be instructions given also to Ephraim, which they should have followed, but which they have not followed.

**12:7–8** / The second charge in the court indictment is therefore stated, 12:7–8b. Ephraim has been like a Canaanite **merchant** who has defrauded his customers and become rich, as the deceitful forebear Jacob was rich. This is one of the few places in Hosea's book where he mentions the commercial injustice that so enriched the northern kingdom and oppressed the poor (cf. Amos 8:5). Because the northern kingdom was prosperous, especially in the reign of Jeroboam II, it counted on its wealth to preserve it and to give it arms and status in the world of nations. But all of Ephraim's wealth cannot cover over the guilt it has incurred. Such is probably the meaning of 12:8c–d, following the LXX, rather than the rendering given in the NIV.

**12:9–10** / "I am the LORD your God from the land of Egypt" reads 12:9a in the Hebrew (so too 13:4). That is the way God is identified throughout the OT. The one true God is the God who delivered Israel from slavery in Egypt and made Israel his own. And because Yahweh is Lord, Israel's deceit cannot go unpunished; otherwise Yahweh would not be the Lord. Therefore, the judgment follows: God will once again make Israel dwell **in tents,** as it did in its first trek through the wilderness. Probably *môʿēd* refers here not to **appointed feasts** but to God's meetings with Israel in the tent of meeting in the desert (cf. Exod. 33:7–11)—a distinctly northern, Mosaic tradition.

Perhaps Hosea is saying that prosperous Ephraim will return to the barren life of the nomad, as some commentators have maintained. More probably, however, this is once again a note of God's covering grace. Israel must certainly undergo the judgment upon its deceitful and faithless ways. But then, God will lead Israel once again into the desert, and there, Hosea has earlier said (2:14–15), God will woo his beloved once again and reestablish his covenant relationship with her. Beyond the judgment which must surely come, there is hope for Israel's future.

**12:11–14** / The court indictment continues, however. The third example of Israel's deceitful ways is its false worship, verse 11. The bloody deeds of its priests at **Gilead** have already been mentioned (see the comment at 6:8), as has its baalistic worship at **Gilgal** (see the comments at 4:15 and 9:15). But its **altars** for sacrifice will become like stone heaps in a field when Yahweh's judgment descends upon it.

In verse 12, Hosea returns to the history of Ephraim's deceitful forebear Jacob, and this time, Jacob the supplanter is shown even further for what he was. He was a servant, a virtual slave, who had to work seven years to gain **a wife,** fourteen years to gain the one woman he loved (cf. Gen. 29:15–30)! That is what all of Jacob's trickery and wealth led to—servitude! But in contrast

to that, by obeying the word of its God, delivered through the
prophet Moses (cf. Deut. 18:15–16), Israel was redeemed from its
slavery in **Egypt,** verse 13. Thus, Hosea has returned to the theme
with which he began (11:12)—that of his prophecy. And what is
implied is that rather than taking its character from its deceitful
ancestor Jacob, Ephraim should take its course from the word of
God, delivered through the prophets in ages past (v. 10) and now
through Hosea himself. That is what preserved Israel in the beginning, verse 13b, and that is what will preserve Israel now in
Hosea's time.

But Israel will not, verse 14. The verse reads, "Ephraim
provoked bitterly, and his blood-guilt will fall on him, and the
Lord (*ʾᵃdōnāy*) will return his shame upon him." With all of
its deceitful ways, following the deceitfulness of its ancestor,
Ephraim has bitterly provoked God's wrath. God therefore will
be *ʾᵃdōnāy*, "master," "Lord," over this people, and will return
their deceitful ways upon them, bringing upon them the sentence of death, which is always the sentence for blood-guilt
(Exod. 21:23–24; Lev. 24:20–21; Deut. 19:21). The deadly results of
their faithlessness will not return upon them automatically, but
will be inflicted upon them by their Lord. What Ephraim has
sown, that it will also reap.

---

### Additional Note §28

---

**12:4** / The NIV's **talked with him** correctly emends "us" to
"him."

## §29 No Other God and Savior (Hosea 13:1–8)

Chapter 13 is clearly made up of four originally separate oracles—verses 1–3, 4–8, 9–11, and 12–16. All four oracles probably date from the last years of Hosea's ministry and from the last years of Hoshea ben Imla's reign, around 724 BC. Thus, they have probably been set in their present place by a disciple/redactor of the prophet's work. Shalmaneser V is on the throne of Assyria, soon to be replaced by Sargon II, who will conquer the last remains of the northern kingdom. It is clear that Ephraim's attempts to free itself from the Assyrian yoke by turning to Egypt are futile. Ephraim's doom is certain.

The redactor, however, has joined verses 1–3 with verses 4–8 by an introductory *waw*—probably an adversative *waw* (**But**)—at the beginning of verse 4. We shall therefore discuss verses 1–8 as a unit.

**13:1–3** / As is so customary with Hosea, he reviews Ephraim's past in order to contrast it with the present and future, verse 1 (cf. 9:10; 10:1; 11:1, 3–4; 12:4, 10, 13). The prophet speaks in verses 1–3, and there was a time, he says, when Ephraim's strength and authority caused others in the realm of nations to tremble. Certainly that was the case during the Syro-Ephraimitic war in 734–733 BC. Isaiah 7:2 records that "When the house of David (i.e., King Ahaz of Judah) was told, 'Syria is in league with Ephraim,' his heart and the heart of his people shook as the trees of the forest shake before the wind" (RSV). And before that, in the beginnings of Israel's history, Ephraim held a preeminent place among the tribes of Israel (cf. Gen. 48:15–20; 49:22–26).

But Israel's history was finally dependent on the guiding of God, and when Ephraim deserted God to worship **Baal,** it **died;** that is, it lost the vital source of life that had given it strength and preeminence. Hosea here sounds the leading motif of verses 1–8: Life comes from God alone, and apart from God there is only death.

Instead of seeking life from God, Ephraim sought it from the fertility rites of baal worship, verse 2. The reference to **idols,** *massēkâ,* in verse 2b, is probably to small molten images (cf. Exod. 32:4, 8), modeled after the bull of Bethel (cf. 8:5; 10:5), which were made of bronze and overlaid with silver, and which were used by individuals. Kissing the idol was part of the ritual of such baal worship (cf. 1 Kgs. 19:18).

The reading of the last three lines of verse 2 is difficult, and along with the NIV and LXX, some commentators have found a reference to the baalistic practice of human sacrifice (cf. Jer. 32:35). However, the Hebrew is better emended to read, "To these they say, sacrifice! Men kiss calves!" Were human sacrifice being practiced in his day, surely this would not be Hosea's only reference to it!

Because Ephraim has deserted the one source of life in God and has tried to find life in Baal, Ephraim will therefore vanish from history, verse 3, like **morning mist** and **dew** that disappear before the heat of the sun (cf. 6:4), like **chaff** that is separated from the wheat on the **threshing floor** and blown away by the wind (cf. Ps. 1:4), like **smoke** that wafts out the **window** of a house (cf. Ps. 37:20). The latter is not properly a window, but a hole in the roof or side of the dwelling, through which the smoke from a cooking fire may escape.

**13:4–8** / In verses 4–8, the Lord speaks directly through the prophet to the people, and once again the past is reviewed. The only God and Savior whom Israel has ever known is Yahweh. The NIV translation has seriously weakened the original. The Hebrew literally reads, in this order:

> But I am Yahweh your God
>   from the land of Egypt.
> And a God besides me you do not know,
>   and a Savior—there is none except me.
> I knew you in the wilderness,
>   in the land of drought.

When the Israelites were enslaved and helpless in **Egypt,** Yahweh delivered them (cf. 11:1). In every crisis and difficulty, Yahweh has been Israel's only **Savior** (cf. Jer. 14:8; Isa. 63:8–9; 43:3, 11; 45:15; 49:26; 60:16). God knew this people when they wandered for forty years in the wilderness (cf. 9:10). God has known Israel, intimately, lovingly, as a member of his family—as a beloved wife (cf. 2:2), as his adopted son (cf. 11:1)—and in that intimate relationship, which characterizes the covenant for Hosea, Israel has known God.

But after the Israelites entered the land and were **fed** to the full by God's gifts of grain and wine and oil (cf. 2:8), they **became proud:** The Hebrew reads, "their heart was lifted up," verse 6. That is, Israel felt self-sufficient, able to get by on its own apart from its one Savior, relying on its idols, its military strength, its kings and princes to enrich and preserve its life. The Israelites forgot all that their God had done for them in the past. The emphasis in verse 6 is on that final line, on Israel's forgetting. As in 2:13, to forget God is to no longer "know" God, to no longer live in a daily, intimate communion with a God who is entrusted with one's life, and to no longer remember all that God has done (cf. Ps. 106:21). Israel turned from the one source of life to the false sources of paganism and self-sufficiency, and thereby lost its life. For the people who would save their own life will lose it. There is no life apart from the one God of the covenant.

The terrible judgment is therefore announced in the similes of verses 7–8, and Yahweh himself will execute the sentence of death. Obviously it is the armed forces of the Assyrian Empire that will destroy Ephraim so that it disappears from history. But propelling that destructive power is God alone.

Because similes are used in verses 7–8, the meaning is not that God *is* a **lion** or **leopard** or she-bear, but rather that God's judging *action* is as destructive as the attacks of those animals would be. And we can have no doubt that the Assyrian siege, destruction, and deportation of the inhabitants of Ephraim were indeed that destructive (cf. 2 Kgs. 17:5–6, 18, 24). Hosea knows the customs and ways of ancient warfare. He therefore uses figures of speech that portray its awful devastation and death. The same figures would be appropriate for the effects of war in our time. War brings death. And Ephraim is going to die.

## §30 No Other Helper (Hosea 13:9–11)

**13:9–11** / The text of the first two lines of verse 9 and of verse 10 is difficult. In the Hebrew, verse 9a reads, "He will destroy you, Israel." This has normally been emended, following the Syriac, to read, "I will destroy you" (unlike the NIV's passive **you are destroyed**), since it is obvious that Yahweh continues to speak in verses 9–11. The Hebrew of verse 9b literally reads, "Against me," but it can also have the meaning of "who." Thus, the two lines read:

> I will destroy you, Israel, (or, reading perfects, I destroy you),
> Who is your helper?

In addition, in verse 10, **in all your towns** should be emended to read "with all your princes." The verse is then read,

> Where is your king now, to save you,
> with all your princes, to defend you (following the LXX)?

In the past, Yahweh has always been the **helper** of Israel against its foes—a tradition as old as the tribal league in the time of the judges (cf. Deut. 33:7, 26, 29) and preserved in the Psalms (Ps. 115:9–11; 124:8). And, as previously stated in Hosea 13:4, Yahweh is Israel's sole helper. When God is for Israel, no one else can finally prevail against it. But when God is against it, no one else can deliver it.

Thus, when Yahweh determines to **destroy** his people, no reliance on political means of defense can turn aside that destruction, verse 9. Ephraim thought that it could save itself by turning to Egypt for aid against Assyria. But its leaders who thought to carry out that strategy—its **king** and princes—have themselves been imprisoned by Shalmaneser V of Assyria (2 Kgs. 17:4). "Where now are your king and your princes whom you thought could save and defend you?" God taunts, verse 10. Because the rulers were chosen apart from any thought given to the will of Yahweh (see the comments at 8:4 and 9:15), they cannot possibly be instruments of salvation. Rather, they serve as instruments of God's **wrath,** verse 11. Ephraim has relied on its kings to save it, rejecting the kingship of Yahweh (cf. 1 Sam. 8:7), and has thereby brought doom on itself.

This short pericope is a forceful statement of who finally rules the affairs of nations and persons. There is one ultimate power in the world, who is the God of Israel and finally the God and father of our Lord Jesus Christ, and unless human affairs are conducted according to the will of *the* ruler, those affairs cannot succeed.

## §31 The Lord of Life and Death (Hosea 13:12–16)

**13:12–16** / The God of Hosea is not only the ruler over all nations and persons. This cosmic Lord commands the very forces of life and death itself. He kills and makes alive (Deut. 32:39; 1 Sam. 2:6). He gives the breath of life (Gen. 2:7) or withdraws it (Job 34:14–15; Ps. 104:29–30; cf. 146:4; Eccl. 12:7). In the hands of God are all powers of life and death.

Death therefore rises up upon Ephraim, according to this passage, because God will not pass over Ephraim's iniquity and sin. The Hebrew of verse 12 reads:

> The iniquity of Ephraim is bound up,
>   laid up his sin.

The reference is to the custom of binding up papyrus and parchment scrolls and of depositing them in a storage place for safe-keeping (cf. Isa. 8:16). Thus have Ephraim's **sins** against the Lord been recorded, bound up, and **stored**. The passage of time cannot erase them or cause God to forget them. Further circumstances cannot mitigate their deserved punishment. The wages of sin is death, and Ephraim must pay for its sins with death (cf. v. 16).

Ephraim, therefore, is like an unwise son, verse 13, who should be born into life, but who instead refuses to present himself at **the opening of the womb** and who dies as a result. God wanted to give the people life (cf. Isa. 66:7–9), but they have chosen death. The figure of speech, with its picture of a child who refuses to traverse the birth canal, is a stunning portrayal of the obstinacy of the Israelites.

The NIV has read verse 14ab as assertions, which is possible, but it is more likely, according to the word order, that they are questions:

> From the hand of Sheol (NIV: **the grave**) shall I ransom them?
> From death shall I redeem them?

Throughout the OT, Sheol is the place below the waters under the earth to which all the dead go. It is variously described as a place of dust and darkness, from which there is no return (Job 7:9–10; 16:22). Those who were formerly alive dwell there as *rĕpāʾîm*, that is, "weak ones," shadows, who chirp and mutter (Isa. 8:19). These beings cannot praise God, because such praise is synonymous with life (Ps. 6:5; 30:9; 88:10–12). In much of the OT, Sheol is beyond the reach of Yahweh, but in Amos 9:2 and here in Hosea, God is sovereign over Sheol as well as over heaven and earth. God could buy back Ephraim from Sheol—both verbs in verse 14a, b involve the thought of payment.

Instead, God calls for death and Sheol, here personified, to loose all their pestilent powers from the underworld upon this faithless people, verse 14c–d. That death is treated as an objective power—an evil force let loose in the world—reminds one of the realism of the Scriptures, mirrored also in the NT (Eph. 6:12; 1 Cor. 15:26). But clearly also throughout the Scriptures, God is sovereign over that evil power (cf. Rom. 8:38–39). And here in Hosea, death is an instrument of judgment (cf. Rom. 6:23). Why? Because, God says, "Compassion is hid from my eyes" (so reads the Hebrew).

The meaning of verse 15a is obscure, and many have emended it to read, "Though he flourishes among rushes," understanding *ʾāḥû* as "reeds" or "rushes" on the basis of Ugaritic (so Wolff, *Hosea*, p. 15; instead of *ʾaḥîm*, **brothers**). The image is then given of a reed plant that flourishes in waters, but that will be dried up by the east wind—the hot, desert sirocco—that Yahweh will send, verse 15b–c.

There is no doubt, then, that the **east wind** in verse 15 is Assyria, which comes across the eastern desert against Ephraim as the instrument of Yahweh's wrath against his people (cf. the "east wind" that Ephraim pursues in 12:1). In the metaphor of verse 15d–e, the water of life will fail for Ephraim. It will die as a waterless plant will die. And leaving behind the metaphor, verse 15f–g pictures the troops of Assyria plundering every valuable thing that Ephraim owns.

As Ephraim's sin cannot be overlooked, verse 12, so Samaria, the capital of Ephraim, must bear its guilt, verse 16. (The Hb. does not have **The people of Samaria**, contra NIV.) Samaria, which has led all the people, and which here in fact stands for the total population, has **rebelled against** its **God**. The verb *mārāh* is used elsewhere of the obstinacy of a disobedient and unmanageable child (Deut. 21:20; cf. Ps. 78:8), as Israel has been obstinate and disobedient (cf. Hos. 11:1–2).

The troops of Assyria will therefore lay siege to Samaria and finally capture it (2 Kgs. 17:5–6), and the last three lines of verse 16 picture the destruction that will follow. Samaria's fighting men will **fall by the sword,** and then the entire populace will be subjected to the rampaging cruelty of the invading army (cf. 2 Kgs. 15:16; Amos 1:13). Ephraim will die. Hosea foresees the end that befalls Ephraim in 721 BC.

The Apostle Paul uses Hos. 13:14 in his great chapter on the resurrection, in 1 Cor. 15:55, but he turns the saying on its head. Because of the death and resurrection of Jesus Christ, death and Sheol have no more power. God is sovereign still, and Christ has won the victory over them. But human sin has not been passed over any more in that victory than in Hosea. No, the wages of sin is still death, and God has paid the penalty by giving up his Son to die on the cross. Perhaps Hosea's words can help us realize the enormity of the punishment that might have been ours except for the sacrifice of our Lord, and the immensity of the love that has saved us.

## §32 *The God of Free Grace (Hosea 14:1–9)*

We can reasonably consider this oracle to be the last message delivered by Hosea in his prophetic career, and therefore to be properly placed by the redactor at the end of the Hosianic collection. The NIV paraphrases verse 1b. The Hebrew of that line reads, "You have stumbled in your iniquity." Israel has stumbled. It is already falling, and its end is near.

Hosea has announced that inevitable end in the oracles that have gone before. The plagues of death and the destruction of Sheol must come upon his people in the judgment decreed by God upon their sin (see the comment at 13:14). But Hosea has also announced that God cannot give up his people—his adopted son—forever (11:1–11); that on the other side of the judgment God will take Israel—his beloved wife—once more into the desert and there woo her again until she is betrothed to him in faithfulness to her covenant bond (see the comment at 2:14, 15). It is out of this latter promise, of an Israel restored to fidelity by God, that this passage in chapter 14 is spoken.

**14:1–3** / In verses 1–3 the prophet exhorts his people to return to their Lord, and he composes a prayer for them to utter upon that return. **Take words with you,** Hosea says; no other sacrifice is now acceptable; Israel's cultic sacrifices have been too corrupted by their worship of Baal, and so now all they have left are words, **the fruit of** their **lips.** Verse 2d–f should be read, "Take away all iniquity, and accept the good, and we will render the fruit of our lips."

That "good" which they then offer is a renunciation of all of their former idolatry—their dependence on foreign nations, on their own military strength, and on their idols, verse 3. They were once the adopted son of God (cf. 11:1), but they have rejected their Father and become orphans. Now, in repentance and renunciation of their former way of life, they once again find $y^e ruham$, "mercy" (NIV: **compassion;** MT v. 4) in their God.

**14:4** / Hosea does not compose such a prayer for his people because he thinks they are capable of such repentance and renunciation of their apostasy. As he has stated before, Israel has no power in itself to return to its God (cf. the comment at 5:4). Rather, he envisions Israel uttering such a prayer *because he believes God will heal and recreate them*. And that is the central announcement of this passage, in verse 4. "I will heal their turning away; I will love them freely; for I will turn my wrath from them" reads the Hebrew of that verse. God here promises to remake Israel, to heal it (cf. 6:11), to love it **freely**, apart from any condition or repentance and turning on Israel's part. What Israel cannot do for itself, God will do. That is the primary good news of the message of Hosea.

**14:5–7** / The effect of Yahweh's healing of this people is then vividly described in the images drawn from nature in verses 5–7. To understand the force of these images, however, we should realize that they are pictures drawn from love poetry (so Wolff, *Hosea*; see the notes below). They are images of Yahweh wooing this people (cf. 2:14), speaking tenderly to them, loving them as a young man loves his betrothed.

God **will be like the dew to Israel.** The abundance of dew was absolutely necessary to life and growth in Palestine's arid climate (Deut. 33:13). In fact, dew was later used as a symbol of God's power to raise the dead (Isa. 26:19). As the dew grants life, God will give new life to this people, verse 5. Consequently, they will blossom like the large-flowered lilies that flourished and spread through the desert valleys. And they will send out **young shoots,** verse 6. The images are intended to portray the fertility and multiplication of Israel's populace, in contrast to the earlier picture in 9:11–14.

In its new life, given by God, Israel will send down roots like those strong and towering trees of Lebanon that were seen as symbols of durability and permanence (cf. Ps. 92:12; Isa. 2:13; Jer. 22:23; Amos 2:9; Zech. 11:1), verse 5. Their **splendor** will be like that of the **olive tree,** noted for its fruitfulness (Ps. 128:3; Jer. 11:16). And they will be pleasing, like the **fragrance** of Lebanon, verse 6. The latter reference is not to the fragrance of the cedars of Lebanon (contra NIV), but to the many fragrant shrubs and herbs that grew on its forest floor.

Verse 7 in the Hebrew reads, "They shall return, dwelling in his shadow," the reference being to the protection and comfort given Israel by God (cf. Ps. 91:9; 121:5; Isa. 25:4; 32:2; 49:2; 51:16). Then follows the enigmatic line, "they shall grow grain," which the RSV, probably correctly, emends to, "they shall flourish as a garden." Israel, given new life by its God, will blossom forth like a spreading vine, becoming renowned for its fruitfulness and vitality and pleasantness, verse 7.

**14:8** / All of the images used are intended to portray vitality given once again to Israel, not by Baal, but by Yahweh, who is Israel's one source of life and good. In a daring switch on baalistic religion's worship of sacred trees, Yahweh is therefore compared to a flourishing evergreen **tree** in verse 8. From God alone comes Israel's fruit; that is, from Yahweh alone can Israel have life and have it more abundantly. God has nothing to do with the idols of self-reliance and military strength and baalistic worship upon which Israel has relied. God alone answers Israel, is responsible for its life, and "encloses" (NIV: **cares for**) it. In God is life (cf. John 1:4).

Thus, beyond the destruction of its nation, beyond the punishment of its apostasy, beyond the reckoning for its sin, Israel is promised a new life by this God of Hosea, who cannot let his people go. In the future, God will begin a new saving history, leading Israel once again out into the wilderness, where he will woo her tenderly, and making her his own, betrothed to him in righteousness and justice, in covenant love and mercy and faithfulness. There Israel will once more "know the LORD" and will once more cleave to God in the intimate and heartfelt love of a faithful wife for her husband, or in the obedient and trusting love of a son for his father (2:19–20, 23).

Surely it is when the Gospel according to Matthew sees Hosea 11:1 fulfilled in the holy family returning up out of Egypt (Matt. 2:15) that God begins the new saving history promised in Hosea—a saving history that is still being worked out among the covenant people. The promise is to the new Israel in Jesus Christ, the Christian Church, that in the only begotten Son of this God of Hosea's we, and indeed Israel (cf. Rom. 11:26), will have life abundant and eternal. The NT gospel looks toward the completion and fulfillment of what Hosea promises, and in the certainty that God will keep this word, we journey forward.

**14:9** / A later scribe of the Wisdom school added this verse to Hosea's book to recommend it to his generation. The last half of the verse echoes vocabulary of the exilic Deuteronomic

Deuteronomic historians, while the two ways—of the righteous and rebels—are typical of wisdom teaching (cf. Ps. 1, for example).

**These things** refers to the entire written book of Hosea, which the scribe wants his readers to understand (NIV: **realize**) and know. The one who takes Hosea's message to heart and walks in the ways of the Lord is wise. The one who rebels against Hosea's message is foolish and will fall. It is still a good admonition for us contemporary readers.

---

### Additional Notes §32

---

**14:2** / The NIV correctly reads *pᵉrî*, **fruit,** for *pārîm,* "bulls."

**14:3** / The NIV misunderstands the reference to **war-horses.** The word "horses" refers not to cavalry, but to chariots drawn by horses.

**14:5** / **Lily:** cf. Song Sol. 2:1, 16; 4:5; 5:13; 6:2, 3; 7:2.

**14:6** / **Fragrance like a cedar of Lebanon:** cf. Song Sol. 2:13; 4:10, 11; 7:8, 13.

**14:7** / **Blossom like the vine:** cf. Song Sol. 6:11; 7:12; **dwell . . . in his shade:** cf. Song Sol. 2:3; **wine:** cf. Song Sol. 1:2, 4; 4:10; 5:1; 7:9.

**14:8** / **Green pine tree:** the words in the Hb. can actually refer to any one of a number of luxuriant conifers.

# *Joel*

# Introduction: Joel

The book of Joel does not ordinarily command a great deal of attention in our modern churches. When it is taught or preached, usually only one of two passages is utilized: either Joel 2:12–19, which is the stated text for Ash Wednesday in most lectionaries, or Joel 2:28–32, which is quoted by Peter in Acts 2 as part of his sermon at the first Christian Pentecost in Jerusalem.

Yet the prophecies of Joel set forth the very heart of the gospel that found its embodiment in the incarnation of Jesus Christ. Paul knew this when he quoted Joel 2:32 in Romans 10:13, and he made it a central thrust of his message: "Everyone who calls on the name of the LORD will be saved."

## Themes

Indeed, it is no exaggeration to say that the two great themes of Joel encompass the two major poles of the gospel. First, Joel announces God's very real judgment on human sin, a judgment that concerns the whole world of nature and nations. Second, however, Joel proclaims the merciful grace of God, who will not give over his covenant people and his creation to final destruction. In proclaiming this message, the prophecies of Joel are never out-of-date.

## Date

Joel's words were probably first spoken between 500 and 350 BC, which are dates based on the internal evidence of the book. To be sure, some earlier scholars dated the book in the ninth century BC because of its position preceding Amos in the canon. Recently, some still argue for a seventh-century BC date. But the situation pictured in Joel is that of the quiet, postexilic time when Judah was a little subprovince of the vast Persian Empire. No external, historical enemy threatens its existence. The Babylonian exile and the dispersion of the Jews is in the past (Joel 3:1–3). The existence of the second temple, which was rebuilt by 515 BC, is taken for granted, along with its priests and daily sacrifices (Joel 1:9, 13–14, 16; 2:14, 17). There is no mention of a king or of courtly officials, and priests and elders are the leaders of the Judean community. The walls of Jerusalem, which were rebuilt in the time of Nehemiah, are standing (Joel 2:7, 9).

On the international scene portrayed in the book, Tyre and Sidon have commercial associations with Philistia (Joel 3:4), which we know to have been the case before 343 BC. Sidon was destroyed by the armies of Artaxerxes III of Persia in 343 BC. Tyre fell to Alexander the Great in 332 BC. The latest possible date for the book, therefore, is 343 BC.

Further evidence of the book's date is also given by Joel's extensive use of earlier prophecy, including that of Obadiah, which was not in existence before the fifth century BC and which constitutes the earliest possible date for Joel. It therefore seems proper to date the book between 500 and 343 BC.

### Authorship

We know nothing of the prophet himself, other than the name of his father, which he gives us in 1:1. Significantly, the name "Joel" is found elsewhere in the OT only in 1 Samuel 8:2 and then seventeen times in the postexilic books of Chronicles, Ezra, and Nehemiah (1 Chron. 4:35; 5:4; 6:28; 7:3, etc.; 2 Chron. 29:12; Ezra 10:43; Neh. 11:9), which would seem to confirm our dating of the book.

The name of Joel's father, Pethuel, is found only here. The LXX and Syr. and L identify Pethuel with Bethuel, the father of Rebekah (Gen. 22:22–23; 24:15, 24, etc.), but the identification cannot be sustained, and the MT is supported by other manuscripts of the LXX, by the Tg. and the Vg.

It is unusual in the prophetic writings to have no indication in the heading of the book of when the prophet carried on his active ministry (cf. e.g., Isa. 1:1; Jer. 1:1–3; Zech. 1:1, etc.). Only Jonah 1:1 is comparable to Joel 1:1, and perhaps the omission of specific dates in both of those books is an indication of their authors' desire to say that their message is for every age.

## *Unity*

The unity of the book was defended up through the nineteenth century. At the beginning of the twentieth century, however, Bernhard Duhm gave the classical formulation of the theory that the original book dealt only with the locust plague and that the eschatological sections in Joel 3, as well as all references to the day of the Lord in Joel 1–2, were later interpolations from the period of the Maccabees. Duhm's theory was widely adopted by scholars such as G. A. Smith, J. Bewer, and T. H. Robinson.

Now, however, it has been convincingly shown that the eschatological passages of the book are integral to its message and that the book as a whole has a remarkable symmetry. Joel 2:27 and 3:17 form two parallel climaxes in the book. Joel 2:21–27 answers 1:4–20; 3:1–17 corresponds to 2:1–11; 2:28–32 answers 2:12–17. The book apparently has been shaped very carefully literarily, and its final form may be the result of some editing. For example, 3:4–8 is probably a later addition to the work, although it may have been added by the prophet himself. As the book now stands, it certainly forms a unity, and it should be treated as such.

The MT of the book is in very good shape, and it needs very few emendations. However, those who study the book in the original Hebrew should be aware of the fact that the chapter and verse numberings differ somewhat in the English versions. Joel 2:28–32 in English versions is numbered 3:1–5 in the Hebrew. Joel 3:1–21 in English versions is chapter 4 in the Hebrew.

## *Use of Prophetic Tradition*

One of the most fascinating aspects of the book of Joel is its use of earlier prophetic tradition. In that use, the prophet shares much in common with us modern students of the Bible. Just as we read the words of the prophets in the Bible and hear God speaking to us through them, so too the word of God is revealed to Joel through the preaching of the prophets who have preceded him. Just as is the case for us, the word of God, spoken through the earlier prophets, is not a thing of the past for Joel. Rather, that word continues to speak and work its influence in the present. Indeed, Joel is sure that many of the words spoken by his earlier prophetic colleagues have not come to pass; their fulfillment lies in Joel's present and in the future that stretches out beyond him.

The word of God is alive for Joel, at work in human history. It is never a dead utterance of the past.

As a result, Joel uses three great complexes of tradition from earlier prophetic writings. First, he uses prophetic tradition concerning the day of the Lord as set forth especially in Zephaniah 1–2, Isaiah 13, Ezekiel 30, Obadiah, and Malachi 4. Second, he uses the traditions concerning the enemy from the North as found in Jeremiah 4, 6. And third, he employs prophetic traditions concerning God's judgment on foreign nations as those are found in Jeremiah 46–51 and Ezekiel 25–32. But Joel also borrows whole sentences from earlier prophets: e.g., 1:15 from Isaiah 13:6; 3:16 from Amos 1:2. And he appropriates smaller word groups: e.g., Joel 3:18 from Amos 9:13 and Joel 2:32 from Obadiah 17. (For a complete listing of Joel's use of earlier prophecy, see Wolff, pp. 10–11.) It must not be thought that Joel is simply updating earlier prophecy, however. He is also given new words from God which not only interpret prophecy from the past but also illumine the present and the future. And that future concerns our time and the days and years that lie out ahead of us.

### Summary

In summary, the book of Joel does not seem a pleasant one for modern eyes and ears to read and hear. It contradicts so much of how we regard ourselves and tells us such unsettling truths: that we are subject to God's judgment every day of our lives and that finally we must stand before God to hear our final judgment; that God can use the very forces of nature itself against us; that our sin corrupts not only ourselves but also the natural world around us; that we are an apostate people, turning to other gods and goddesses, or making even ourselves our own deities, and thus violating God's loving covenant with us. In all of that, Joel is a very realistic book.

But Joel's realism also sets forth the nature of the God who is true God, and in doing so it foreshadows the heart of the gospel. Even now, it says to us—even now, though we be lost in our apostate secularity, the Lord of the covenant holds open the door by his free grace to our repentance and return to him. We do not earn that return, not even by our repentance, but God offers it to us in his mercy. He is above all else a God of love for us.

At the same time, Joel shows us that the true God is a God of power, the ruler of all nature and history, who has the might to offer effective love. God can do away with rebellion and his enemies on earth, and he will establish his good kingdom. No human sin or opposition will stand in the way of God's completion of his purposes.

All of that realistic message, then, is made flesh for us in our Lord Jesus Christ. By Christ's cross, the sentence of death for our sins is carried out, and that judgment still is at work in our lives every day. And when Christ comes again, we will indeed face God's final judgment. But at the same time, and through that one man Jesus Christ, the offer of mercy is extended. Through faith in the work of God in his Son by the cross and resurrection, we can be grafted into an everlasting covenant relation with our Lord that nothing in heaven or on earth can take away.

Surely our response to that message can only be the grateful rending of our hearts in repentance and turning to our Lord. Teach all of this to your children and their childrens' children, Joel bids us in the beginning of his book. And at the end, his invitation to us is, "Come!"

## §1 The Interpreting Word (Joel 1:1)

**1:1** / It may be that the name **Joel** is more than just the proper name of the prophet. In the Hebrew, "Joel" combines two words, *Yah*, which is an abbreviated form of *Yahweh*, the Hebrew name for the Lord, and *ʾēl*, which means god. Thus, the name "Joel" signifies "*Yahweh* is God," and while many pious parents could have affirmed their faith by giving their son that name, "Joel" may also point to one of the major concerns of the book, namely, apostasy or the worship of false gods. Joel condemns Judah in the strongest terms for its sin, but he never says what that sin is. Yet, in the two climaxes of the book, in 2:27 and 3:17, the statement is, "Then you will know that I am . . . the LORD your God." The implication is that Judah has not hitherto known. Rather, if the prophet's name is any indication, Judah has gone after other gods. Apostasy has been its sin, in violation of the first commandment.

**The word of the LORD . . . came to Joel.** All of the prophets make that claim—that they are speaking words that the Lord God has given them to speak. When we study the writings of the prophets, it is clear that the word of God comes to them from outside of themselves. This is emphasized in Jeremiah 15:16 and Ezekiel 3:1–3, where it is said that the Lord has given the prophet the word to "eat." The word of the Lord is not the product of the prophet's own inner musings or of his meditations on the events of his day, but rather a word that comes solely from God, often without any preparation by faith or experience, on the part of the prophet (cf. Jer. 1; Amos 7:14–15).

This is important for the interpretation of Joel. Most commentators have maintained that Joel derived his prophecy by reflecting on the severe locust plague that afflicted Judah. The locust plague has reminded Joel, they maintain, of the coming day of the Lord, when God will come to judge the earth and to set up his kingdom. But that turns the Bible's understanding of prophecy exactly upside down.

The Bible never maintains that events interpret the word of God. Rather, the word of God interprets events, and it is the prophet's function to tell just how and why God is involved with any event. The prophet is one who says, on the basis of the transcendent word given him, "Here God is at work, in this event," or "Here God is not at work." For example, Jeremiah and Ezekiel both point to the fall of Judah and Jerusalem to the Babylonians in 587 BC and proclaim that the destruction is not just a military defeat but the punishment of God for Judah's sin; God has had a hand in Judah's fall. So, too, Joel points to the locust plague and proclaims that it is not just a natural disaster like those that often came upon the Mediterranean world; rather it is the work of God in judgment on his sinful people. God's word illumines and gives meaning to human and natural history because it tells where God is at work in that history.

In our day, that means the events and experiences in our time are not to be used to interpret the Bible. Rather, the Bible is to be used to interpret experiences and events. Only by such an approach to the Scriptures are we able to live by God's word and not by our own.

## §2 *The Locust Plague (Joel 1:2–4)*

**1:2–4** / **Tell it to your children,** verse 3. Joel proclaims that he has a message that should be handed down to **the next generation,** and indeed to all following generations for all time to come. At first reading, that message would seem to concern an unprecedented **locust** plague that has stripped Judah bare of every scrap of wood and vegetation and left her land wasted and desolate, so that her very existence is threatened.

If that were the primary import of Joel's message, it might be compared to old folks in our time telling of "the snows of yesteryears" or of the hardships that they endured growing up during the Great Depression.

But Joel's message concerns much more than the preservation of the memory of some hardship. That which Joel wants told is the message of his entire book. Verses 2 and 3 form an introduction to the entire work, and it is the whole of that prophecy that must be handed down, even to our day.

Usually when the OT talks of handing on a story or a tradition to the next generations, the subject is the good news of God's mighty or saving acts (cf. Exod. 12:26–27; 13:8; Deut. 4:9; 6:20–23; 32:7; Ps. 22:30; 78:4). Here, however, the subject is first of all God's judgment. And the reason the message must be handed on is that it is a message about God. That is what Israel always found worth preserving—the message of God's acts within its history. All else was of secondary importance.

What has been revealed to Joel by the word of God is that the locust plague, which has ravaged Judah's land, is the work of God's judgment upon them for their sin (cf. Exod. 10:4–6, 12–15; Ps. 78:46; 105:34–35; Amos 4:9). God's word to Joel has interpreted the event and revealed it to be a work of condemnation (cf. Amos 7:1) and a call to repentance (cf. 1 Kgs. 8:37–38).

As we shall repeatedly see, Joel's prophecy has as its context the covenant of Israel with God. In that covenant, Israel promised to be God's people, and God promised to be Israel's

God. But attached to that covenant, as preserved in Deuteronomy, was a list of covenant curses that would fall upon Israel if
it abandoned its God (Deut. 28:15–68). One of those curses concerned a locust plague (Deut. 28:38–42), and Joel proclaims that
the locust curse has now fallen on Judah because of its apostasy.
Such a message is only intimated in these opening verses. Joel
will develop it throughout what follows.

Such prophecy immediately raises difficult questions for
us, of course, because of our view of the natural world. Most of
us modern, twentieth-century Christians believe that we live in
a closed universe, that is, that the universe is a closed system in
which everything proceeds according to natural law. There is no
place where God intervenes. Rather, if a natural disaster occurs,
we believe it to be the result of natural causes, independent from
the hand of God. Thus, we have almost totally secularized the
sphere of nature, so that for us God's working is absent from it.

The Bible, however, does not share such views. Throughout the Scriptures, God is the Lord of nature, who has created the
natural world, who sustains all of its workings and processes, and
who is able to use it for divine purposes (cf. Neh. 9:6; Ps. 104; Jer.
31:35; Amos 4:7–10 among multitudinous references). God is
quite able, therefore, to turn the processes of the natural world
against us as a means of judgment upon us (cf. e.g., Amos 8:9;
Luke 23:44–45; Hab. 3:6; Matt. 27:51–52), and Joel is saying that
God has done so by bringing the locust plague upon Judah in
fulfillment of the word in Deuteronomy.

This does not mean, however, that every natural disaster
that comes upon us in our time is intended as a judgment by God.
Some natural disasters are the consequence of orders God has set
up within the natural world. For example, if you build your
house upon a flood plain, you are liable to get flooded out. This
is not a judgment but a natural consequence of the order of the
world. Further, Jesus has made it very clear in Luke 13:1–5 that
when some other person suffers a catastrophe, we are not to
point the finger at them and say that they are being judged by
God for their sin. As our Lord makes clear, all of us are sinners,
and all of us deserve God's judgment.

But the Bible's view of the natural world and of God's
working in it should lead us always to ask the question when we
suffer a natural catastrophe, "Is the Lord God trying to tell me
something? Do I myself have need of repentance?" And Joel is
saying that with the locust plague God is indeed delivering a

message. The locust plague is God's judgment on an apostate
people, and they have need of repentance.

Our difficulty, of course, is increased by the fact that we no
longer have prophets like Joel to point to specific events and tell
us, "This is the work of God in judgment." We have left to us only
the word of God that has come down to us through the Scriptures. But that word reminds us that we must continually examine our lives, especially when we suffer catastrophe, and ask
what it is that God wants us to do and be.

---

### Additional Notes §2

---

**1:2** / **Elders:** The word can be read either as the NIV has it, or
as "old men," and given the context, the latter reading is probably best.
Joel is appealing to the elderly to search their memory of past events.

**1:4** / There has been much discussion among biblical scholars
as to what kinds of locusts Joel is describing in this verse, and the NIV
notes that the meaning of the terms is uncertain. The prophet uses four
words for locust out of the nine words that were available to him in
the Hb.—**locust swarm** (or "cutting locusts," *gāzām*); **great locusts** (or
"swarming locusts," *ʾarbeh*); **young locusts** (or "hopping locusts," *yāleq*);
and **other locusts** (or "destroying locusts," *ḥāsîl*). Some scholars maintain that Joel is describing the four stages in the locust life cycle: pupa,
adult, wingless larva, and winged larva. Certainly *ʾarbeh* is the usual
term for the insect, and refers to the fully developed, winged migrant of
some six centimeters in length. More probable, however, is the view that
Joel is simply piling up terms for locusts to emphasize the overwhelming
nature of the catastrophe. Judah has been subjected to one swarming,
chewing, cutting enemy after another.

It should also be mentioned that earlier exegetes sometimes interpreted the locusts to be symbols of attacking foreign nations, but the
content of the whole book makes it clear that Joel is referring to an actual
locust plague that has taken place in the recent past.

## §3 Three Gifts Withdrawn (Joel 1:5–12)

Joel has to convince his apostate people that the catastrophe they have suffered is from the hand of God. He therefore summons three groups in Judah to lament for three gifts of God's grace and favor that have been withdrawn. Using extremely strong verbs, he calls upon them to **weep** and **wail** (v. 5), to **mourn** or keen (v. 8), and to be dismayed (**despair,** v. 11) and **grieve** over the loss of these gifts. Contrary to the usual interpretation of these verses, this is not yet a call to a communal lamentation, but rather the prophet's attempt to get his people to understand that their relation with their God has been broken by their sin.

**1:5–7** / Surprising to us, the first group that Joel addresses are the alcoholics. In their perpetual drunkenness, they are those least likely to realize what is going on around them, and yet they are also the ones who will first notice their lack of **wine.**

It is important to pay attention to the possessive pronouns in verses 6 and 7. *My* **land,** *my* **vines,** *my* **fig trees,** God proclaims, have been laid waste and ruined. God's possessions have been devastated by the locust horde, which is compared in verse 6 to an invading army that is numberless and irresistible, and to savage beasts with **fangs** and **teeth** like saws. The question implied is, How could God allow such a thing to happen?

Throughout the OT, the land is considered to belong to God (cf. Lev. 25, especially v. 23; Ps. 24:1). Even in Genesis 1:28, where it is said that human beings are to have dominion over ("subdue") the earth, that dominion remains always secondary to God's, because the whole earth belongs to God (cf. Deut. 10:14; 1 Chron. 29:10–13; Ps. 50:10–11; 60:7–8; 89:11; 95:4–7; Isa. 66:1). Out of grace, however, God conveys the land to Israel as a precious gift (cf. Jer. 27:5). But Israel is merely a steward of the land, and it must care for the land according to God's wishes. It therefore is given numerous laws about how to treat the land and its creatures (e.g., Exod. 20:8–10; Deut. 22:6–7; 24:19–22, etc.). Most importantly, Israel is given the land only as long as it is faithful to its God (Deut. 30:15–20; Ezek. 33:23–29). If Israel turns to other gods, it pollutes the land, for in the OT, idolatry is the ultimate pollution (cf. Num. 35:33; Jer. 16:18; Ezek. 36:18). And when Israel engages in that pollution, it loses its land and is taken into exile (cf. Jer. 7:5–7; 22:26–27; 35:15)—in Leviticus' powerful figure, the land "vomits" Israel out (Lev. 20:22; cf. 18:22–28).

Here in Joel, Israel is not expelled from the land, but it does lose the land's gifts of grapes and figs. The locusts have even stripped the bark off of those vines and trees, which often grew in the same field together, so that the branches are left barren and white. And the drunkards in the populace will be the most acutely aware of the deprivation, for they can no longer have "new wine"—that first juice from the wine-press which satisfies their desperate craving for drink even before all of the grapes have been processed.

**1:8–10** / The second gift that God has withdrawn from the people of Israel is the means of communion in worship with himself; God has taken away the **grain** and wine necessary for the daily **offerings** in the temple, verses 9–10. We know that in the temple worship, grain moistened with oil and a libation of wine accompanied the morning and evening burnt offerings of lambs (cf. Exod. 29:38–41; Num. 28:3–8). God had prescribed these as the means by which Israel could enter into communion with him. So important were these daily sacrifices to Israel's life that they were not discontinued even when the Romans laid siege to Jerusalem in the first century (Josephus, *War* 6.1–8).

Unlike many of the earlier prophets, Joel does not criticize Israel's sacrificial worship (cf. Isa. 1:11, 13; Jer. 7:21–22; Hos. 6:6; 8:11). Indeed, it must be remembered that such earlier prophetic criticism was a condemnation not of sacrifices as such but of Israel's faithlessness and disobedience that accompanied the sacrifices. Joel therefore is attacking Israel's worship on much the same grounds. However, the insincere sacrifices are not merely criticized. They are removed, by God, through the means of the locust plague. Judah's communion with its covenant Lord is thereby made impossible. No wonder that **the priests are in mourning**!

The call to lamentation of verse 8 is directed not only to the priests, however. The verb is feminine and is probably addressed to Jerusalem, here personified as a betrothed **virgin** whose marriage has not yet been consummated (cf. 2 Kgs. 19:21; Lam. 2:13).

Betrothal was the first stage in marriage in biblical Israel and had the same binding commitment attached to it, although the sexual union of husband and wife did not take place until after the marriage ceremony (cf. Gen. 29:18–21; Matt. 1:18). Jerusalem is therefore called to **mourn** here, as a betrothed virgin would mourn over the death of her promised **husband,** with her loins girded with the rough, burlaplike material of **sackcloth.** Jerusalem can no longer have fellowship with its God. Therefore it is to weep.

**1:11–12** / The third gift that God has withdrawn from faithless Judah is the gift of **joy,** verses 11–12—joy at the harvest and joy in the worship service. The **harvest** was always a time for rejoicing in Israel (cf. Ps. 4:7; Isa. 9:3), but Israel's worship was no less a joyful affair. Indeed, Deuteronomy says that whenever the Israelites brought their sacrifices to Jerusalem, they were to "rejoice before the LORD" (Deut. 12:12, 18; 14:26; 26:11; 28:47). But now all joy has **withered away,** verse 12, because the gifts and presence of God have been withdrawn from them. That thought forms the climax of the strophe, verses 11–12.

We hear in this strophe of verses 11–12, however, that a second catastrophe besides that of the locust plague has come upon Judah, and the phrase **dried up** in verse 10 prepares us for it. Judah is also experiencing a severe drought, so devastating in its effects that all of the crops that had begun to recover from the locusts have withered, and there is nothing for the farmers to eat or sell; there is not even seed available for replanting. God, the LORD of nature, has withheld the rain, and Judah bakes under calamitous judgment.

Just as the rain that brings fertility and abundant harvests is a sign of God's covenant favor (Deut. 28:12; Lev. 26:3–5, 9–10), the withholding of the rain is a working out of God's covenant curse (Lev. 26:19–20; Deut. 28:23–24; cf. 1 Kgs. 17–18; Jer. 14:1–6). Originally, biblical Palestine was a rich and fertile land, so abundant in produce that it could be said to flow with milk and honey and furnish its inhabitants with every necessity (Deut. 8:6–9). The **pomegranate,** prized for its large, red, juice-yielding fruits, grew in the Jordan Valley. **Wheat** and **barley** were abundant and the most important cereals. Even apples were grown and prized for their refreshing and restorative properties in illness, although they were inferior to the apples we know today, and some have suggested that we read "apricot" instead of **apple** in verse 12. But all of these goods have withered under God's sentence on Israel's sin, and the result is that "the ground mourns," which is the proper reading of verse 10b.

We do not often realize that nature too is affected by our sin, but from beginning to end, the Bible affirms that human sin ruins the natural world. In the beginning, the ground is cursed because of human disobedience (Gen. 3:17–18), and in the NT the whole creation groans together in travail because of human corruption (Rom. 8:22). In the intervening pages, the prophets repeatedly tell us that nature's ruin is the result of our sin (cf. Jer. 12:4; 3:3, 24; 9:10–11, 12–13; 23:10; Hos. 4:2–3; Isa. 24:4–5; 33:7–9). Perhaps we can realize from that just why we have an ecological crisis. But nature is affected not only outwardly by our ecological indifference and rapacious actions toward it. The Bible's view is more radical than that: the very being of nature is corrupted—every seed, every gene, every process. As Paul phrases it in Romans 8:21, all are subject to the "bondage of decay" and to the final death that is the wages of sin.

---

## Additional Notes §3

---

This passage (1:5–12) may be divided into three strophes or stanzas, on the basis of the imperative calls for lamentation: vv. 5–7, 8–10, and 11–12. The English translation has obscured two features in the Hb. First, in vv. 4 through 10, there predominates the figure of "cutting." The "cutting locust" of v. 4 has "cut off" the sweet wine in v. 5, so that the temple offerings are "cut off" in v. 9, as is the oil in v. 10 (NIV reads **fails**). By the language he uses, the prophet vividly portrays the cutting action of the locusts' teeth.

**1:10** / A second feature present in the Hb. but obscured in the English is that the catastrophe that Judah has suffered is emphasized in v. 10 by a series of three staccato lines: "For destroyed the grain, dried up the wine, cut off the oil." The lines each contain only two words in the Hb., as if the prophet's words themselves were cut off along with everything else.

## §4 A Call to the Priests (Joel 1:13–20)

This entire section, which may be divided into five strophes (vv. 13, 14, 15–16, 17–18, 19–20) is directed at the priests in the Jerusalem temple, for if communion with God has been lost in Judah, the priests are those primarily responsible.

**1:13** / It was the priests' duty in biblical Israel to teach and maintain their people in the ways of the Torah. But that did not mean simply teaching the people the law. Rather, the priests were responsible for preserving and handing on to the people all of the stories and traditions concerning Israel's relationship with God throughout its entire history, and those traditions included the commandments that God had given. In short, the priests were responsible for passing on what now makes up much of our OT. Only if Israel knew what God had done in its past could it be faithful in the present. Thus, Hosea could say in his time that the people were rejected by God for lack of knowledge, and the blame for that was laid on the priests (Hos. 4:6).

The priests were also responsible for mediating between the people and God—for representing the people's worship before God, and for representing God's will to the people. As Leviticus says, they were to distinguish between the holy and the profane, between the clean and the unclean; and they were to teach the Israelites all the decrees the Lord had given them through Moses (Lev. 10:10–11). Thus in Exodus the priests are commanded to wear on their breastplates the names of the twelve tribes of Israel, symbolically bearing them into worship before the Lord (Exod. 28:21, 29–30, 38). So Joel turns to the priests in his preaching of repentance and points again to his primary concern: The means of communion with God through the sacrifices have been cut off (v. 13).

There are possible only two faithful responses to that situation. First, Joel summons the priests themselves to lamentation and repentance, asking them to gird themselves in the **sackcloth** of repentance and to undergo even the unusual discipline of repenting in the temple through the night, verse 13.

**1:14** / Second, Joel directs the priests, as the leaders of the covenant congregation, to call a public **fast** of repentance in which the entire populace comes to the temple, verse 14.

Such fasts of lamentation and repentance are known throughout the OT, and they were ordered by the leaders of the community whenever Israel suffered any calamity—war, famine, pestilence, captivity, here a locust plague and drought (cf. Judg. 20:26; 1 Sam. 7:6, etc.). We also know that such fasts were held in commemoration of past catastrophes, such as the destruction of the temple by the Babylonians in 587 BC (Zech. 7:1–7).

During the usual one-day fast, the people abstained from all normal activities—from eating and drinking, from work, and from sexual intercourse. Instead, they devoted themselves to prayer in loud weeping and wailing before God, often rending their clothes or striking themselves on the cheek, sprinkling themselves with dust and ashes (cf. our use of ashes on Ash Wednesday), prostrating themselves on the ground, or stretching out their hands to heaven in supplication to God to forgive and to turn aside the calamity (cf. 1 Sam. 7:6; Jer. 3:25; 4:8; 6:26; 31:19; Lam. 2:10, 19, etc.). Joel wants the priests to proclaim a ceremony of such repentance. But Joel's concern is not just with the calamities of locusts and drought that Judah has suffered. His principal concern is with the fact that those calamities, which have made sacrifice impossible, are signs of Israel's rupture of its covenant relationship with God.

**1:15–16** / More than that, the natural catastrophes bringing the cessation of the daily sacrifices are to Joel harbingers of a greater calamity to come—namely, final judgment day, **the day of the LORD** *(yôm Yahweh)*, verse 15. Judah's loss of communion with its God is not a temporary judgment, according to the prophet. It is the beginning of a final loss that threatens Judah with ultimate **destruction** because of God's wrath upon Judah's apostasy.

This all seems very foreign to modern ears, of course, because many in our age do not believe in sin or in a God who judges anyone. God, for many modern Americans, is rather an agreeable deity largely devoted to helping us out of difficulties, easily assuaging any guilt we may have, and making us feel as comfortable and secure as possible. As for sin, we would rather attribute evil or "socially unacceptable" actions to a poor environment, to faulty parenting, to inadequate schooling, and to the common human propensity for occasionally making mistakes. We "goof," or we have "psychological hangups," we "fall in with the wrong crowd," or we take bad advice. But we hesitate to call anything sin, because sin involves a reciprocal relationship with God, and we blithely believe that God approves of us.

According to the Bible, however, God is not mocked (Gal. 6:7). God has made us to live in a trusting and obedient relationship. We are created to glorify and enjoy God forever. We must cleave to God all our days, walk according to God's will, and love, serve, and praise God with all our hearts and minds and strength and will (Deut. 10:12–21; Mark 12:28–34; Rom. 12:1–2). Sin, then, is rejecting that relationship and following our own ways and wills. Sin is refusing to let God be God and trying to be our own gods and goddesses instead (Gen. 3). And that sin God will not allow, because God will never be anything less than Lord and King over us (cf. Ezek. 20:33–38; Matt. 28:18; Phil. 2:10–11).

The Bible therefore tells us that we not only face God's little judgments of every day, borne in upon us in our anxieties and trials, our broken homes and broken lives (cf. Isa. 28:13; Hos. 5:12; Rom. 1:28–32). It also tells us that we face a final judgment of our ways in the day of the Lord. Both Jesus and Paul refer to that day (Mark 13 and parallels; Matt. 25:31–46; Rom. 2:5; 1 Cor. 1:8; 3:13; 5:5; 2 Cor. 1:14; Phil. 1:6, 10; 2:16; 1 Thess. 5:2, etc.). And throughout the NT we are told that we all will stand before the judgment seat of God, accountable for our love and trust and obedience or lack thereof (Matt. 12:36; Rom. 14:10–12; 2 Cor. 5:10; 1 Pet. 4:5). The day of the Lord is near and is coming. The entire Bible affirms Joel's message.

**1:17–18** / Joel then returns to the evidence of the first hints of the coming of the day—to the drought that is baking Judah in judgment, verses 17–18. Because of the covenant curse embodied in the lack of rain, **the seeds** under the soil simply wither and do not germinate. No **grain** grows to feed man or beast, and the **granaries** fall into ruin. The **cattle** low and **mill about** in their hunger, and even the **sheep,** who could live from the dry grasses of the steppes and would not need moist pasture, suffer for want of food. The Lord of nature has withdrawn all gifts because of Judah's sin, and the effect is felt by all of nature.

**1:19–20** / The beasts of the field know, however, to whom to cry. As Isaiah had said, "The ox knows his master, the donkey his owner's manger" (Isa. 1:3; cf. their presence in every Christmas crèche), and so the beasts of the field (**wild animals**) **pant** or "long for" God, verse 20.

Joel wants the priests to learn a lesson from the beasts and to cry to God as the animals of the field cry to their Lord. The prophet therefore composes a prayer for the priests to pray on the day of repentance, verse 19. But the **fire** mentioned in the prayer is not a natural manifestation of the drought—some commentators have believed that the dry fields have simply ignited by spontaneous combustion. No, fire is associated throughout the OT with God's judgment (Isa. 47:14; 66:15–16; Jer. 4:4; 5:14, etc.), and the priests are to lead the people in contrition and turning to plead for an end to that judgment.

## Additional Notes §4

**1:13** / **Sackcloth** was worn in biblical times as a sign of both mourning and penitence (cf. Joel 1:8; 1 Kgs. 21:27; Neh. 9:1–2; Jonah 3:5–6). The custom was to wrap the sackcloth around the loins, with the upper body of males left bare, in order that the chest might be struck in grief, which is the meaning of **mourn** in v. 13a.

**1:14** / The fact that the entire populace could be gathered together in the temple may be an indication of the small size of the postexilic Jerusalem population.

**1:15** / **The day of the LORD:** Found throughout the Bible, the concept of the day of the Lord had its beginnings in the times of the Judges and of Saul (1220–1020 BC; 1020–1000 BC) when Israel was often attacked by surrounding peoples and was forced to fight what scholars call the "holy war." The name derives not from the fact that war was considered good, but from the practice of conducting such wars according to fixed cultic rules. The picture that we have of such wars in the OT shows us that they were largely conceived as the wars of God, who was the principal combatant and to whose aid Israel merely lent its service. God fought in the battles at the head of supernatural hosts (Josh. 10:11; 24:7; Judg. 5:4–5), often instilling in the enemy terror and panic (Exod. 15:14–16; 23:27; Josh. 2:9, 24; 5:1; etc.). The belief therefore arose in Israel that God would always be on its side, and that when God came on the day of the Lord finally to destroy all enemies and to inaugurate a kingdom over all the earth, Israel would enjoy a blessed peace and prosperity as the favored and exalted people. The day of the Lord was therefore not one day, but a time when all of Israel's enemies would be defeated and Israel would enjoy salvation (Isa. 32:16–20).

It was the prophet Amos, in the eighth century BC, who first upset this happy expectation of Israel's. The day of the Lord was not light, he told the people, but darkness for them because of their sin, and it would mean for them not salvation but judgment (Amos 5:18–20). In this prophecy of woe, Amos was followed by Zephaniah (ch. 1), Isaiah (2:6–22), Ezekiel (ch. 7), and Malachi (4:5; 3:1–5; cf. Lam. 2:1, 21–22). Joel is taking these earlier prophecies and envisioning their fulfillment in his time.

**1:17** / This is one of the few places in Joel where the text is conjectural, because it contains two Hb. words that are found nowhere else in the OT. The LXX reads "the cows stamp about in their enclosure." The Vg. has "the beasts of burden rot in their dung" (?). The LXX rewords the entire v., but only the first two lines are questionable, and the reading given in the NIV is probably the best to be had.

**2:1–11** / In 1:15, Joel announced the imminence of the day of the Lord. He now tells what that day will be like. Some scholars have maintained that this section does not concern God's final judgment and is instead a description of the invasion of the locusts of chapter 1. In such a view, the locust plague would be not a past event, but a present one.

Several features of this passage would, on the face of it, seem to support such a position. It describes **a large and mighty army,** verse 2 (cf. v. 11), and that would seem to fit in with the characterization of the locusts as a "nation," "powerful and without number," in 1:6. The reference to **clouds and blackness** in 2:2 fits locust hordes, which are often so large that they block out the sun. The shape of locusts could be compared to that of horses, 2:4, and Revelation 9:7 specifically draws that comparison. The sound of locusts eating might be likened to the **crackling** of the **fire** of 2:5. Certainly locusts swarm into settlements, scaling walls and invading houses, as in 2:7, 9, and their march forward is steady and irresistible, as in 2:8. And they certainly leave the total devastation behind them that is described in 2:3.

We therefore have to say that Joel's description of the day of the Lord has probably been influenced by the sights and sounds of the locust horde that invaded Judah, just as the day pictured in Revelation 9:2–11 was similarly influenced. But it must also be said that the locust plague is a thing of the past in Joel—that is absolutely necessary for understanding the book. And the army portrayed in Joel 2:1–11 is no natural foe or even an historical one.

No, the army that approaches in the prophet's vision is the enemy from the North, foretold by Jeremiah (Jer. 1:13–15; 4:5–22, 29–31; 5:14–17; 6:1–8, 22–26). It is God's apocalyptic army, come to wreak God's long-prophesied judgment, and there is no escaping from it (cf. Amos 5:18–20; 9:1; Zeph. 1:18). It is an army unlike any other before or any that will follow (Joel 2:2), and therefore

Joel's description of it is only approximate: **They have the** *appearance* **of horses** (v. 4); **they gallop along** *like* **cavalry** (v. 4), **with a noise** *like* **that of chariots** (v. 5), *like* **a mighty army drawn up for battle** (v. 5). When the OT describes the things of God, it does so in carefully guarded language (cf. Exod. 24:10; Ezek. 1:26–28), because God is not of this earth and cannot be identified with it (John 3:12–13, 31), contrary to the many solely immanental theologies so current in our time.

God's army comes on the day of the Lord, and so Joel summons unnamed watchmen on the walls of Jerusalem to sound the war **trumpet** to warn of the approach of the enemy (2:1). In fact, Joel himself also serves here in the prophetic role of a "watchman" who warns God's people of coming disaster (cf. Ezek. 3:17–21; 33:1–9; Isa. 21:11–12; Jer. 6:17; Mic. 7:4).

The description that the prophet gives of the day of the Lord has elements typical of prophetic descriptions of the day. The **darkness and gloom** of 2:2 reminds us of Zephaniah 1:15. The fear of the populace evidenced by their **pale** faces, from which all blood has drained, recalls Nahum 2:10 (contrast Isa. 13:8). The prophets preserved a fairly stereotypical tradition about the day of the Lord which was handed down from generation to generation—a tradition that can be seen in much of its entirety in Isaiah 13, for example.

By the same token, those prophets that proclaimed the day of the Lord did so by drawing on the traditions of the holy war. For example, here in Joel, God leads **at the head of his army**, fighting with supernatural means (v. 11). And as throughout the OT, the whole cosmos is shaken and trembles at God's coming (v. 10; cf. Exod. 19:16–19; Ps. 97:1–5; Hab. 3:3–11; Matt. 27:45, 51–52; 28:2). When God leads the apocalyptic forces against his foes, **sun and moon are darkened** (v. 10; cf. Mark 13:24–25; Luke 23:44–45). The fire of judgment goes before God (Joel 2:3), and the land that was like Eden becomes a desolation (v. 3; a reversal of the thought of Isa. 51:3 and Ezek. 36:35).

We cannot conclude from this passage that we know exactly what God's final judgment will be like. The prophets and apostles of the Bible draw on traditional descriptions to tell us of it. We do know, however, that the day of the Lord comes. It began with the death of our Lord on the cross, when the sun was darkened at the sixth hour until the ninth hour, and death was shown to be the judgment for our sin. The day will be fully present when our Lord returns to set up his kingdom on earth and we all stand before his tribunal. The question that Joel asks, therefore, is the question for us all: **Who can endure** the day of the Lord when it comes, verse 11 (cf. Mal. 3:2)? Who will stand, and who will be told, "Depart from me, you who are cursed" (Matt. 25:41)? In mercy, God warns us before the coming of this day. According to Malachi 4:5, Elijah will be sent before the day comes, but Jesus tells us that Elijah has come (Mark 9:13 and parallel) in the person of John the Baptist. Our Lord's word to us therefore is "Watch" (Mark 13:35–36 and parallel). Be prepared, by faith and trust and obedience, for we do not know when the day comes. It may come in the evening, or at midnight, or at cockcrow, which is the hour of temptation (Matt. 26:34), or at dawn (Mark 13:35). But "what I say to you, I say to everyone: 'Watch'!" (Mark 13:37 and parallel).

## Additional Notes §5

The passage may be divided into four strophes (vv. 1–2, 3–5, 6–9, 10–11), and it is bracketed by references to the day of the Lord in vv. 1 and 11.

**2:1** / The **trumpet,** or *šôpār* in the Hb., was made from a curved ram's horn. Watchmen were stationed on the walls of fortified cities, such as Jerusalem here in Joel, and when the *šôpār* was sounded at the approach of an enemy, the alarm was spread from place to place, and the people gathered within the city walls for protection (cf. Jer. 4:5). The enemy that approaches here in Joel is, of course, God with a mighty army (cf. Ezek. 13:1–7, where false prophets have failed to serve as watchmen).

**2:2** / **Dawn:** Some commentators suggest we should read "blackness" as in the NRSV. The NIV's translation is better.

## §6 "But Even Now" (Joel 2:12–14)

**2:12–14** / This is one passage in Joel where it is absolutely necessary that we understand what the original Hebrew says, because the NIV translation has missed the force of the opening words. Verse 12 begins with "*But* even now," the "but" being translated from what is known as a *waw* adversative, and it is that "but" that is all important.

If God had not said "but" in human history, the human race would be lost. That lostness is pictured for us in the primeval hamartiology (doctrine of sin) of Genesis 3–11, where it is shown that we have corrupted God's good world by trying to be our own gods and goddesses. We have made all human community—between husband and wife, brother and sibling, nation and nation—impossible. The good gift of work has been turned into drudgery; the relation between the sexes has become a battle; the beauty and the fertility of God's good earth have been lost to thorns and thistles; and over it all lies God's curse on our sin and God's sentence of death because of our rebellion. Yet God said "but" and called one man named Abraham out of Mesopotamia, and through Abraham's descendants God began a salvation history in which the curse would be turned into the blessing.

Abraham's descendants in Israel, however, also rebelled against God's purpose, and so the human race was left the wages of death for its sin. Yet God said "but" by a cross on Golgotha and by an empty tomb in a garden, and hope and the promise of new and eternal life were granted forever to us all.

Still today, we will not accept that good news, and we try to turn away from God's loving lordship. Therefore violence walks our city streets, and loneliness sits in our living rooms. Blood pollutes the ground, and fears and hatreds haunt our loves. Yet God says "but" and promises us a kingdom of good in which mourning and crying and pain, hatred and evil will be done away forever.

Thus when God says "but" to us here in Joel 2:12—and
God speaks directly in the first person to us, through the
prophet Joel in verses 12 and 13a—God is signaling the possibility of a reversal of all our sinful fortunes. The following words
are **even now**—even now, in our situation, in our sin-pocked
and violent world; in whatever corner of evil we find ourselves,
God can work transformation.

Not only that, however. These verses are telling us that if
we allow God to change us we can escape that final judgment,
when a new kingdom is set up on the day of the Lord. That is the
message given here to Judah—that its apostasy can be overcome,
and that when the day of the Lord comes upon it, it can stand and
endure. And that is the message, too, of the cross and resurrection—that by the sacrifice and victory of our savior, our apostasy
from our God can also be overcome, and we too can stand before
the bar of God and be counted righteous.

But the condition laid upon both Judah and us is that we
**rend** our **hearts and not** our **garments**—in short that our repentance be not empty show, but the sincere turning of our hearts
and lives. Tearing of the garments in ancient Israel was a sign of
lamentation, expressing exceptional emotion in times of grief or
terror or misfortune (cf. Gen. 37:29, 34; Num. 14:6; 2 Sam. 3:31;
1 Kgs. 21:27; Ezra 9:3, etc.). And repentance, throughout the
Bible, has the literal meaning of "turning around," of walking in
the opposite direction from how we have previously walked. So
God here calls for that turning, and it is to be done in the heart.

Throughout the Scriptures, the heart is the seat of faith,
equivalent in its functioning in Hebrew anthropology to our
brain. Everywhere, the OT appeals to our hearts. Love God
with all your hearts, reads Deuteronomy's central command.
"Write these words on your heart" (Deut. 6:5–6). "Circumcise
your hearts," proclaims Jeremiah (4:4; cf. Rom. 2:29). "Get a new
heart," commands Ezekiel. "Why will you die, O house of Israel"
(18:31). If the heart is centered on God, faith and obedience will
follow, for as in the NT, it is what comes out of the heart that
determines the whole manner of life (Mark 7:18–23).

Therefore, we must be changed in our hearts if we would
change our sinful lives to good (cf. Jer. 31:31–34; Rom. 10:8). And
that change is wrought in us by God working in us, to be sure
(2 Cor. 4:6). But it is also a deliberate working of our own will,
a determined taking of ourselves in hand—getting out of bed
every morning and deciding to be faithful. As Paul says, we work

out our own salvation, for God is at work in us, to will and to work his good pleasure (Phil. 2:12–13). God's work—and ours; both are necessary for salvation.

According to this passage in Joel, and indeed, throughout the Scriptures, is it only because of the character of our God that we have this possibility of turning and transformation, and finally of standing in the day of the Lord. We can return to God from our apostasy, according to verse 13, only because God **is gracious and compassionate, slow to anger and abounding in love.** We do not deserve God's acceptance of our turning, *but* God receives it anyway.

The description that Joel gives of God in verse 13 is a credal statement from Israel's tradition about God that is found eight times in the OT. (Exod. 34:6–7 gives the full form; cf. also Num. 14:18; Neh. 9:17; Ps. 86:15; 103:8; 145:8; Jonah 4:2; Nah. 1:3. The form Joel uses is probably taken from Jonah 4:2, because Joel 2:14 also comes from Jonah 3:9.)

God's graciousness in verse 13 is expressed in the totally unmerited favor that is bestowed on the people. **Compassionate** in that verse could probably better be read "merciful," and it has the most intimate love connected with it, like the love of a mother for the child of her womb. **Slow to anger** includes in its meaning God's patience—an incredible long-suffering patience with us sinful folk, a constant refusal to give up on us and to consign us to death, a yearning love to include us in his kingdom.

The NIV's translation of the Hebrew words *rab ḥesed* by **abounding in love** in 2:13 has obscured their meaning, however. They could be translated literally "great covenant love." The term *ḥesed* is used many times throughout the OT, and it is most often to be understood in the context of the covenant that God has made with the people of Israel. The word is translated in the NRSV by "steadfast love," in the KJV by "great kindness," but neither of those translations captures the covenant context. *Ḥesed* signifies that loving faithfulness to his covenant with Israel that God steadfastly maintains. Even though Israel promised, when the covenant was made at Mt. Sinai, "We will do everything that the LORD has said" (Exod. 19:8; 24:3, 7; cf. Deut. 5:27), the people constantly break their promise. But in the covenant relation God has promised to be Israel's God and he does not go back on his word. Instead, when Israel deserts God and its relation with him lies in shambles, God promises a new covenant, in which he will write his words on the people's heart so that they will remain

faithful to him (Jer. 31:31–34). And it is that new covenant that
Jesus Christ offers to his disciples—and also to us—at the Last
Supper (1 Cor. 11:25).

God's willingness to uphold his covenant relation with us
is his *ḥesed,* and it is that loving and willing faithfulness to which
Joel 2:13 is pointing. God not only is gracious, merciful, patient,
and faithful to his covenant, however. He is also free. God's love
for us is never earned, but given only as free and undeserved gift.
Joel therefore frames 2:14 in a conditional: It "may" be that God
will restore the grain and wine for the sacrifices and thus make it
possible for Judah to commune with him once more. Judah is
entirely dependent on God's free grace, as are all of us. "I will
have mercy on whom I will have mercy," God tells us, "and I
will have compassion on whom I will have compassion" (Exod.
33:19). No act of our repentance and turning coerces God; nothing forces God to accept us back into his fellowship. Always we
are totally dependent on the Lord of our lives; we can only wait
for God's action. As it is written:

> I wait for the LORD, my soul waits,
>    and in his word I put my hope.
> My soul waits for the Lord
>    more than watchmen wait for the morning,
>    more than watchmen wait for the morning.

> (Ps. 130:5–6; the entire Psalm fits with the situation and
> thought in Joel)

---

### Additional Note §6

---

**2:12** / **Declares the LORD:** This is the prophetic formula,
"Oracle of *Yahweh,*" which indicates that God is speaking through the
prophet. The formula is found only here in Joel, and it emphasizes that
vv. 12–13a are the personal invitation of the Lord.

## §7 The Call to a Fast of Lamentation (Joel 2:15–17)

God's word in 2:12–13a has assured Judah and Jerusalem that it is possible to return to communion with God. Joel now wants his people to act on that word. He therefore first addresses an imperative call to the priests to take the leadership in calling the people to a fast of repentance, 2:15–16.

**2:15–16** / The religious leadership of any community is first of all responsible for that community's relation to God, for it is the religious leaders who have been set apart by special call and office to lead the people in the way of the Lord (cf. Exod. 5:22; 33:12). Priests in Israel were to "distinguish between the holy and the common" (Lev. 10:10) in a society very much like ours that did not know the difference between the things of God and the things of a secular world. So too in our time the clergy and especially the pulpit, entrusted with the word of God, must make that distinction and point the way. As Hermann Melville wrote in *Moby Dick*, "The world's a ship on its passage out . . . and the pulpit is its prow." Where the preacher leads, the church will follow, toward either the holy or the common.

In the name of the Lord, Joel therefore commands the priests to **blow the trumpet,** this time not to warn of war (cf. 2:1), but to **declare a holy fast** and **call a sacred assembly,** verse 15. The NIV translation obscures the meaning somewhat. Verse 15b–c in the Hebrew reads, "Sanctify a fast, proclaim an assembly," and the thought is then repeated in verse 16a: "Gather the people, sanctify the congregation." To be sanctified, in biblical usage, is to be set apart for the purposes of God. So the priests are commanded to assemble the people to a fast of lamentation and repentance that serves not the people's purposes, but God's. In short, the assembly is called not just to relieve the people of their suffering under the effects of locust plague and drought, but to bring about God's purpose for them.

No one is exempt from the call—not the aged (the NIV reads **elders**) or children **at the breast,** not the **bride** in her cohabitation chamber or the **bridegroom** in his private room alone with his beloved (Judg. 15:1; 2 Sam. 13:10; 2 Kgs. 9:2; Ps. 19:5; Song Sol. 1:4).

It seems strange that these are the ones named. Does a suckling infant need repentance? We might ask the same question when we bring a child to infant baptism. But the Bible knows that every child is born into a sinful world that fastens its grip on that child's life (cf. Ps. 51:5), and God alone can break the power of that bondage and lead the child in the paths of righteousness.

But why, then, bride and groom? Newly married men in Israel were even excused from military service for a year following their marriage (Deut. 24:5). But a far greater war descends upon Judah with the advent of the day of the Lord, a war from whose threat of death no one is exempt (cf. Luke 14:16–24, especially v. 20). Indeed, Jeremiah proclaimed that when God's judgment came, there would cease from the cities of Judah and from the streets of Jerusalem "the voice of mirth and the voice of gladness, the voice of the bridegroom and the voice of the bride" (Jer. 7:34 RSV; cf. 16:9; 25:10). And to avoid that final fate, bride and groom also have need of repentance.

The encompassing nature of the judgment and need for repentance puncture our self-righteousness, of course. We Christians almost automatically assume that we are free of any final condemnation, and we take on a rather unholy carelessness before the throne of grace, ignoring any need for preparation before we enter the church sanctuary or sit at the table of the Lord. But much has been given to us, and much shall therefore be required (Luke 12:48), and even when we have done all that is required of us, we are still unworthy servants (Luke 17:10). Therefore, judgment begins with the household of God (1 Pet. 4:17), and we too have need of repentance (cf. Matt. 6:12).

**2:17** / To lead that repentance for Judah and Jerusalem, Joel composes a prayer for the **priests,** 2:17. It is framed in the typical phrases of communal laments (cf. Ps. 79:4, 8, 10), but it is profound in its total dependence on the mercy of God. There is first of all the plea to God's pity to **spare** this sinful **people.** Those are the words of those who know that their own righteousness is nothing but filthy rags, who realize that they are but dust in the hands of a God who commands their life or death (cf. Gen. 2:7; 3:19; Job 10:8–9). Second, the prayer begs the mercy of God on the basis of the covenant relation. Israel, intone the priests, is God's **people**, and God's **inheritance** or heritage (Deut. 9:26, 29; 1 Kgs. 8:51; Ps. 28:9; 33:12; Jer. 12:7, etc.). Therefore the plea is that God remember the covenant with his people, though they have forgotten it and turned to other gods.

A new note enters the preaching of Joel in the third plea of the prayer, however. There is a reminder that God's honor is at stake **among the nations** of the world, for if Israel dies, other nations will believe that the Lord is powerless to save the chosen people. Is such a prayer simply appealing to a self-interested God, jealously protecting a shaky reputation?

That is not the meaning. Rather, the third plea in the prayer is a profound recognition of the sole purpose of Israel's life and of ours, namely, to glorify God (cf. Ps. 6:5; 30:9; 88:10–12; 115:17; Isa. 38:18). When our lives are preserved and transformed, God's power and mercy are magnified before the world. When we are saved by the undeserved love of God, that salvation resounds to God's glory (cf. Ps. 98; Isa. 52:13–53:12). God's light shed upon the people draws all nations to its shining (cf. Isa. 60:1–3). God's working in this chosen folk causes all peoples to seek and honor God (cf. Zech. 8:20–23; Matt. 5:14–16). So this third petition in the priest's prayer is not an appeal to God's selfish concern but an acknowledgment that God is to be honored and praised for his work in his people Israel. The priests here confess that, yes, they are concerned that God be glorified throughout the world, much as Christians also pray, "Hallowed be thy name."

---

### Additional Notes §7

---

The one critical question that needs to be asked of this passage is whether it concerns the past or the future. Some commentators translate vv. 15–17, not as imperatives, but as perfects, showing action in the past: "They blew the trumpet in Zion, they declared a holy fast," etc. What follows, then, in 2:18 is conceived as the direct result of this repentance on the part of Judah. The people repented, therefore God relented, in a kind of holy tit-for-tat. But we must remember from 2:14 that repentance does not coerce God, and mercy does not automatically follow petition. Therefore the NIV translation is correct, and vv. 15–17 and what follows in 2:18 are all in the future. Joel calls the priests and the people to their proper work of repentance. But the work of God is never an automatic response to that turning. God's action to save can only be promised; it cannot be coerced.

**2:15** / **Declare,** properly "sanctify": The verb in the Hb. is *qādaš*, which has the basic meaning of "to cut" or "separate" or "set apart." It can also have the meaning "to be holy"; i.e., to be separated out of the profane realm and reserved in God's holy realm for divine purposes alone. When translated into NT Greek, it could be rendered with the word "saint" (1 Cor. 1:2). Saints, therefore, are not those who are morally perfect—certainly Paul could not address the church at Corinth as "saints" if that were the meaning. Rather, saints are those who have been separated out from the world to be used for God's work. In this sense, every Christian is a saint.

**2:17** / The NIV translation makes it very clear that prayers of lamentation by the priests were customarily offered in the large space in the temple between the porch or vestibule of the inner court (1 Kgs. 6:3; 7:21) and the altar of burnt offering that was found there (1 Kgs. 8:22, 64).

## §8 God's Zeal for Salvation (Joel 2:18–27)

**2:18–20** / We now come to the turning point of the book of Joel—the point at which God's jealousy leads to pity for the chosen people. God removes both the everyday judgments and the threat of final judgment from their lives, verse 18.

This passage too, however, is not to be understood in terms of some sort of self-seeking on God's part. Rather, God's "jealousy" could also be translated as God's "zeal"—the word has both meanings in the Hebrew. The God of the Bible is a zealous God, with a purpose that is being worked out in the world. God will not be deterred or turned aside from fulfilling that purpose. This purpose is the restoration of the good and abundant life that he intended for his world in the beginning—the life that was corrupted and destroyed by human sin. And God's means of working out that purpose is to make a covenant people who know how to live in righteousness and trust under God's guiding lordship (Exod. 19:3–6; 1 Pet. 2:9–10). Into that covenant fellowship, then, God works to draw all peoples, that the earth may be filled with the glory and knowledge of God, as the waters cover the sea (cf. Isa. 2:2–4; Hab. 2:14; Zech. 8:20–23).

Israel, in the time of Joel, has deserted its God and turned to other deities. But God is **jealous** (Exod. 20:5)—that is, zealous—for the purpose of recreating his world (Exod. 34:10; Isa. 9:7). Therefore, Israel's apostasy will not change the fact that Israel is God's **people**, living in God's **land** (v. 18), and God will use Israel in spite of itself. God will maintain his covenant with Israel in spite of Israel's unfaithfulness. The Lord will enter into communion with Israel, in spite of its desertion. The covenant remains unbroken. God is faithful to it. That is the message of this passage.

As evidence of that covenant faithfulness, God will therefore restore the **grain** and the **wine** and the **oil** that will make it possible for Israel to enter into the communion of the temple sacrifices once again (v. 19), and the nations will no longer be able to say that Israel's God has deserted it. But more than that, God will remove the threat of judgment on the day of the Lord, verse 20. (The NIV reads **northern army**, but the Hebrew has "the northerner," referring to the enemy from the North, cf. 2:1–11).

Such **pity** is totally unearned grace, occasioned not by Israel's repentance but solely by God's zeal for his purpose and mercy toward Israel in using it in that purpose. Thus, while all of those gifts of mercy mentioned in 2:19–27 correspond to Israel's need detailed in 1:2–2:17, it is not Israel's need or its turning that prompts God's actions toward it. Verses 2:17–20 have the standard form of a communal lament (v. 17), followed by an oracle of assurance (vv. 19–20), but the two sections are bound together theologically by the "pity" of God.

Some commentators have maintained that 2:20 refers once again to the locust horde. In their view, God drives the locusts into the Dead Sea on the east and into the Mediterranean Sea on the west, and the stench of the locusts' rotting bodies on the seashores then fills the air. Once again, however, the enemy from the North is intended, and the mentioned stench simply reaffirms that the fearful enemy is dead and that the final judgment on Israel has been turned aside forever.

**2:21–27** / Because God will maintain his covenant with his chosen people, covenant blessings will therefore be restored to them, and the hardships that Judah has experienced in the past will be reversed by God's **great** acts, verse 21. The promises of 2:21–27 overcome the sufferings specifically mentioned in chapter 1: The ground will be restored (cf. 2:21 with 1:10); the wild animals will be fed (cf. 2:22 with 1:20); joy will return to Judah's harvests and worship (cf. 2:23 with 1:16); the drought will be a thing of the past (cf. 2:23 with 1:10, 12, 18–20); the fruit trees will bear (cf. 2:22 with 1:12, 19); threshing floors and wine vats will be full (cf. 2:24 with 1:5, 17). All are covenant blessings that God will again bestow on this people (cf. Deut. 11:13–17; 28:3–5, 11–12; Lev. 26:3–5). All make up part of the blessed future to which Judah can look forward. As a result, Judah will be able once again to rejoice in the fellowship of the Lord its God (vv. 21, 23), and will praise God's name (v. 26).

Best of all, however, Israel will **know** that the Lord is its God, dwelling in its midst (v. 27; cf. 3:17) in fulfillment of the ancient promises (cf. Exod. 25:8; 29:45; Lev. 26:11; 1 Kgs. 6:13; Isa. 12:6; Ezek. 37:27–28; Hos. 11:9; Zeph. 3:15, 17). No longer will

Israel seek after other gods and goddesses, but it will know that
the Lord alone is God, because he alone has saved it (cf. Isa. 45:5,
6, 18, 22; 46:9). Israel's apostasy will be done and gone, replaced
with commitment to an everlasting covenant (cf. Gen. 17:7–8;
Hos. 2:16–23).

These are all future promises in Joel, but, as with all of
God's promises in the OT, they have "found their yes in Christ"
(2 Cor. 1:20). He now has restored us to communion with the
Father (2 Cor. 5:17–19). His cross and resurrection have now
imputed to us that righteousness in which we may stand in the
day of the Lord (Rom. 8:31–39; 1 Cor. 1:8; Eph. 4:30; 6:13). His
gospel has given us joy in his abundant life and worship (John
15:11). His resurrection has made it sure that at the end, the
whole creation will be healed (Rom. 8:19–22).

---

## Additional Note §8

---

There are two poems in this section, vv. 18–20 and 21–27. Verses
18–20 divide into two strophes, vv. 18–19 and 20. Verses 21–27 have four
strophes, vv. 21–22, 23, 24–25, 26–27, with the speech of God alternating
with that of the prophet. This second poem of vv. 21–27 has something
of the form of a standard oracle of salvation, as found for example in Isa.
41:8–13. Such a salvation oracle included a statement of God's past
dealings with Israel (Isa. 41:8–9), an imperative "Fear not!" and a promise of God's intervention (Isa. 41:10), a description of the results of God's
actions (Isa. 41:11–12), and an explanation of God's actions (Isa. 41:13).
As he does with all standard forms, Joel uses the genre of the salvation
oracle with great flexibility.

**2:28–32** / The promise of abundant life and rescue from the judgment of the day of the Lord has been given out of the free grace of God (2:18–27). Joel now turns to tell of the signs that will precede the coming of the day. Thus, **afterward** in 2:28 refers not to events that will take place after the coming of the day, but before its imminent arrival (cf. **before** in v. 31).

As found also in NT tradition, the day will be preceded by both cosmic and earthly signs (cf. Mark 13:7–8, 24–25 and parallels; Luke 21:20, 25–26). Mark speaks of "wars and rumors of war" (Mark 13:7), and the **blood, fire,** and **smoke** of Joel 2:30 probably refer to the burning of cities and the slaughter of their populace. The darkening of the **sun** and the changing of the **moon to blood** in 2:31, on the other hand, are not natural disasters such as an eclipse or sandstorm, but supernatural signs of the approach of the day (cf. Amos 8:9). As in Malachi 4:5 and Luke 21:25–28, God will give warning of the approaching judgment.

Most important in this passage, however, is God's promise that before the day comes, **I will pour out my Spirit,** literally in the Hebrew, "on all flesh." By reading **on all people,** the NIV has tended to emphasize a universal note in this promise, just as Acts 2:38–39 emphasizes that the gift of the Holy Spirit may be given to those of all nations. But the repeated use of **your** in verse 28, spoken to Judah, limits the promise in Joel to that covenant people. The Acts 2 account of the first Christian Pentecost takes the gift limited by Joel to Judah and extends it to all nations in a universal offering that is one of the glories of the Christian gospel.

The gift of the Spirit to Judah will enable its populace to prophesy, to dream the dreams and see the visions given to the earlier prophets (cf. Jer. 23:25; 24:1–3; Amos 7:1–9, etc.). It was characteristic of the early nonwriting prophets of Israel that their revelations were given to them by the Spirit (cf. 1 Sam. 10:6, 10; 19:20; 2 Sam. 23:2; 2 Kgs. 2:9, etc.). However, such a means of revelation was almost entirely replaced among the classical, writing prophets by revelation through the word, and it is not until the time of this passage in Joel that revelation by means of the Spirit is once again emphasized. Thus, when revelation by the Spirit once again occurs, according to Joel, it is a sign that the day of the Lord is very near.

The gift of the Spirit, throughout the Bible, was given to persons for the purpose of enabling them to accomplish a task for God. The Spirit lent them power to do God's bidding (cf. Exod. 31:2–5; Judg. 6:34; Mic. 3:8; Hag. 1:14, etc.). Such is the understanding of the gift in Acts 2. The disciples are given the Holy Spirit in order that they may be witnesses to Christ "to the ends of the earth" (Acts 1:8; 2:4). But that does not seem to be the emphasis of this passage in Joel. Rather, consonant with Joel's entire concern, the Spirit here signifies a new relation with God. "All flesh" in Judah, including manservant and maidservant, will once again have that intimate relation to God characteristic of prophets (cf. Isa. 50:4; Jer. 15:16; 20:11). Surprisingly, therefore, the cult with its sacrifices, so often referred to by Joel, will no longer be necessary. No priest will be needed to mediate between the people and their God. All will be brought into intimate relation with the Lord.

When such a relation with God is established, the day of the Lord is near. Indeed, Acts 2 understands that with the gift of the Spirit to the disciples, the day has begun; the new age of the kingdom has broken into human history and will now exercise its influence until the kingdom comes in its fulness. According to the gospels, the kingdom was already present in the person of Jesus of Nazareth (cf. Mark 1:15; Luke 11:20). Participation in its power is now offered to all who repent and are baptized in the name of Jesus Christ for the forgiveness of sins. When that takes place, the gift of the Holy Spirit, promised here in Joel, will be given (Acts 2:38–39).

Judah will be given the free gift of the Spirit in a new relation with its God. But Judah must then respond to the gift— and so must we. We are given the Spirit apart from any deserving or working on our part. And it is the Spirit, then, *which allows us to call on the name of the Lord* (Joel 2:32): Throughout, the prophecies of Joel emphasize God's prevenient grace; that is the meaning of **whom the LORD calls** in verse 32; it signifies "those to whom God has given the Spirit of God."

It is quite possible to be given the Spirit of God, however, and to do nothing with it: thousands of persons in the Christian

Church, who received the Holy Spirit at their baptisms, are evidence of that fact. We can stifle the Spirit, quench it (1 Thess. 5:19 RSV), do nothing with it. And if that is our response, we will not survive in the judgment on the day of the Lord. For the judgment still comes. We all will still have to stand before the bar of God. In verse 32, Joel reiterates the promise of Obadiah 17 that there will be a remnant saved in Judah on the day of the Lord. But that remnant will be those who have used the Spirit's power to call on the name of the Lord.

According to other passages in the OT, to call on God's name means to worship God (Gen. 12:8), to acknowledge that we belong to him alone (Isa. 12:2–4; 44:5; Ps. 105:1; Zech. 13:9), and to depend on him for all life and good (Prov. 18:10; Zech. 2:5). Thus, to call on the name of the Lord in the last judgment is not a desperate, last minute attempt to save one's life from eternal destruction, but rather is the natural fruit of a heart-felt dependence on God that one has known throughout one's life.

This salvation from the dark judgment of God's day, when the kingdom is set up over all the earth, is now offered by the gospel to all persons (cf. John 3:16–17). But that gracious offer, recorded here in Joel, is now centered in Jesus Christ, and those who call on his name are the ones who will stand in the last day (Rom. 10:9–13).

That means, in our time and in every time, that we are therefore to worship only the God revealed to us in Jesus Christ through the Scriptures. Many false gods and goddesses claim our allegiance in our society. But "there is no other name under heaven given to men (and women) by which we must be saved" than the name of Jesus Christ (Acts 4:12). To call on his name means to live by his will and not by our own, and to depend on his commandments for daily guidance (cf. John 14:15). "Apart from me you can do nothing," he tells us (John 15:5); that is, we can do no good act that accords with the will of God except through Christ. And so we call on him constantly to guide and empower us, not only when we are in difficulty, but every day, consistently, in order that we may be obedient.

Finally, to call on the name of the Lord means, according to the Bible, to tell others what God has done (cf. Ps. 105:1; Isa. 12:4), to be witnesses to the ends of the earth (Acts 1:8). In that witness, we proclaim a total worldview that sees everything in terms of God's working in this world; we announce that God's alone are the kingdom and the power and the glory forever; we bear the glad news that out of free grace, God offers to all persons salvation in the day of the Lord. Paul uses Joel 2:32 in Romans 10:13. But then he goes on to ask how anyone can call on one in whom they have not believed. "And how can they believe in the one of whom they have not heard? And how can they hear without someone preaching to them?" Faith comes from hearing the gospel message, says Paul, and that message is heard through our witness to and our preaching of what God has done in Jesus Christ. It is to these tasks that we are called by Joel's Lord and our Lord.

## §10 God's Case against the Foreign Nations (Joel 3:1–8)

**3:1–3** / The NIV has eliminated two important words in the translation of verse 1. In the Hebrew, the verse begins, "For behold," which not only connects this passage with the preceding poem, but also emphasizes the content of verses 1–4. In 2:28–32, Joel has announced those signs that will precede the coming of the day of the Lord. He now tells what will happen at the time of the day itself. When the day comes, God will save Israel (v. 1) but will gather together the other nations and take them into the **Valley of Jehoshaphat** to go to court with them for their sins.

The name "Jehoshaphat" is a symbolic name, made up of two Hebrew words: *Yah* (which is a shortened form of the divine name *Yahweh*, used throughout the OT), and *šāpaṭ*, which means "to judge." Thus, the Valley of Jehoshaphat means "the valley where the LORD judges." From the fourth century on, this was identified with the Kidron Valley, but the Kidron is a narrow wadi and not a plain. It is not identical with the Valley of Beracah, where King Jehoshaphat won a victory (2 Chron. 20:20–28), nor is it the Valley of Ben Hinnom (Jer. 7:31–32). Thus, since we cannot locate any such valley geographically, the Valley of Jehoshaphat must be the symbolic name given to the place where God will judge all nations in the time of the day of the Lord.

God's judgment of all nations will be carried out in terms of the promise to Abraham in Genesis 12:3. God promised the patriarch, "I will bless those who bless you, and whoever curses you I will curse." Joel foresees that God will judge all nations, including ours, in terms of their attitude toward Israel. Or put another way, our life or death before God depends on how we have regarded the descendants of father Abraham.

The reason for that is not that Israel is inherently valuable in herself. Rather, we are to be judged in relation to Israel because

Israel is the instrument of God's purpose in the world, so that by our rejection or acceptance of Israel we reject or accept the purposes of God (cf. Rom. 9–11). It is no accident that the world has always persecuted the Jews. Lying deep in the subconscious of sinful humanity is the thought that if it can just get rid of the Jews, then it can also get rid of God's rule over it; thus anti-semitism is finally the attempt to be our own gods and goddesses. But the promise of Genesis 12:3 is finally focused for us in that decisive descendant of Abraham, Jesus of Nazareth, and we now will live or die eternally according to how we react to him (Mark 9:37 and parallels; John 13:20; Matt. 25:31–46).

God will level three charges against the nations in this court case against them. First, they will be accused of scattering Israel **among the nations** in the exiles of 721, 597, 587, and 582 BC. When the northern kingdom of Israel fell to the Assyrians in 721 BC, many of its inhabitants were carried away to Assyria and foreigners moved in to take over the land. In 597, 587, and 582 BC, the southern kingdom of Judah likewise fell, this time to the Babylonians, and all but its poorest peasants were exiled and subsequently scattered among the neighboring nations. Some Jews returned to Judah after 538 BC, after the decree of Cyrus of Persia, the Babylonian Empire having been conquered by that ruler; but many Jews settled abroad and remained dispersed throughout the ancient Near East. All of the prophets preceding Joel considered the exiling of Israel to be punishment for its sin, but verse 2 here also understands Israel's captivity as a sinful work of the foreign nations.

Second, God charges the foreign nations with taking portions of *God's* land of Palestine for themselves, verse 2. As we saw in connection with 1:5–7, the OT never considered that Israel owned the land of Palestine. Rather, God was its owner (cf. Lev. 25:23; Ezek. 33:23–29; Deut. 30:15–20) and bestowed the land as a gift on Israel. When foreigners took portions of Israel's land, they were therefore robbing God's possession, and they stand guilty before God for that usurpation.

Third, God charges the foreign nations with slave trading, verse 3. Merchants and traders often followed conquering armies, buying captives from them to be used as slaves. The foreign soldiers considered Israelite captives to be of such little account, however, that they sold a boy for the price of an hour with a prostitute, or they sold a girl for the price of a drink of wine. But no people, much less God's chosen people, may be treated with such contempt.

**3:4–8** / In verses 4–8, God's charge becomes even more specific, and is leveled directly at **Tyre** and **Sidon** to the north of Israel, and at the Philistines along the coastal plain who have engaged in slave trafficking with the Greeks from the fifth century BC on, verse 6. In addition, God adds one more charge: They have robbed the temple of some of its precious **gold** and **silver** ornamentation and equipment and carried it back to decorate their own temples. One does not mock the Lord of the universe with impunity!

In verses 7–8, therefore, God pronounces judgment on Tyre and Sidon and Philistia, and their punishment will fit their crime. The enslaved Jews will be brought back from their captivity and will themselves become the middlemen, selling the Phoenicians and Philistines into slavery in distant Seba.

Such a sentence gives us pause, because it seems simply to substitute one evil for another. Would God do such a thing? Two answers may be given. First, throughout the Scriptures, God's punishment of evil often consists in letting the evil return upon the sinners' own heads (Cf. 1 Kgs. 8:31–32; Jer. 50:29; Obad. 15; Ezek. 35:11; Hab. 2:8; Matt. 18:23–35; Rev. 18:4–17). And this is exactly what we see in the world around us: Hatred brings hatred in return; war breeds vengeance; suffering causes lust for vengeance; oppression cries out for retaliation. And God displays a certain permissiveness in such a system: God lets it operate, as an instrument of divine judgment. That brings us to the second thing that may be said: As Paul has written, sometimes God simply gives us over to sin in order to punish us for it (Rom. 1:24–32), as much as to say, "All right, if that is what you want, you can have it and suffer the consequences. Wallow in your evil ways. I give you over to them as the punishment of your wrongdoing." In short, according to Scripture, to be free, self-governing, autonomous individuals is to live under the wrath of God. God's loving grasp has let us go and we have been turned over to our own evil devices. Surely that is one of the most terrifying judgments that can befall any individual or nation! To be free of God, the Lord and sustainer, the guide and redeemer of all of life—that is not a situation to be desired!

## Additional Notes §10

**3:1** / **In those days and at that time** is found elsewhere only in Jer. 33:15; 50:4, 20, which also deal with the coming of the kingdom.

**3:2** / **The Valley of Jehoshaphat:** Both the Targum and Theodotion interpret the meaning of the name by reading "the plain of judicial decision" and "the country of judgment" respectively.

**3:4–8** / These verses are very likely a later addition to the book of Joel, but they may have been added by the prophet himself. Certainly they are prose, as in the NIV, and not poetry.

**3:8** / The Sabeans from Seba are not geographically located in the OT, and Seba is called only a distant country (Jer. 6:20), but we know from archaeological evidence that it probably was located in the southwestern portion of the Arabian peninsula now called Yemen. The point in Joel is that Seba is far away, in the opposite direction from Greece.

## §11 Evil's Resistance and God's Victory (Joel 3:9–17)

Christians welcome God's judgments of them, because they know that God is working with them, purging out the sin in their lives and making of them new creatures in Christ. Christians willingly take up a cross and have their old self crucified, for then God can raise up a new person.

**3:9–12** / Evil people, on the other hand, always try to resist God's judgments, to deny them, and to fight against them (cf. John 3:20). And that is what we have pictured in Joel 3:9–10. The speaker summons the evil nations to do battle with God, in order to resist divine judgment upon them. But verse 9 is ironic of course, because the prophet is speaking the part of one who summons the wicked to war.

Playing the role of a leader of God's enemies, Joel calls everyone to battle—the **warriors** from their peaceful laziness, the farmers from their fields, even the weak, who are unfit to fight—for the wicked will need everyone they can muster to stand up to God the warrior. And every weapon will be needed. Thus, in a deliberate reversal of Isaiah 2:4 and Micah 4:3, the farmers are bidden to heat up the forge and beat their **plowshares into swords** and their **pruning hooks into spears.** After all, they face a formidable enemy!

Then in the last line of verse 11, the prophet cries to God to bring down those angelic warriors who make up the army of the Lord (cf. Zech. 14:5; Ps. 103:20). The final battle is about to begin in the Valley of Jehoshaphat.

**3:13–17** / God speaks in verses 13 and 17, which frame the second poem in this section. With God taking a seat in verse 12, as commander over angelic hosts and as judge over all the nations, the fearsome battle commences. This will not be the proximate judgment found in 3:8. Now there will take place the final sentence on all flesh.

The two dreadful figures used to portray God's final judgment are both taken from agriculture. In one, God's army mows
down the nations like a farmer swinging a **sickle** through grain
(cf. Isa. 17:5; Mark 4:29; Rev. 14:15–16, 18–19). In the other, God's
army tramples the wicked like a vintner treading down grapes in
a **winepress** (cf. Isa. 63:3; Jer. 25:30). Both figures are frequently
used in the Scriptures to picture God's judgment against enemies.

Joel even heightens the figure of trampling grapes by saying that there are so many wicked to be destroyed that their
lifeblood overflows the vats used to catch the juice of the grapes.
There are **multitudes** and **multitudes** in the valley, verse 14. The
NIV has missed the connections between the verses by substitut-
ing "so" for the original reading of "for" at the beginning of the
last line of verse 13. But "for" holds the whole poem together at
13b, 13d, 13f, and 14c. And the immense number of the wicked is
emphasized by the repetition of "multitudes."

Significantly, too, the name of the valley has changed. It is
no longer "Jehoshaphat" but **decision**—the Valley of Judicial Decision, verse 14. That which was promised in the day of the Lord
now becomes reality in this vision of the future. God the judge
imposes the sentence, and the sentence is death.

We recoil at that, of course, and think that it is one more
evidence of the primitive nature of the OT. We have domesticated
God into nothing more than a friend, a lover, a helper, one who
bails us out of our difficulties and looks the other way when we
sin. But the church father Tertullian in the third century, knew
better. "What a prevaricator of truth is such a god," he wrote.
"What a dissembler with his own decisions. Afraid to condemn
what he really condemns, afraid to hate what he does not love,
permitting that to be done which he does not allow, choosing to
indicate what he dislikes rather than deeply examining it! This
will turn out an imaginary goodness, for the true God is not
otherwise fully good than as an enemy of evil" (*Adv. Marcion*
1.26–27). The true God of the Bible is an enemy of evil, who will
finally do away with those who have rebelled against divine
lordship, and the NT too is fully aware of that fact. "It is a fearful
thing to fall into the hands of the living God," says the Epistle to
the Hebrews (10:31 RSV). Or in Ephesians, "Our struggle is not
against enemies of blood and flesh, but against the rulers, the
authorities, against the cosmic powers of this present darkness"
(6:12)—against evil grown so enormous and menacing that it is a
cosmic shadow darkening the earth. A God who is merely a

helper or friend is no match for such evil. But the God of the Bible is its match and will do away with the powers of evil in the end.

The wages of sin is death (Rom. 6:23). Joel knew that, as did Paul. And we see it finally pictured for us in the death of our Lord on the cross. Evil must die in order for God to reign over all, and our Lord died that death, taking upon himself the destruction that we deserved.

On the other hand, the gift of God can be eternal life in Christ Jesus, our risen Lord (Rom. 6:23). And Joel 3:16 gives the foretaste of that glad announcement. God can be a refuge or fortress or stronghold (cf. 2 Cor. 10:4) for repentant people, shielding them from death on the final day, as the resurrection of our Lord can shield us from eternal death at the day of the Lord.

Repeating some of the words of 2:27, Joel 3:17 gives a foretaste, then, of the assurance of Rev. 21:3–4. The communion of the faithful with their covenant Lord will be complete, and God will dwell in their midst, and never again will their lives be threatened by any enemy alien—whether by locusts or armies, unbelievers or idolaters (cf. Isa. 52:1; Zech. 14:20–21), or, in the words of Revelation, "death or mourning or crying or pain." God's good kingdom will have come on earth, even as it is in heaven.

### Additional Notes §11

The whole section may be divided into two poems, with 3:9–12 making up the first, and 3:13–17 the second. The second poem then has two strophes, vv. 13–14, and 15–17.

**3:13** / **Sickle:** The word could be translated "pruning knife." The figure of harvesting grapes would then be the only one, but the figure of harvesting grain is also used of God's judgment, and the NIV translation need not be corrected (cf. Rev. 14:15–20).

**3:14** / **Multitudes, multitudes:** Commentators have long noted that the sound in the Hb. of this repeated word imitates the hum or roar of a distant assembled army.

**3:15** / Once again Joel refers to the cosmic darkness that will occur on the day of the Lord (cf. 2:10). Watching the battle scene, the Lord will roar, so that the cosmos will tremble before such wrath. Verse 16a–b is a quote from Amos 1:2, and all of vv. 13–16b are similar to Jer.

25:30–31. Joel is reclaiming past prophecy and projecting its fulfillment into the future.

**3:16** / **Refuge, stronghold:** Such metaphors of protection are frequent in the Psalms (Ps. 18:2; 46:1; 61:3; 62:7, etc.), but here Joel goes beyond the Psalmists' thoughts to envision that protection in the day of the Lord.

## §12 The Glorious Future (Joel 3:18–21)

Joel ends his book by portraying the glorious future that awaits the people of God. Their enemies have been destroyed, and peace reigns on the earth (cf. Ps. 46:8–11). In the place of the catastrophes that they knew in the past, they have become inheritors of abundant life. Indeed, Joel's portrayals of that life, borrowing partially from Amos 9:13, pick up the themes of his first chapter and show their exact opposite. Once the sweet, new wine was cut off from Judah (1:5), but now the mountainsides with their vineyards will yield it in abundance. Once the cattle gave no milk, because there was no pasture for them (1:18), but now in God's kingdom abundant pastureland on the hills will ensure copious supply. Once, in the drought, there was no water (1:17–20), but now even the dry wadis of Judah will be filled abundantly. More than that, a fountain will flow forth from the temple and water the dry Valley of the Acacias.

In referring to the river issuing forth from the temple, Joel is once again picking up a prophetic theme from the past and envisioning its fulfillment in the future (cf. Ezek. 47:1–12; Zech. 14:8; Ps. 46:4; Rev. 22:1–2). Joel is similarly drawing on the prophetic theme used earlier in Isaiah 55:1–3, in which wine, milk, and water depicted God's salvation.

**3:18–19** / As the NIV points out in a footnote, Joel 3:18 reads literally in the Hebrew, "the Valley of Shittim," which is that deep and rocky portion of the Kidron Valley or wadi that begins northwest of Jerusalem, bends around east of the city, and then continues through a deep gorge southeast toward the Dead Sea. Usually the valley is dry, but acacias grew in abundance in its dry soil in biblical times, and the valley was often named the Wadi or Valley of the Acacias, as the NIV has correctly interpreted.

The OT rarely is satisfied with generalities. When it pictures all of Israel's former enemies destroyed, it must also specifically name two, in verse 19. The mention of **water,** in verse 18, brings to mind the enemy **Egypt,** which was so abundantly supplied with the waters of the Nile. Thus, in the reversal of Israel's fortunes, plentifully watered Egypt will become dry and desolate. The mention of the continuing inhabitation of **Judah** in verse 20 connects with the thought of **Edom,** who took advantage of the fall and exile of Judah and Jerusalem to Babylon in 587 BC (cf. Obad.). In the reversal brought in the kingdom of God, Edom will become a **desert** without inhabitants, verse 19. Verses 18, 19, and 20 are all linked closely together. Moreover, Egypt and Edom are typically named in earlier prophetic oracles against the foreign nations (cf. Ezek. 30–32; Jer. 46; Isa. 34), and Joel is indicating that no prophetic word concerning the day of the Lord will be left unfulfilled in the future.

**3:21** / Verse 21 is perplexing in this context and has been variously translated and interpreted (see the additional note below). The NRSV takes the meaning to be that God will avenge the slaying of the Israelites by their enemies. If that is the proper interpretation, then the line may belong after verse 19, as many scholars have suggested. On the other hand, the NIV understands the verse as referring to God's forgiveness of the people for their **bloodguilt,** i.e., for their shedding of innocent blood, but such a thought has appeared nowhere else in Joel and is intrusive here. One can either omit the line, or place it after verse 19, with the NRSV's reading, or confess inability to deal with it. This commentator would choose the latter course. Perhaps some day the meaning will be clear, but it is not at this time, and we sometimes have to acknowledge our inability to deal with the word until God sheds further light.

The most important statement in verse 21 is that with which the verse ends, however: **The LORD** will dwell **in Zion.** And surely it is to be read in the future tense. Joel looks forward to the Kingdom of God, when God's enemies will have been eliminated from the earth, when abundant life will be given to his people, and when the Lord will dwell in the midst of his faithful people, bound to them by an everlasting covenant. The vision is really one of Genesis 17:7–8 fully fulfilled.

## Additional Note §12

**3:21** / The LXX reads "And I will avenge their blood, and will not leave it unavenged," a reading presupposed also by the Syr. and Tg. On the basis of manuscript evidence, the NRSV approaches the proper meaning: "I will avenge their blood, and I will not clear the guilty." The Hb. is: "And I will avenge their blood not avenged." Perhaps the v. should be moved to the end of v. 19 to form a meditation on the shedding of innocent blood, v. 19d.

# *Amos*

# Introduction: Amos

## Amos's Place in Prophecy

Amos, whose ministry took place about 760 BC, is the first of the classical or writing prophets. As such, he stands in a certain continuity with the nonwriting prophets who preceded him—Elijah, Elisha, Micaiah ben Imla, Ahijah, all those others mentioned in the Samuel books and Kings—through whom God guided the course of his covenant people during their first two centuries of monarchy. Amos acknowledges that the early prophets were divinely guided (Amos 2:11), and certainly they were the ones who kept the Mosaic covenant faith alive in a time of syncretism, internal and external war, and absolutist claims on the part of the rulers of both the northern kingdom of Israel and the southern kingdom of Judah.

Yet Amos represents the most radical break with the prophets who have gone before him. First of all, most of the early nonwriting prophets earned their daily bread from their prophesying and were professional members of prophetic guilds, although a court prophet like Nathan seems to be an exception to the latter. But Amos disavows any connection with prophetic bands or guilds (Amos 7:14–15). Instead he is a Judean, a somewhat wealthy sheep-breeder and owner of sycamore fig orchards (see the commentary on 1:1), who has been suddenly yanked out of his customary life by the hand of God and told to journey northward to Israel in order to proclaim there the judgment of God on that sinful kingdom.

Second, the means by which the Lord's will is revealed to Amos is different from that used with the early prophets. Their revelation came to them usually by means of the Spirit (cf. 1 Sam. 10:10–11). Amos, however, is the recipient of the *word* of God, sometimes accompanied by a vision (Amos 7:7–9), and revelation by means of the Spirit drops almost totally out of the prophetic experience until the time of Joel in the fourth century BC. God speaks to the prophet—we do not know how—and the prophet is thereby set under an almost irresistible compulsion to proclaim God's word (Amos 3:8; cf. Jer. 20:9).

Third, unlike the early prophets, who devoted their entire lives to their profession, Amos serves as a prophet of the Lord for only a limited amount of time. He is given a task to do and the words from the Lord by which to do it. Once the task is accomplished, he is released to return to Judah and to resume his normal life as "a herdsman, and a dresser of sycamore trees" (7:14 RSV).

Fourth, the recipients of Amos's message are usually different from those addressed by the early prophets. They most often directed their messages to the rulers of their country, and the earliest form of the prophetic oracle was that of a judgment oracle to an individual. (See Westermann, *Basic Forms of Prophetic Speech,* pp. 129–62). But the majority of Amos's oracles take the form of judgment speeches to the nation, in which there is an initial indictment detailing Israel's sins. This is followed by some form of the prophetic formula, "Thus says the LORD God" (Amos 3:11 RSV), or "Therefore this is what the Sovereign LORD says" (3:11 NIV), or "The Sovereign LORD has sworn by his holiness" (4:2 NIV), or "Therefore this is what I will do to you" (4:12 NIV). Then there is the announcement of the judgment. But the important point is that Amos begins that long line of classical prophecy primarily directed not against individuals but against the nation as a whole.

Above all, however, in the fifth place, Amos is given a new and radical message from God that has never been heard before in Israel: God is coming to bring Israel's life to an end (Amos 8:2). God will spare this people no longer. The prophet's task is no longer simply to expose the people's sin and call them to repentance and return to their God. Repentance is no longer possible. The nation's sin is now so severe that it can be corrected only by their being wiped out.

In short, Amos is a prophet of total judgment, announcing the death of the northern kingdom. He is not a social reformer but an exposer of rebellion against God. He is not a humanitarian but a herald of God's coming action. He is not announcing new ideas about God but rather is proclaiming that the God of the covenant is on the move, toward the goal of the day of the Lord, when God will set up his kingdom on earth.

God is coming personally to do Israel to death, according to Amos, and so throughout the prophet's oracles, the divine "I" predominates: "I will send fire . . ." (1:4); "I will not turn back . . ." (2:1); "I will punish . . ." (3:2); "I will stir up a nation against you . . ." (6:14); "I will kill . . ." (9:1); and so on.

Indeed, perhaps the central word of Amos is, "Prepare to meet your God, O Israel" (4:12).

### The Covenant Context of Amos's Message

The God whom Amos sees coming to destroy his sinful people is undeniably the God of Israel's covenant past. Some commentators have denied Amos's connection with the covenant tradition, but such a denial is invalid. Amos stands firmly in Israel's Mosaic, hexateuchal tradition. Amos 3:2 can mean nothing other than the election of Israel. Nor can Amos's references to the exodus, wilderness wanderings, and gift of the land in 2:9–10 be termed nongenuine. It is with the central covenant commandments that the prophet is dealing. In Amos's book, God is the Lord of the covenant who comes to judge his people precisely because they have broken their covenant with their God.

In the covenant, Israel promised to be God's people (cf. "my people" in 7:8, 15, and 8:2). They swore that they would reflect God's justice, righteousness, and mercy in their communal life. They promised that they would do God's "good" (cf. 5:14–15), that they would be God's folk, serving God's purpose, set apart from every other nation on the face of the earth by their obedience to their God alone. Thus, they would honor God's name as Lord, the one God over all the hosts in heaven and on earth.

In the message of Amos, then, that honor due to God is encapsulated in Amos's repeated use of the title, "Yahweh, Adonai Elohim Sebaoth" ("Yahweh, Lord God of hosts"), and it is that title or some variation on it that appears at every crucial point in the collection of Amos's writings. Indeed, it is by the use of that title that the central oracles in Amos 3:13–9:7 are structured into larger sections. Let us demonstrate:

> 3:13–4:13: The Indictment and Punishment of Israel Spelled Out
> Subunits: 3:13–15; 4:1–3, 4–13.
> Begins and ends with "Yahweh Elohim Sebaoth (is God's name)" in 3:13 and 4:13.

5:1–17: The Sentence of Death
  Subunits: 5:1–9, 10–13, 14–15, 16–17.
  Bracketed by funeral mourning in 5:2 and 5:16–17.
  Begins with "Thus says Adonai Yahweh" in verse 3, followed
    by "Yahweh is his name" in verse 9, and "Thus says
    Yahweh Elohim Sebaoth Adonai" in verse 16.

5:18–6:14: Israel's Ill-Placed Confidence
  Subunits: 5:18–20, 21–24, 25–27; 6:1–7, 8–11, 12–14.
  With Yahweh Elohim Sebaoth (is God's name) in 5:27; 6:8
    and 6:14.

7:1–8:3: The Prophet's Visions and Encounter with Amaziah
  Subunits: 7:1–3, 4–6, 7–9, 10–17; 8:1–3.
  Begins and ends with Adonai Yahweh in 7:1 and 8:3.

8:4–9:6: The End and the God of the End
  Subunits: 8:4–8, 9–10, 11–14; 9:1–4, 5–6.
  Bracketed by reference to the rising and sinking of the land
    in 8:8 and 9:5, with "Adonai Yahweh Sebaoth" in 9:5,
    "Yahweh is his name" in 9:6, forming the climax.

Thus, from their beginning to their end, the central oracles are affirmations of the lordship of Yahweh and of the honor due his name.

In the light of this, we might almost call the book of Amos a great doxology and exposition on the name of Adonai Yahweh Sebaoth as the only God, who is Lord of nature and of history, and who judges all nations, as well as the people of Israel, for their idolatrous worship and their corrupt practices in society which dishonor his name.

Many commentators have held that the hymnic portions celebrating Yahweh's name in 4:13, 5:8–9, and 9:5–6 are late additions to the book, perhaps all belonging together in a hymn of three strophes, and therefore not integral to the prophet's theology. I cannot agree. While Amos may indeed be borrowing from an ancient hymn, his use of the hymnic assertions is an integral part of the structure and theology of his book, which then could almost be understood as an explanation of the third commandment of the Decalogue, "You shall not take the name of the LORD your God in vain; for the LORD will not hold him guiltless who takes his name in vain." In Amos, Yahweh confronts Israel with its guilt, which earns its death.

The fact that Israel has broken its covenant with God by refusing to honor God's name and has joined the other nations of the earth in rebellion against God's lordship is then set forth at the beginning and end of the book. In 1:3–2:16, Israel is to be judged like the other nations. In 9:7, the elected people, who were to be set apart, are now no different than any other people. Israel has rejected its electing God, and significantly, Amos never calls Yahweh Israel's God. Israel has rejected its calling, and that rejection is shown primarily in its injustice toward the helpless, in the corruption of the courts in the gates of the towns and cities, and in insincere and meaningless worship. Thus, God now comes to reject Israel and to bring its salvation history to an end. It is a simply stunning message, and we can perhaps feel the force of it by imagining that a prophet were to tell us Christians that the cross and resurrection of Jesus Christ are no longer sufficient to save us.

## Historical Specificity in Amos

The prophet and his message are located firmly in the history of the ancient Near East, and we are not to comfort ourselves by thinking that his words are not to be taken seriously. About 760 BC, Amos prophesied the death of the northern kingdom of Israel, and in 721 BC that kingdom was swallowed up by the empire of Assyria and disappeared from history. "The end has come upon my people Israel" (8:2 RSV), God said through his prophet, and that end came. Amos is concerned with the state of affairs that led to that end, and as heirs of the message of Amos and members now of God's covenant people, we Christians need to examine carefully the causes of Israel's demise.

The superscription of 1:1 places Amos's ministry in the time of Jeroboam II (787/6–747/6 BC) of the northern kingdom of Israel and Uzziah of the southern kingdom of Judah. Uzziah reigned from 787/6 until 757/6, when he contracted severe leprosy and the responsibility of government was turned over to his son Jotham as co-regent. The fact that the latter is not mentioned in the superscription probably means that Amos dates from before 757/6 (cf. Hos. 1:1).

The book is not earlier than about 760 BC, however, because Assyria is never mentioned in it, although we know that Assyria under Adad-nirari III (806–783 BC) was strong enough to subdue the kingdom of Aram to the northeast of Israel. After Adad-nirari's death, however, Assyria became occupied with the advances of the kingdom of Urartu from Asia Minor, and the Arameans were free once again to move into Israelite territory (Amos 1:3), as were the Ammonites from the east (Amos 1:13).

Supporting the date of about 760 BC is archaeological evidence from Strata VI at Hazor, showing that it suffered a violent earthquake about that time. This could very well be the earthquake mentioned in Amos 1:1.

During the early part of Jeroboam II's reign, when Assyria had subdued Aram, the Israelite king was free to expand both his territory (2 Kgs. 14:25; Amos 6:13) and his economy. The result was a lively commerce (Amos 8:5) that nourished a growing wealthy class. Elaborate dwellings, sumptuously furnished (3:15; 6:4), housed a pleasure-loving elite that was indifferent to the plight of those less fortunate (6:4–6). Indeed, the rich prospered at the expense of the poor (4:1), taking possession of the land of those who had fallen into debt or subjecting them to slavery (2:6; 8:4, 6), denying them justice in the lay courts at the city gates (2:7; 5:10, 12), and cheating them in the marketplace (8:5). As the structures of community broke down, immorality and debauchery increased (2:7–8; 6:5–6), while at the same time the consciences of the rich were placated by participation in an elaborate cultus (4:4–5; 5:21–23). The "beautiful people" enjoyed their *vita dolce*, while in the hovels and dark alleys of Jeroboam's realm the needy suffered unnoticed. The situation was not too different from that found in any prosperous modern nation.

## The Source of Amos's Language

Amos, though a fairly wealthy man himself, was incensed by the conditions he saw. But it was not from his own sympathies and sense of justice that Amos derived his words. Rather, his words were given him by God, and he had no choice but to speak them (3:8). Indeed, the Lord often preempted the prophet's words, speaking in the first-person directly to the sinful people: "I . . . ," "I . . . ," "I . . . ," says the Lord.

God was incensed with the conditions in Israel. The language of Amos is sharper than any two-edged sword, delivered in numerous brief judgment oracles, with concrete images and imaginative metaphors driving home the condemnation. A God of justice could find no justice in this people's society. A God of righteousness roared out against a people grown totally unrighteous. A good God looked in vain for any in Israel who sought goodness. The Israelites failed to reflect anything of the nature of the Lord to whom they were bound in covenant. They lost their God. And of course, if a people loses the Lord God, they also lose their life.

### The Redaction and Text of the Book

There can be no doubt that somebody other than the prophet himself contributed to the book of Amos. Just the presence of the third-person account of 7:10–15, which has been inserted into the series of visions found in 7:1–8:3 along with the oracle in 7:16–17, and which probably comes from an eyewitness to the encounter with Amaziah, makes that certain.

In the heyday of liberal biblical criticism at the beginning of this century, many verses in the book were deemed secondary. In our time, Hans Walter Wolff, who is one of the major contemporary interpreters of the book, theorizes that the book as we now have it went through a six-stage development (*Joel and Amos*, pp. 106–13):

A. Three eighth-century literary strata, from Amos himself or his contemporary disciples:
1. "The words of Amos from Tekoa" (1:1): most of the oracles in chapters 3–6.
2. The literary fixation of the cycles of visions and oracles against the foreign nations, probably by Amos himself: 7:1–8; 8:1–2; 9:1–4; 1:3–2:16.
3. The additions from a circle of Amos's disciples of the second clause of the superscription ("which he viewed concerning Israel two years before the earthquake"); the insertion of 7:10–17 into the vision cycle; the addition of some verses in chapters 5–6 and 8–9, all probably between 760 and 730 BC, in Judah, although it is very difficult to separate these from the words of Amos himself.

B. Later additions that actualized the text's message for new situations:
1. References to Bethel, in keeping with Josiah's destruction of that sanctuary (2 Kgs. 23:17; cf. 1 Kgs. 13), solemnized by the additions of the hymn pieces in 4:13, 5:8–9, and 9:5–6.

2. Deuteronomic redactions that expanded the superscription and added the oracles against Tyre, Edom (1:9–12), and Judah (2:4–5), along with 2:10–12, 3:7, and 5:25–26.

3. A postexilic addition of the promises in 9:11–15.

While Wolff's analysis has been accepted in its broad outlines by commentators such as James L. Mays, I repeat that one cannot remove the hymnic portions (4:13; 5:8–9; 9:5–6) from the work without doing violence to the basic theological thrust of the prophet's work.

Further, I have to agree with Brevard S. Childs *(Introduction to the Old Testament as Scripture)* that additions to the text of Amos are not dependent primarily on later events in the life of Judah. In such a hermeneutic, historical events are dictating the content of the word of God, and that is to turn the OT's understanding of prophecy upside down. Rather, the word of God determines events. It may very well be, therefore, that passages that we think reflect events, such as 2:4–5, which supposedly echoes the fall of Jerusalem in 587 BC, actually were present in the Amos book *before* the events took place. As Childs points out (p. 408), in Amos's oracles, both the announcement of the destruction of Israel and the promise of its rebirth speak of events lying still in the future.

The primary task of the interpreter of Amos is therefore to ask after the theological meaning of this message, as it has been handed down and now lies *in its entirety* before us. Additions to the work there may be, but the whole now is given to us as authoritative word of God—as canon, as ultimate rule for our faith and practice. It is with that whole that we must deal.

Aiding us in our task is a fairly well-preserved Hebrew text. Despite the fact that the Septuagint (LXX) gives different readings at many places, only a few verses in the MT require emendation, and many of the variant readings can be ignored. We will note only *necessary* emendations in the commentary.

Very frequently there is also reference in the commentary to readings found in the Revised Standard Version. I believe the RSV to be more faithful to the original Hebrew than the translations in the New Revised Standard Version and in the New International Version. I have therefore employed the RSV as a corrective for readers of the NIV.

**1:1** / Amos is introduced to us by a number of editors, probably from Judah, who have, over a period of time, formulated the superscription as we now have it. Probably the original heading of the book read something like, "The words of Amos from Tekoa." The NIV mistakenly connects the **shepherds** with Tekoa, but **of Tekoa** modifies **Amos,** and the reference to the shepherds simply states Amos's occupation. The facts that the reign of **Jeroboam** II of Israel is synchronized with that of **Uzziah** of Judah, and that Uzziah is mentioned first, point strongly to an addition by the southern kingdom's postexilic Deuteronomic editors, who framed the entire history of Israel and Judah in such terms in the books of Kings (e.g., 2 Kgs. 14:23; 15:1). **Two years before the earthquake** makes the date of the book very specific for its readers, who evidently were familiar with the event (cf. Zech. 14:5), but the phrase dates the book only approximately for us, about 760 BC, on the basis of archaeological evidence (see the introduction). The reference to the earthquake may indicate, however, that Amos's ministry took place within the span of one year.

There is no other person named **Amos** in the OT, but his name is surely an abbreviated form of Amasiah, another person mentioned in 2 Chronicles 17:16. Often the father of a prophet is named in a superscription (cf. Isa. 1:1; Jer. 1:1), but the omission here does not need to be understood as an indication of lowly birth.

**Tekoa** was a small village located some ten miles directly south of Jerusalem on the ridge dividing the cultivated land to the west from the steppes and wilderness of Judah on the east. Second Chronicles 11:5–6 indicates that it was fortified by Rehoboam (cf. Jer. 6:1), and 2 Samuel 14:2 connects it with the practice of wisdom, although Wolff has probably gone too far in ascribing much of Amos's use of tradition to wisdom teaching. George Adam Smith, *The Book of the Twelve Prophets,* pp. 72–74, eloquently proposed that the geographical setting of Tekoa had much to do with shaping Amos's thought, but it is bad theology to ascribe a prophet's words to the influence of his surroundings.

Calvin (*Joel, Amos, Obadiah,* p. 149) finds that the "poor shepherd" from a "mean village" who is sent to challenge the pride of the king of Israel and the wealth of Israel's inhabitants is prophetic of 1 Corinthians 1:27–28 ("God chose the foolish things of the world to shame the wise . . ."). But while Tekoa may have been lowly, it is doubtful that Amos was poor or an ordinary shepherd. He is called a *nōqēd* in 1:1, a word that is found elsewhere only in 2 Kings 3:4. There the word is properly translated "sheep breeder" (RSV) and is used of Mesha, the king of Moab, who was able to deliver annually to the king of Israel one hundred thousand lambs and the wool of a thousand rams. Amos may similarly have been the breeder and trader of large herds, traveling about the countryside on his business. In addition, in 7:14 (RSV), Amos terms himself "a dresser of sycamore trees." The phrase refers to the fact that sycamore figs had to be individually punctured in order to ripen properly. Sycamore fig trees could not be grown on the hills around Tekoa, but only in the warm lowlands around the Dead Sea and along the Mediterranean coast. Thus, the prophet was probably a rather wealthy land owner, who traveled frequently to carry on his business of producing and selling two popular products.

Some commentators have waxed eloquent about the simple country shepherd who traveled to the big city and was enraged by the opulence and injustice that he found, but as James Mays has written, ". . . it is time to lay to rest the ghost of the wilderness shepherd who reacts to city culture and cult because he sees it as an outsider whose sensitivities are outraged by its contrast to the simple life" ("Words about the Words of Amos," p. 266).

Similarly, the fashion in some liberation theologies of the present day has been to claim that only the poor can properly understand the word of God. Such a view would eliminate Amos from the canon, not to mention Isaiah of Jerusalem, with his entrance to kings' courts. God chooses those to whom he will reveal himself.

The superscription says that Amos **saw** the words of the Lord, a conventional term for the revelation given to the classical prophets (cf. Isa. 1:1; Mic. 1:1), and an indication that we present-day interpreters can never fully understand how God spoke to the prophets. Certainly Amos had prophetic visions (cf. 7:1–9; 8:1–3; 9:1–4), but "saw" refers to all of the words of Amos. Perhaps the most important point for us is that the term is a clear indication of the fact that Amos's oracles were given him from outside of himself; they were not the product of his own meditations, convictions, and musings; they came from God.

Amos is set under the command of God to travel from his home in Judah to the northern kingdom of Israel, there to speak to the heirs of the old northern tribal league, the possessors of the original Mosaic covenant (cf. 7:15). It is a fateful journey, under an awful command.

## §2 Introduction to the Oracles (Amos 1:2)

**1:2** / This verse forms a summary statement that sets the tone of the whole Amos corpus. The editors have joined it to the superscription by the phrase, "And he said" (RSV) but it really stands alone. Many commentators have attributed 1:2 to the editors, but I believe it comes from Amos himself, because the figure presented is used by prophets who follow Amos, some almost immediately.

The Lord is portrayed with the simile of a lion roaring after its prey, a figure of speech that Amos repeats in 3:4, 8, and 12, and Hosea uses the same figure some two decades later (Hos. 5:14; 11:10; 13:7). Jeremiah 25:30 then employs the figure in a manner almost identical with that of Amos: the Lord roars from Jerusalem against all peoples and nations of the earth (Jer. 25:30–31; cf. 25:38; Ps. 50:22). Joel 3:16 quotes the first two lines of the oracle, but uses the figure to reassure the people of Israel of God's protection. Related to these passages also are Joel 2:11, where Yahweh "utters his voice before his army" (RSV) on the day of the Lord (cf. Amos 5:18), and Isaiah 42:13, where "he shouts aloud" (RSV) as he prepares war against his foes. Thus there seems to be a complex of tradition, begun by Amos, in which God is portrayed by the figure of a lion, roaring from the temple on Zion against all foes, which is connected with the coming of the day of the Lord and subsequently, though somewhat loosely, with the thought of Yahweh as a "warrior" (cf. Exod. 15:3). It seems doubtful that this trajectory of tradition would exist if Amos 1:2 were just the product of a later editor.

The single verse foreshadows all that follows in the book. God has broken out in a roaring against his covenant people. In our day, we are apt to complain about the silence of God. That is not the Israelites' problem. Their difficulty is that their Lord has broken out in a wrathful roaring against them, a roaring that will leave them dead, with only a few fragments of their former life remaining (Amos 3:12).

Many commentators have written that the effect of God's roaring will be drought, with the plentiful forests, the rich vineyards, and the fruitful orchards of Mt. **Carmel** dried up, and the lush meadows of the lowlands withered and devoid of herbage. But the effect of the divine lion's roaring will be much more serious than that. God's judgment is almost universally throughout the OT likened to fire (Amos 5:6; 7:4; cf. Isa. 66:14–16, et al.)—fire before which the very earth melts (Ps. 46:6), and fire before which all nature mourns (Jer. 12:4 RSV). It is that effect that is pictured here. The prosperity of Israel has been no sign of God's favor toward it, and we should never view ours as such a sign either. All will become ruin before the fire of an angry God.

Significantly, God's voice comes **from Jerusalem**—not from Bethel or Dan, where Jeroboam I had earlier erected the temples of the northern kingdom with their golden calves (1 Kgs. 12:26–33), but from the temple on **Zion**, where God dwelt in the midst of his people above the ark in the Holy of Holies and where alone he would put his name, according to Deuteronomy (12:5 et passim). The worship of northern Israel was no worship and would soon come to an end. Deuteronomy learned its exclusive lesson well from the prophets.

---

### Additional Notes §2

---

**1:2** / The NIV has omitted the "And," that is at the beginning of the v. in the original Hb.

Because Yahweh's voice is often connected with thunder in the OT (Ps. 29; Exod. 19:19 RSV), the NIV has translated **thunders,** 1:2c, where the RSV correctly translates "utters his voice."

The Hb. reads "mourn" instead of **dry up,** 1:2d. The RSV has the proper reading of the line.

## §3 Oracles against the Foreign Nations (Amos 1:3–2:16)

In the prophetic corpora, oracles of judgment against the foreign nations usually follow a prophet's oracles to his own people (Jer. 46–51; Ezek. 25–32). Here in Amos, however, the prophet begins with the announcement of judgment on the foreign peoples immediately surrounding Israel, and his purpose in doing so is entirely theological. These foreign nations posed no serious threat to Israel's life in the time of Jeroboam II, although that king may have carried on sporadic border warfare with the Arameans on the northern border of Gilead (1:3) and with the Ammonites on the southern border of that tribe (1:13). Amos's theological purpose in beginning with the foreign nations, however, is to show that Israel, the covenant people of Yahweh, has joined with the rest of the nations in a common rebellion against the authority of the Lord of all the hosts of heaven and of earth.

The nations of Israel's world refuse to let God be God, that is, they refuse to acknowledge God's lordship over them. They do not follow God's will for the relation between nations, and thus they profane God's holy name. But the Israelites are supposed to be different. They are the inheritors of the Mosaic covenant (3:2). They are supposed to be a people set apart for God's purposes and thus obedient to divine will (cf. Exod. 19:4–6). Israel is, as the ancient oracle of Baalam has it, "a people dwelling alone, and not reckoning itself among the nations" (Num. 23:9 RSV). It is no accident that the stress on Israel's election in 3:2 follows immediately after the oracle against Israel in 2:6–16, for that is the theological point being made—Israel is the elected nation, who is to be different from the surrounding peoples (cf. Ezek. 20:32). Instead, Israel has become like every other nation in refusing to let God be God, Lord over its life. Amos therefore first details the rebellions of the foreign nations, to which he will then add the rebellion of Israel in 2:6–16.

Amos's oracles against the foreign peoples are all given in the standard form of the speech of a messenger from Yahweh, and thus they all begin with the messenger formula, "Thus says the LORD" (RSV) or "This is what the LORD says" (NIV), and with three exceptions (1:10, 12; 2:5), they end with the formula, "says the LORD." Like a diplomatic messenger, entrusted with a message from his king (cf. 2 Kgs. 18:19; 19:3), Amos speaks the words that his Lord has given him to speak.

The indictments contained in the messages are set forth in a series of graduated numerical sayings, a form frequently found in wisdom literature (cf. Prov. 30:15–16, 18–19, 21–23, 29–31), but it seems strange that only one crime is then charged to each of the nations. Again the reason is theological. The nations have rebelled frequently against God, but God has been "slow to anger" (Nah. 1:3), frequently suspending deserved judgments and forbearing in mercy, until pushed too far (cf. Amos 7:1–9). Finally, for one crime, the nation is indicted and its punishment announced.

In each of the oracles, the nature of the punishment is summed up by saying that God will send the fire of wrath (a general term always for God's judgment) upon the people. But then the specific nature of the punishment is spelled out in terms of exile, warfare, or death.

The oracles on the Arameans (1:3–5), Philistines (1:6–8), Ammonites (1:13–15), and Moabites (2:1–3) all have the identical form, but that uniformity is broken in the case of Tyre (1:9–10), Edom (1:11–12), and Judah (2:4–5). The announcement of punishment for these three is very short, the consequences of Yahweh's intervention are not spelled out, and the concluding messenger formula is omitted. In the case of Judah, its sin consists not in crimes against humanity, as in the other oracles, but in sin against God.

On the basis of these form critical and literary differences alone, Wolff and others have concluded that the oracles against Tyre, Edom, and Judah are later additions to the book, intended to apply its message to later circumstances. But considerations of form are not sufficient in themselves to justify such a conclusion. Probably only the oracle against Judah is a later addition, since it seems to mirror the events of 587 BC, and even then we must ask, with Childs, what the function of the Judah oracle is in the book as it now lies before us.

**1:3–5** / **Aram,** with its capital of **Damascus,** lay to the northeast of Israel, on the northern border of **Gilead,** which was

Manassite territory (1 Kgs. 4:13). Aram was the principal enemy of Israel in the border wars of the middle of the ninth to the beginning of the eighth century BC. The **Valley of Aven** (or "wickedness") probably refers to a region in northern Aram. **Beth Eden** (or "house of pleasure") may be identified with the petty state of Bit-Adini, which was located on the Euphrates downstream from Carchemish and was probably under the control of Aram. **Ben-Hadad** and **Hazael** are both dynastic names, so we are not sure to which Ben-Hadad the text refers. Probably the reference is to the son of Hazael mentioned in 2 Kings 13:24.

The crime with which Aram is charged is excess in time of war. It has treated the inhabitants of northern Gilead much more cruelly than necessary to take over some of their territory, raking them as heavy wooden threshing **sledges,** studded beneath with **iron teeth,** rake through the grain in order to separate the wheat from the chaff. Even in the secular military contests between nations, there is a divine mercy that is to be shown in acknowledgment of a higher will than that exercised by human beings.

Aram's punishment will therefore fit its crime, but its attacking enemy will be God, whose **fire** of wrath will eat up its defenses, break down its barred gates, cut down the population of its annexed territory and the occupant of its throne, and send its inhabitants into exile in Kir.

**Kir** was located in Mesopotamia, near Elam, and Amos 9:7 designates it as the original home of the Arameans. Thus, Yahweh the Lord of nations will reverse Aram's history. God brought the Arameans up out of Kir (9:7); God will return them there. International relations are finally subject to the will of God and not the will of human beings.

**1:6–8** / The **Philistines,** from whom the name Palestine is taken, dwelt in five city-states on or near the coast of Palestine. **Gaza** was the principal city, on the border with Egypt. Some ten miles to its north was **Ashkelon,** then were **Ashdod** and Gath, with **Ekron** the northernmost settlement. Gath is not mentioned in this oracle, and it may have fallen to Uzziah of Judah in the time of Amos (cf. 2 Chron. 26:6).

The Philistines' crime was that they captured the entire population of small settlements and sold them to **Edom** to be used as slaves, either in Edom's own mining and maritime industries or by other peoples for whom the Edomites acted as middlemen. Which small settlements were thus denuded is not said, but they were probably in Israel or Judah. Such stealing of human beings deserved the death penalty in Israel's law (Exod. 21:16), and even the law codes of foreign peoples, such as the Code of Hammurabi and the Nuzi texts, set limits on the treatment of captive peoples (cf. Exod. 23:9; Neh. 5:8; Job 31:13–15; Joel 3:6, 18). The helpless were not to be misused and abused as mere material objects to profit the mighty.

In the NT, of course, the grace of God reaches even further to make the slave a beloved brother or sister in the Lord (Phlm. 15–17; cf. Gal. 3:28). Here in Amos, God's wrath will wipe out the Philistines and their rulers, so that not even a remnant will be left to them.

**1:9–10 / Tyre** was located on the Mediterranean coast just north of Ashur and was the leading city of Phoenicia in the middle of the eighth century, noted for its far-flung maritime trade. It emerges into importance in the OT already in the tenth century BC and figures prominently in relations with Kings David and Solomon of Judah (2 Sam. 5:11; 1 Kgs. 5:1–12; 7:13–46) and Ahab of Israel (1 Kgs. 16:29–31). Thus, the **treaty of brotherhood** probably refers to a political treaty (cf. 1 Kgs. 9:13), but with whom the treaty was made is not specified.

Tyre's crime is identical to that recounted in the preceding oracle—they **sold** whole villages of men, women, and children into slavery. Their fortifications will therefore fall in the warfare brought upon them by the fire of God's wrath. The brevity of the announcement of judgment makes the oracle suspect, but it now exists in the Amos corpus, and its word stands: God watches over even the faithfulness with which international treaties are kept, a sobering word to all nations of whatever time. One could apply it to our dealings in the past with North American Indians or to those with any modern state in the present.

**1:11–12 /** The oracle against **Edom** has exactly the same structure as that in 1:9–10. Further, there is a whole cluster of texts in the OT that condemn Edom for its vengeful pillage, extradition, and slaughter of the inhabitants of Jerusalem immediately after the fall of Jerusalem to the Babylonians in 587 BC (Obad. 10–14; Isa. 34:5–8; Jer. 49:7–22; Ezek. 35; Joel 3:19; Ps. 137:7). For these reasons, this oracle too has been termed a later addition to Amos.

But the enmity of Edom against Israel began already in the time of Moses (Num. 20:14–21), when Edom threatened to come

out against the Israelites with a **sword** (cf. Amos 1:11) if they
passed through Edomite territory. Though Saul and David
both subdued Edom (1 Sam. 14:47; 2 Sam. 8:12–14), Hadad the
Edomite continually harassed Israel in the days of Solomon
(1 Kgs. 11:14–25), and Edom was the constant enemy of Judah
following the accession of Jehoram (853 BC; 2 Kgs. 8:20–22). Since
Amos 1:11 states that Edom "kept his wrath forever" (RSV), a long
period of enmity seems to be indicated, and it is not necessary to
judge the oracle to be secondary.

Edom, whose forebear was Esau, was **brother** to Israel,
whose forebear was Jacob (Gen. 25:24–26), and Edom is judged
in this oracle because it has never honored the bond of brotherhood. God watches over not only the relations between nations,
but also those within the circle of the family. The God of Amos is
concerned with large affairs, but also with small. No area of
human life lies outside of God's rule.

**1:13–15** / **Ammon** lay on the eastern side of the Jordan
River, between Moab on the south and **Gilead** on the north, and
from the time of the Judges on, Ammon constantly tried to expand its territory into the fertile grazing land to its north (Judg.
11:4–5; 1 Sam. 11:1–11; 2 Sam. 10:1–14, et al.). We cannot be sure
just when the awful incidents mentioned in verse 13 occurred,
but we do know that the slaughter of **pregnant women** and their
unborn children was sometimes a feature of ancient warfare
(2 Kgs. 8:12; 15:16; Hos. 13:16). During World War II, the same
atrocity against the Jews was attributed to Hitler's S.S. troops. In
the savagery of warfare, ancient or modern, human life is very
cheap, and anything is possible. But the crime is especially odious
because it attacks the most dependent, the pregnant woman, and
the most helpless, the unborn child, for whom God throughout
the Bible demands the most merciful care.

Significantly, therefore, the judgment in this oracle is to be
worked by God alone, who will personally **set fire to the walls of
Rabbah,** the capital city on the upper course of the Jabbok, rather
than sending fire, as in the other oracles. Moreover, Yahweh will
fight against the Ammonites by means of a tempest and whirlwind; both of these are indications of God's personal appearance
or theophany as a warrior fighting foes (Ps. 83:15; Isa. 29:6; 66:15;
Jer. 23:19; Nah. 1:3). The result will be that Ammon's **king** and
leaders will be carried **into exile,** though it is not said where.

**2:1–3** / **Moab** was located to the east of the southern half of the Dead Sea, with Edom bordering it on the south. In these oracles against the foreign nations, the prophet has been moving from one compass point to another—first to the northeast (Aram), then to the southwest (Philistines), the northwest (Tyre) and finally to the southeast (Edom, Moab), with the oracles against Judah (2:4–5) and Israel (2:6–16) returning to the center. **Kerioth** is mentioned elsewhere in Jer. 48:24, and may have been a royal city of some sort, since its **fortresses,** which may also be translated "palaces," are mentioned. Line 13 of the Moabite stone tells us that Kerioth was the site of the sanctuary of the Moabite god Chemosh.

The crime of the Moabites was that they "burned to lime the bones of the king of Edom" (RSV). The NIV has correctly interpreted the meaning of the text by translating **as if to lime;** that is, to ashes as fine and white as powdered chalk. Death by fire was a form of capital punishment in Israel, reserved for particularly repulsive crimes (Gen. 38:24; Lev. 20:14; 21:9; Josh. 7:25), but the body of a royal person was not to be treated in such a manner (cf. 2 Kgs. 9:34).

The citizens of Moab, along with its political leaders, will therefore be annihilated in warfare, whose battle sounds the prophet vividly pictures in verse 2 (cf. Isa. 13:4; Hos. 10:14). The God of Israel controls the military movements of nations and orchestrates their defeats.

**2:4–5** / This is the only oracle in the series of prophecies against the nations that mentions only crimes against God and none against human beings. All but the most conservative commentators label it secondary, because of its Deuteronomic language and its reference to the fall of Jerusalem in 587 BC. Certainly the prophet could have foretold the fall of Jerusalem in the general terms given. But the **law** or *tôrâ* **of the Lord** refers to the Deuteronomic corpus of the seventh century BC, and the **decrees** or *ḥuqqîm* are its individual statutes. The oracle probably is a later addition to the Amos book.

The question, therefore, concerns the function of the oracle. Childs maintains that it shows that there is no difference in the divine plan for the northern and the southern kingdoms; both will be punished by God for their rebellions against divine will. But the oracle does more than that. In a series that lists crimes against human beings, it emphasizes that finally all sins are sins against the majesty of God. To sin against other human beings is to reject the rule of God as surely as following after other **gods** (or "lies," cf. NIV note) is to reject it. The foreign nations and Judah are equally guilty, as Israel will also be shown to be guilty in the following oracle of 2:6–16. All rebellions against God's will are offenses that try to make God less than God and Lord of all. That is the major point that Amos emphasizes.

**2:6–16** / Ending the series of oracles against the foreign nations is this oracle against **Israel** itself, and it should be understood as an integral part of this series. Israel has deserted its calling as the elect, covenant people of God. It has become like every other heathen nation. Therefore it will be judged as they will be.

In typical fashion, the NIV has interpreted the text of this oracle in its translation of it. The NIV has largely preserved the intended meaning, but the RSV translation is much closer to the original Hebrew, although even it omits some important conjunctions.

Especially to be deplored is the NIV's omission of connecting and contrasting conjunctions and exclamations that are found in the original Hebrew and that highlight the emphases of the original prophecy. For example, lines 7d, 8a, and 8c in the NIV should all begin with "and," as the prophet piles one sin upon another. Verse 9 should begin with "But I," emphasizing God's faithfulness in contrast to Israel's unfaithfulness. Lines 9d, 10a, and 11a should all also begin with "and," emphasizing one grace piled on top of another. And at the beginning of the announcement of punishment, in verse 13a, there is in the Hebrew the word "Behold!" followed by an emphatic pronoun, "I." All of these small words are exceedingly important for getting at Amos's meaning, and the NIV has tamed the original.

Israel is accused of oppression of the poor and **needy** by the rich and influential. This oppression has taken several forms. First, the wealthy have corrupted the courts in the gates of the cities, so that the poor, even though they are **righteous** or innocent of any crime, are judged guilty and sold into slavery to pay their debts, even if their debts are as insignificant as the cost of **a pair of sandals,** 2:6–7. It is as if the influential upper class is trampling "the head of the poor into the dust of the earth" (RSV) and turning "aside the way of the afflicted" (RSV) in the gate-courts.

Second, the upper class is taking **garments** pledged for surety in the place of debts and keeping them overnight (2:8), in violation of the law (Exod. 22:26–27; cf. Deut. 24:12–13). Similarly, they are using the **wine** that was given as a payment-in-kind for debts simply for their own debauched pleasure—and in the house of worship at that, 2:8.

Third, the wealthy are oppressing the poor by sexually abusing them, 2:7d–e. The reference to a **father and son** going into the same maiden probably refers to both of them forcing themselves upon a concubine slave-girl in their household.

All of these are profanations of Yahweh's holy name—line 7e is intended to refer to all of the sins that have been previously mentioned. And this is emphasized, then, by the reference to syncretistic worship in verse 8. The upper class are drinking wine **in the house of their god.** They are not worshiping the true God. Their actions have nothing to do with loyalty to the one Lord of heaven and earth.

In verses 9–11, Amos will therefore tell who God really is. God is all-powerful, as is shown by the Israelites' complete victory over the Amorites, the original inhabitants of Canaan. **Amorites** is a general term, used loosely of the peoples who were in the land given by God to the Israelites in the thirteenth century BC. Though they were a **tall** and **strong** people, like proverbial **cedars** and **oaks** (cf. Num. 13:28; Deut. 1:28; 9:2), God **destroyed** them, fruit and roots (cf. Isa. 37:31), or, as we would say, "root and branch."

The one true God is also merciful, delivering the helpless and oppressed, and so Israel was delivered out of slavery in **Egypt** before it had done one thing to deserve its redemption and before it even knew such a God, verse 10a. The real God is faithful, leading Israel through the terrors of the wilderness for **forty years,** verse 10a; despite its constant murmuring and rebellion, God provided manna to eat and water to drink, showed where Israel should pitch its tents, protected it from every kind of enemy, and finally brought it to a land flowing with milk and honey, verse 10b. The true God is also a guiding God, raising up **prophets** and **Nazirites** to teach the Israelites the way to walk in their life with their God and with one another, verse 11a–b.

To all of these facts of its history, Israel surely has to agree, verse 11c. The question is rhetorical. And yet, to all of the gracious history that has clearly revealed the character of the

Lord, Israel has said "no." And its "no" is symbolized by the fact that it has debauched the Nazirites and silenced the prophets, verse 12.

**Nazirites,** two of whom are named in the OT (Samuel, 1 Sam. 1:28; Samson, Judg. 13-15), were those set apart by special vows for service exclusively to the Lord. As a mark of separation, they vowed not to cut their hair; as a mark of self-denial, they abstained from **wine;** and as a mark of purity, they did not go near the dead (Num. 6:1-21). They thus bore witness to Israel's early life in the desert when it swore sole allegiance to the person and ways of its God at Sinai (cf. Hos. 2:15). Along the same line, the early, nonwriting prophets like Elijah and Elisha were called out by God to preserve for Israel the covenant faith and to demand that it live in accordance with that faith. But by leading the Nazirites to break their vow, by either force or subtle influence, and by silencing the **prophets,** usually by force (cf. 1 Kgs. 18:1-4), the Israelites have signaled that they will not be separated to the Lord as a holy nation and kingdom of priests (Exod. 19:4-6), but will instead walk in the ways of the heathen nations who do not know the one God.

The Lord, however, is true God, all-powerful, faithful, providing, and guiding, who delivers the oppressed and needy, including those so afflicted within his covenant people and those who will not let God's word be silenced by any human power, or God's name be profaned by any human sin. Israel cannot be permitted to diminish God, the one Lord of heaven and of earth.

Therefore, God has no choice but through his prophet Amos to manifest his lordship and to bring his judgment upon a people who, in complete ingratitude for God's grace, have totally abandoned their history, their calling, and their Lord. They will be bogged down, as a **cart** full of sheaves of **grain** bogs down in the soft earth and cannot go forward, verse 13. There will be no **escape** from the coming wrath: fast runners will be paralyzed; the powerful will become weak; soldiers will be defenseless, stripped **naked** of their armor and weapons, verses 14-16. Israel will meet its God, and Israel will be destroyed.

This oracle against the covenant people of the OT serves as a warning to Christians and all others who profane God's holy name by trying to make him less than God. These thoughts can perhaps be summarized by excerpts from a prayer of John Calvin, prayed as he lectured on the prophecies of Amos:

Grant, Almighty God, that since we see so grievous punishments formerly executed . . . we may be warned by their example, so as to abstain from all wickedness, and to continue in pure obedience to thy word; . . . grant that we may ever be attentive to that rule which has been prescribed to us by thee in the Law, as well as in the Prophets and in the gospel, so that we may constantly abide in thy precepts, and be wholly dependent on the words of thy mouth, and never turn aside either to the right hand or to the left, but glorify thy name, as thou hast commanded us, by offering to thee a true, sincere, and spiritual worship, through Christ our Lord. Amen. (Calvin, *Joel, Amos, Obadiah,* pp. 183–84)

## Additional Notes §3

**1:15** / **Her king will go into exile:** The Hb. text has been read, "And Milcom will go into exile," referring to Molech, the god of the Ammonites. The LXX reads "her kings," followed by "her priests" in place of "he." The Tg. and Vg. support the MT, which is properly translated in the NIV.

**2:1** / The Tg. reads, "Because he burned the bones . . . and used them for plaster on his house," inferring that the body of the human king was treated like basic building material (cf. Deut. 27:2, 4).

**2:3** / **Ruler:** The word for "king" is *šôpēṭ,* probably indicating a regent, but Moab had a monarchy from the earliest times (cf. Judg. 3:12–19), and the regent probably had the power of a king.

**2:6** / It has been suggested that the reference to sandals has to do with the sandal-transfer that sealed an agreement to buy land (cf. Ruth 4:7–8), but in context it is more probable that the low price of sandals is intended.

**2:7** / The word for **girl** (better, "maiden" RSV) is a neutral term, not used of a temple prostitute, so that the reference is not to the idolatrous fertility cult. Nor is it probable that the father is violating the son's love affair with a maiden whom the son is then obliged to marry (Exod. 22:16; cf. Lev. 18:15; contra Wolff, *Joel and Amos*).

**2:13** / The verb **crush, crushes** is unusual and has been interpreted by some to mean "break," or "break open," so that the ground breaks open under Israel as in an earthquake, echoing 1:1, 8:8, and 9:1. Stuart's rendering, "bog down," makes much more sense in the context (*Hosea–Jonah,* p. 319).

# §4 Summarizing Oracles (Amos 3:1–12)

By including both Israel and Judah in the series of oracles against the foreign nations in 1:3–2:16, Amos has shown that the people of God have joined with the rest of the nations in a common rebellion against the lordship of Yahweh, thereby profaning God's holy name. The prophet will then in 3:13–4:13 spell out the specific indictment against Israel. But before he does so, as Amos's book is now arranged, he must first include some summarizing statements, in 3:1–12, that lay the foundation for what follows. Verse 3:2 is an independent oracle, with an introduction in 3:1, that states the basic presupposition of the entire Amos corpus. Amos 3:3–8 is the prophet's justification for his ministry. Verses 9–11 summon foreign nations to act as jury for the court indictment that follows. Verse 12 foreshadows the awful fate that awaits the people of God.

**3:1–2** / The understanding of this brief oracle is essential for understanding and interpreting the theology of Amos's work. The speech of Yahweh in 3:2 is preceded by the call in 3:1 to hear the important message that is to follow (cf. 4:1; 5:1), and the summons to listen to the message is addressed not just to the northern kingdom of Israel, but to the whole people of God, to **the whole family I brought up out of Egypt.**

While it is probably true that only the forebears of the northern Rachel tribes were actually involved in the exodus from Egypt, throughout its history Israel considered that the deliverance wrought for a few tribes was a redemption won for them all (cf. Deut. 26:5–9). Every member of the old tribal league and every subsequent generation appropriated that event by hearing the story of it recounted in worship and by participating in that story through faith (cf. Exod. 12:43–49; 13:3–10; Deut. 16:1–8, et al.). Just as the redemption effected by Christ is appropriated by the faithful Christian when the story of the cross and resurrection is recounted during worship, so too the redemption wrought by the exodus was in the setting of worship appropriated by all of Israel as its own story. Thus, Amos addresses not just the northern kingdom of Israel in 3:1, but the whole of Israel, the whole people of God who were elected in the redemption wrought at the exodus. And the repetition of **against** in 3:1 emphasizes that the message to follow is one of judgment.

God speaks in the first person in 3:2, in a direct address to this elected nation. The prophet is merely a mouthpiece. No mediator stands between the Lord and the elect, no intermediary softens God's words or introduces mitigating circumstances. These are Yahweh's own words against his chosen people.

The words point out that from among all the families or nations on the face of the earth, God singled out Israel to be his *sᵉgullâ,* or "peculiar treasure" (Exod. 19:5 KJV), as was evidenced by its deliverance from slavery in Egypt. The exodus was the election of Israel, the event by which God adopted Israel as a son (cf. Hos. 11:1; Exod. 4:22–23; Jer. 3:19; 31:20). Such is the meaning of the verb "known" in verse 2 (RSV) which the NIV translates **chosen** (cf. Hos. 13:5; Deut. 32:10). That is the same thought that is implied in the introduction to the Decalogue in Exodus 20:2.

Just as in the Decalogue, however, that election meant obligation for Israel. The implication of Exodus 20:2, 3, and 7 is *"Therefore* you shall have no other gods before me," and *"Therefore* you shall not take the name of the LORD your God in vain," just as in Exodus 19:5–6 the presupposition is that Israel can be to God "a kingdom of priests and a holy nation" *if* it will obey God's voice and keep God's covenant. Israel was elected not to privilege but to responsibility, namely, to the responsibility of being set apart (as "holy") in order to mediate the knowledge of God to the rest of the world (as a "kingdom of priests"). But Israel has not fulfilled its responsibility; it has not met its obligation as God's chosen people; it has not worshiped God alone and honored God's name. Those are Israel's **sins** in 3:2. It has not rendered to God the response God's election requires of it.

When interpreting the specific sins that Amos recounts in the following oracles, the reader should always keep this basic failure of Israel in mind. The book of Amos can be, and often has been, interpreted by preachers and teachers much too narrowly, as if it is concerned only with social justice and proper worship. The prophet has much more in mind. He is concerned more broadly with election and with the obligation that election places on the people of God.

That God will judge us for failing to meet the responsibilities of our election should be a sobering thought for the Christian Church, for like Israel, we too have been chosen by God to be a kingdom of priests and a holy nation, that we may declare God's wonderful deeds to all the world (1 Pet. 2:9–10). Like Israel, we too in our redemption have been adopted as sons and daughters of God, and have been allowed to call God "Father" (Gal. 4:4–7). Because of the work of Jesus Christ, which has grafted us into the root of Israel (Rom. 11:17–24), made us citizens of Israel's commonwealth (Eph. 2:11–22), and allowed us to share the name of "the Israel of God" (Gal. 6:16), we Christians can now claim to be among the elect (cf. Rom. 8:33; 2 Tim. 2:10; 2 Pet. 1:10). But as our Lord tells us in Luke 12:48, "From everyone who has been given much, much will be demanded; and from the one who has been entrusted with much, much more will be asked."

Election carries with it responsibility. We have been chosen by God not merely to enjoy the privilege of God's company in the Spirit, although there is no greater gift that could have been given us. We have been elected not merely to know the joy of forgiveness and the certainty of eternal life, although those gifts make it possible for us to go on day by day. We have been chosen rather to serve God's purpose of bringing salvation to his beloved world (John 3:16). We have been elected to make disciples of all nations, teaching them to observe what Christ has commanded us (Matt. 28:20). We have been singled out to be God's witnesses (Acts 1:8), glorifying God's holy name, until every knee bows and every tongue confesses that Jesus Christ is Lord (Phil. 2:10–11) and the knowledge of the Lord covers the earth as the waters cover the sea (Isa. 11:9). When we entered into the Christian Church by baptism and accepted that covenant responsibility at the Lord's table, we promised to do such things. God's word to us from Amos now is that God expects us to fulfill our promise, and that judgment awaits us if we prove unresponsive and unfaithful in our use of the marvelous gifts that have been given us. The message is little different from that found on the lips of our Lord (cf. Matt. 24:45–51; 25:14–30).

**3:3–8** / Amos met opposition in his ministry, as all of the prophets met opposition (Isa. 28:9–22; 50:4–9; Jer. 20; Ezek. 2:7; Hos. 9:8; cf. Luke 6:22–23; 2 Cor. 11:24–27). That is not only evident in 7:10–13, but it is also implied in 2:12, 6:3, and 9:10. Amos's message was not comforting for the populace of the northern kingdom to hear, especially when they were sure that their lavish cultic practices earned them Yahweh's favor (Amos 4:4–5).

As the Amos book is now arranged, this defense of his legitimacy as a prophet (3:3–8) is therefore placed before the oracles beginning in 3:13, which spell out Israel's sin, just as so many of the prophetic books place the account of the prophet's call toward their beginning (Jer. 1; Isa. 6; Ezek. 1–3). It is probable, however, that the arrangement stems from an editor of the book, and that Amos had already begun to announce his oracles of doom, which are preserved for us after 3:12. Hearing Amos's announcements, his listeners immediately challenged his authority to speak on behalf of God.

Amos's answer to that challenge is a well-reasoned argument in the form of a didactic disputation that traps his hearers in their own logic. Amos asks seven rhetorical questions in verses 3–6, and the obvious answer to all of them is "no." Effect always follows cause. Persons do not **walk together** unless they have **agreed** to meet; lions do not **roar** unless they have captured some **prey;** birds do not **fall** to the ground for no reason; trumpets do not sound alarms without causing fear. Indeed, disasters come not from happenstance, but from God's governance of the world, verse 6 (cf. Isa. 9:13; Hab. 1:5–12). The prophet's audience must agree with all of that. Amos therefore sets out one more cause: "The Lord GOD has spoken," (RSV) and the effect must therefore follow: **who can but prophesy?** (v. 8).

Amos is not speaking out of his own heart and mind and conscience. He probably did not even want to be a prophet. But the Lord simply "took" him and told him "Go, prophesy" (7:15). He was compelled to obey, as his predecessors and successors in the prophetic office were equally compelled (cf. Exod. 4:11–17; Jer. 1:6–7; 20:9; Ezek. 2:8–3:3). So there is no escape for the Israelites from the prophet's awful words. The words are from God, and Amos is simply a messenger. Israel's "end" will come (8:2, RSV), whether the people like the message and its deliverer or not.

Several theological points are noteworthy in this dispute saying. First, in the parallelism of verse 8, Yahweh is compared to a **lion** who is roaring over some **prey** that it has caught. Lions do not roar while stalking, but only after capturing their meat, and so in Amos's thought, Israel is as good as dead. It is the same daring figure that Amos employed in 1:2; it further illumines the meaning of that verse, and it is picked up again in 3:12. Hosea then employs the figure in 5:14 (cf. Hos. 6:1) and 13:7–8 (cf. Isa.

31:4). For a sheepbreeder like Amos, lions were devastating enemies, and it is jarring to use such a simile in connection with God. But the figure is a healthy corrective for any society that believes that God is only a sweet lover or tender mother or succoring friend who overlooks every wrong. The God of the Bible is a terrifying foe of those who would make him less than Lord over every life and every thing.

Second, God's absolute sovereignty over history is affirmed in verse 6. While the Bible does recognize that some events take place by chance (Gen. 38:1; Ruth 2:3; 1 Sam. 6:9; 2 Sam. 1:6; 20:1; Jer. 41:3), it finally refuses to divorce any happening from the governance of a God who uses all events, good and evil, to work out his divine purpose (Isa. 45:7; Phil. 1:12; 2:13; Rom. 8:28–30). It therefore behooves believers to ask, when evil befalls an individual, city, society, or nation, if the Lord has done it, and to inquire just what the Lord intends by such an event. Amos 4:6–11 understands some historical and natural catastrophes to be God's means of calling to repentance (cf. Isa. 9:13). And that too is a healthy corrective for a secular age that believes God to be totally absent from the world.

Third, verse 7 is a profound summary of the nature of revelation in the Scripture. Throughout the Bible, God is revealed by means of history—by the deliverance of Israel from Egypt, for example, or by the resurrection of God's Son. But in order for those events to be understood and truly revelatory of his nature, God also furnishes **prophets** to interpret the events. Moses interprets the exodus as an event wrought solely by God; the NT writers, playing the role of prophets, interpret the resurrection as God's defeat of death. The event in itself is not sufficient to be revelatory; the prophetic word must interpret the event. To give another example, the Babylonian exile of Judah in 587 BC would have been understood as nothing more than a crushing military defeat had Jeremiah and Ezekiel not spoken the words that revealed that the exile was God's punishment of Judah for her sins. In order to be known, God not only acts in history; God also sends prophets to interpret that history. This does *not* mean that God is not otherwise active in human history and in nature (so too Calvin). This verse does not imply God's freedom is limited (contra many interpreters). Rather, verse 7 points to the means God uses in self-revelation.

Verse 7 also underscores God's incredible mercy toward his chosen people. Israel is not dealt with in the same way as other nations; God sends them prophets to tell them what will happen, just as God has sent the Christian church the prophetic writings of the NT to tell us what the outcome of all history will be. And those prophets and prophetic writings warn Israel and us ahead of time to repent before catastrophe strikes and before our fate is forever sealed (cf. Mal. 4:5; Matt. 11:14; Mark 9:11–13; Luke 1:17). God does not desire the death of the wicked; God desires that we repent and live (Ezek. 18:32).

**3:9–11** / Few oracles in the book of Amos are more relevant to our modern society than is this one. The general charge against the Israelites here, in verse 10, is that **they do not know how to do right.** That is, nothing is straight, upright, honest, just, in the northern kingdom; nothing accords with a God-given moral standard. Indeed, the people have no comprehension of a moral standard binding together their society, no consensus about what is right and what is wrong. If ever there were a picture of modern American society, that is it.

Amos spells out two general evidences of such amorality and immorality and attributes them both to Israel's upper classes, who "store up" (RSV; **hoard,** NIV) "violence" and "robbery" (RSV), verse 10. The NIV has missed the meaning of "violence" and "robbery" by translating them **plunder** and **loot.** "Violence" *(ḥāmās)* refers to mortal attack, to assault against life and limb (Job 19:7; Hab. 1:2). "Robbery" *(šōd)* refers to the destruction and plunder of material goods (Hos. 7:1; Isa. 13:6; 16:4). Thus, the wealthy urban classes are guilty of assaults against both persons and their property. These constitute the great **unrest** (better translated "terror") and **oppression** mentioned in verse 9. No one is secure from the violence perpetrated by those in power.

In a summons deliberately intended to be an insult against Israel's leading citizens, the prophet therefore calls for unnamed messengers to travel to the Philistine city of **Ashdod** and to **Egypt** in order to call those pagan peoples to assemble themselves on the **mountains** that surround the city of **Samaria.** From there the pagan nations will view with horror what is happening in the society of the chosen people—things far worse than they know in their own cultures.

**Ashdod** and **Egypt** are probably intended to serve a judicial function here as the jury that hears God's evidence against Israel. There is no formal evidence of a court case in this oracle, and some have termed it a messenger speech, others a prophetic judgment speech. But certainly the judicial overtones are present, mixed though the oracle appears in its genre.

The sentence that Yahweh the judge gives in verse 11 is a general one that will be made more specific in the oracles that follow. An unnamed foe will surround Israel, so that there is no escape. Its defenses will be destroyed, and its strongholds will be plundered.

The word for **strongholds** (*ʾarmᵉnôt*) can be variously translated as "palaces" or "fortresses," but apparently here refers to multistoried, multichambered houses of the wealthy, which were used both as residences and as places of defense, sometimes being built right into the fortifications of the city (cf. Ps. 48:13; 122:7). The word forms an inclusio for this oracle, verses 9 and 11. The wealthy heathen are summoned from their strongholds to hear what will happen to Israel's strongholds. There is no defense against Israel's God, and finally the unnamed foe that will surround the capital city of Samaria and destroy it will be the Lord of hosts.

**3:12** / This final summarizing prose oracle uses a vivid image taken from the life of a **shepherd** (cf. 1 Sam. 17:34–35) to portray the northern kingdom's ultimate fate. After their enemy, God the **lion** (3:4, 8; 1:2), attacks them, there will be nothing left of them but fragments, like the two bloodied legs and shredded ear of a sheep that has been killed and eaten by a lion.

Some commentators have maintained that Amos here holds out the hope of a small remnant. Given Israelite legal custom, that cannot be the case. According to Exodus 22:10–13, if someone was entrusted with the care of an animal which was then torn by a beast, in order to prove the animal had fallen victim to a predator, fragments of the animal had to be produced (cf. Gen. 31:39). The fragments left of Israel here are proof that it has been totally lost.

The oracle is directed against the luxury-loving upper class in Samaria, who loll about on their comfortable couches while the average Israelite sits and sleeps on the floor, sometimes in prison. Yet here, and in what follows, the poor are not rescued from the fate that awaits the rich: all in Israel will fall prey to Yahweh's destruction; the whole nation is at an end. We either live together as a community of righteousness or we all perish together, whether from an invading enemy, nuclear holocaust, or the anarchic collapse of an immoral society. God works judgment and no one is immune; we all are responsible for one another, whether we be rich or poor or middle class.

---

## Additional Notes §4

---

**3:5** / The meaning of **snare** is uncertain. Some translate "wooden missile," such as a boomerang, that strikes the bird, which then falls into a net. Others read "throw-net." Most agree that **trap** refers to a net that springs up from the ground.

**3:6** / One LXX minuscule (534) correctly reads "battle" for **city**.

**3:7** / On the basis of its form and vocabulary, many commentators hold that this verse is a later addition from the Deuteronomic editors. However, it contributes greatly in its present setting, and thus the argument is not very significant to our interpretation.

**3:9** / The LXX reads "Assyria" instead of **Ashdod**, but Amos nowhere else mentions Assyria, and the MT is supported by the Tg. and Vg.

The LXX presupposes that the MT reads "Mount Samaria" instead of the "mountains of Samaria." Samaria was located on a plain, with mountains some miles distance surrounding it, but there is no compelling reason to change the MT text.

**3:12** / The final phrase of this oracle is unintelligible in the Hb. and has been variously emended and interpreted. The RSV reading represents one widely-held view: "with the corner of a couch and part of a bed"; the NIV reading represents the other. Probably the NIV is nearest the original intention of the garbled text.

Some commentators have attached this verse to the oracle in 3:9–11, but the messenger formula in v. 12a indicates the beginning of a new oracle. Others have maintained that v. 12d–f begins the oracle in 3:13–15, but Hb. oracles do not normally begin with participles. Verse 12 should thus be seen as an independent unit. The oracle is an expanded *māšāl*, a wisdom saying, which illumines one thing by comparing it with another. The form is often found in the book of Proverbs (Prov. 25:25–26; 26:7–11 etc.).

## §5 The Indictment and Punishment of Israel Spelled Out (Amos 3:13–4:13)

Introductory and summarizing material has been concluded. We now enter into the principal collection of Amos's oracles, encompassing 3:13–6:14, interrupted by the visions and encounter with Amaziah in chapter 7 and 8:1–3, and resuming with 8:4–9:6. This section of 3:13–4:13 forms the first large unit in the collection.

**3:13–15** / Clearly, the setting in this oracle is a court of law. Unnamed witnesses are summoned to hear the court proceedings and to **testify against the house of Jacob,** verse 13. We do not know who these witnesses are intended to be. This oracle is independent of both 3:12 and 3:9–11, and the witnesses are not those of 3:9. Probably the summons is a rhetorical device intended to gain the attention of the prophet's audience.

We can say, however, that verse 13 actually forms the introduction to the whole unit of 3:13–4:13, since 3:14–15 details some of the punishment that is going to come upon Israel, as does 4:2–3 and as did 3:12. The recounting of Israel's sins, which the witnesses are to hear, comes only in 4:1, 4–11. Thus, at one time, God both presents the case against Israel and tells what will be done to them, and the prophet then issues the final warning in 4:12: "Prepare to meet your God, O Israel." The final judgment of the court will then be given in the following chapters.

The testimony that the witnesses will hear is **against the house of Jacob,** 3:13. By using the name of the northern patriarch (cf. 6:8, 7:2, 5; 8:7) as well as those of the northern Isaac (7:9, 16) and Joseph (5:15), Amos is once more emphasizing the tradition of the election, which took place when the forebears of the northern tribes were delivered out of Egypt, and which finally was appropriated by all of the covenant people. Once more Amos has the whole of Israel, the elected people, in view (cf. 3:1).

Yet what God attacks in the first-person speech in verses 14–15 are also specific sins in the northern kingdom, namely, false worship and injustice. Northern Israel relies on a lavish cult to keep the favor of God (cf. 4:4–5), but the center of that cult, the **altars** of sacrifice at **Bethel**, will be desecrated by having their horns hewn off.

The **horns** of altars were protrusions up from their four corners and were perhaps symbols of special holiness and strength, but they also were associated with refuge for criminals (1 Kgs. 1:50; 2:28, but see Exod. 21:14), with blood sacrifice (Lev. 4:7), and much later, even with revelation (Rev. 9:13). None of those benefits will be left to Israel. The horns of its altars will be cut off, and that will take place at "Beth-el," "the house of God." That false house will fall.

In the same manner, the luxurious houses of royalty and of the wealthy will be demolished, verse 15. In Jeroboam II's time the upper classes have become so rich that they can have two houses, one warm for the **winter**, one cool for the **summer** (cf. the two houses of Ahab, 1 Kgs. 21:1, 18), and perhaps both containing furniture luxuriously adorned with engraved ivory plates. But those houses too will fall, smitten by God. The verb in verse 15a (**tear down**, NIV; "smite," RSV) denotes wrecking that leaves nothing but broken pieces. Thus will be ended the "many houses" (**mansions**, NIV)—the houses of the rich, the house of worship, the house of Jacob. This will all take place **on the day**, verse 14, that is, on the day of the Lord (cf. 5:18–20), when God comes to put down all enemies and to establish rule over all the earth.

**4:1–3** / Throughout history women have served as "decorations" for the rich and powerful. In Western society, the more beautiful the woman, the more status is lent to her male escort or husband. The more lavishly the woman is outfitted and pampered, the more evidence there is of her man's wealth and power. So it was too in Amos's time apparently, and indeed, in the following century (cf. Isa. 3:16–26). The **women** in this oracle in Amos are symbols of the godless pride and dissoluteness of Israel's upper classes, and it may be for this reason that the imperative in 4:1 is in the masculine and that masculine pronouns occur in the following lines, even though the oracle seems addressed to females. The women are symbols of a deeper corruption that has led to the oppression of the **poor** and the crushing of the **needy**.

The indolent wives are evidences of the sins corrupting both male and female.

Amos therefore attacks the women-symbols and what they represent, and declares that their end has come. He does so by turning them into nonhuman objects. They are not beautiful; they are fat **cows,** like those of **Bashan,** which was noted for its lush pastures in Transjordan (Ezek. 39:18; Deut. 32:14; Jer. 50:19, etc.). And they will not die natural deaths of old age and be properly buried. They will die violently before the onslaught of an enemy who will breach their walls. Their corpses will be dragged away, one after another, **with hooks,** like so much meat, to be cast forth toward Mt. Hermon (see additional note), which was situated in the Bashan range, verses 2–3. As in 3:9–11, the enemy who will do the women to death is not named, but this whole section of 3:13–4:13 is framed by the name of Yahweh Elohim, the God of hosts (3:13; 4:13), and it drives toward the proclamation of that name.

Further, the truth of the message proclaimed in this oracle is attested by the oath of Yahweh Elohim, who **has sworn by his holiness,** verse 2. Nothing stronger could be said (cf. 6:8). God's holiness is his divinity, his absolute otherness from everything that he has made, and so this oath is immutable (cf. Ps. 89:33–35; Num. 23:19; Heb. 6:13; 7:20–22). **The time will surely come**—that is, the final days, the day of the Lord—when the pampered and indolent women of Israel will be nothing but dead carcasses and when all that they represent will therefore be done away. Israel, by its injustice toward the poor and needy, has profaned God's holy name, violating the third commandment of the Decalogue. They cannot continue such profanation and live.

**4:4–13** / Some commentators have held that Amos 4:4–5 forms an oracle that is independent of 4:6–13, and that "But even I" at the beginning of verse 6 (omitted in the NIV) has been added to join the later material of verses 6–13 to the original Amos oracle of 4:4–5. Such a view completely misses the theology of this passage, which I would attribute in its entirety to the prophet.

The point is that the Israelites believe that their lavish cultic ritual allows them to meet and enter into communion with God, enjoying God's favor and fellowship. Amos contradicts that belief by labeling their worship "rebellion" *(pešaꜥ)* against God and by recounting all of those times in Israel's past when the Lord has tried to get Israel to return in spirit and in truth, but when

Israel has refused to do so. The result is that in the coming days, God will indeed come to meet Israel, but in judgment. And the concluding hymn in verse 13 says just who that God will be. The whole pericope is a carefully formulated theological statement about true communion with the one true God.

It is significant in this connection that all of the ritual practices mentioned in verses 4–5 may be used as peace offerings or as communion meals. **Sacrifices** in verse 4c may be a general term for the offering of animals, but probably here refers to the peace offering (cf. Lev. 3; 7:11–13), as do **thank offering** and **leavened bread** in 5a (Lev. 7:11–15). Portions of all of these could be eaten in communion meals with the deity (Lev. 22:29–30). Similarly, **tithes** (v. 4d) were a tenth of the annual yield of the land, which were taken to the sanctuary, and there eaten in a festive meal "before the LORD" (Deut. 14:22–29). **Freewill offerings** (v. 5b) were voluntary sacrifices that were specialized uses of the peace offerings (Lev. 7:16–17; 22:18–23). The Israelites, through their sacrifices, believe themselves to be at peace with their God.

Amos turns that belief upside down. When Israel offers its sacrifices and tithes, it rebels against its God—the verb *pāšaʿ* ("to rebel"; NIV: **sin**) is a political term, denoting subversion of God's rule. The force of these verses is comparable to having some one say to a contemporary Christian congregation, "Come to worship—and sin!" Israel's worship is nothing but an empty show (v. 5b–d), a way of gaining status in the wealthy community, the individual's means of displaying the means to sacrifice grandly and often.

Israelite worship was carried on by means of pilgrimages to the shrines such as **Bethel** and **Gilgal. Sacrifices** were offered on the morning of the day of arrival; **tithes** were given on the third day, before departure. The NIV has imposed the later Deuteronomic law of Deuteronomy 14:28 on verse 4d by reading **every three years** instead of "three days," as the MT has it. The Hebrew of verse 4c–d does not say that the sacrifices and tithes were given "every" morning and "every" three days, but that may be the intended meaning—that the Israelite worshipers were repetitious in their offerings in order to show off their wealth. We encounter the same sort of pride in the modern church when a rich person makes a show of a lavish gift.

Both Bethel and Gilgal were important shrines in the northern kingdom. **Bethel,** which lay to the south of the capital city, was taken over from the Canaanites already in the time of

Jacob (Gen. 28:10–22). It was a sanctuary in the time of the Judges (Judg. 20:18), and it was made one of the two chief cultic centers of the northern kingdom in the time of Jeroboam I (1 Kgs. 12:29), becoming then "the king's sanctuary and the temple of the kingdom" by the eighth century BC (Amos 7:13). **Gilgal,** lying on the eastern border of Jericho (Josh. 4:19) was connected with Israel's entry into the promised land (Josh. chs. 4–5), was the site of Saul's anointing as king, according to one of the traditions (1 Sam. 11:14–15), and was a place of pilgrimage and sacrifice in the eighth century BC (Amos 5:5; Hos. 12:11). Israel had long worshiped at these sites, but its upper classes loved themselves and not the Lord. They practiced their piety before others in order "to be seen by them" (Matt. 6:1, 2–6), not in order to commune with or give glory to God.

The following verses of 6–11 testify to the long-suffering patience of God with the northern kingdom. God has repeatedly tried to discipline them by sending tribulation upon them—famine (vv. 6–9), pestilence (RSV; v. 10), and **sword** (v. 10): the categories are traditional curses for the violation of the covenant with God (cf. Lev. 26; Deut. 28); that is, for failing to live up to the responsibilities mandated by one's election to be God's covenant people. Verse 11 then forms a summary statement of such divine cursing: the destruction of **Sodom and Gomorrah** (Gen. 19:24–29) became the archetype in biblical tradition of God's judgment on sin (cf. Deut. 29:23; Isa. 1:9; 13:19; Jer. 23:14; 49:18; Lam. 4:6; Matt. 10:15; 11:23–24; Rom. 9:29; 2 Pet. 2:6, etc.). Yet, despite God's frequent discipline of them, and despite the fact that God always then plucked them out of disaster, **like a burning stick snatched from the fire** (v. 11c), Israel did not absorb the lesson that its life belonged totally to God, who could both destroy and rescue it, just as we modern, scientific Americans do not absorb that lesson when some disaster strikes us. So Israel pursued its own course and did not turn to submit itself to God's sovereign rule.

As a result, though Israel has not returned to God, God will return to it, verse 12a—such is the meaning of this line. The Hebrew reads, "Therefore, thus I will do to you, O Israel," and many commentators have thought that the mention of some specific punishment has dropped out of the text. But "thus" refers to "return" in the preceding line. God will "return"; God will never again "pass by" (7:8; 8:2 RSV). In total judgment God will meet this rebellious folk, and of that meeting, Amos now warns them. **Prepare** in verse 12c is often used of preparation for cultic worship (cf.

Exod. 19:11, 15; 34:2), and the context of a "meeting" in worship is maintained. But this "meeting" will mean death for the elected, covenant people of God; Israel should be prepared to die!

Who is the God who comes to meet Israel? Verse 13 breaks into hymnic celebration of the name of Yahweh Elohim Sebaoth, the Lord God of all the hosts of heaven and earth. (The NIV incorrectly translates **LORD God Almighty**). This God has done many things: shaped the mountains, like a potter working with clay; given to humankind and to all creatures their breath or spirit of life (reading "spirit" instead of **wind** for *rûaḥ* in verse 13b; cf. Job 10:12; Ps. 104:30); revealed the plan for the world, so that all are without excuse. Ominously, this God can bring **darkness** over the face of the earth (cf. 5:18, 20) and tread (in the sense of "conquer," cf. Judg. 20:43; Ps. 91:13; Isa. 66:3, etc.) all its worship sites (or **high places**). This is the God who creates and rules all nature and nations (cf. 1:3–2:6), and Israel has refused to worship and obey him, and thereby to honor his name. God therefore comes to meet and judge Israel.

---

### Additional Notes §5

**3:14** / Later tradition considered this prophecy fulfilled when the altar at Bethel was destroyed in the time of King Josiah of Judah (2 Kgs. 23:15, 17).

**3:15** / It was the interesting custom in some of the cities of America's Old South that the more prominent had winter and summer houses, sometimes located side by side. They differed in their furnishings, the winter houses containing heavy drapes and rugs and furniture, the summer houses much lighter decorations. Or if only one house was owned, all of the furnishings were changed to be appropriate to the season. The latter custom could still be found in Richmond, Virginia, in 1970.

**4:2** / The word for **hooks** is not found elsewhere with this meaning, and some have read "ropes" and then "harpoon" or "cattle prod" for "fishhooks," portraying the women being led into exile. But the final verb, "cast out," is used of corpses (cf. 8:3; 1 Kgs. 13:24–25; Jer. 14:16!), and the portrayal is much more gruesome than that of exile.

**4:3** / The MT reads **Harmon**, which is unknown. The LXX has "Mt. Rimmon." Most emend to read "Hermon." The women's bodies join those of any other cattle that die in Bashan.

## §6 *The Sentence of Death (Amos 5:1–17)*

This section is only arbitrarily broken into subunits for the purpose of convenience. Actually it constitutes a whole in the form of a funerary lament, and it begins (v. 2) and ends (vv. 16–17) with wailing over the dead. In addition, the proclamation of the divine name begins (v. 3, Adonai Yahweh), divides (v. 8, Yahweh), and ends (v. 16, Yahweh Elohim Sebaoth Adonai) the lament. But the theme is the same throughout: Israel's death, brought on by its failure to honor Yahweh by true worship and just dealings in its courts of law. Verses 2–3 and 11 presage the result of verse 17. Verses 4 and 6 anticipate verses 14–15. Verse 7 sounds the theme of verses 10–13 and 15. Verses 16–17 form the final sentence of death handed down by the divine judge because of all the sins mentioned in verses 4–12, 15. The whole hangs together as one unit. We shall divide it only to make it easier to analyze.

**5:1–9** / The pronoun **I** is a separate Hebrew word in verse 1, emphasizing the fact that it is Yahweh who speaks in verses 1–2, just as at the end of the unit, in verses 16–17. Chillingly, what the divine voice does is to utter a funeral **lament** over the people. Israel is dead. Though it yet lives in Amos's day, its death is a foregone conclusion and already mourned. An unnamed enemy (cf. 2:14–16; 3:11) will invade its land, totally defeat its armed troops, verse 3, and leave its dead on the ground, with no restoration possible, verse 2. Israel is a **virgin,** its life yet incomplete in the land God has given it (cf. Judg. 11:39–40), but it shall die unfulfilled and forsaken.

Israel's military units were divided into groups of thousands and hundreds (cf. 1 Sam. 22:7; 2 Sam. 18:1), but having some left after the battle, verse 3, does not indicate the existence of a remnant. An army so diminished was totally defeated. Israel was as good as dead.

The fact that in the prophecies of Amos Yahweh is the one who mourns over his fallen people is evidence of his love for them. As is so often the case in the holy history, God's reaction to the people's sin is not wrath but grief (cf. Gen. 6:6), and judgment on them is carried out in the sorrow of a disappointed lover (cf. Matt. 23:37–38 and parallel). We shall encounter the same tenderness in 7:1–6, and it is a good note to keep in mind when interpreting Amos's judgment oracles.

Verses 4–5 continue the divine speech and point out to Israel what it should have done. Scholars have interpreted these verses in a variety of ways—as irony, as spoken only to the under classes; as offers of hope for the future—but their meaning is similar to that set forth in 4:4–13: Israel's worship at its cult sites has been totally false, without ever involving any true communion with God, and those sites of worship will be destroyed. So what Israel should have done was to seek that true communion. Israel should have sought Yahweh, who alone could give it life. To **seek** the Lord normally had the meaning of going to the sanctuary where saving blessing could be found (cf. Ps. 24:6; 27:8; 105:4). Yahweh is now substituted for the cultic site.

**Beersheba** is added to the two cult sites of **Bethel** and **Gilgal** previously mentioned (4:4). It was located in the far south of Judah and was originally connected with the religion of the patriarchs (Gen. 21:31; 26:23–25; 46:1). But it was also a place of pilgrimage for those in the northern kingdom (cf. 8:14; 2 Kgs. 23:8). Amos's condemnation of Israel's worship at its sanctuaries is all-encompassing.

To reinforce what has been said in the first-person Yahweh speech of verses 4–5, Amos reminds his listeners, in verse 6, of what they have always heard from Israelite sacred tradition—that Yahweh alone is the source of Israel's life, but that he is also a consuming **fire** (cf. Deut. 4:24; 9:3; Isa. 33:14; 2 Thess. 1:7; Heb. 10:27, 31; 12:29) who will brook no disregard of his holy will or of the honor due his name.

Then in verse 7, Amos states why Bethel will be destroyed: because its inhabitants have turned justice to "wormwood" (RSV; NIV reads **bitterness**) and cast righteousness to the ground, thereby making of their worship a sham. The participle beginning verse 7 connects it with **Bethel** in verse 6, as in the RSV. The lines in the Hebrew order read, ". . . Bethel, who turns to wormwood justice."

Wormwood was a bush that grew in the southern part of Judah and in Transjordan. Though not poisonous, its pulp had a bitter taste, and Amos is drawing on a medicinal metaphor.

**Justice,** by which Amos means the legal restoration of those wronged and oppressed, was to be the medicine that healed Israel's society (cf. Exod. 23:6–8; Lev. 19:15; Deut. 1:17; 10:17; 16:19–20). Instead, it has been turned into a foul-tasting draught. **Righteousness** throughout the Old Testament (and the New) is a relational term, standing for the fulfillment of the demands of a relationship. Israel was always required by God to show mercy to the poor and helpless (Exod. 22:21–27; 23:9; Lev. 19:33–34; Deut. 24:19–22)—that was the requirement of its relationship with them. Instead, its upper classes have ignored their obligation, as if throwing it to the ground. Because verses 6–7 charge Bethel specifically with such sins, Amos probably preached this oracle in that city, and it is no wonder therefore that he comes into conflict with Amaziah, the king's priest at that worship site (7:10–17).

The inhabitants of Bethel can turn justice into wormwood, but they are dealing with a God who can turn **blackness into dawn** or **day into night,** verse 8. Indeed, this is the God who created in the beginning by controlling the chaotic **waters of the sea** (cf. Gen. 1; Ps. 104:5–9). As in the hymn of 4:13, God's lordship over all creation is celebrated and the sacred name is proclaimed. In verse 8, Yahweh **is his name** specifies with whom Israel has to deal and that will lead in verse 16 to the proclamation of God's lordship over all the hosts of heaven and earth. Israel will be met by a God who can destroy it, verse 9. It has missed its opportunity to seek God and live, forfeited its calling to serve God and prosper.

**5:10–13** / Many commentators have maintained that the text of Amos 5:1–17 has many later additions. Verses 6, 8–9 should be omitted as secondary, they say, as should verse 13 and the connecting **For** at the beginning of verse 12. Separate oracles are then left in verses 7, 10–11, 12–13, 16–17, and 14–15. Others make 5:7, 10–12, 16–17 one oracle, while some rearrange the text to form an oracle consisting of 5:12, 11a, 16b, 17. We have, instead, taken 5:1–17 as a unit, dividing it into subunits only for the purpose of convenience of exposition. Finally the task of the interpreter is to try to make sense of the canonical text as it now stands.

In this section, in which the prophet himself speaks, the subject is the fate of the righteous in Israel, and the thought of the verses might be summarized by a quotation from Ps. 11:3 RSV: "If the foundations are destroyed, what can the righteous do?" For Amos, the foundation of justice in Israelite society was supposed to be in its courts of law. Such courts were made up of the male elders of each city, who met together to hear the case presented by a plaintiff against one accused, along with their witnesses. The court met in the city gate, which was a fortified building set into the wall of the city, and which had rooms or recesses on its interior side in which benches were set (cf. Deut. 21:19; 25:7; Ruth 4:11). All elders could speak in the court (cf. Job 32:12), and they were expected to uphold the innocent and decree punishment for the guilty (cf. Prov. 24:23–25). They were the final recourse given to the poor and helpless in Israelite society.

These verses tell us, however, how corrupt the courts had become. There were elders still left in the northern kingdom who spoke the **truth** and sought justice for the innocent, verse 10, but they were drowned out by a sea of dissenting voices that catered to the rich and accepted **bribes** for their deceit, verse 12. Indeed, the just elders became objects of such hatred, scorn, and social ostracism in their society that they were forced into unwilling silence, not out of cowardice but out of the inability to make their voices heard above the roar of the avaricious, verse 13: That thought brackets this section, in verses 10 and 12. The picture reminds one of those shouted down and not allowed to speak on "politically correct" university campuses in the United States, or of those whose influence is rejected by some group because they do not toe the party line (cf. Isa. 29:21). Or most tellingly, the picture reminds one of the mob that shouted, "Crucify him," when innocence stood before them (Mark 15:13–14).

As an example of the **poor** being trampled in the courts by the powerful and corrupt, Amos mentions the exacting of fines of **grain** from poor farmers, verse 11a, b (cf. Prov. 17:26; Exod. 21:22). The rich then sold such grain commercially and used the proceeds to build houses for themselves out of **stone**—an art learned from the Phoenicians in the time of Solomon (cf. 1 Kgs. 5:17; 6:36; Isa. 9:10)—rather than out of the clay bricks that crumbled so easily. And they could afford **vineyards** with the best layouts in the choicest locations (cf. Isa. 5:1).

The tables would be turned, however, Amos proclaims, for the corruptions of human courts were breaches of Israel's covenant with its Lord (cf. Deut. 16:18–20)—"rebellions" (v. 12, NIV: **offenses**) against the rule of the one whose name was "Yahweh," verse 8, LORD of the hosts of heaven and earth, verse 16. The consequence would be the falling of covenant curses upon the people: an unnamed enemy would overwhelm them, and they would not enjoy the fruits of their greed, verse 11 (cf. Deut. 28:30,

38–41). They had gotten rich at the expense of the poor; now others would become rich at their expense.

The repetition of **therefore** in verses 11 and 13, a word that normally introduces the announcement of the judgment pronounced by God, points toward a climax in the final announcement of that judgment in verse 16, which also begins with "therefore." As in verse 2, the judgment is death. As Calvin remarks in his commentary on this passage's picture of the silencing of those who speak the truth, "When licentiousness has arrived to this pitch, it is certain that the state of things is past recovery, and that there is no hope of repentance or of a better condition" (Calvin, *Joel, Amos, Obadiah*, p. 271).

**5:14–15** / Once again Amos reminds his hearers of the traditions embodied in the Yahweh faith of the past. In verses 4–5, they were reminded that they were to seek the presence of their Lord in their worship and not substitute for that presence false and empty ritual (cf. Isa. 48:1). Here the prophet reminds them that they were to seek **good** in their society, especially by rendering **justice** (cf. "justice, and only justice" Deut. 16:20 RSV) in their **courts** of law.

When Amos or the other authors of the OT speak of seeking "good" (cf. Ps. 34:12–14; 37:3; Isa. 1:16–17; see also Rom. 12:9), they have in mind no set of virtues or standards outside of God. The "good" in Hebrew thought was what Yahweh commanded, and it was good because he commanded it. No ethical code, no set of religious rules, no ideals existed apart from their grounding in the will of God. Life could be had only in relationship with the source of life, and apart from trusting and loving and obedient communion with the Lord, life was impossible. Thus, in the great assize of Matt. 25:31–46, no act is good in itself and deserving of life. Rather it is good, only because it is an act done toward Jesus. At the heart of biblical faith is not a code of ethics, but a personal relationship with God.

The Israelite was commanded to "love" the Lord (cf. Deut. 6:5), as is the Christian (Mark 12:30 and parallels), but part of that love is to be exercised by justice toward one's neighbor, as Deuteronomy so vividly spells out throughout its pages, and as Jesus emphasized when he joined the second great commandment to the first (Mark 12:31 and parallels). This is the age-old tradition, present from the first in biblical faith, which Amos recalls in verses 14–15.

Such love does not coerce God, of course, who will "be gracious to whom [he] will be gracious, and will show mercy on whom [he] will show mercy" (Exod. 33:19 RSV). Because God's grace and favor are always undeserved and cannot be commanded by any imperfect human love or obedience, Amos states that God's promise of undeserved help was always conditional in the past, verse 15 (**perhaps**). We are always "unworthy servants" (Luke 17:10), and never earn the right to be among even a **remnant** when God judges the earth. Of that too Amos reminds his listeners, verse 15d.

The Israelites knew no condition, however. These two verses give us a picture of what Amos's hearers believed and of what their tradition from the past had told them. They assumed that God was with them, though they corrupted both their worship and their courts. They assumed God would always be gracious to them and no evil would come upon them (cf. 6:3; 9:10), verse 14. But there is no softening of the sentence of death in these verses. Amos cites the past only in order to contrast it more forcefully with the words that follow in verses 16–17.

**5:16–17** / The oracle of 5:1–17 ends here, as it began in verse 2, with the words of the Lord, and with the picture of a funeral lamentation over the corpse of the unjust and apostate virgin Israel. Three times the word **wailing** is repeated (see the RSV for the reading of the original Hebrew). We hear the repetition of "Ho! Ho!"—the Hebrew of "Alas!" (RSV). The sound of grief echoes through Israel's open squares and narrow streets, across its fields and down the rows of its vineyards. Professional **mourners** are not numerous enough to bewail all of Israel's dead (cf. Jer. 9:17), and so even the **farmers** have to join voices with the mourning women, verse 16. But finally all will fall victim to the sentence of death, for Israel has made an enemy of its God, and that God now comes in judgment. God will never again pass by (cf. 8:8). Now God comes into Israel's midst to destroy it.

## Additional Notes §6

**5:5** / **For Gilgal will surely go into exile:** God's absolute judgment on Gilgal is emphasized by an alliteration in the Hb.: *gilgāl gālōh yigleh.*

**And Bethel will be reduced to nothing:** Hosea 4:15 and 5:8 continue this condemnation of Bethel by naming it "Beth Aven," that is, "house-of-nothing" or "house-of-wickedness." For the Hb., evil was equivalent to nothingness, void, chaos, nonbeing, as contrasted with God's gift of life, order, being.

## §7 Israel's Ill-Placed Confidence (Amos 5:18–6:14)

In the preceding group of oracles, Amos announced that God would pass through Israel's midst to do them to death. Undoubtedly that message met with skepticism on the part of those who bothered to listen to this prophet with a Judean accent. Like everyone who is prosperous and comfortable, most of those in Israel who counted for anything felt that they were enjoying the results of God's favor toward them, or, if they took no thought of God, that their good life was secure. In 5:18–6:14, the prophet therefore sets about to show how ill-placed is Israel's confidence in every area of her life. And significantly the section begins with an oracle concerning the day of the Lord, because finally it is the day of the Lord that will bring Israel's death.

**5:18–20** / Amos was the first of the writing prophets to preach about **the day of the Lord,** but he was followed in the practice by Zephaniah, Isaiah, Jeremiah, Ezekiel, Joel, and Malachi. When the OT speaks of the day, it is referring not to a definite extent of time, but to a definite event in time, whose nature will be determined entirely by the Lord. It is that event which is referred to when we read the phrases, "on that day" (Amos 8:9 RSV) or "at that time."

The concept of the day of the Lord arose out of the theology of Israel's ancient Holy Wars, which were conducted during the times of the tribal federation (ca. 1220–1020 BC) and of the early monarchy (1020–1000 BC), and which have been labeled "holy" by scholars because they were conducted according to fixed cultic rules.

In such wars, it was considered that Yahweh was the divine warrior (cf. Exod. 15:3; Isa. 59:15–18; 63:1–6; 66:15–16; Jer. 20:11; Joel 2:11; Zeph. 3:17), who fought on behalf of his beleaguered people against their enemies, winning the battle for them by employing cosmic weapons (Josh. 10:11; 24:7; Judg.

5:4–5; 1 Sam. 7:10, cf. Exod. 14:24–25) and by bringing terror and panic upon the enemy (Josh. 2:9, 24; 5:1; 7:5; cf. Exod. 15:14–16; 23:27; Zech. 14:13).

The optimistic belief therefore arose in Israel that God would always fight for it and that on a climactic day, when God came to establish a kingdom over all the earth, he would destroy all of its enemies and exalt Israel above all nations. It is that confidence in the day that Amos attacks in 5:18.

The prophet's announcement is that Israel, in desiring the day of the Lord, is longing for its own doom, for on that day there will be **darkness** and **not light,** death and not life. God will fight not only against his enemies outside of Israel, but also against those within it. Though Israel has previously escaped God's wrath, like a man fleeing from a **bear** or a **lion** (cf. Hos. 13:8), and though it now feels secure, like a man inside his own **house,** there death will strike, like a poisonous serpent (cf. 9:3). As a result, the oracle opens with **woe!** which is a funerary lament over the dead.

From the time of Amos on, the day of the Lord is characterized by the prophets as a day of **darkness** and gloom (Zeph. 1:15; Joel 2:2) or of clouds and thick darkness (Zeph. 1:15; Ezek. 34:12; Joel 2:2; cf. Ezek. 30:3), when all the heavenly bodies will give no light (cf. 8:9; Joel 2:10; cf. 2:31; 3:15; Isa. 13:10)—a fact significant for the story in the NT of the crucifixion of Christ (Mark 15:33 and parallels). As our Lord says of his death, "Now is the judgment of this world, now shall the ruler of this world be cast out; and I, when I am lifted up from the earth, will draw all men to myself" (John 12:31–32 RSV).

In the oracles that follow in this section, Amos will also deal with two other aspects of the day of the Lord that became traditional; namely, with the facts that wealth cannot save and is useless before God's wrath (6:4–7; cf. Isa. 2:20; 13:17; Ezek. 7:11; Zeph. 1:18), and that human pride is destroyed (6:1–3, 8; cf. Isa. 2:11–17; 13:17; Ezek. 7:10, 24; Obad. 3–4; Zeph. 3:11–12).

**5:21–24** / The purpose of worship is to nurture the relationship with God by means of praise and prayer, offering and intercession and petition. Israel in Amos's time apparently felt that its lavish cult ensured its peaceful relation with its deity, just as modern worshipers sometimes believe that going to church always puts them right with God.

Judging from the cultic practices described in this passage, the northern kingdom was not neglecting its worship life. The **feasts** referred to in verse 21 were the three great festivals— Tabernacles, Passover or Unleavened Bread, and Weeks (Exod. 23:14–17; 34:22, 25; Deut. 16:1–16)—which Israelites celebrated with pilgrimages, probably to Bethel or Gilgal (see the comment on 4:4). "Solemn assemblies" (RSV) were feast days celebrating sabbaths, new moons, and other less important occasions, when all work ceased and the people gathered together to worship and sometimes to eat (cf. 8:5; Lev. 23:36; Num. 29:35; 2 Kgs. 10:20; Isa. 1:13; Joel 1:14).

The listing of sacrifices is quite comprehensive, verse 22. **Burnt offerings** were those entirely consumed by fire and sent up in smoke to the deity (Lev. 1:3–17). *Minḥâ*, which the NIV translates as **grain offerings,** could refer to any type of sacrifice (Lev. 2). "Peace offerings" (supplied in the NIV margin as an alternative to **fellowship offerings**) were only partially consumed by fire, the remainder being eaten at a communion meal (Lev. 3). And the latter could include singing, accompanied by the lute, which had an angular yoke and a bulging resonance chamber and was the oldest musical instrument known in Israel (Wolff, *Joel and Amos,* p. 264).

Amos details Israel's worship life only to announce that God rejects it all. The three verbs that the prophet employs in verses 22b–23b are significant. God will not **accept** the burnt offerings; literally, the verb means "savor" or "smell," as in Genesis 8:21, so God closes his nostrils to Israel's offering. God **will have no regard** for the grain offerings; that is, God will not "look upon" them, so he closes his eyes. And God **will not listen** to the singing and playing on lutes, so he closes his ears. Indeed, the festal **songs** are nothing but **noise.** Of the worship that Israel believes wins favor in God's sight, God says, **I hate, I despise** them, verse 21, and he closes himself off from it all (cf. Isa 1:10–15).

As long as Israel will not practice justice and righteousness in its courts and commerce, fulfilling its covenant obligations toward the poor and oppressed, its worship is not acceptable to its God. The Lord wants *mišpāṭ* (**justice**) and *ṣᵉdāqâ* (**righteousness**) literally to "cascade" through Israel's daily life like a mighty **river;** God does not expect them to dry up like some desert wadi that runs full only during the rainy season, verse 24.

In short, what we do in our relations with our fellow human beings always affects our relations with God, and we cannot love God if we do not also love our neighbor: the first and the second great commandments are inextricably joined (Mark 12:28–31 and parallel), and from beginning to end, the Scriptures affirm that joining. (See, e.g., Mal. 2:13–16 or Matt. 5:23–24 or James.)

**5:25–27** / This prose passage (RSV) is probably the most difficult pericope to interpret in the book of Amos, and it is a real question as to whether or not it belongs to the prophet. It seems to continue Amos's condemnation of Israel's false worship in verses 21–24, yet it shares in the Deuteronomic view that Israel offered no **sacrifices** in the wilderness (cf. Jer. 7:21–23), and its mention of **forty years** is traditional with that source (cf. Deut. 2:7; 8:2, 4, etc.). It interrupts the series of woe oracles in 5:18–20 and 6:1–7. It mentions Assyrian astral deities, but we do not know otherwise if Amos knew the names of such gods or if they were worshiped in his time. Certainly 5:21–24 forms a complete unit without these verses.

Some scholars have therefore termed the entire passage an addition made to the book after 721 BC, when Israel was exiled to Assyria. Others omit only verses 25–26 and take verse 27 as the pronouncement of judgment, following verses 18–24, but it should be noted that there is no **therefore** at the beginning of verse 27 in the Hebrew text (contra NIV and RSV) and thus no customary introduction to the judgment announcement (cf. 6:7). My own inclination is to judge the passage a later, probably Deuteronomic, prose addition that borrows Amos's use of Yahweh Elohim Sebaoth (v. 27) and that anticipates his later references to exile (7:11, 17). The passage has been added to the book in order to explain further the fall of the northern kingdom.

But whether or not the passage is authentic, its message is that sacrifice per se was not willed by God, and that Israel's sacrificial system is at odds with the ideal time in the wilderness (cf. Hos. 2:14–15; Jer. 2:13) when there was no sacrifice. God rejects it totally. Therefore Israel will be exiled to an unnamed foreign land in the northeast beyond Damascus, where it will be forced to worship the idolatrous images of its conqueror.

**6:1–7** / Amos continues to attack those aspects of Israel's life in which it rests its confidence, and here he treats one of the standard themes found in the prophetic writings concerning the day of the Lord, namely, the inability of fame and wealth to save in that day of Yahweh's wrath and sovereignty (cf. e.g., Isa. 2:12–21).

This passage has the shape of a woe oracle, a funerary lament over the dead, with the **woe** or "alas" pronounced (v. 1), a series of participial phrases detailing over whom the woe is announced (v. 1), why it is announced (vv. 3–6), and the pronounced judgment (v. 7). However, verses 3 and 4 interrupt this form, and their interpretation has been a matter of debate.

Who speaks in verse 2? If the prophet addresses the wealthy and influential here, then his questions obviously deserve the answer "no." **Calneh** and **Hamath** were both city-states to the north of Israel and were apparently under Israelite influence in Amos's day, though they would be conquered by Tiglath-pileser III of Assyria in 734 BC. **Gath** was a Philistine city-state on Judah's border and subject to it, but it would be conquered by Sargon II of Assyria in 712/1 BC. Is Amos pointing to the good fortune of Israel and Judah by his questions and yet predicting the future loss of their supremacy? Or has verse 2 been inserted after 734 BC as an interruption of the form of this woe oracle? If verse 2 is intended to be a prediction, it is a vague one, to say the least.

Some have suggested that Amos is quoting the words of the wealthy and influential, who are bragging about their supremacy over their neighbors. But in that case, one would think that the two questions would read, "Are they better off than *our* two kingdoms? Is their land better than *ours*?" My inclination is to see verse 2 as an insertion added after the Assyrian conquests and prompted by Amos's reference to the **evil day** in verse 3.

Those addressed in this woe oracle are the **notable men** of the northern kingdom's capital city, who feel themselves fully as important as the leaders of the southern kingdom of Judah. Amos addresses both the northerners and southerners, but his concern is really with the former and he mentions **Zion** only for purposes of comparison. Sarcastically, he calls Israel "the first of the nations" (in the Hebrew; so too the RSV).

The leaders addressed are those to whom everyone in Israel looks, those to whom the populace flocks—the "beautiful people" of Amos's day, who determine policies and set the fads and "call the shots" about what is "in" and what is "out," what is "politically correct" and what is not. They determine the morale and morality of the nation, and they feel themselves smugly secure, confident that if the day of judgment that Amos announces is coming, it is in the very distant future (cf. Ezek.

12:26–27), verse 3. In the meantime, they can just continue their practice of oppressing the poor in the courts: Verse 3b does not refer to a **reign of terror,** as the NIV has it, but speaks of "the seat of violence," as in the RSV, which is a reference to judicial or governmental injustice.

The leading citizens of Israel are not only smug and influential, however; they are also dissolute. In verses 4–6, Amos gives us a remarkably detailed description of their banquets. They sprawl about on couches **inlaid with** costly **ivory.** They enjoy meals of the choicest meats, although eating meat of any kind was a rarity in Israel. They amuse themselves by improvising songs accompanied by lutes and timbrels. They get thoroughly drunk by drinking wine mixed with spices, not from cups, but from bowls (cf. Prov. 20:1; 21:17; 23:20–21, 29–35; 31:4–7). And they stimulate themselves by anointing their skin with fragrant oil (cf. Song Sol. 1:3; 4:10). Yet they take no thought for the fact that their society is rotten to the core, blackened and decaying in its commerce and courts and worship, giving no heed to the covenant demands of a God who is Lord over all. Those who are first in the land will therefore continue to be first, Amos announces—**first into exile** in an unnamed foreign land, verse 7. Their proud confidence fostered by their wealth and fame will come to an end.

It has been suggested that 6:8b, which reads "oracle of Yahweh Elohim Sebaoth" belongs at the end of verse 7, and that is probably correct. The God who is truly the first and the last can speak the end of the people who will not honor his holy name.

**6:8–11** / Some commentators have maintained that this passage joins the fragments of two original oracles. Others point out that verse 8 forms a complete unit in itself. However, in the Hebrew, each line of verses 8c through 10c (**and detest his fortresses . . . the name of the LORD**) begins with a connective *waw,* and this progression culminates in verse 11 with an emphatic, "For behold, the LORD is commanding . . . ." The picture is of God, the commander of army hosts, destroying Israel's military defenses, which are as inadequate to give it security as is its worship (5:21–24), its sacrifices (5:25–27), its fame, and its wealth (6:1–7).

God swears by his own eternal and almighty nature, which is the strongest guarantee that can be given (cf. 4:2), that he hates Israel's **pride,** verse 8. Pride is the root of Israel's sin—as it is the root of most human sin. In its pride, Israel believes itself

self-sufficient, able to rely on its own sources of security instead of relying on God (cf. Gen. 3:5; 11:4; Mark 8:35 and parallels; John 12:25). As stated above, verse 8b probably belongs at the end of 6:7. It is omitted in the LXX.

In verse 8, Israel relies on its military fortifications to turn back any enemy. But when God is the enemy he cannot be turned back, and God will surrender Samaria and all its proud inhabitants to an unnamed foe. **Ten men** constituted the smallest military unit (cf. 5:3), and even if they **are left,** they will all **die,** though they try to hide in the innermost recesses of a house, verse 9. When their kinsmen come to fulfill their function as relatives by disposing of the bodies, they will find none left alive. And they will not permit the name of Yahweh to be mentioned, lest the name invoke Yahweh's fearful and destroying presence once again among them, verse 10.

"The LORD is commanding"—the verb in verse 11 is a participle, and Amos sees God's destruction of the people as already begun with his word to the prophet. Indeed, that is the function of the prophetic word: It begins the action of which it speaks. And so, with Amos's words, God's deathly attack on Israel's life is initiated. That attack will destroy the **great** stone **house** (probably a reference to the palace of the king) like some giant fist smashing down upon it (cf. 3:15), and it will destroy the little houses made from clay. No one will survive, for Israel is allowed no pride except its pride in God (Wolff, *Joel and Amos,* p. 120; cf. Jer. 9:23–24; 1 Cor. 1:31; 2 Cor. 10:17).

**6:12–14** / Sin is a mysterious force let loose in the world, according to the Scriptures. Despite the story of sin's beginning in Genesis 3, that chapter never really explains why men and women turn their backs on God and paradise, any more than the NT explains why we repeatedly reject the abundant and eternal life offered us in Jesus Christ. Rationally considered, sin is senseless, a dark corruption defying explanation, a festering rejection of all logic and order.

That is what Amos says in verses 12 and 13 of this oracle. In the manner of wisdom teaching, he asks two foolish questions, verse 12: "Do horses run upon rocks? Does one plow the sea with oxen?" (reading with the RSV; see additional notes). And the answer to the questions is, "Of course not. The rocky terrain would ruin the horses legs, and the oxen would drown in the sea." But that foolishness is what Israel has practiced in its courts and society. It has **turned justice into poison:** When the oppressed have turned to the courts, the one place where they could expect to find relief, they have experienced deadly injustice instead. And when righteous acts have been expected to bear **fruit** in the society, they have been rewarded only with bitter disappointment, in a terrible reversal of ethical standards. The normal, God-given order of Israel's society is out of whack, distorted by corruption and sin (cf. Jer. 5:7; Jer. 2:31–32; 8:6–7; 18:13–15). A mysterious force of evil has seized hold of Israel and made it captive. The prophets in the Old Testament, along with Paul in the New, knew the deadly power of sin (cf. Jer. 13:23; Hos. 5:4; Rom. 7:15–24).

Some scholars have thought to divide verse 12 from verses 13–14, but verse 13 begins with a participial, and those accused in verse 12 of corrupting justice and righteousness are the braggarts of verse 13. Clearly the root of their sin lies in their pride (cf. the comments on 6:8). Under Jeroboam II, God gave Israel control of the territory from Hamath in the north to the Brook of Zered at the southernmost tip of the Dead Sea (2 Kgs. 14:25). Similarly, from the Arameans, Jeroboam recovered territories around **Lo Debar,** in the eastern part of Gilead (cf. Josh. 13:26; 2 Sam. 9:5; 17:27), and around **Karnaim** to the northeast on the upper reaches of the Yarmuk. But the Israelites, in their pride, claim that it was all their own doing, the fruit of their own strength. They have forgotten their God, who alone sustains their life (cf. Ps. 33:16–20).

In a final divine reversal of Israel's fortunes, God therefore announces that an unnamed enemy will be raised against them and will take their whole land, verse 14. The one who declares this reversal is Yahweh Elohim Sebaoth, the Lord of all military hosts, the Lord over all nations, the Lord of heaven and earth. With its failure to honor that divine name and to obey that almighty sovereign, Israel's doom is sealed.

## Additional Notes §7

**5:22a–b** / These lines read in Hb., "Even if you offer me burnt offerings . . ./ Your offerings I will not accept." The protasis has no apodosis. Most translations, including the NIV, follow the LXX.

**5:23** / The verbs are sing., and it has been suggested that they are directed at the small class of festival musicians.

**5:25–26** / The LXX reads, "Have you offered to me victims and sacrifices, O house of Israel, forty years in the wilderness? Yea, you took up the tabernacle of Moloch, and the star of your God Raephan, the images of them which you made for yourselves." The vocalizations of the names, *sikkût* and *kîyûn*, have been taken from *šiqqûṣ*, which means "abomination." They probably are to be equated with *Sakkuth* and *Kaiwan*, which were Babylonian names of the astral deity Saturn (Mays, *Amos*, p. 112). The NIV indicates an alternative reading for v. 26, "lifted up *Sakkuth* your king / and *Kaiwan* your idols, / your star gods."

**6:4** / The verb for "lie" here is used elsewhere only of the spreading tendrils of a wild vine (Ezek. 17:6) or of loose hanging of fabric (Exod. 26:12). Thus, Amos pictures the wealthy sprawling lazily about on their couches.

**6:10** / Cremation was not a customary burial practice in Israel. It has therefore been suggested that *dôd* signifies the father's relatives and *mᵉsārēp* the mother's, but the latter is speculative. As the v. stands, with its reference to the burning of a corpse, it is very strange.

**6:12** / By separating one consonant from the word for **oxen**, our more suitable reading, given above, is gained, with no changes in the MT. See the RSV. The NIV supplies the word **there**.

**6:13** / Amos works a sarcastic pun on the name of the city of Debir, calling it *Lōʾ-dābār*, which means "no word," or "nothing." In God's eyes, Israel's military victories are insignificant.

## §8 The Prophet's Visions and Encounter with Amaziah (Amos 7:1–8:3)

While this section contains two different types of visions and a biographical insert, it should be regarded as a unit that has been given its present form by the disciples of the prophet.

The first two visions, in 7:1–3 and 7:4–6, are "event visions," portraying what is about to happen, and they are identical in their form. The third and fourth visions, in 7:7–9 and 8:1–3, are "wordplay visions," in which the meaning of what is seen depends on Yahweh's interpretation of the word used. The biographical account of 7:10–17 shows the reaction of the priest Amaziah to the judgment announcement in 7:9 and is bound to the third vision by the use of "sword" in both 7:9 and 7:11 and by the reference to "sanctuaries" in both 7:9 and 7:13. Thus the whole unit holds together by its common subject matter of visions and the reaction to them.

Visions were frequent means of God's communication with the prophets. In an ecstatic state of heightened consciousness, the prophet was granted to see and to hear God's voice and actions, of which others were unaware. For example, Isaiah sees and hears God in the heavenly court (in Isa. 6). In an account similar to that in our passage, Jeremiah sees and hears God's future judgment upon the people in the form of a military attack by the mysterious enemy from the North (Jer. 4:19–22). Or in Jeremiah 1:11–12, he is asked what he sees, and the Lord then interprets the meaning of the "branch of the almond tree" for him. There is no way we moderns can analyze or explain such prophetic experiences. We can only say that they were validated by Israel's subsequent history, and we accept them at face value as belonging to the traditions of our faith.

It is not necessary that we consider the visions in this unit to have been granted Amos all at one time. Nor do the visions form a "call" to the prophet, marking the beginning of his ministry. Indeed, the first vision (7:1–3) takes place in the late spring, the second (7:4–6) in midsummer, the fourth (8:1–3) in autumn. Amaziah's reference to "all" of Amos's words, in 7:10, implies that the prophet has been preaching for some time. And the content of the visions, which proclaims the exile and end of Israel, is consonant with the prophet's preaching in 5:2, 5, 17 and 6:7. The implication is, therefore, that the visions occurred in those days when Amos was also given the messages now found in chapters 5 and 6.

Like all of the prophets, Amos undoubtedly experienced opposition to his announcements of judgment—no people like to hear that they are going to die at the hand of their God. The encounter with Amaziah in 7:10–17 portrays that opposition brought to a head in the objection of the royal priest at the king's sanctuary. Amos's life was in danger.

In one sense, however, the first two visions in verses 1–6 form an apologetic for the prophet's ministry, as did 3:3–8. By telling of his intercessions on behalf of his sinful compatriots, intercessions that have twice turned aside the wrath of God, Amos shows that he has had no desire to see the death of his people. Like so many of the prophets both before and after him, he has vigorously exercised the prophetic function of interceding for the good of his nation.

We do not often realize that the prophets of the OT not only proclaimed God's judgment on their sinful folk but also defended that folk in tearful intercession before the throne of God (cf. Jer. 9:1). Moses, the first and greatest of the prophets, undertook strenuous asceticism to turn aside God's judgment (Deut. 9:17–20, 25–29). Jeremiah pleaded so frequently with God for the forgiveness of his people that God finally had to tell him to be quiet (Jer. 7:16–17; 11:14; 15:1). Ezekiel likened prophetic intercession to a soldier filling up a breach in a fortification that Israel might stand in battle in the day of the Lord (Ezek. 13:5). Thus Amos, by his prayers in 7:2 and 7:5, is fulfilling the role of a true prophet.

It is interesting to note in this section that Amos is the only one in Israel who sees the condition of his people correctly. "Jacob," Amos's favorite name for the northern kingdom (3:13; 6:8; 8:7; 9:8), is "so small," he says (7:2, 5). That is, Jacob is so weak, so helpless, so pitiful. But this is the people who boasted in their pride of their security and wealth, their military prowess and their lavish cult (see the comments on 5:18–6:14). In the light of God's word, Amos sees their true condition; they are pitiful and small. We can be grateful that God saw our real natures behind all of our equally foolish and proud claims, that God pitied us as a father pities his children and came to rescue us in Jesus Christ.

**7:1–3** / While the NIV has drastically altered the original text here (cf. the RSV), it has correctly interpreted the meaning of the original and made verses 1–2 considerably easier to understand.

The time of this vision of **locusts** is late spring, when the second planting of seeded crops, as well as wild growth, are just appearing—all vegetation is meant. Apparently the royal house had first claim on what was planted, although the evidence for this is scanty. (First Kings 18:5 is usually mentioned but has no bearing on the practice.) The produce from this planting sustained Israel's life during the dry summer months, and were it to be lost, both humans and cattle would die. In short, the locust horde threatened Israel with extinction.

Locusts could and sometimes did literally strip Israel clean of every scrap of vegetation, eating even the bark from the trees and other wood that might conceivably be consumed to stave off hunger. A vivid picture of such a locust invasion is given in Joel 1, and it is significant that those who shaped our canon placed the book of Amos after that of Joel. Amos's words, they implied, should be read in the light of Joel's, because both have to do with the day of the Lord. Thus, those catastrophes that Amos sees the Lord preparing here in this vision and the ones that follow are not just natural and historical events but manifestations of God's wrath in the awful day of the Lord.

Amos's intercession, verse 2, persuades the Lord to "repent" (NIV: **relented**), that is, to change his mind about loosing the locusts, verse 3. God listens to human appeals (cf. Gen. 18:22–32; Josh. 7:6–13), especially when he sees how small and pitiful are the objects of his wrath. In the Bible, there is nothing foreordained that God, the Lord of history and nature, cannot change. The sacred history is really one long dialogue between God and human beings in which there is constant action and reaction. It is doubtful, however, that verse 3 implies forgiveness of Israel's sin by God; the judgment is merely turned aside for the time being.

**7:4–6** / It is very likely that Amos's second vision was granted him in midsummer, when heat and drought lay over the land, but the judgment that he sees the Lord preparing is no natural **fire.** The fire of God's wrath is a supernatural fire that can burn up even the **great deep,** the waters under the earth (cf. Deut. 32:22). And that fire, too, is associated with the day of the Lord (cf. Joel 1:19–20; 2:3, 5, 30).

Amos's intercession is not for forgiveness, as it was in 7:2. No forgiveness was granted then, and perhaps the prophet has learned by this time that no forgiveness will be forthcoming. Rather, Amos simply begs, "cease" (RSV), **stop!** That is, halt the judgment! And God, in pity for this little people, heeds the prophet's cry. (See the comments on 7:1–3 above.)

**7:7–9** / Evil cannot remain in God's sight (cf. Hab. 1:13), and when the people do not repent, God's cleansing judgment must wipe out the wrong (cf. Josh 7:6–15; Isa. 1:18–20; Jer. 8:4–13). Amos is therefore granted a third vision of the Lord standing beside a **wall** holding a **plumb line.** In the dialogue of verse 8, the Lord explains to Amos the meaning of what he sees.

A **plumb line** is a builder's tool consisting of a string with a weight on the end that is used to determine whether or not a structure is "plumb"; that is, "straight" or absolutely vertical. The implication of the vision is that Israel once was upright but now has become crooked. Measured by the commandments and will of God for justice in society and for true worship, Israel has deviated from the Lord's covenant norms for its life and thereby profaned God's holy name. God can therefore spare it no longer; literally, God cannot again pass by its sin (see the RSV). Instead, God will "pass through" the midst of Israel (5:17), wreaking final judgment on it, verse 9. Israel's **high places,** its local worship sites throughout the countryside, will become empty of people (i.e., "desolate": the RSV reading is correct), because they have all gone into exile. Its **sanctuaries,** its temples at Bethel and Dan, will be destroyed. And its monarchy will fall victim to the **sword,** called here the sword of Yahweh—a prophecy that was fulfilled by the assassination of Jeroboam II's son Zechariah, ca. 746 BC (2 Kgs. 15:10; cf. 14:29).

**7:10–17** / In the visionary oracle of Amos 7:7–9, the prophet has foretold the death of King Jeroboam II by the sword and the destruction of all of the northern kingdom's worship sites, including those royal sanctuaries at Bethel and Dan. Amos's words have now become politically unbearable, verse 10, because they threaten the throne with insurrection.

Such was the fear of the priest **Amaziah,** who was in charge of the royal sanctuary at **Bethel,** and his fear was well-founded. In Israel's history, at the command of the Lord, prophets had repeatedly instigated the overthrow of a reigning monarch (1 Kgs. 11:25–40; 2 Kgs. 8:7–15), and indeed, Elijah and Elisha were the ones who finally caused the fall of the powerful Omri dynasty (1 Kgs. 19:15–18; 2 Kgs. 9:1–14).

Moreover, the worship sites of the northern kingdom were intimately connected with the power of the throne. Jeroboam I founded the sanctuaries at Bethel and Dan, with their idols of golden calves. He changed the time of the autumn New Year festival. He rejected the levitical priesthood in favor of ordained lay priests, and he himself offered sacrifices upon the altar at Bethel (1 Kgs. 12:26–33). In short, Jeroboam founded a state religion different from the religion of Israel's covenant past, a civil religion over which he himself ruled supreme. King and cult had become joined together, and state power was thereby absolutized. It was as if worship services whose content and order were dictated solely by the President of the U.S.A. were held in the White House—a practice known in our past.

Jeroboam I's priest at Bethel therefore sends a message to that king in his palace, some fifty miles away in Samaria, to report what Amos has been preaching, verses 10–11. It is noteworthy that in his message Amaziah does not attribute Amos's words to Yahweh: **This is what *Amos* is saying.** In short, Amaziah does not believe Amos's words are divinely inspired. However, Amaziah is responsible for preserving peace and stability in the social and religious order by maintaining loyalty to the throne, so he does not wait for the king's reply, but takes matters into his own hands, verses 12–13.

Amaziah's aim is to get rid of the problem, and the problem is the *place* in which Amos has chosen to preach. Amaziah does not care a whit if Amos returns to **Judah** and mouths his oracles, because Amaziah does not believe the oracles. The priest has seen lots of professional prophets earning their living by preaching, giving oracles in return for money. Amaziah accepts that as a customary occurrence in society. But such professional prophets become dangerous if they start stirring up the people against the king. God will not do anything subversive, Amaziah believes, but the aroused populace may, and it is that threat that Amaziah wishes to be rid of.

Amos's reply to Amaziah, in verses 14–15, is therefore a response to the priest's unbelief, and it is an emphatic response. "No professional prophet (am) *I*," reads the Hebrew, "and no member of a prophetic guild (am) *I*. *I* am (still) a herdsman and a cultivator of figs." (See the comment on 1:1 for the meaning of these terms.) "But Yahweh took me . . . and he said . . . 'Go prophesy to my people Israel'." In short, Amos contradicts Amaziah by maintaining that he is a man under divine compulsion with a message from the Lord of the covenant. (Note **my people,** v. 15). His authority is not that of a prophetic institution or of an accepted social role but an authority given him solely by the word of his God, and when Amaziah opposes him, the priest is opposing God. It is not Amos who is the rebel, but Amaziah, and Amaziah is rebelling against the real king, Yahweh.

As a result, Amos pronounces a divine oracle of judgment against Amaziah for his lack of faith in the word of God, verses 16–17. An enemy will come against **Isaac,** the term used here for the northern kingdom to emphasize its covenant responsibility. Amaziah's **wife** will become a harlot for the invading soldiers. His children will fall before their **sword.** Amaziah's own property will be **divided up** among the conquerors. Amaziah will be exiled, along with his countrymen, to an unclean land that worships foreign deities (cf. 5:25–27), and there Amaziah will die. Such will be his punishment for his lack of faith in the word of God.

**8:1–3** / This fourth vision, after the confrontation with the priest Amaziah, serves to reiterate and make final what Amos has already proclaimed in his third vision, 7:7–9: Reading literally, as in the RSV, the "end" has come upon God's people Israel. Or in the NIV, she is **ripe** for punishment. The Lord will no longer pass over Israel's sin or pass by their faithlessness. The wages of their sin is death, and that wage will be paid. Amaziah's warning has not deterred the prophet. God has shown Amos the vision of the end, and the fulfillment of the vision is irrevocable.

In his commentary on Amos, James Mays has suggested (p. 141) that the vision is prompted by the sight of a **basket** of **fruit** brought to the temple as an offering at the autumn festival. Perhaps so, though the prophets needed no external stimuli to prompt the word of God to them. Rather the wicker **basket** (cf. the same word used for "cages" in Jer. 5:27) is just there, attached to no one, an object in space, suspended, filled with **fruit** that

ripens late in the fall, such as olives or figs. (The text literally reads
"summer fruit," as in the RSV.)

The significance of the summer or ripened fruit is explained
by God by means of a wordplay. The Hebrew word for "summer
fruit" is *qāyiṣ*, the word for "end" is *qēṣ*, and both were probably
pronounced in a similar manner at the time of Amos. Thus the
emphasis of the oracle of Yahweh, in verses 2–3, is on "end," finis,
close, termination of Israel's life in the dark day of the Lord that is
coming, a judgment that Ezekiel later pronounces also on Judah
by means of a deadly repetition (see Ezek. 7:5–7).

The OT rarely speaks in generalities, however, and so Amos
spells out three graphic details of the end, in verse 3. There will
be funeral lamentations or **wailing** instead of joyous **songs** (cf.
8:10). Corpses will be everywhere, shamefully unburied food for
the dogs and the birds (cf. 1 Kgs. 14:11; Jer. 16:4). Deathly silence
will prevail throughout the land—the still, sad silence of sin
punished by the Lord over all life and death. Israel has refused to
honor God's sovereign name in obedience and faith. Its death
will therefore show forth the fact that God is Adonai Yahweh,
ruler of heaven and earth.

---

### Additional Notes §8

**8:3** / The text of this v. is somewhat corrupted. The plural form
(*šîrôt*) for **songs** is not elsewhere found, and it is unusual to say that the
songs themselves will **wail**. Perhaps the reading was *šārôt*, for female
singers (cf. 2 Sam. 19:35; 2 Chron. 35:25; Eccl. 2:8), and the line should
be rendered, "The female singers of the temple will wail." Or the verb
could be transitive and the line read, "They will wail the temple songs
at that time," although the NIV reading is a third possibility.

There is also a question as to whether *hêkāl* should be read as
**temple** or "palace." Female singers are elsewhere always associated with
the royal court in the references cited above. But 8:10 supports the
reading as "temple."

## §9 The End and the God of the End
## (Amos 8:4–9:6)

In 7:8 and 8:3, Amos has announced the end of Israel, and the thought of that end dominates this whole section. One by one, the prophet will take up those aspects of Israel's life that will come to an end, until finally the totality of Israel's existence will be seen to be fated for extermination by the God who is Lord both of its beginning (cf. 2:9–11) and of its end.

8:4–8 / By their unjust business practices, the merchants of Israel are bringing "the poor of the land to an *end*" (reading the Hebrew, as in the RSV). With the growth of urban culture in the northern kingdom, many peasants were left without land and were at the mercy of those who sold them food. Here we see the avarice of the merchants. They cannot wait for the holy days, with their periods of rest, to end so they can get on with their unjust commerce.

The **New Moon** was a festival celebrated at the beginning of every lunar month, and the text implies that commerce was forbidden on it. Certainly the celebration of the **Sabbath** on every seventh day was from the earliest times commanded as a day of rest from any sort of labor (Exod. 20:8–11; 23:12; 34:21; cf. 35:3; Num. 15:32–36; Neh. 13:15–22; Jer. 17:21–27). Moreover, the command to rest from work was understood as a gracious gift of God, who gave human beings both their labor (cf. Gen. 2:15) and their rest from labor. But heedless of the lordship of God, the merchants of Amos's time chaffed at the interruption in their greedy pursuit of wealth.

To line their own pockets with unjust gain, the merchants falsified the size or content of the ʾêpâ (NIV: **measure**), which was a forty-liter vessel used to measure out a standard portion of grain. They added to the size of the "shekel" (see the RSV), which weighed about 11.5 grams, and which was placed on a balance scale to determine how much silver was owed for the grain. And

they even bent the balance scale out of shape in their own favor—the verb ʿût has the meaning "to bend" or "to distort," verse
5. All such dishonest practices were specifically forbidden in
Israel's law (Lev. 19:35–36; Deut. 25:13–16; cf. Mic. 6:10–11) and
were an "abomination" to the Lord (Prov. 11:1; 16:11; 20:10, 23),
finally violating the covenant command not to steal (Exod. 20:15)
and profaning the name of the Lord of the covenant.

With such dishonest gain the greedy merchants then could
purchase the debt-ridden poor as slaves for as little as the price
of **a pair of sandals,** verse 6. And so desperate were the helpless
poor for food sometimes that they would even buy swept up
grain-leavings from the floor that had chaff mixed in with them,
verse 6. The powerful had taken for themselves the lordship over
human life that belonged to God.

The oracle therefore announces that the true Lord will
bring an end to such injustice and the land that harbors it, and
that announcement is sealed by God's oath, verse 7. The Lord
swears by the **Pride of Jacob,** and the NIV has capitalized the
name to indicate that it is a divine title. That is, Yahweh is Israel's
Pride, just as in 1 Sam. 15:29 Yahweh is its glory, and Yahweh is
swearing by himself, as in 6:8 and 4:2. Such an interpretation has
been rightly questioned. In 5:18–6:14, the prophet has dealt with
Israel's proud self-confidence. Some commentators have therefore suggested that "the pride of Jacob" is ironic: Yahweh's oath
is as unalterable as Israel's false arrogance. Others have maintained that the "pride of Jacob" refers to the land of Israel, as in
Ps. 47:4, but given the fate of the land in Amos 8:8, this seems
questionable. Probably the second solution is best: over against
the proud self-confidence of Israel God sets his oath, and that will
mean the end of Israel's possession of its land. Not only will they
go into exile, which has been previously stated, but the very
ground on which they set their feet will rise up against them.

Recalling 1:1, many have interpreted verse 8, along with
9:5, to refer to an earthquake, but Amos is not dealing with
natural events. He is announcing the shaking of the land and of
the whole cosmos by the coming of the day of the Lord. It is
appropriate therefore that this oracle is followed by 8:9–10.

**8:9–10** / Once again Amos prophesies that the end of
Israel's life will come about at the time of the day of the Lord (cf.
5:18–20 and the comment there). Verse 9 reiterates what he has
said in 5:18, 20: the whole cosmos will be affected by God's final

wrath. But this time the darkness is perhaps also creation's participation in the mourning that will come upon Israel (cf. Rom. 8:22). More than that, perhaps it is also sign of God's mourning (cf. Gen. 6:6), for Yahweh speaks in the first person in this oracle, and each verb emphasizes "I" . . . "I" . . . "I."

The *end* that is emphasized in this passage, however, is the end of Israel's joy (cf. Isa. 24:8; Jer. 7:34; 16:9; 25:10–11). The religious festivals, with their hymns of rejoicing, will be turned into fasts of lamentation (cf. Ezek. 26:13; Lam. 5:14–15), with the donning of **sackcloth** and the shaving of the head (cf. Ezek. 7:18; see Joel 1:8, 13 and the comments there). Rather than sing, Israel will weep—bitterly, as if weeping for the loss of an **only son** (cf. Jer. 6:26; Ezek. 27:30–31; Zech. 12:10).

At the time of Amos, and indeed, up until the time of Daniel in the second century BC, Israel had no formal belief in life after death. The essence of one's personality was contained in one's name (cf. 1 Sam. 25:25), and the only immortality expected was to live on in one's name, passed down to one's son (cf. 1 Sam. 24:21). Thus, if an **only son** died, not only was the son lost, but one's own immortality, embodied in the preservation of one's name, was at an end. To weep for the death of an only son was therefore to weep without hope for the future. That is the *end* that God here sets before Israel, a total end, with nothing to follow.

**8:11–14** / Israel has refused to hear **the word of the LORD** delivered by the prophets (2:11–12), and the priest Amaziah has tried to put an end to Amos's preaching in the northern kingdom (7:12–13, 16). Indeed, the book of Amos as a whole gives evidence that Amos's preaching went largely unheeded by the indolent wealthy who ran and ruled Israel's society (cf. 5:18–6:14). But there will come days, God announces in this oracle, when the Israelites will finally realize that disaster is coming upon them, and then—too late—they will seek the word of the Lord.

Few passages in Amos are more poignant than this one, which might be compared to the tragic Saul's futile quest for some word from the Lord (cf. 1 Sam. 28:5–15). We have pictured here a desperate population, staggering, that is, running to and fro in an agitated state of distress, wandering the length and breadth of their land, like a starving man seeking food or a dehydrated wanderer in the desert seeking water. Frantically they search for the word of God, but that word has been withdrawn from them, because God has withdrawn from them (cf. Hos. 5:15). The Lord has abandoned them to their fate (cf. God giving over sinners in Rom. 1:24, 26, 28).

"Man shall not live by bread alone, but by every word that proceeds from the mouth of God" (Matt. 4:4 RSV; cf. Deut. 8:3). Apart from the word of God, human life knows only chaos (cf. Gen. 1:2; John 15:5). It is the word that speaks order into creation and that sustains all the processes of nature (Neh. 9:6, etc.). It is the word that motivates all history and brings it to fulfillment (Isa. 55:10–11; John 19:30). It is the word alone that gives guidance (Ps. 119:105) and forgiveness (Ps. 27:7; 143:7) and blessing (Num. 6:22–27) and fruitful life (Ps. 1:2–3). It is in the word that God draws near to his chosen people (Deut. 4:6–8; John 14:9) and abides with them (John 15:10). Nothing more clearly signals the end of Israel than the fact stated in this oracle that it will no longer be given the word of God.

The phrase at the beginning of verse 13, **in that day,** normally marks the beginning of a new oracle, but as they now stand, verses 13–14 must be interpreted in continuity with verses 11–12. Thus, the **thirst** referred to in verse 13 is the same thirst mentioned in verse 11—thirst for hearing the words of the Lord. And because the word of the Lord cannot be found, even the vigorous youths, the promise for the future in Israel, will be utterly weak and helpless (such is the meaning of **faint** here, cf. Jonah 4:8). The fairest and strongest too will be swept away in the holocaust of the day of the Lord.

Israel swears here not by the name of its God but by its own worship practices, at Bethel and **Dan** and **Beersheba** (cf. 5:5). **Samaria** is named instead of Bethel to signify the royal house's worship at Bethel (cf. 7:13). **Dan** is the other royal site, along with Bethel, where Jeroboam I erected a golden calf (1 Kgs. 12:28–29). **Beersheba** was a place of pilgrimage, and the Hebrew reads "the way of Beersheba" (so too the RSV), not the **god of Beersheba** as the NIV has it. In short, Israel's trust is in its own cultic exercises at the three sites; in those it places its confidence (cf. 5:21–23; 4:4–5; 5:4–5). But if the word of the Lord is withdrawn from worship, Israel has nothing and no one upon whom to rely. It is bereft of all help and salvation. It shall fall and never rise again. That funeral dirge first uttered in 5:2 is affirmed once again.

**9:1–4**  /  In his great paean of praise of the love of God in Christ Jesus, Paul writes, "If God is for us, who can be against us?"

and he assures us that nothing in all creation can separate us from that love—neither "famine" (cf. Amos 8:11–12) nor "sword" (cf. Amos 9:1, 4), "neither the present nor the future, nor any powers, neither height nor depth . . ." (Rom. 8:31, 35, 38–39). But what Israel learns in this vision and its oracle is that none of those things can separate it from God's wrath. When trust and obedience are missing, when the name of the Lord has been profaned by empty worship and oppression of the poor and helpless, when human pride has thought to form its own means of security, when responsibility within the covenant with God has been totally ignored, then the divine love takes the form of radical judgment, and there is nothing in all creation that can rescue Israel from that judgment. If God is against it nothing and no one can be for it.

In a fifth and final vision, Amos sees the Lord **standing beside** an **altar** of burnt offering in an unspecified temple—judgment begins with the household of God (1 Pet. 4:17). He hears the Lord command the heavenly beings (cf. Isa. 40:1) to "smite" (RSV) the capitals of the **pillars** that support the roof of the temple with such force that the **thresholds** of the temple **shake** (cf. Isa. 6:4). The capitals are shattered and fall along with the roof onto the heads of the assembled worshipers.

Thus begins the final judgment of Israel. But the divine words that follow the command tell the ominous events that are to follow. Anyone who escapes from the temple will be personally slain with a **sword** by God. They may try to hide in the farthest reaches of the universe, in the heights of the heavens or in **the depths** of Sheol under the earth, but from there the **hand** of the Lord of heaven and earth will **take them,** verse 2. They may ascend Mt. **Carmel** and try to hide themselves in its deep forests, but there the maker of mountains will find them. They may plunge to **the bottom of the sea** to be lost in its depths, but there they will be bitten by the deadly sea-serpent whom God has tamed, verse 3. They may even think that they can be rescued by a foreign army that will take them into **exile,** but there God's **sword** will find them out and **slay** them, verse 4. For no one can escape from God's sight (cf. Job 34:21; Ps. 11:4; 66:7; 139:16; Prov. 5:21; 15:3; Jer. 16:17; 32:19, etc.), and God's **eyes** are set upon Israel **for evil and not for good** because of its rebellion.

**9:5–6** / Biblical authors frequently borrowed pieces of ancient hymns and other liturgical materials to use as integral parts of their message (cf. Num. 10:35–36; Rom. 1:3–5; 1 Cor. 16:22; Phil. 2:6–8, etc.). Amos may have borrowed these two verses from the last stanza of an ancient hymn made up of 4:13; 5:8–9; and 9:5–6. The prophet has, however, made the hymn stanza an integral part of his proclamation and, indeed, has used the hymnic material to frame his announcement of Yahweh's judgment. Thus, though these two verses may originally have been independent of 9:1–4, they now form the climax of that oracle and should be deemed neither late additions nor extraneous to it. Amos put these verses in their present position.

The prophet has joined verses 5–6 with verses 1–4 by a consecutive *waw* ("and," omitted from both the NIV and the RSV) and by the repetition of the name Adonai (**Lord**) from 9:1. Thus 9:5–6 is intended to illumine the nature of the God who speaks in 9:1–4. Because of the repetition of "Adonai," however, the formulaic appellation in verse 5a has had to be changed from Amos's usual usage. Elsewhere he has spoken of Yahweh Elohim Sebaoth (4:13; 5:27; 6:8, 14; cf. 3:13; 5:16). Here the name is Adonai Yahweh Sebaoth. But verses 5–6 tell who God is.

Obviously this Adonai's hands contain all power. The fire of Adonai's wrath **melts** the earth with just a touch (cf. Ps. 46:6; 104:32; 144:5; Isa. 64:1–2; Mic. 1:3–4; Nah. 1:5) so that all peoples are plunged into mourning. Indeed, Adonai, as the Lord of the earth, verse 5, can cause the whole earth to heave up and sink (8:8). But Adonai is also the Lord of the heavens, establishing a dwelling in the vastness above the sky, lifting up the blue arc of the firmament and anchoring it at each end upon the earth, verse 6. And this Adonai is Lord of the seas, commanding the waters above the firmament to pour through the windows of heaven as rain, verse 6. This Adonai, this God, who controls earth and skies and sea, this God is named Yahweh—the God of the covenant with Israel. And so this is not only Lord of Israel's life and of the life of all nations. This is also Lord of the cosmos, who commands all things and peoples. This is the God who is coming to bring an end to Israel's life.

---

## Additional Notes §9

---

**8:6** / **Selling even the sweepings with the wheat:** Some have suggested that this line properly belongs at the end of v. 5.

**8:8** / Instead of **like the Nile,** the MT reads "like the light," omitting only a *yod*. The versions support the NIV translation.

**9:2** / In the Israelite worldview, Sheol was the place of the dead, that dark and gloomy place of dust (Job 17:16) that lay below the waters under the earth. There was no return from Sheol (Job 7:9; 16:22), and in some Israelite thought, it was a realm beyond Yahweh's grasp or finding out (Job 14:13; Isa. 38:18). But here and elsewhere (Job 26:6; Ps. 139:8; Prov. 15:11), Sheol lies open to Yahweh, who is Lord of all the regions of the universe.

**9:3** / The word for **serpent** is *nāḥāš* as in 5:19. The LXX usually translates *nāḥāš* with *ophis*, but here it reads *drakōn*, i.e., sea-serpent, and that is obviously the meaning, echoing the language of the ancient chaos dragon myth, in which the great deep was portrayed as a dragon or serpent (cf. Ps. 74:13–14; Isa. 51:9–10). As in Ps. 104:26, however, the dragon, sometimes called Leviathan or Rahab (cf. Ps. 89:9–10), has become a servant of Yahweh.

**9:6** / The LXX correctly interprets 9:1–6 by adding Elohim Sebaoth to the last line after the name Yahweh.

# §10 A Misplaced Oracle (Amos 9:7–10)

**9:7–10** / Clearly, the praise of Yahweh as the Lord of earth, skies, and seas in 9:5–6 has formed the climax of the prophecies of Amos. Verses 9–10 therefore appear as anticlimactic addenda to what has gone before. In addition, they seem to contradict what has previously been said. Amos has, throughout his oracles, announced the end of Israel, but in verse 8c, that announcement seems dissipated by mention of a remnant. What should we make of this passage?

A frequent solution has been to maintain that these verses are from the disciples of Amos and that they arise from the questioning and disputation of the prophet's words that followed his preaching in 760 BC. In the process of disputation, Amos's proclamation of absolute judgment was softened to give room for the survival of a remnant, verse 8c; only the **sinners** in Israel would be done to death, verse 10.

Actually, however, only verse 8c softens the prophet's original message. When that line is removed, the rest of the oracle is consonant with the judgment that Amos has announced. Its message is that Israel has joined the rest of the nations in their common rebellion against God (as in 1:3–2:16), and as a result, Israel too will be judged, and even more harshly than the others, verse 8. The Israelites need not plead that they are Yahweh's special people, created at the exodus, for the God who is the Lord of all nations has brought the **Philistines** from their original home in Crete to the coastal plain of Palestine. Similarly, God has brought up the **Arameans** from their place of origin in Egypt and Nubia to their home in Syria, verse 7. Israel can base no special pleading on its election at the time of the exodus. Rather, its election marked it with special responsibility for obedience and trust (cf. 3:2).

Israel, like all the nations, will be shaken in the **sieve** of God's judgment, **as grain is shaken** over a coarse mesh to sift it out from debris and pebbles, verse 9. But none in Israel will fall through the sieve; none are good **grain.** And so the people of

Israel **will die by the sword** of the Lord, because in their pride they have believed themselves their own invulnerable lords, whom judgment cannot touch, verse 10.

In short, only verse 8c comes from a later hand. The rest of the oracle is consonant with Amos's total preaching. Certainly, however, verses 7–10 (minus 8c) seem out of place, and they probably belong after 7:17: in 7:16–17, Amos pronounces judgment on Amaziah himself, but he then goes on to reiterate his judgment on Israel as a whole, and 9:7–8ab, 9–10 are the words he uses to do so. In the process of transmission, however, they have been disarranged and placed in ch. 9 because of their connection with the catchwords **shake** (9:1, 9), **sword** (9:1, 4, 10), and "evil" (RSV 9:4, 10).

## §11 The Last Word (Amos 9:11–15)

These are actually two separate oracles, their beginnings marked by the standard eschatological phrases, **In that day** and **The days are coming.** Elsewhere in Amos, these phrases had specific reference to the coming day of the Lord. Here they point to an indefinite eschatological future not envisioned by the prophet himself.

These two brief passages are undoubtedly the work of a later hand, and the same author is probably responsible for both. In addition, both of these oracles stem from Judah sometime in its exilic or postexilic period, for after the fall of the northern kingdom of Israel to Assyria in 721 BC, the northern kingdom was a thing of the past.

**9:11–12** / The first oracle, in verses 11–12, promises the restoration of the Davidic empire. While the meaning of "booth" (RSV; NIV has **tent**) is uncertain in verse 11, it probably refers to the city of Jerusalem (cf. Isa. 1:8 RSV). The promise is that Jerusalem's walls and ruins will be restored to their former glory (cf. Isa. 61:4), and the new Davidic king will repossess the territory of **Edom,** which had so ravaged Judah after its fall to Babylonia in 587 BC (cf. Obad. 10–14). But the new Davidic realm will encompass other **nations** as well in a universal kingdom (cf. Ps. 72:8–11).

**9:13–15** / The second oracle, in verses 13–15, promises the restoration of all of the fortunes of the people of God (cf. Jer. 30:18) in a reversal of Amos 5:11: labor will be rewarded (cf. Isa. 65:21–22; Jer. 31:5) and there will be agricultural abundance beyond imagining (cf. Ps. 72:16; Joel 3:18). So plentiful will be the grapes that hang from the vines on the mountainsides that it will seem as if **the mountains** are flowing with their juice. There will be a return to the land of Palestine. Never again will the people be exiled, but they will enjoy a secure future for all time (cf. Isa. 60:21; Jer. 24:6; Ezek. 37:25).

In short, despite the fact that the life of the northern kingdom is at an end, God still has a future for this people. Those who assembled the prophetic books of the OT knew that if God's judgment was the last word, then God was defeated. God promised to Abraham in the beginning of the history of Israel (and from here on, we use the term to refer to the whole people), that all the families of the earth would be blessed through it (Gen. 12:3). During the reign of David, God promised that there would never be lacking a Davidic heir to sit upon the throne (2 Sam. 7).

Similarly, in the beginning, God intended human life and his world to be "very good" (Gen. 1:31). But when human sin corrupted God's good creation (Gen. 3–11), God set out to make his world good again, beginning a history of salvation by calling Abraham out of Mesopotamia. And God's intention was to form, through Israel its cornerstone (cf. Isa. 28:16), a universal people, encompassing all the nations of the world in a faithful community that knew how to live in justice and righteousness under God's lordship (cf. Isa. 2:2–4; 19:24; 44:2–5; 45:22–25; Mic. 4:1–4; Zeph. 3:9–10; Zech. 8:20–23).

In other words, in answer to human sin, God set out to establish a kingdom on earth even as it is in heaven. But if God's judgment on this sinful people is the last word, then human sin has won, God has been unable to attain his original goal for the universe, and is finally *not* Lord of heaven and of earth.

Above all else, however, the prophecies of Amos are a proclamation of the fact that the God of Israel is sovereign over all—that this is Yahweh Elohim Sebaoth—the Lord God of all the hosts of heaven and of earth. It therefore is very appropriate that a later hand has appended these two oracles to the preaching of Amos, for they are a witness and a confirmation of that which Amos proclaimed: that God is indeed the Lord God Sebaoth who will bring all his good purposes for humanity and his world to fulfillment.

God can never overlook human sin (cf. Jer. 7:16–20; Hab. 1:13). The inhabitants of the northern kingdom could not profane the name of Yahweh and go unpunished; otherwise Yahweh would not be the Lord. But human sin is never the last word. God has the final say. And because God is a good God of love, the final word is always one of hope and restoration and salvation.

With God alone, however, rest all our hopes for salvation. Significantly, Amos 9:12 emphasizes that it is the Lord alone **who will do these things.** Enslaved to our sinful injustice and empty worship practices and proud claims that we can save ourselves, we cannot bring in the kingdom of God on earth. But Yahweh Elohim Sebaoth can bring it and is doing so.

The promises of Amos 9:11–15 center on the fulfillment of the promise to David and on God's intentions when Abraham was called. But Christians now know that the new David, the Messiah or anointed Davidic king, has come. And he is the fulfillment of the promise to Abraham (cf. 2 Cor. 1:20), the one through whom God will bring blessing on all the families of the earth (Acts 3:25–26; Gal. 3:8). Through the church's preaching of Christ, therefore, God is calling all nations into a covenant people (Acts 15:16–18), that the abundant life promised in this appendix to Amos may belong to all people under the lordship of the one God, Yahweh Elohim Sebaoth.

# *Obadiah*

# Introduction: Obadiah

## Obadiah's Place in History

Obadiah is made up of the words granted to the prophet in an ecstatic vision (v. 1) sometime during the Babylonian exile of the kingdom of Judah, 587 to 538 BC. Many scholars would date the book a century later than that, but it may well come from the middle of the sixth century BC.

Obadiah's words are directed to the nation of Edom, which was located to the south-southeast of the southern tip of the Dead Sea. The Brook Zered formed Edom's northern border, while the northern shore of the Gulf of Aqabah marked Edom's southern border. The important trade route to the Gulf of Aqabah ran through Edom, and in the times of both David and Solomon, Edom was controlled by Israel. After their reigns, kings of Israel and Judah were characterized by whether or not they could hold onto Edom (cf. 2 Kgs. 14:22; 16:6), and wars were frequent (cf. 2 Chron. 20; 21:8–10).

The forebear of Edom was Esau, brother to Jacob (Gen. 25:19–26), and from the first the relation of the two brothers was marked by deceit and hatred (Gen. 25:29–34; 27; 32–33), an enmity that continued between the peoples descended from them. Nevertheless, the Edomites were brothers to the Israelites, and the law of Deuteronomy 23:7 forbade Israelite abhorrence of an Edomite. But in violation of that brotherly relationship, Edom turned against Judah at the time of the Babylonian capture and destruction of Jerusalem, even joyfully joining in the betrayal and pillaging of Judah (vv. 12–14). For that act, Obadiah announces God's judgment on Edom.

The name Obadiah is a familiar one in the OT (1 Kgs. 18:3, 7, 16; 1 Chron. 27:19; 2 Chron. 34:12, etc.), having the meaning "servant" or "worshiper of Yahweh." But none of the other references refer to the prophet, and we know nothing about him.

## Message

At first reading, the book appears to be nothing but a nationalistic testimony to Judah's vengeful hatred of Edom for its calumny. But that is a shallow reading of this shortest book of the OT. Rather, the book is a powerful witness to the sovereignty of Yahweh, the God of Israel, and for that reason it deserves careful attention.

In this book, nations pursue their apparently independent ways: Babylonia captures and exiles Judah; Edom takes advantage of its brother-nation's downfall; Judah languishes hopelessly in its captivity. But nations are not independent at all, Obadiah is telling us, for over them all reigns a sovereign Lord to whom belong all kingdoms of the earth (cf. v. 21). And it is finally the Lord's will that determines the fate of peoples. Thus, Obadiah announces that God, as the sovereign power, will reverse the fortunes imposed upon Edom and Judah by history. On the day of the Lord, God will destroy Edom and exalt the people Israel, who will then reign secure from Mt. Zion.

## The Unity of Obadiah

Many scholars have questioned the unity of the book. Their view is that the original work consisted of verses 2–14, 15b, and was delivered shortly after the fall of Jerusalem in 587 BC. Later, they maintain, verses 15a, 16–18 or 16–21 were added, perhaps in the time of Nabatean raids against Edom that forced it from its territory. The addition, then, sets the original oracle of verses 2–14, 15b in the context of God's universal judgment in the day of the Lord. In support of this theory, such scholars point out that in verses 2–14, 15b, Edom is punished by means of foreign nations, whereas in verses 15a, 16–21, Israel is the instrument of judgment on all nations.

Literary and rhetorical features found in the book argue against such conclusions. Edom is the central object of judgment throughout. The day of the Lord figures in both verse 8a and verses 15–18. The theme of the reversal of fortunes is prominent from beginning to end. In addition, the particle *kî*, translated "for" at the beginning of both verses 15 and 16 (RSV), inseparably points back to what has gone before. One of the most important words in Hebrew language, *kî* is followed by the theological rationale for what has previously been said. The book, as it stands before us in the canon, may justifiably be read as a unity. I will divide it into sections in the commentary that follows only for the purpose of analysis.

With the exception of corruptions in verse 20 especially, and in verses 19 and 21, the text of Obadiah is in good shape. A passionate and poetic style characterizes the Hebrew of the book, with interrupting exclamations (cf. v. 5c) and repetitious verbal clauses (cf. the Hebrew of v. 2) giving emphases to the thought.

There are parallels between some portions of the book of Obadiah and later portions of Jeremiah: Obadiah 1–4=Jeremiah 49:14–16; Obadiah 5=Jeremiah 49:9; Obadiah 8 echoes Jeremiah 49:7. Some scholars have therefore theorized that either an older oracle was known to both prophets or, more probably, that Jeremiah 49:7–22 is a later addition to that book and is dependent on Obadiah. There are also echoes of Joel in Obadiah: cf. verse 10 with Joel 3:19; verse 11 with Joel 3:3; verse 15 with Joel 1:15; 3:4, 7, 14; verse 17 with Joel 2:32; 3:17. But Joel is undoubtedly the later work, and the likenesses illustrate how prophets used earlier traditions and adapted them to their own situation. The word of God never spoke only to the time in which it was given, but continued to exercise its influence on subsequent ages.

## Fulfillment of Prophecies

Did Obadiah's prophecies come to pass? While Edom's history after the time of Obadiah is rather obscure, we do know that it was driven from its land during the first half of the fifth century, probably by Nabatean raiders from the desert. It moved farther into the desert region south of Judah and established there the kingdom of Idumea, with a capital at Hebron (1 Macc. 4:29; 5:3, 65; Mark 3:8). Then, according to Josephus (*Ant.* 13.9), it was incorporated forcibly into the Jewish commonwealth in the time of the Maccabean John Hyrcanus (135–104 BC). In prophetic thought, however, Edom became a type of all of those opposing God, and similarly as in Obadiah, its downfall was understood as an indispensable part of the messianic age (cf. Isa. 34:5–6; 63:1–6).

God rules the ways of nations—that is the affirmation of Obadiah. Nations are expected to fulfill their covenant relations. Their injustice is punished; their evil deeds are returned upon their own heads. God protects and saves those who are elected to serve God's purpose for all peoples. And the Lord God works such things steadfastly and irresistibly toward a future when all the kingdoms "of the world have become the kingdom of our Lord and of his Christ" (Rev. 11:15). In that future kingdom, all persons will live once again in faithfulness and peace with one another. Enmity and hatred will be no more. Suffering and death will be done away. And the goodness of God will be all in all. Thy kingdom come, O Lord, even as it is in heaven!

# §1 Pride Brought Low (Obadiah 1–4)

Edom enjoyed natural fortifications. Its highlands rose southeast of the Dead Sea in three great steps of sandstone cliffs to a height of more than 5,000 feet. A maze of mountains, cliffs, chasms, rocky defiles, and stony plateaus, with arable land mostly on the east and in its wider defiles, Edom was easily defended. In Obadiah's time, it was densely populated, with abundant water in its gorges and ample food for all. It thought itself secure and independent, superior to its conquered brother-nation Judah.

**1–4** / But cliffs and mountains are no barrier to the God who has made them. Significantly, God is named ᵃdōnāy Yahweh in verse 1, "Lord Yahweh," and is Lord over Edom. Obadiah therefore reports what he has heard in his vision: A messenger has been sent to unnamed **nations** to mount a military attack against Edom, but really it is Yahweh who is going to bring its ruin. By using pronouns separate from the verbs in verses 2a and 4c, the Hebrew emphasizes that Yahweh is the actor: "*I* will make small, *I* will place you among the nations, who will jeer at you," verse 2a; "*I* will bring you down," verse 4c. Like the king of Babylon boasting of his invincible deity in Isaiah 14:13–14, Edom has boasted, verses 3–4. Its **pride** in its own strength and self-sufficiency has deceived it in its **heart,** the seat of its intellect and will, verse 3. But such pride is a challenge to the sovereignty of God, and God will not put up with it (cf. Mark 8:35 and parallels; Ps. 51:17; Isa. 57:15). Thus, the judgment of God that follows in the rest of the book is not only a defense of the people Israel, but a vindication of God's lordship.

These verses are characterized by images of high and low. Edom, who has set itself on high, will be brought low. It dwells in the heights, but nations will rise up against it to bring it down. And commanding it all is Yahweh, who makes high and makes low, who humbles the proud and exalts the lowly—a theme found throughout the Scriptures (cf. 1 Sam. 2:7; Job 40:12; Isa. 2:9; 5:15; Ezek. 17:24; 21:26; Luke 1:48; 14:11; 18:14). God brings the reversal of human history.

## §2 Edom Plundered and Defeated (Obadiah 5–7)

**5–7** / The NIV has translated these verses in the future tense, but they are better rendered in the present, as in the RSV, for in his vision Obadiah sees Edom already plundered. Thus, verse 5c should be read, "How you have been destroyed!" What the prophet speaks is as good as accomplished.

Obadiah deals in contrasts. If **thieves** stole, they would leave something behind; if **grape pickers** harvested, they would leave some fruit behind for the poor (cf. Deut. 24:21). But Edom's **treasures** have all been taken, verse 6. Edom carried off Judah's wealth, verses 11, 13. In God's reversal, Edom's own goods are lost to the plunderers.

Similarly, Edom violated its covenant of brotherhood with Judah, verse 10. Now those who entered into military covenants with Edom, and those friends who ate bread at its table, violate their covenants, betraying Edom's trust and driving it from its land. At God's instigation, the covenant-breaker becomes the broken.

The last line of this section, verse 7d, reads in the Hebrew, "There is no understanding it." The reference is not to the fact that Edom does **not detect** the trap laid for it by its friends and allies, as the NIV has interpreted, but rather to the fact that covenant-breaking defies all that is rational. Why, Edom wonders, would its friends betray it? There is no sense to such an event, and history is out of joint. But the thought serves to emphasize what comes after—Edom's own perfidy in breaking its covenant of brotherhood with Judah, verse 10.

## §3 The Wisdom of the Wise Destroyed (Obadiah 8–10)

**8–10** / The Edomites apparently enjoyed a reputation among the peoples of the ancient Near East as cultivators of wisdom tradition (cf. Jer. 49:7). But picking up the catchword **understanding** from the previous verse (RSV), God declares that understanding will depart from Edom, because all its **wise men** will perish, verse 8. Its warriors at **Teman,** the northern district of Edom, here used as a synonym for the whole country, will be no help in its defense. All of them will die, verse 9. And Edom will be noted among the nations not for its wisdom but for its shameful violation of its covenant of brotherhood with **Jacob,** the name used here of Judah, verse 10.

All will be Yahweh's work, for it will take place on **that day,** on the day of the Lord, verse 8. Obadiah here employs the popular and traditional understanding of the day of the Lord as the time when God would exalt the people Israel and destroy all of their enemies. (See the exposition of Amos 5:18–20 and of vv. 12–16 below.)

## §4 Edom's Day (Obadiah 11–14)

**11–14** / The NIV translation of the verbs in this section is rather odd. It renders verse 11 in the past tense, verses 12–14 in the present tense. Actually, all of the verbs should be read in the past tense; we have here a vivid description of Edom's attitudes and actions during and immediately after the Babylonian destruction of Judah and Jerusalem in 587 BC.

Edom did not deplore the destruction of its brother-nation Judah. Rather, it reveled in it, gloating over Judah's downfall, boasting that it was mightier than Judah, rejoicing over Judah's ruin. The NIV has softened the meaning of the verbs in verses 12 and 13. **Look down** in 12a and 13b should be "gloated"—a vivid picture of Edom's vengeful attitude toward its sibling (cf. Ps. 137:7; Ezek. 35).

Indeed, when the Babylonian troops entered Jerusalem and divided up its booty and populace by lot, Edom entered into the gambling, verse 11. And those persons whom the Edomites won, they then sold into slavery, along with the Judahites whom the Edomites captured as the former fled the city, verse 14. In addition, Edom engaged in its own looting, stealing what goods it could find, verse 13.

Edom totally violated the covenant of brothers, and that Edom should not have done. Despite the long history of enmity between Esau and Jacob and their descendants, Edom was related to Judah, with the obligations of a relative, and those obligations were not to be dismissed.

In short, God takes human covenants seriously. The pledges between husband and wife, the obligations of siblings, the responsibilities of neighbor for neighbor, of communities for each other, of nations for nations—all are ordained and guarded by God, intended to be used for divine purposes. When Edom betrayed Judah, it defied the will of God.

But more is involved than merely the obligations of human relationships. The people Israel, represented by the nation of

Judah in the time of Obadiah, is the chosen people of God. Elected by its deliverance from slavery in Egypt, Israel is God's adopted son (cf. Exod. 4:22–23; Jer. 3:19; Hos. 11:1), the chosen medium for bringing God's blessing on all the families of the earth (Gen. 12:3) and for shedding abroad the knowledge of God (Exod. 19:6) until it covers the earth as the waters cover the sea (cf. Isa. 11:9). To attack Israel is therefore to attack God's purpose for this world. Edom has challenged the very lordship of the ruler of all human history, and that challenge will be put down by the destruction of the Edomites.

## §5 The Day of the Lord (Obadiah 15–16)

**15–16** / As a consequence, in contrast to the day of Edom (above), there will be the **day of the LORD.** Verses 15–16 should actually be connected with verses 11–14 in an unbroken stanza, but I have separated them here simply to emphasize the contrast between Edom's day and God's. Verses 15 and 16 are connected rhetorically with verse 14 by *kî*, "for," an important word that the NIV has omitted from the beginning of both verses 15 and 16. Thus, the sense is: Edom should not have betrayed Judah, *for* or *because* the day of the Lord is near, and *because* it will be judged along with all the nations on that day.

The concept of **the day of the LORD** had its roots in the wars fought by Israel's tribal federation during the time of the Judges and of the early monarchy. In those wars, called "holy wars" by scholars because they were fought according to fixed cultic rules, it was believed that Yahweh fought for Israel with cosmic weapons. The popular belief therefore arose in Israel that Yahweh would finally bring in a time or day when all of Israel's enemies would be defeated and Israel would be exalted among the nations. Most of the prophets denied that popular belief and declared that disobedient Israel would also be judged. Rather than being a time of Israel's triumph, the day would bring wrath and darkness and destruction, leaving perhaps a remnant of its people (cf. Amos 5:18–20; Isa. 2:6–22; Ezek. 7:5–27; Joel 1:1–15; 2:1–11; Mal. 4:5). Obadiah reverses that usual prophetic picture of gloom and declares that the day of the Lord will be a time of salvation for the chosen people, while Edom, and indeed all of Israel's enemies, will be no more, verse 16.

Obadiah uses two traditional pictures in these verses. First, he employs what scholars have called a "synthetic view" of sin, in which the sin of Edom returns **upon** its **own head** as its punishment, verse 15. It is a common view in the Scriptures (cf. Jer. 50:15, 29; Ezek. 35:15; Joel 3:4, 7): evil returns upon the evil doer, not automatically, but as a consequence of Yahweh's working (cf. 1 Kgs. 8:31–32; Rom. 1:24, 26, 28). As Edom has done to Judah, so it shall be done to Edom.

Second, Obadiah uses the figure of **all the nations** forced on the day of Yahweh to drink of the cup of wrath (cf. Jer. 25:15–29; 49:12; Lam. 4:21). Edom, God says, profaned the holy hill of Zion with drinking and boisterous celebration of Judah's fall, verse 16. But Edom and all nations will have another draught—the draught of God's wrath from the cup of God's anger, and they will drink and gulp and swallow that draught until they have disappeared from history.

## §6 A Remnant to Judah, None to Edom (Obadiah 17–18)

**17–18** / Judah, of course, has already drunk of God's wrath in its exile to Babylonia. But that is not the end of Judah. God still has for it, as Jeremiah would say, "a future and a hope" (Jer. 29:11). There will be left a remnant to Judah—a thought that the NIV translation has totally obscured, verse 17a. The Hebrew reads, "But on the mountain of Zion (there shall be) those who escape" (see the RSV). The mountain itself will become **holy,** that is, it will become an inviolable sanctuary through which conquerors will never again pass (cf. Joel 3:17). And the Judeans will once again possess their own land (**inheritance**).

More than that, a reunited Israel, symbolized in verse 18 by the **house of Jacob** (the southern kingdom of Judah) and **the house of Joseph** (the northern kingdom of Israel) will be reconstituted by God, who will then use the new Israel as a means of judgment on Edom. Like a fire burning up straw **stubble,** a figure often used of God's judgment (cf. Mal. 4:1), the renewed Israel will consume Esau until no remnant (NIV: **survivors**) of them is left. Presumably a military victory is meant, although it is not specified. But all of this is certain future, because Yahweh has spoken it, and Yahweh's word does not return void (cf. Isa. 55:10–11).

## §7 The Kingdom of Israel and the Kingdom of God (Obadiah 19–21)

**19–21** / The picture that Obadiah finally paints is that of the kingdom of God come on earth, with a united Israel once again in possession of the whole ideal kingdom from Halah in the north to Edom in the south, from the western coast of Palestine and Syria to the eastern limits of Gilead and Edom beyond the Jordan, verses 19–20.

Many of the prophets' pictures of the glorious future of Israel portrayed the northern and southern tribes of the covenant people restored and united once again in a single nation (cf. Ezek. 37:15–23, 24–28). That is, the ten northern tribes, lost to history in the Assyrian exile of 721 BC, would once again be found and restored to their homeland, as would also all of the dispersed exiles of the Babylonian conquests of the 6th century BC. In the kingdom of God, the people of God would once again be whole.

Further, no enemy would threaten Israel's borders or claim its territory. Thus, the Israelites in the southern desert, which was called the **Negev**, would possess Edom, verse 19. Those in the Shephelah or **foothills** of Palestine would have the coastal regions from the **Philistines. Ephraim** and **Samaria** in the north would belong to Israel, as would Ammon and **Gilead** on the eastern side of the Jordan. Instead of reading with both the NIV and RSV, **and Benjamin will possess Gilead,** the second half of verse 19 should be read, "They shall possess the land of Ephraim and the land of Samaria and Ammon to Gilead," reading *bᵉnê ʿammôn* for *binyāmin*. Otherwise the mention of the single tribe of Benjamin, which originally owned land between Ephraim and Judah, is very strange.

Verse 20a–b is so corrupted in the Hebrew as to be indecipherable. The RSV reads *ḥalaḥ* for *haḥēl* (**company** or "host") and translates, "The exiles in Halah who are of the people of Israel (shall possess) Phoenicia as far as Zarephath." **Zarephath** was to the north, on the coast between Tyre and Sidon. Thus, this reading speaks of the ownership of northern territory, while verse 20c–d speaks of ownership of the **Negev** to the south by Israelite exiles in **Sepharad,** the name given to Sardis in Asia Minor. If the RSV reading is accepted—and it seems more probable than that of the NIV—the picture is one of scattered Israelite exiles returning from their dispersion and reclaiming and enlarging their homeland from the far north to the south. This is Israel exalted among the nations indeed!

As Obadiah has centered on Edom, however, it returns once again to that concern, in verse 21. The NIV translates **deliverers,** but the verb should be read "delivered" or "saved," referring to the Israelites—we have heard nothing of deliverers otherwise, and Yahweh is the one who will save Israel for a future glorious kingdom.

The "saved" Israelites will once again be able to go up to Mount Zion, in full control of their former enemies, the Edomites. But finally, as in the picture of the future found in Isaiah 2:2–4, God will be the ruler over all the nations, in a kingdom of righteousness and covenant faithfulness and peace.

# *Jonah*

# Introduction: Jonah

Although it is placed among other prophetic writings in the book of the Twelve, the book of Jonah is different from all other prophetic books. Instead of being a collection of prophetic oracles, it is a story *about* a man named Jonah, who is never called a prophet in the book. To be sure, it opens with the familiar prophetic phrase, "The word of the LORD came to Jonah" (1:1), but there is only one brief prophetic oracle in the whole work (3:4).

Unlike the other prophets, Jonah is sent to preach not to Israel but to the foreign city Nineveh in Mesopotamia. A covenant context for his preaching is entirely missing. The story, with the exception of 2:2–9, is in prose rather than in the familiar poetry of the other Minor Prophets. And far from being a mouthpiece for the word of God, Jonah is a disobedient and angry servant.

While we do have some other narratives about prophets, such as Elijah, Elisha, and Jeremiah, those stories never constitute the whole of the information about them. Other prophets, such as Jeremiah and Ezekiel, preach oracles against foreign nations, but their primary audience is Israel. And all of the prophets except Jonah carry on their ministries within the context of God's covenant with the chosen people. Jonah is unique among the "goodly fellowship of the prophets," to say the least.

## The Prophetic Message of the Book

There is one sense in which the book of Jonah is rightly placed in the canon of prophetic literature, however. The book reveals who God is and what God does. Prophets in the OT were not only those who "stood in the council of the LORD to perceive and to hear his word" (Jer. 23:18 RSV) and who were then sent to Israel to proclaim that word. Prophets also had the function of proclaiming, on the basis of that word, just where and how and why God was at work, and it is this general function of prophecy that the book of Jonah fulfills. It tells where and how and why the

God of Israel is at work. Indeed, the central character in the story is not Jonah but God. And through this story, God's character and purpose are revealed.

## The Theology of the Book

The theology in Jonah is based primarily on a doctrine of creation. God is the creator of all things and persons (1:9; 4:10). God creates the storm, the fish, the plant, the worm, the scorching east wind. And God is the creator of Jonah and of the inhabitants and animals in Nineveh. As a result, God is the sustainer and sovereign over all of them, "hurling" the storm, "appointing" the fish and plant, the worm and wind.

As its creator, God alone is the source of life. God is the only one who can save the sailors (1:6, 14) and Jonah (2:2, 6, 9, 10), and Nineveh (3:9; 4:11). The sailors' gods (1:5) and heathen idols (2:8) cannot do so. God can take away Jonah's life (4:3), and Jonah and the sailors both know or learn that they are entirely dependent on God for their existence (1:10, 12, 14, 16; 2:6–7). To be separated from God, or to flee from "before his face" means death (1:12; 2:4), a thought that is emphasized by the repeated use in the Hebrew of the verb, "to go down" (1:2, 3, 5; 2:6) from God. "To rise up" (1:2, 3, 6; 3:2, 3, 6) or "to lift up" (1:12, 15) in obedience to God or in God's direction is to be pointed toward life.

Thus all life is dependent on the creator's mercy in preserving it (4:7), and it is only God's mercy that sustains the life of a disobedient Jonah or a wicked Nineveh. Life is not granted to people because of their goodness or obedience, their repentance or piety (3:9). God is free to do anything with creation; it all belongs to him (4:10–11). And the true miracle in the book of Jonah is not that he is saved by being swallowed by a great fish but that the creator of the universe deals with creation in mercy and not with the stern justice that human creatures so richly deserve.

## The Setting

Jonah is named as the "son of Amittai," and though he is not called a prophet in this story, this title immediately identifies him with the "prophet" and "servant" of the Lord mentioned in 2 Kings 14:25, who prophesied that Jeroboam II (786–746 BC) would greatly expand the territory of the northern kingdom of

Israel. Thus, Jonah is to be understood in that eighth-century BC setting. According to 2 Kings 14:25, he hails from Gath Hepher, a city fifteen miles west of the Sea of Galilee, in the territory of Zebulun (cf. Josh. 19:13).

The fact that Jonah was written *after* Jeroboam's time becomes clear, however, from the story's description of Nineveh. It is called a "great city," verse 2, and while it was one of the oldest cities in Mesopotamia, located on the east bank of the Tigris River opposite Mosul, it did not have great importance during the reign of Jeroboam II, when Assyria was ruled by a series of weaklings. It was not until the resurgence of Assyrian power under Tiglath-pileser III (745–727 BC) that Nineveh began to grow in importance. In 701 BC, the Assyrian emperor Sennacherib (705–681 BC) made Nineveh his capital; it became perhaps the most powerful city in the Near Eastern world. But Nineveh was reduced to ruins by the Medes and Babylonians in 612 BC, and it was never rebuilt.

Archaeology has revealed that at the height of its power Nineveh had a perimeter of 7½ miles, which shows that it would not take three days to walk across it, despite the notice of that in Jonah 3:3. (The NIV has emended the text at 3:3 to soften the disparity).

Certainly from the time of Tiglath-pileser until the fall of the Assyrian Empire, Nineveh was the symbol of the overwhelming and ruthless power of that empire—"the place of man's omnipotence" (Ellul, *The Judgment of Jonah*, p. 27). Its pride in its power is vividly set forth in Isaiah 10:12–14, while the book of Nahum, which depicts Nineveh's fall, tells us that Nineveh was a "city of blood" (3:1) and of "endless cruelty" (3:19). It was the Assyrian Empire that first carried out a systematic policy of deporting captured peoples and of replacing them with foreigners, a policy that led to the disappearance from history of the ten northern tribes of Israel when they were defeated by Assyria in 721 BC.

What we have in Jonah, therefore, is a distant recollection of Nineveh, hazy and exaggerated in its details, but nevertheless to be understood in the light of the cruelty of the Assyrian Empire in the latter part of the eighth century BC. It is that "wickedness" that has "come up before" Yahweh (Jonah 1:2). And it is such a bloody symbol of the Assyrian Empire to which Jonah is commanded to "arise, go," and "preach."

## Getting the Purpose Straight

Arguments over the historicity of Jonah, especially as they center on the probability of the big fish swallowing Jonah, are therefore misguided. Like the parables of Jesus, the book of Jonah conveys its revelation of God in the form of a story. Brevard Childs has even described the story as "parable-like" (Childs, *Introduction to the Old Testament as Scripture*, p. 421) while pointing out its differences from prophetic legend, midrash, and allegory (p. 422). I think it is quite sufficient, however, to term the book a "didactic story" as many commentators have done.

In view of the fact that the book is primarily concerned with God, it is also an error to think its purpose centers around the issue of false prophecy. Some hold that Jonah flees from God because he knows God will not judge Nineveh and he does not want to be a false prophet. But since prophecy is never mentioned in the book, this seems less than likely.

Similarly, the widespread understanding of the book as a protest against the exclusivism of Judaism, as that is mirrored in the work of Nehemiah and Ezra, is not to be adopted. Jonah says nothing about the problems with which those Israelite leaders dealt. Certainly there is some missionary emphasis in the book, and that will be discussed in the commentary. But the missionary note is secondary to the book's primary purpose of revealing the character of the creator and sovereign of the world.

Indeed, rather than dating the book after the time of Nehemiah and Ezra in the latter half of the fifth century BC, it is probably more correct to date it, with Terence Fretheim (*The Message of Jonah*, p. 36), in the first half of that century, during the time reflected in the prophecies of Malachi. The statement of the Judeans in Malachi 3:14—"It is futile to serve God"—is precisely the attitude of Jonah in Jonah 4:3, as we shall discuss in the commentary.

## Text and Unity

Fortunately, the Hebrew text of Jonah is in excellent shape. Until the discovery of a partial Hebrew text at Wadi Murabba'at in the Dead Sea area in 1955, the best manuscript that we had of Jonah dated from AD 1008. But Murabba'at revealed only 13 minor differences from the eleventh-century manuscript, a testimony to the care with which the book was transmitted through centuries of time.

In my estimation, scholars have raised only two significant questions with regard to the unity of the book. (a) Was the psalm in 2:2–9 part of the original composition? Certainly it could be removed without disturbing the flow of the story. It is a typical individual psalm of thanksgiving. On the other hand, it is not inconsistent with the portrayal of Jonah in the rest of the book, as we shall see, and there is no reason why it should be removed from the text.

(b) Is 4:5 out of place, and should it be put after 3:4, as von Rad (*Old Testament Theology* II, p. 289) and others have suggested? It does seem inconsistent with its context, especially with 4:2 and 4:6. But I am always reluctant to alter clear texts, and we shall deal with the arrangement of chapter 4 as it stands.

The reader should especially note one fact. Throughout its treatment of Jonah, the NIV consistently has translated the Hebrew text very freely, producing what borders on a paraphrase. Indeed, so free is the translation that I have not tried in every instance to correct the NIV's reading. Most of the time, the NIV does not alter the essential meaning of the text, but there will be instances when it will be necessary to give the proper rendering of the Hebrew in order to get at the original meaning. The reader is advised to consult the RSV for an accurate translation of the MT.

## §1 The Command and the Flight (Jonah 1:1–3)

**1:1–3** / The NIV has omitted several rhetorical devices in these first three verses that are significant for an understanding of Jonah. Verse 1:1 begins with *wayᵉhî*, which may be translated, "Now it came to pass," or simply "Now." The word is a sure indication that what follows is a story or narrative (cf. MT of Josh. 1:1; Judg. 1:1).

Verse 2 begins with "arise" (RSV; NIV: **go;** *qûm*), and this verb is repeated at the beginning of verse 3: "But Jonah rose *(qûm)* to flee to Tarshish" (RSV). He obeys the Lord's command to arise but goes in the opposite direction from Nineveh.

Verse 3 emphasizes that Jonah's disobedience is a *descent* from the Lord by repeating the verb *yārad*, "to go down": "And he went down to Joppa . . . and he went down on it (the ship) to go with them to Tarshish. . . ." The verb will then recur in verse 5, "But Jonah went down to the hold of the ship . . . ," and in 2:6, "I went down. . . ." Jonah, in his disobedience, is descending vertically from the presence of the Lord, and in the poem of chapter 2 that descent is down toward Sheol, the place of the dead. The author of this story is therefore using word symbols to portray the terrible implication of Jonah's disobedience. To flee from the Lord means death. In good storyteller fashion, that is not spelled out for us at the beginning but is revealed gradually as the narrative proceeds.

The NIV has also omitted one use of the word "Tarshish" in verse 3b, which reads, "and he found a ship going to Tarshish." Three times the name of that destination occurs in verse 3. The author is impressing the direction of Jonah's flight upon us. Similarly, the phrase, "before the face (or presence) of Yahweh" or "before my face" occurs three times in verses 2 and 3. Nineveh's sin has risen up before Yahweh's face, verse 2, but Jonah flees to Tarshish "from before the face of Yahweh," and that phrase occurs twice in verse 3. By such repetitions, the author is emphasizing that Jonah is separating himself from the Lord.

Thus, from the beginning, an ominous note is struck for the careful reader in this charming and sometimes humorous tale.

Although Jonah does "arise," he then goes to the port of **Joppa,** which was near modern Tel Aviv, and takes a ship to flee in exactly the opposite direction of Nineveh, to the west rather than to the east. The exact location of Tarshish has never been definitely settled, but most scholars are inclined to identify it with Tartessus, a Phoenician colony on the southwestern coast of Spain. In biblical times, it was famous for its sea traffic (1 Kgs. 10:22; Isa. 23:1, 14; 66:19; Ezek. 27:25), and its ships were noted for their size and grandeur (Isa. 2:16). It tends to be mentioned as a distant place (Isa. 66:19; Ps. 72:10), so that our story is emphasizing that Jonah was fleeing to the farthest point in the opposite direction from Nineveh.

The story says that Jonah was fleeing "from before the presence of Yahweh" (MT, verse 3), but it is questionable that Jonah believed he was escaping the Lord's presence. Jonah was a good Jew, and he probably knew Amos:

> Not one will get away,
> none will escape.
> Though they dig down to the depths of the grave,
> from there my hand will take them.
> Though they climb up to the heavens,
> from there I will bring them down.
> Though they hide themselves on the top of Carmel,
> there I will hunt them down and seize them.
> Though they hide from me at the bottom of the sea,
> there I will command the serpent to bite them.
> (Amos 9:1–3)

Perhaps Psalm 139 was familiar to him:

> Where can I go from your Spirit?
> Where can I flee from your presence?
> If I go up to the heavens, you are there;
> if I make my bed in the depths, you are there.
> (vv. 7–8)

The Lord of Israel is an inescapable God, and Jonah probably knew that. But Jonah can flee to a distant city where Yahweh of Israel is unknown, where the society knows nothing of God's word spoken through his prophets and psalmists, where the covenant with Israel is not acknowledged, and where other gods and other commitments guide daily life. Jonah can place himself

outside of the elect people and live with a people for whom
Yahweh is not the Lord, much like people in our day can choose
to immerse themselves in a totally secular culture. A place where
God and God's word are unknown, or ignored and forgotten—
that is the society Jonah seeks. It is a good picture of our modern
preference for such a society.

But why does Jonah flee? Multiple answers have been
given to the question. The ancient historian, Josephus, said Jonah
was afraid (*Ant.* 9.208). Others believe the task was too difficult—
after all, Nineveh was five hundred miles away, as the crow
flies—but there is no mention of Jonah's inadequacy for the task.
Very frequently, scholars have held that Jonah knew God
would not punish Nineveh, and Jonah did not want to be known
as a false prophet. We are not immediately given the reason for
his flight. Rather, we are left simply with a good story's tension
of wondering what will happen to this disobedient prophet and
what will happen to wicked Nineveh.

Certainly the reader can begin to identify with Jonah's
disobedience, however. Why on earth should anyone want to
carry God's word to a city like Nineveh? The ways of this God of
Jonah seem inexplicable, to say the least. But of course, when
Jonah decided that he, rather than Yahweh, knew what was the
best course of action, he set himself to correct God, and that is
always dangerous.

**1:4–6** / The author lets us know immediately that Jonah can neither escape nor defy God. Verse 3 ends with Jonah fleeing "from before the face of Yahweh." Verse 4 begins, "But Yahweh." Into the path of Jonah's horizontal flight from God, the Lord "hurls" (MT) a great wind onto the Mediterranean, which causes a **violent storm** with enormous waves. Thus Jonah's flight is brought to a dead stop only shortly after it is begun.

Disobedience rarely has consequences only for the sinner, however. The ship, laden with its cargo, threatens to break up, drowning not only the disobedient Jonah, but also the ship's pagan crew and captain. As a result, as any human being is wont to do in a life-threatening situation, the sailors pray, each of them **to his own god** or goddess. At the same time, they take the mariner's familiar precaution of throwing their **cargo** and equipment overboard to lighten the ship and thus keep it from being swamped and sunk by the enormous waves. (The MT reads, "and they hurled the equipment which was on the boat into the sea," repeating the verb "hurl" from verse 4).

When he goes down in the hold to fetch some of the cargo, the ship's **captain** discovers **Jonah** sleeping a deep **sleep** (cf. Isa. 29:10; Gen. 2:21) among what were probably bales and jars. In an ironic touch, he awakens Jonah with the same command that Jonah had received from God, "Arise! Call . . ." (cf. MT 1:2). That word of God is pursuing Jonah, try as he may to escape it.

The captain summons Jonah to pray to **your god** and then calls Jonah's god "the God" (MT; the NIV reads simply "he"). The sailors have already prayed to their various gods with no saving result. Perhaps the unknown God of Jonah will hear and keep them all from perishing. The captain hopes to locate at least one god who has power to say to the storm "Peace, be still!" (cf. Mark 4:39 RSV) and thus rescue them all from perishing. But of course the captain does not know that Jonah, in his disobedience, has turned his back on God. Jonah cannot abruptly shift and pray to

Yahweh when he finds himself in a jam—a caution to every reader of this story. And so there is no mention of Jonah uttering any prayer.

There are several notable points to be made in relation to these verses. First, it is quite clear that Yahweh is not *in* the storm. Yahweh is not some nature god, bound up with or contained in the elements, as a storm-god would be. Rather, Yahweh is Lord over nature and able to command the wind and storm. Second, it is quite clear that the pagan gods do not share that lordship over the natural world. The sailors' prayers have no efficacy in stilling the storm. Yahweh here is the only God, the Lord over creation. Third, it has been suggested by some commentators that the sailors were making sacrifices to their gods when they threw the cargo into the sea. But anyone who has read histories of sailing knows that the jettisoning of cargo is a frequent measure of mariners when they are threatened with swamping. Fourth, Ezekiel 27:3–9 gives a description of a Phoenician ship in the sixth century BC. It is very likely that the ship that the author of Jonah had in mind was similar, made of pine, cedar, and cypress, and that it had oars as well as sails (cf. Jonah 1:13), but it apparently was a cargo ship and may not have had fine linen sails or a deck inlaid with ivory. We do not know.

Finally, there has been a great deal of speculation about why Jonah was asleep. According to the pluperfect verb in verse 5, he had gone down into the hold and fallen into a deep sleep as soon as he boarded the ship. The text says nothing about his being tired. Rather, it seems that we simply have a picture of a man who is content with his decision and who therefore is able to fall asleep. Indeed, he is so fast asleep that the storm does not arouse him, and he returns to consciousness only when addressed rather roughly, and certainly loudly over the noise of the storm, by the captain: "What do you mean, you sleeper! Arise, call upon your God!" (MT and RSV). But of course, this is the one thing that Jonah cannot do.

## §3 The Lot (Jonah 1:7–12)

**1:7–8** / That which the NIV translates with **calamity** in verse 7 and with **trouble** in verse 8 is the Hebrew word for "evil." The sailors realize that the storm which threatens their lives is no ordinary storm, but an "evil" that a divine being has brought upon them. As throughout the Scriptures and the ancient Near East, the forces of nature are not divorced from the action of God. The violent and sudden storm did not come upon them by chance, the sailors reason. Some divine being is punishing someone. They therefore turn to the ancient universal custom of casting lots in order to determine who is the guilty party, verse 7.

While the casting of **lots** is frequently mentioned throughout the Bible (Num. 26:55; Josh. 14:2; 1 Sam. 10:20–24; 14:42; 1 Chron. 24:5; 25:8; 26:13; Mark 15:24 and parallels; Acts 1:26), no detailed description of the actual procedures used or of the instruments utilized is given. Small objects (stones or pieces of pottery), each inscribed with a name, have been discovered at the first-century AD mountaintop fortress of Masada, and perhaps something similar is implied in the story of Jonah. The important point is that the deity determines upon whom the lot falls (Prov. 16:33). By casting the lot, the sailors therefore learn that Jonah is responsible for the evil that has come upon them, verse 7.

Immediately the sailors barrage Jonah with questions, verse 8. They want to know his occupation, home town, country, and ethnic background, but they are not interested in Jonah's biography. They want to know what god he serves, for it is that god who is punishing Jonah by means of the storm. To the sailors' way of thinking, every god or goddess is attached to a particular location or people, and the sailors desperately need to identify the deity, in order to take measures to appease him or her.

**1:9–11** / Jonah's reply in verse 9 shakes the sailors to the depths of their being. "A Hebrew am I," Jonah replies, using the appellation that was employed when addressing foreigners

(Exod. 2:7; 3:18), "and I fear Yahweh, God of heaven (cf. Gen. 24:7; 2 Chron. 36:23; Neh. 1:5) who made the sea and dry land" (MT). The sailors are not dealing with some localized deity. They are being subjected to a storm sent by the God who made their entire world and who therefore is Lord over it.

That Jonah makes such a confession of faith is totally ironic. He says that he "fears" (NIV: **worship**) Yahweh. "To fear God," in biblical usage, can have two meanings. It can mean simply "to obey" (Deut. 5:29; 6:2, 13, 24; 10:12, passim), and Jonah certainly has not obeyed Yahweh. "To fear God" can also mean to stand in awe of God (Ps. 33:8; Lev. 19:14, 32, etc.) or to reverence or honor God (Exod. 1:17; Ps. 55:19; 66:16, etc.), and Jonah has not been in awe of God; he has deliberately disobeyed Yahweh and then gone soundly to sleep, with not a disturbing worry. So Jonah is an Israelite who knows all the right words but who pays his God lip-service only (cf. Isa. 29:13). He is an orthodox believer who is not acting according to his beliefs, a message that the author undoubtedly wants to convey to his readers.

That Jonah is disobeying the Lord of heaven and earth terrifies the pagan sailors; they stand more in awe of that supreme God than does Jonah. And through the words of pagans, God confronts Jonah with his responsibility. "What is this that you have done?" the sailors ask Jonah, verse 10 (RSV), which was the same question God asked Eve, according to Gen. 3:13. Despite his disobedient flight, despite his indifference as he slept through the punishing storm, Jonah is responsible to God. And he cannot escape that responsibility any more than could Adam and Eve, or any person whom the Lord God has created. Human beings, made in the image of God, are related always to their maker, no matter what their situation, and they are responsible for their actions in relationship to God.

Jonah is an orthodox believer, however, and so he should know what to do to appease his God and thus quiet the raging **sea,** verse 11. He has two choices. He can repent, get off the boat at the next harbor, and return to his mission to Nineveh. Or he can accept the just punishment for his disobedience: death.

**1:12** / Some commentators have maintained that Jonah's statement to the sailors in verse 12 is his final way of escaping his mission. In one sense, that is true. Jonah will not go to Nineveh. He would rather die than preach to that wicked people (cf. 4:3). Others have lauded Jonah for his willingness to give his life in order to save the sailors. Perhaps there is also some justification for that view. But principally, Jonah realizes that he cannot escape or defy the Lord of heaven and earth and get away with it unscathed. That Lord is not mocked (cf. Gal. 6:7) and cannot be defeated. God's is "the kingdom and the power and the glory"; the author wants the readers to absorb that truth also.

So Jonah instructs the sailors to "hurl" him overboard, as they "hurled" their cargo and equipment (v. 5). That will bring the just retribution of Jonah's sin. The wind that Yahweh has "hurled" over the sea (v. 4) will be stilled, and the waters will return to their normal state, verse 12.

## §4 The Sailors Converted (Jonah 1:13–16)

**1:13–14** / Contrary to Jonah's instructions in verse 12, the sailors do not immediately hurl Jonah overboard. Instead, they try to **row** the ship to land where they can beach it, verse 13. Probably their motives were not entirely altruistic, as indicated by verse 14. They did not want to take the risk of incurring bloodguiltiness, and they reasoned that if they could deposit Jonah on land, he and God could work out their dispute between them without the sailors being involved. In short, they wanted a no-fault disposal of the troubling Jonah!

We must remember, however, that God controls the raging wind and storm (cf. Ps. 89:9), and so God thwarts the sailors' attempt to reach land. God, it seems, wants Jonah hurled overboard. The sailors finally realize that they too are powerless against the will of Yahweh. He has **done as** he **pleased,** verse 14: That one sentence should be seen as the theme that runs through the book of Jonah (cf. Ps. 115:3; 135:6).

The sailors' one concern, therefore, is that they not be held responsible for Jonah's blood, if the case be that he is an innocent man, for then God's condemnation would fall on them (contrast Matt. 27:25). Israel's law forbade the shedding of innocent blood (Deut. 19:10, 13; 21:8), and those who shed it were cursed (Deut. 27:25; Jer. 26:15). So the sailors have learned a healthy respect for the power of Yahweh, and their prayer to him in verse 14 is couched in the language of urgent entreaty. "Please, Yahweh," they entreat, "let us not die for the life of this man, and do not lay upon us innocent blood, for you, Yahweh have done as you desired" (MT). The sailors have been pawns in the contest between Jonah and his God, and they do not want to be held accountable to Yahweh for the results of that contest.

**1:15–16** / God wants Jonah hurled into the sea. God wants Jonah to experience the condemnation and punishment of sin—the punishment that might fall on Nineveh for its wickedness. So the innocent sailors bow to God's will and cast Jonah forth to a watery grave, verse 15. Justice is done for Jonah's disobedience, punishment is administered. "The wages of sin is death" (Rom. 6:23). The reason for the wind and storm is gone, and **the raging sea** grows **calm** (cf. Ps. 107:23–30).

In utter relief and gratitude, and with overwhelming awe at the sovereignty of Yahweh, the pagan sailors offer an animal **sacrifice** to Yahweh and make **vows,** verse 16. There has been some discussion among commentators about how it would have been possible to offer such a sacrifice on a ship, but again, those who are familiar with the history of sailing know that animals were often carried on ships to provide fresh meat for the crew, and the fire of a sacrifice could easily be contained. The notice of a sacrifice really is not unbelievable.

We are not told what the content of the vows was or what the future relation of the sailors to Yahweh would be. In fact, the sailors now disappear from the story and are not mentioned again. But certainly the Lord of the world has used Jonah to convert one small group of heathen, and so Yahweh's purpose has begun to be fulfilled. The focus of the story now shifts to Jonah, who is sinking to his deserved death.

## §5 *The Great Fish (Jonah 1:17–2:10)*

**1:17** / Cast overboard from the ship by the sailors, Jonah is drowning. His death, the just punishment for his disobedience of God, is certain. However, 1:17 opens with the phrase, "But Yahweh . . ." and that makes all the difference. The Lord ordains **but,** and the course of human events is reversed. Jonah thought to flee from the presence of his God, but Yahweh purposed "but" (1:4) and Jonah's flight was abruptly halted. Now Jonah is sinking to certain death in the depths of the sea, and once again God decides "but . . . ," and the situation is totally changed. Left on our own, we human beings think we can determine the course of our lives and history, but our plans and destiny are always being changed by that divine and decisive "but." This God of Jonah is in control of human life and its outcome.

This God is also in control of all of the forces of nature. The Hebrew text says "But Yahweh *appointed* a great fish to swallow Jonah." The fish was God's servant, and the fish's sovereign singled him out to do this task. **Swallow Jonah,** God commanded, and the fish obeyed, verse 17.

Other than stating that it was a **great fish,** the text does not specify the species of fish. The author repeatedly describes objects as "great"—Nineveh is the "great city," 1:2; the wind is a "great wind," the storm is a "great storm," 1:4; and the sailors fear of Yahweh is "great fear," 1:16. The adjective enhances the storyteller's art. So it is a great fish that gulps down Jonah, and the hearer or reader is left to imagine the kind of fish.

Certainly it is futile to argue over whether such a thing would be possible. The author is telling us a story in order to say some very important things about God, and all arguments over the fish tend to divert our attention from the main points being made. The important fact is that Jonah, despite his disobedience, inability to pray, and acceptance of his just sentence of death, has been saved from a watery grave by the totally undeserved grace of God. In the belly of the fish for **three days and three nights,** he is preserved alive by his Lord.

**2:1–9** / Jonah's reaction to his deliverance is finally to utter the prayer that he has so far been unable to utter (cf. the comment at 1:6). What is more, the prayer is prayed to **the LORD his God,** 2:1. The prayer that we find in 2:2–9 is a typical song of thanksgiving with which any pious Israelite could identify. The type is found frequently in the Psalter (Ps. 30; 32; 34; 92; 116; 118; 138). While this passage in Jonah alters the typical structure to some extent, such songs of thanksgiving were made up of an introduction (v. 2), a description of distress or trouble in which the psalmist found himself (vv. 3–6b), a report of God's deliverance (v. 6cd), and a conclusion that sometimes included reference to a vow (v. 9). The songs were sung in response to some specific deed of deliverance, and were usually intended to be sung in the worshiping congregation. The basic meaning of "to give thanks" in Hebrew thought was "to confess," and so God was not properly thanked until the deliverance was recounted in the congregation and it too was inspired to praise God's name.

To comprehend the content of this psalm, we need to have some understanding of the Hebrew worldview, of the symbol of the sea/deep/flood, and of the OT conception of death. According to the portrayal of the world that we find in Genesis 1 and throughout the Scriptures, the universe was three-storied, with heaven above, earth in the middle, and Sheol, the place of the dead, under the earth. The earth floated on subterranean waters and was anchored in those waters by pillars or mountains, and below the subterranean waters was the realm of Sheol.

The waters under the earth (as well as the waters above the solid arc of the firmament) were not ordinary waters, however. They were the great *tᵉhôm,* the primeval deep, the waters of chaos that were bound when God created the world (Gen. 1:2, 9; Ps. 104:7–9; Job 38:8–11; Prov. 8:29). And connected always with those chaotic waters was the thought of evil, darkness, and death, as opposed to God's created order of good, light, and life. Thus, to sink into the waters was to sink toward death and the realm of Sheol or of the pit, as it was sometimes called (Ps. 69:1–2, 15; 124:4–5; 144:7).

Such is the picture of Jonah that is portrayed in this psalm. He has been cast into the sea, and the chaotic waters (*tᵉhôm,* v. 5 [MT v. 6]) are closing around him (Jonah 2:3, 5) as he sinks down through them toward Sheol (v. 2 RSV, NIV margin) or the **pit** (v. 6). Thus, while the author speaks of Jonah sinking in the actual sea—for example, with his reference to **seaweed** in verse 5—he also portrays by his vocabulary Jonah's descent through the waters of chaos toward Sheol, the place of the dead.

The NIV has done a disservice by translating "Sheol" in verse 2 with **grave**. A grave was dug in the earth or carved out in rock. Sheol was the place to which the dead person descended. It was the realm to which all the dead went (Gen. 37:35 RSV, NIV margin) and is described throughout the Scriptures in the MT (contra NIV) as a place of darkness (Job 10:21–22; 17:13), of dust (Ps. 22:15, 29), from which there is no return (Job 7:9–10), where life is but a shadow, and the shades (Job 26:5 RSV) just chirp and mutter (Isa. 8:19 RSV). There was no return from Sheol, and so Jonah will be imprisoned by the "bars" of the "land" (not **earth** as the NIV has it), that is, of the land of Sheol. Worst of all, Yahweh could not be worshiped in Sheol (Ps. 6:5; 88:11–12), and so Jonah will be driven out from Yahweh's presence forever and will never again be able to look toward Yahweh's dwelling in heaven or on earth, verse 4 (RSV).

Jonah is sinking toward death. In Hebrew thought, every sort of distress or illness or trouble was considered to be a weak form of death. Thus, while Jonah is not yet dead, he can say that he has been in Sheol, and that Yahweh has delivered him from there, verse 6. Jonah "went down"—once again the vertical descent from the Lord is emphasized (see the comment at the beginning of ch. 1)—to Sheol, to death, and it is from there that God's appointment of the great fish rescued him. Jonah finally prayed (vv. 2, 4, 7), and God heard his prayer, verse 7.

That Jonah criticizes those who rely on **worthless idols**, verse 8, is an ironic note. Until the time of this prayer, Jonah has not relied on Yahweh at all. But now, seemingly, he has realized his dependence on God for his life, and the verse accords with the rest of the thanksgiving song.

The second line of verse 8 reads, in the Hebrew, "they forsake their *ḥesed*." The meaning can be that idol worshipers forsake their own faithfulness to God, or it can be, as the NIV implies, that they deprive themselves of the steadfast love of God, which manifests itself in God's gracious acts. Jonah promises, in verse 9, to offer a thank-offering sacrifice in response to the Lord's deliverance of him. But that is a future vow which he promises he will fulfill.

**2:10** / The difficulty with this song of thanksgiving is that it is sung inside the great fish! Jonah has been delivered from Sheol's death, but he is still inside the fish, and so in one sense, he has not been delivered at all. It seems reasonable to think that Jonah would pray this prayer *after* verse 10. But by the arrangement of the text, we are perhaps to take verse 9 as an indication of Jonah's certainty that he will be delivered from the fish's belly.

In one way, this thanksgiving song marks a conversion of Jonah. In another, as we shall see, Jonah's problem with God has not at all been resolved. But Jonah has turned to his God, and the result is that the Lord speaks a word to the fish, and the fish promptly vomits Jonah out on **dry land**, verse 10. The sailors could not reach dry land to get rid of Jonah (1:13), but one little word from Yahweh enables the fish to rid his aching belly of him. As Terence Fretheim wrote, "Three days of undigested Jonah!" (*The Message of Jonah,* p. 96). The fish was glad to get rid of him. Wherever he goes, Jonah just seems to cause difficulties, whether for human beings or God's other creatures.

## §6 The Patience of God (Jonah 3:1–4)

**3:1–4** / Though undeserving, Jonah has been delivered from death by God's merciful working through a fish. The book of Jonah is, before all else, a lesson concerning God's free grace. But it is also a portrayal of God's incredible patience. As Jonah confesses in 4:2, Yahweh is a God who is "slow to anger," and it is amazing that God says nothing to Jonah in 3:1–2 by way of rebuke or admonition. Instead, God simply calls Jonah again, using the same words that he used in 1:1: "Arise, go to Nineveh, that great city . . ." (RSV).

Previously, Jonah was to cry out against the city, 1:2. This time he is to **proclaim** the words that Yahweh will speak to him, but we do not hear the content of the proclamation until 3:4. The word for "proclamation" (*q<sup>e</sup>rî<sup>ʾ</sup>â*) is found only here in the Bible, and is translated by the LXX with *kērygma*.

Jonah's obedience to this second word of the Lord is emphasized by a repetition of the verbs in verse 2: "And Jonah arose and went . . . ," verse 3 (RSV). He goes "according to the word of the LORD" (MT and RSV), in obedience and subservience to it. His futile attempt to flee from the presence of his God is done. Now he will obey.

We can suppose that Jonah obeys Yahweh as a grateful response to the deliverance that God has afforded him (ch. 2). So it is always with God's deliverance. It affords no "cheap grace" that allows its recipient simply to bask in the salvation won. Rather, along with the grace there is always the demand—God's expectation of obedient response—because God does not save for no purpose. God has a plan for this world, and God saves in order to further that purpose. As Psalm 130:4 puts it, "There is forgiveness with thee, that thou mayest be feared"—God expects the obedient response of those who are saved.

We are told that **Nineveh** is so great a city that it takes **three days** to walk across it (see the comment in the introduction; the NIV has greatly altered the text), verse 3. Jonah journeys one day into the metropolis and calls out the message that God has given him. He cannot invent his own message. He can speak only God's word: After 40 days, Nineveh will be "overthrown" (NIV: **overturned**), as Sodom and Gomorrah were "overthrown" (Gen. 19:21, 15). The verb signifies total destruction.

Contrary to most prophetic oracles, no reason is given for Nineveh's destruction: Its sin is too well known to the readers of Jonah to need further elaboration. Further, the author has no interest in explaining what language Jonah uses to speak to the foreign Ninevites. For the author, such details are unimportant. Primary is the portrayal of God being set forth.

Nineveh is given a grace period of **forty days** before God will destroy it. Once again the patience of Yahweh and his slowness to anger are emphasized. "Forty days" is a traditional timespan, referred to throughout the Scriptures (Exod. 24:18; Num. 13:25; Deut. 9:9; 1 Sam. 17:16; 1 Kgs. 19:8; Mark 1:13 and parallels).

The most amazing fact, however, is that God gives Nineveh time to repent at all. Why should God be concerned with Nineveh, that symbol of human evil and "will to power"? Why does God not destroy it immediately and be done with it? That certainly would be Jonah's wish. But here the book of Jonah looks into the heart of God and finds there only love, even for the worst of sinners. God does not want to give up on the Ninevehs of the world—the message for all readers of the book! God cares about even the most wicked, and cannot endure their loss. This is a God of justice, to be sure, whose lordship cannot be mocked. But above all else, this is a God of love who has no pleasure in the death of anyone, no matter how evil they may be (Ezek. 18:32), and who will send even his only begotten son because of his great love for our wicked world (John 3:16).

## §7 Nineveh's Repentance (Jonah 3:5–10)

**3:5** / The name of God in the text now switches from "Yahweh" to "Elohim," because the Ninevites know the deity not by his covenant name, but simply as **God**. Verse 5 emphasizes the overwhelming power of the word of God. Jonah proclaims only one brief message from God, and the Ninevites believe it on the first day of his preaching. That is, they believe that what God says through his prophet will come to pass. Such is the nature of faith in many parts of the Bible—to hear the word of God, to count it true, and to act as if it will be fulfilled (cf. Gen. 15:6). But obviously, such faith is not the result of the preacher's skill or persuasive power (cf. 1 Cor. 2:1–5). Jonah probably would rather not have spoken the word at all. Rather, such faith is the product of the working of the word itself, which has the power to make itself be received. The word of God creates its own reception, inspiring faith in its hearers (cf. Rom. 10:17). We have here a brief theology of preaching.

So the word of God spreads by word of mouth from Ninevite to Ninevite, from the least of them to the greatest, until all of the inhabitants of the great city believe it and begin a **fast** of repentance, donning **sackcloth**—a rough burlaplike material—as a sign of their penitent mourning over their sin.

**3:6–9** / Finally, the word reaches **the king of Nineveh**— a fictitious note, since Nineveh was not a city-state with a king—and he too sheds his royal mantle, wraps sackcloth about his loins, and joins the fast of penitence, verse 6. But he makes the fast more strict than it apparently was at its inception by issuing a royal **decree** governing the fast's rules. Neither humans nor animals are to eat or drink anything; all are to pray to God for forgiveness; and most important, all are to renounce **their evil ways** and the **violence** for which Nineveh and the Assyrian Empire have been so noted. As in Isaiah 58:3–7, the king is calling not merely for ritual observance, but for a transformation of life.

The king and his subjects are therefore later made a model of repentance in the preaching of Jesus (Matt. 12:41; Luke 11:32). Fasts of repentance are mentioned throughout the OT and could be acts of individuals (2 Sam. 12:16) or of the community as a whole (Jer. 36:9; Joel 1:14; 2:15–17; see the comment there). They were proclaimed when any sort of danger threatened the community. They were designed to turn aside God's wrath, manifested in the danger, to beg divine forgiveness, and to enlist divine aid.

That animals are also to join in the fast by being covered with sackcloth and kept from food and water is a profound note in this story. First, it acknowledges that the natural world is affected by human sin, that nature falls as we fall (cf. Jer. 12:4; Hos. 4:1–3; Isa. 24:4–5). Second, the story is underlining the fact that God is sovereign over the world of nature (cf. Ps. 148:1–10; Jer. 27:6), as well as over the realm of human beings, and that the natural world too needs redemption from its corrupted state (Rom. 8:19–23). Its cries too are heard by God (Job 38:41; Ps. 147:9; Joel 1:10, 18, 20; 2:21–22), and so here in Jonah, animals join in the fast of repentance.

There is in the Scriptures no automatic link between repentance and salvation, however, and the statement of the Ninevite king in verse 9 acknowledges that fact. Who knows, he says, whether God will turn from destroying them for their wickedness? God will choose the recipients of divine grace and mercy (Exod. 33:19). God's actions and purposes are entirely self-determined, and human actions cannot bind that freedom. We can only throw ourselves on the mercy of God and pray for forgiveness (cf. Luke 18:9–14).

**3:10** / God's forgiveness is an undeserved act of mercy, and verse 10 emphasizes that fact. God **saw** Nineveh's transformation of its ways. Throughout the Scriptures, nothing escapes God's sight, especially not the actions of human beings (Exod. 2:25; Job 34:21–22; Ps. 11:4, etc.). In free mercy, God therefore decides to have **compassion** *(nāḥam)* on the Ninevites. Many commentators and the RSV read the verb as "repented" or as "changed his mind" (NRSV), and that turn about is implied in the verb. But **had compassion** emphasizes that God's change of mind is an act of free grace and not an automatic response to Nineveh's penitence.

The fact that God does decide not to fulfill the word of judgment on Nineveh shows clearly that God is sovereign over the divine word. When the word is released into history, it is an active, effective force that shapes the course of history until the word is fulfilled (cf. Isa. 55:10–11). But God can recall the word, as happens here in verse 10, or can delay its working (cf. Ezek. 12:28). Always God is Lord over the situation.

The main emphasis of verse 10 is on God's incredible mercy, however. This capital city of the most wicked nation in the eighth-century BC ancient Near East is forgiven by God and spared punishment for its sins. God's love extends not just to his chosen people, but to the Ninevehs of the world. That is the fact that the author of Jonah wants Israel—and us—to understand.

## §8 *Jonah's Angry Prayer (Jonah 4:1–4)*

**4:1–4** / God has forgiven the great city of Nineveh, that symbol of human ruthlessness and evil; Nineveh will no longer be judged. That decision now sends Jonah into a paroxysm of anger, verse 1. Jonah's preaching has brought about the result that every prophet should hope for—repentance and transformation of life in those to whom the message of judgment has been announced. Jonah has been successful—and he is furious.

The reason for his fury, as well as for his initial flight from Yahweh to Tarshish, is stated in verse 2. Jonah knew the character of God. He knew it would do no good for him to preach judgment upon Nineveh, because he knew that God is "gracious and merciful, slow to anger and abounding in love" and that therefore God's grace would prevail over judgment, and God would forgive.

Jonah's orthodox theology and his place in the traditional piety of Israel are revealed by his angry prayer. His description of God is a description found in numerous places in the OT, occasionally with variations in the wording, and it is one that virtually has the status of a canonical creed (Joel 2:13—see the comment there; Ps. 145:8; Exod. 34:6–7; Neh. 9:17; Ps. 86:15; 103:8; 111:4; 2 Chron. 30:9; cf. Num. 14:18; Nah. 1:3; Ps. 112:4 margin). The adjectives "gracious" and "merciful" (NIV: **compassionate**) both appear thirteen times in the OT and are used only of God (Limburg, *Jonah*, pp. 90, 91).

In short, the heart of Israel's understanding of God is set forth here in one brief sentence. Yahweh of Israel is a God who would rather forgive than destroy, who takes pity on all who have need, who is not quick to condemn and when condemning is not quick to act in judgment, and who loyally loves all the creatures and beings created in this world. That God of an absolutely unique compassion and love, which are unachievable by human beings, is the God who has forgiven Nineveh. And Jonah is angry.

Finally the reader learns from verse 2 the reason for Jonah's flight to Tarshish (see the comment at the end of 1:3). Jonah has disobeyed Yahweh's initial command to him (1:2) not because he would be branded a false prophet when Nineveh repented; Jonah is not interested in his own reputation here (contra a number of commentators). Rather, Jonah is interested in the character of God, and Jonah has disobeyed because he does not want God to be a God who forgives Nineveh. Nineveh has been too evil to deserve forgiveness. Justice demands that Nineveh be destroyed. Otherwise there is no ultimate structure of right and wrong in the world, no guide for faithful living that a person can count on.

For that reason, Jonah asks that Yahweh, the Lord over life and death, take away his life, verse 3. His world has crumbled around him. There is no point in being good or in obeying God (cf. Mal. 2:17; 3:14; Ps. 73:13) because God will just forgive those who do evil anyway. And without a God-given structure of justice in his world, Jonah does not want to go on living. Jonah, like Abraham, demands that the judge of all the earth do right (Gen. 18:25; cf. Job), and the judge has refused. Jonah's attitude could be compared to that of all those who, weary of evil, ask, "Why does God permit such evil to continue?" (cf. Hab. 1:1–4), and the answer comes back, "The LORD is gracious and merciful, slow to anger, and abounding in steadfast love."

Jonah, from the first, has set himself up as the human judge of his divine God, thinking that he knows what is proper and right and acting accordingly. Jonah believes justice and right are in his hands and not in the hands of God. Jonah, like Adam and Eve in the garden, wants to be his own god, knowing good and evil (Gen. 3:5). And when God has not bowed to Jonah's definitions of justice and right, Jonah has become angry.

But Yahweh, that patient, forgiving, compassionate, steadfastly loving Lord, who already has graciously delivered this petty prophet from death, is still very slow to anger. Once again, God does not rebuke Jonah, but simply asks him a quiet question, "Do you do well to be angry?" (v. 4, RSV).

## §9 A Little Grace and a Little Judgment (Jonah 4:5–8)

Jonah is a stubborn man. He is sure that he is right and that Yahweh is wrong. Nineveh should have been destroyed for its wickedness. That would have been the just course of action on God's part. Through clenched teeth, Jonah has told God that in so many words in his angry prayer in 4:2–3.

**4:5–8** / Thus, like an angry parent rebuking a child, Jonah does not even bother to answer Yahweh's question in verse 4. Instead, he hopes that Yahweh has gotten the point and will be convinced to return to the original judgment (cf. 3:10) and destroy Nineveh. So Jonah goes outside of the city to the east, makes himself a little temporary **shelter** (literally, "booth"; cf. Gen. 33:17; Neh. 8:15), to shade himself from the sun, and sits down to see if Yahweh will act justly after all, verse 5. Surely God has understood by now!

If the reader can smile at such foolish impertinence on Jonah's part, surely God must have smiled also. And as in 1:17, the Lord, "the God of heaven, who made the sea and the dry land" (1:9 RSV), exercises sovereignty over the world of nature, this time to "appoint a plant" (MT) to grow up and **shade** Jonah's **head.**

The type of plant is a *qîqāyôn,* and we are not sure exactly what species is intended. Most commonly, it has been understood as a castor oil plant, with leaves large enough to provide shade. Or some have suggested a unique species is intended, created by God for this specific purpose.

The question has been raised as to why Jonah needs a plant to shade him from the sun when according to verse 5 he already has a booth that serves that purpose. Thus, some commentators have maintained that verse 5 belongs after 3:4, and that the plant in verse 6 then provides the only shade. But that probably is to miss the author's subtle symbolism here. In other places in the OT, God's grace is compared to **shade** (Ps. 121:5; Isa. 4:6; 25:4; cf. Isa.

32:2; Mark 4:32), to mercy and protection that no human shelter can provide. So the plant here in verse 6 is both literal and symbolic, the evidence of God's grace sheltering Jonah. Its purpose is, according to the MT, to save Jonah from his "evil" (*rāʿâ;* NIV: **discomfort**). The plant is a little gift of grace to turn Jonah from his stubborn course. It is a symbol here of God's continuing, merciful working with the angry prophet. And Jonah, basking in that grace, is very happy.

But then, having let Jonah experience a little gift of grace, Yahweh, the Lord of nature, "appoints" a **worm** to "attack" (MT) the plant at dawn, just when the temperature begins to rise, so that the plant withers. The **sun** comes up, blazing forth with its heat on the head of Jonah, and at the same time, Yahweh "appoints" (MT) a sirocco, a hot east wind that blows in over the desert with its dust and that can parch a man to death. Jonah grows faint, as he was faint in the belly of the fish, 2:7 (MT). In short, Jonah is once again threatened with death. He himself has a taste of what the judgment of God means.

Once more, therefore, Jonah wishes to die (cf. 4:3). He thinks he has been in the right, and by bringing judgment upon him, God is once again showing that he is unjust. God is destroying a good man, while forgiving all of those wicked in Nineveh. There is no structure of justice in the world, and Jonah just wants to be quit of it.

**4:9–11** / Once again God asks Jonah if it is right for him to be angry, this time because God's grace in the form of the plant has been removed from him (v. 9, cf. v. 4). Does Jonah deserve no punishment? And Jonah, sticking to his conviction that he has been right and God has been wrong, replies that he indeed has just cause to be angry and, indeed, just cause to die in a world where God is unjust.

The NIV has drastically softened God's words to Jonah in verses 10–11. The verb is not "to be **concerned**," but rather "to pity" *(ḥûs),* and the basic meaning of *ḥûs* is "to act with tears in one's eyes." Jonah has gotten all worked up over a plant for which he did not labor, which he did not cause to grow, and which is here today and gone tomorrow. The plant has been solely an undeserved gift from God, its creator and owner. Jonah has had no claim on it whatsoever. Yet Jonah has had not a shred of pity for the great city of Nineveh, in which there are 120,000 people too ignorant and helpless to know **their right hand from their left,** not to mention all of their innocent cattle, verse 11.

Nineveh and its animals belong to Yahweh, however. Yahweh has created them and owns them. Jonah has no say in their fate whatsoever. If Jonah can get upset over a mere plant, should not Yahweh be upset over Nineveh and weep over what would happen to them if he brought his judgment upon them? The question is emphasized by the emphatic pronoun at the beginning of the sentence: "And I, should I not pity Nineveh . . . ?" Like Jesus weeping over the city of Jerusalem (Luke 19:41; cf. Matt. 23:37; Mark 6:34 and parallel; Mark 8:2), should God not weep over the helpless creatures in the capital of Assyria and show mercy to them?

Jonah is being told three things by his God. First, it is being pointed out to him that he has no right at all to say what should happen to Nineveh. That city and its animals do not belong to him. They belong to God, who can act freely with them. God could have said, "Am I not allowed to do what I choose with what belongs to me?" (Matt. 20:15 RSV). The sovereignty of God over creation is strongly affirmed here, as it is affirmed throughout the story of Jonah.

Second, God is telling Jonah that he is totally ungrateful for the grace and mercy that have been shown him repeatedly. Twice God has saved Jonah's life, though Jonah has been totally unworthy of salvation. Always God has treated him with astonishing patience and forbearance, putting up with his disobedience and arrogance and anger. Any punishment that Jonah has experienced has been transitory and overcome by grace. And Jonah has been made exceedingly glad by God's mercy and salvation toward him. But despite God's tutelage of him, Jonah himself has not learned the spirit of mercy toward others. He has reveled in being forgiven, but he wants no other wicked persons like himself to share in the same forgiveness. He is the model of the unforgiving servant in Jesus' parable (Matt. 18:23–35).

Third, Jonah is being told—as are we and all readers—that God's love extends to the whole sinful, wicked world of violence and wrong. Jonah, who is really a symbol of all of God's elect in this story, full of piety and orthodoxy, is not the only one to whom the Lord of heaven and earth extends forgiving mercy. God reaches out to shed saving grace on all the Ninevehs and creatures of the world.

The God of the Bible weeps over this sinful world (cf. Gen. 6:6). And so while divine love for that world is set forth here in the book of Jonah only in a story, that love becomes incarnate in the person of Jesus Christ. On a cross and by a resurrection, God acts out the forgiveness of all the world that is foreshadowed here in this prophetic book. "God so loved the world that he gave his only begotten Son . . . ," and Nineveh and Jonah and you and I are offered forgiveness for our sin. Perhaps our one task therefore is to receive that grace, and then to go out and tell the world the story of Jonah and of Jesus Christ.

# *Micah*

# Introduction: Micah

## The Critical Approach to the Prophets

It has been the fashion in dealing with the prophetic writings of the OT to assign each oracle in a prophetic book to a particular historical period or date on the basis of evidence within the oracle. For example, Micah 4:10 seems to be a clear reference to Judah's deliverance from Babylonian exile, and therefore Micah 4:9–13 is assigned to the period after 538 BC. Or Micah 7:11–13 is similarly dated because of its mention of the rebuilding of the walls of Jerusalem.

On the basis of such dating, then, and considering also linguistic, stylistic, and theological evidence, scholars have decided what material within the prophetic book originated with the prophet himself and what materials were later additions to the original prophetic message. As L. C. Allen wrote, "The authenticity of each oracle is bound up with its applicability to, and reflection of, its historical setting" (*The Books of Joel, Obadiah, Jonah, and Micah*, p. 241).

By the use of such a critical method, and following the work of B. Stade in 1881–1903, many scholars have arrived at the conclusion that only chapters 1–3 in Micah's book come from the prophet himself, and that even within those chapters minor additions and revisions were made at a later time. Chapters 4–5 and 6–7 were added to "update" the prophet's message for later situations, reaching into postexilic times. And some material, such as Micah 7:8–20, fitted the book for later liturgical use. Indeed, even conservative critics have admitted that Micah 4:1–4, 6–8, and 7:8–20 cannot be credited to the prophet (Allen, 251), and there are few who would dispute the view that the book of Micah has been subject to later addition and revision.

Because the book has thus been edited and enlarged, scholars have therefore been pressed to define the process by which Micah achieved its final form, and theories concerning the redaction and formation of the book are numerous. (See, e.g.,

Mays, *Micah*, pp. 21–33). No consensus about the process has
been reached, however, which is perhaps an indication of the
tenuous nature of such reconstructions.

In fact, there is not even any scholarly agreement as to
how the book is structured or how it is therefore to be divided.
Some scholars divide the work into two parts: chapters 1–5; 6–7.
Others maintain that it is tripartite: chapters 1–3; 4–5; 6–7; or
1–2; 3–5; 6–7. Still others find four separate sections: chapters
1–3; 4–5; 6:1–7:7; 7:8–20, or chapters 1–2; 3:1–8; 3:9–6:1; 6:2–7:20.
I, however, favor the division shown below.


## Micah Confounds the Critics

The lack of consensus about the structure, formation, and
origin of the Micah oracles is perhaps the best indication of the
inability of a purely historical-critical approach to deal with the
book. Certainly there is no doubt that the prophet's own oracles
have been revised or supplemented with later material over a
number of years: few critics would dispute that fact. Equally,
there is no doubt that the book exhibits a structure in which
oracles of judgment and of salvation alternate. Thus, we find
1:2–2:11 (judgment) followed by 2:12–13 (salvation); 3:1–12
(judgment) followed by 4:1–5:15 (salvation); 6:1–7:7 (judgment)
followed by 7:8–20 (salvation).

But to divide Micah into atomistic oracular units, to judge
them genuine or nongenuine, and to separate them on the basis
of the supposed historical background of each unit is to miss the
overriding, unified message of the book.

The book of Micah represents at least two centuries of
Israel's meditation on its God-given role in the world of nations.
As is true also in the Isaiah tradition (cf. 19:23–25; 52:13–53:12),
Micah recalls the promise to the fathers (Mic. 7:20) that Israel
will be a source of blessing for all the nations of the earth
(Gen. 12:3; Mic. 5:7). But hindering that role is Israel's continual
sin, for which it must be judged by the Lord of all the earth.
The Lord wishes for all peoples peace (Mic. 4:3–4; 5:5) and a
glorious future, governed by God's anointed ruler, and under
God's universal lordship. But how can such a desire become
reality when Israel's rebellious iniquity hinders the Lord's
work through it? Micah's answer is that God's plan for all
peoples can be accomplished only through the gracious forgive-

ness of an incomparable God, who alone can fulfill the promise to the fathers.

Such a message is not discernible in what at first sight seems to be Micah's rather chaotic structure until one takes into close account the rhetorical indications throughout the book—indications that are not arbitrary but rather carefully planned. For example, Hebrew rhetoric frequently emphasizes a message by beginning and ending it in the same way. Thus Micah begins and ends with the subject of the nations (1:2; 7:16). Similarly, endings often show the principal concern of the material, and Micah ends with the thought of the promise to the fathers (7:20), a sure indication that such promise is not just a careless afterthought but is to be tied to the future envisioned in the preceding prophecies.

In addition, each of the divisions of the book is carefully marked out by the introductory imperative "Hear" (1:2; 3:1; 6:1), followed then by judgment oracles directed against Israel—judgment that is subsequently overcome by the gracious saving work of God—a repeated pattern giving an indication of the overall theme of the book.

The result is that the message of Micah, to be understood, must be discerned from the entire book, in the final form in which it now has been handed down to us. To be sure, there are some oracles that can be placed in their original historical contexts and connected with specific events in the life of Israel. But that specificity is subject in Micah to a larger purpose—namely, that of presenting to the world God's overarching plan to use Israel in bringing blessing on all the families of the earth, in fulfillment of God's promise.

## The Living Tradition of the Prophets

As an example of Israel's meditation over the centuries on its God-given role in world history, Micah is an excellent example of the extent to which the words of the prophets of the OT formed a living tradition that was handed down from generation to generation. It has often been remarked how much Micah has in common with Isaiah of Jerusalem, whose ministry preceded his by perhaps some forty years. Both of them share the vision of God's coming peaceful kingdom (Isa. 2:1–4=Mic. 4:1–4), utilizing a common tradition. Both deal with the figure of a Messiah, with a remnant, and with the overarching plan of God. Both include liturgical sections and utilize similar phrases, such as "in that day" or "from now and evermore" (see Childs, *Introduction to the Old Testament*, pp. 434–36). In short, Isaiah's prophecies did not just concern his own time but formed an ongoing, living tradition that could be taken up and incorporated in the Micah corpus. And Micah 7:16–17 certainly shows the influence of Second Isaiah, whose ministry followed Micah's by some two centuries. Indeed, the fact that Micah's words from about 701 BC, are quoted in defense of Jeremiah almost a century later (Jer. 26:18; Mic. 3:12) shows to what extent the preaching of the prophets formed not dead letters from the past but living tradition by which Israel understood its present life. Thus Micah's words from the close of the eighth century BC could be incorporated into a Micah book that found its final form sometime after 515 BC.

Prophetic oracles were not isolated pronouncements concerning only their immediate historical period, although they certainly concerned that also. But finally they must be understood as incursions of the word of God into an ongoing plan for the world—a plan that began to be worked out long before the time of the particular prophet in question and that would continue to be executed long after the prophet was dead. As the word of God, prophetic oracles cast God's light on the particular period to which they were directed. But they also formed part of the dynamic power by which God moved along salvation history. They entered into and shared in the moving, historical stream of events by which God is driving toward the goal of a kingdom come on earth. Micah, perhaps more than any other prophetic book, lets us perceive that.

This all means for the reader and student of Micah, however, that we too stand in that historical stream of the saving history. We too live in one era of time included in God's plan for the world. The stream of God's plan flows around us, moving toward a future salvation of the world. And we can, by faith, enter into the movement and direction of the stream, or we can, by disobedience, try to fight against it. But one thing is sure. The stream will finally find its destination in the ocean of God's kingdom, which will cover the earth.

## §1 The Superscription (Micah 1:1)

**1:1** / The superscription has been affixed to the prophecies of Micah by an unknown editor and is, in its initial phrase (**The word of the LORD that came to Micah**) the same form as that found in Hosea 1:1; Joel 1:1; and Zephaniah 1:1.

The claim that what follows is "the word of the LORD" is intended to apply to the entire book. Not just selected portions of the book, and not just portions that scholars judge to stem from the prophet himself are to be understood as words from God. No. All seven chapters are "the word of the LORD," bearing the authority of the Lord of heaven and earth and therefore still authoritative for us and for the reader in any age (cf. Luke 16:31). Because Micah 1–7 bears such authority, it has been preserved and carefully handed down to us over almost 2,700 years.

The superscription says that the word of the Lord "came" to Micah. That is, it came from outside of the prophet himself. In our age, which so credits subjective experience as a source of revelation, it is noteworthy that Micah's prophecies were not the result of his own experience or inner musings or of his sagacious insight into the signs of his time. His prophecies were given to him by God, communicated from God's person to his.

Unlike Isaiah (ch. 6) or Jeremiah (ch. 1), Micah gives no account of his call to be a prophet, and there is only one passage in which he gives a hint of how God's words were communicated to him (3:8). There his words are attributed to his inner filling with the Spirit of God. This superscription, on the other hand, says that Micah **saw** *(hāzāh)* the words of the Lord, and, by emending the text, the NIV has taken that to mean that Micah had a supernatural vision of some sort. The original Hebrew reads simply, "The word of the LORD that came to Micah . . . which he saw concerning Samaria and Jerusalem." As is evident in Numbers 24:4, 16, *hāzāh* can refer to an auditory revelation as well as a visual one. Thus, there is no reason to emend the text here to emphasize that Micah received the word of the Lord in a vision.

We do not know how the prophets were addressed by God; when Isaiah says, for example, "The LORD of hosts has revealed himself in my ears" (22:14 RSV), we have no notion of what that means. What we do know is that the word of the Lord came to the prophets as an objective, effective reality and power (cf. Gen. 1; Ps. 147:15; Jer. 20:9; 23:29). Once the prophets released that word into history by proclaiming it, the word worked, shaping events and effecting a new situation, until it was fulfilled (cf. Isa. 55:10–11; Ezek. 12:26–28; 1 Cor. 1:18, 24; 2 Cor. 5:17). The prophetic preaching was therefore an instrument of the *working* of God in nature (cf. Mark 11:12–14, 20–21) and in history.

The word came to **Micah of Moresheth.** Micah is a common name in the OT and is attached to other individuals at least eight times. It is the shortened form of *mîkāyāh* (cf. Jer. 26:18) and has the meaning, "Who is like Yahweh?" Thus, it is an appellation designed to praise the Lord.

Unlike other prophets, Micah is identified not by the family to which he belongs (cf. Isa. 1:1; Jer. 1:1), but by the hometown from which he comes, an indication of the fact that his ministry was carried on outside of Moresheth, probably in Jerusalem. Although Moresheth's exact location is uncertain, it most likely is to be identified with Moresheth Gath (1:14), which was located some 25 miles southwest of Jerusalem, 1,200 feet above sea level, on the edge of the Shephelah, overlooking the coastal plain. The city was ringed by a circle of fortifications, built first by King Rehoboam, the son of Solomon (2 Chron. 11:7–11), and designed to protect Judah from attack by the Philistines and major powers of the ancient Near East. Thus, Micah was not from a simple peasant background but was familiar with the civil officialdom and military authorities that supplied such fortifications.

Beyond this notice of his geographical roots, nothing further is told us of Micah's cultural context, because the editor deems it unimportant. Far from being the outdated product of their own time and culture, as some today would label the Scriptures, these prophetic books give little attention to cultural and sociological contexts of the word of God. The word comes from outside of those contexts, from God, and is never thought to be limited, determined, or bound by them. God's word is an objective word, and though it is always directed to a specific person or persons, in specific times and places, it transcends those specificities to speak also to our age and every age.

The NIV translates **during the reigns of,** rather than a more literal "in the days of," but the meaning is the same. Micah's ministry is said to take place during the reigns of Kings **Jotham** (742–735 BC), **Ahaz** (735–715 BC), and **Hezekiah** (715–687 BC) of Judah, a span of some 55 years. Perhaps Micah was known to be a prophet residing in Jerusalem during all of that time, but judging from the length of his book and the internal evidence of his oracles, he almost certainly did not actively preach for 55 years. His oracles anticipate the fall of the northern Kingdom of Israel in 721 BC (1:6–7), as they anticipate the destruction of Jerusalem (3:12), but probably the latter passage is to be set in the context of the Assyrian devastation of Judah in 701 BC by Sennacherib (2 Kgs. 18:13–18), since the superscription mentions no reign beyond that of Hezekiah.

Certainly it was a turbulent and uncertain time. After the prosperous and stable reigns of Uzziah in Judah (783–742 BC) and of Jeroboam II in Israel (ca. 786–746 BC), Assyria gained new power and dominance in the ancient Near East under the leadership of Tiglath-pileser III, whose armies marched west to conquer the small states of the Fertile Crescent. In 735 BC, Kings Rezin of Syria and Pekah of Israel formed a coalition to turn back the Assyrian advance, inviting Ahaz of Judah to join them (cf. Isa. 7:1–9). When Ahaz refused, they invaded Judah with the intention of putting a puppet on the Judean throne, but Ahaz appealed to Assyria for aid, and Judah became a vassal of that empire. Israel, however, continued to try to form alliances against Assyria, and in 722 BC Tiglath-pileser's successor, Shalmaneser V, captured the northern capital of Samaria, deporting, according to his own report, 27,290 inhabitants to Mesopotamia. Apparently, however, it was Shalmaneser's successor, Sargon II, who wrought the complete destruction of the northern kingdom, replacing its population with foreigners, while its original inhabitants from the ten northern tribes simply disappeared from history (2 Kgs. 17). It is such a downfall of the northern kingdom that Micah predicts in 1:6–7.

Judah remained a faithful vassal of Assyria for the next decade, but from 712–701 BC, under the rule of Hezekiah, Judah joined a coalition that included Egypt, Phoenicia, and Philistia and that made repeated attempts to shake off the Assyrian yoke. The result was that the Assyrian armies under Sargon's successor, Sennacherib, marched west and between 703 and 701 BC overran each member of the coalition in turn. They captured and destroyed forty-six cities of Judah and laid siege to Jerusalem, that capital being saved only by Hezekiah's payment of a huge tribute (2 Kgs. 18:13–16). Second Kings 18:17–19:37 gives two further accounts of the means by which Jerusalem avoided capture at this time, but whether they have any basis in historical fact is unknown. What we do know is that Hezekiah's successor, Manasseh, remained a faithful vassal of Assyria throughout his long reign.

Micah predicts the final fall of Jerusalem (3:12), but in his day, Jerusalem still stands. It therefore seems reasonable to suppose that he was occasionally preaching during the reigns at least of Ahaz and Hezekiah, and more exactly, occasionally between 735 and 701 BC. Whether he preached also during the reign of Jotham is unknown. At any rate, his ministry occurred in a time of uncertainty and upheaval in both the northern and southern kingdoms.

The superscription says that the word of the Lord given to Micah concerned **Samaria and Jerusalem,** the capital cities of the north and south. The capitals, however, are intended to stand for their entire kingdoms. While Micah's ministry is carried on in the south, in Jerusalem, and while he has only one oracle dealing with Samaria, his words from the Lord concern Israel as a unity, as one people in relation to its God. Indeed, it is this unified understanding of Israel that allows Micah's words to be appropriated and reflected upon by Israel over the next two centuries, just as it is the same understanding that makes them still relevant for the church, the new Israel in Jesus Christ.

## §2 God's Appearance in Judgment
## (Micah 1:2–5b)

Scholars are not in agreement as to the limits of this first oracle in Micah's book. Some take verses 1–7 as the complete unit. Others divide the passage into three parts: verses 1–2, 3–5, 6–7. In my estimation, verses 2–5b form the first announcement of the book.

**1:2–5b** / We have in these verses a proclamation to all the peoples and living things on the earth that Adonai Yahweh—that is, the master of the world whose name is Yahweh—will enter into a judicial court proceeding with all flesh both as a witness against them and as their judge. And the form which that witnessing will take will be Yahweh's coming forth from his holy place to judge the earth. In short, the court proceeding will consist not in words but in God's action.

The NIV describes such action in the present tense, but probably verses 3–4 are to be translated with future verbs, as in the RSV. Yahweh will come forth from his holy temple, from his "place"—the NIV has interpreted the last word to mean **dwelling place.** Both "holy temple" and "place" can refer either to God's heavenly temple (cf. e.g., Ps. 11:4) or to the Jerusalem temple (cf. e.g., Ps. 5:7), but probably the former is intended here, because verse 3 (RSV) says that Yahweh will "come down" (cf. Isa. 31:4; 64:1; Ps. 18:9=2 Sam. 22:10, etc.).

When he comes, Yahweh will tread upon the high places of the earth. Throughout the OT, **high places** often refers to the pagan worship sites of the Canaanites, but that is not the reference here. Rather, the phrase is synonymous with **mountains** in the following line, verse 4. According to the ancient Hebrew view of the world, mountains formed what we might call the "skeleton" of the universe. They held up the solid arc of the firmament (cf. Job 9:5–6; Ps. 18:7), and they anchored the flat earth in the waters beneath the earth (cf. Deut. 32:22; Ps. 18:15; 46:2–3; Jonah 2:6; Hab.

3:10). But when Yahweh comes to judge the earth, the mountains will melt when he treads upon them (Ps. 97:5; Nah. 1:5).

The Lord's intervention in judgment, therefore, will have a devastating effect upon the very structure of the cosmos. The **valleys** will **split apart,** and the melting of the **mountains** will be like the liquefaction of **wax** before a **fire,** so that they will run down as **water** runs **down a slope.** The reference to **wax** and **water** in verse 4c–d refers not to the **valleys** of verse 4b, but once again to the **mountains** of verse 4a.

It has often been noted that this description of Yahweh's coming incorporates standard features of a divine theophany or appearance, as can be seen when the reader compares it with Judg. 5:4–5; Ps. 18:7–15=2 Sam. 22:8–16; 68:7–8; 97:3–5; Isa. 64:1–3; Hab. 3:3–15. That does not, however, diminish the fearfulness of the description. The prophets and psalmists of the OT knew the awfulness of God's holy presence and influence upon the cosmos (cf. Mark 13 and parallels). When the sovereign of the universe comes, it changes the world.

Why is Yahweh coming? Verse 5a–b supplies the answer. God comes in judgment because of the "rebellion" of Jacob. The NIV translates the Hebrew *pešaʿ* with **transgression,** but the word is much stronger than that. It is a political term, with the meaning of rebellion or subversion against a ruler. The master of the universe comes because Jacob-Israel has rebelled against his rule. **Jacob** and **Israel** here both refer to Israel as a whole, to both the northern and southern kingdoms.

Scholars have been bothered by the fact that the address in verse 2 is to all **peoples,** and yet Yahweh's coming is the result of Israel's sin. Some have therefore conjectured that verses 2–4 are later additions to the oracle, which originally dealt only with Israel and which began at verse 5c. Others have accounted for the dissonance between verses 2–4 and verse 5 by proposing that the judgment on Israel is understood as a model or foretaste of the judgment that will come upon all nations. Neither proposal seems correct.

Rather, this proclamation in verses 2–5b encapsulates the thought of the Micah book as a whole and furnishes an overview of Yahweh's plan (cf. 4:12) for the nations, which is being worked out through Israel in fulfillment of Yahweh's promise to the fathers (7:20; cf. Gen. 12:3).

The Lord Yahweh is coming down to judge the earth. And that coming will very soon—even in the time of Micah himself—result in God's judgment upon Israel for its rebellion against his lordship. But that is not the end of the story. Despite its sin, Yahweh will also save Israel, as the salvation announcements in the book make clear. As a result, some of the nations will see the salvation of Israel and repent and turn to Yahweh (7:10, 16–17), but some will not, and they will be destroyed (4:11–13; 5:5–6, 8–9). Then those who remain—the peoples and Israel together—will inherit a blessed realm of peace in the kingdom of God (4:1–4; 5:2–5, 7). First through God's judgment upon Israel, but then through God's salvation of it, God will fulfill his purpose for all peoples, in fulfillment of his word.

This initial oracle therefore joins the imperative **Hear!** to all peoples (v. 2) with the notice of Israel's rebellion (v. 5a–b). Both form a part of that universal scheme of judgment and salvation which the Lord of all is working out through his chosen people.

---

### Additional Note §2

---

1:3 / For further references to Yahweh's shaking of the mountains, see Ps. 114:4, 6; Isa. 42:15; 45:2; Ezek. 38:20.

## §3 The Future Destruction of Samaria (Micah 1:5c–7)

**1:5c–f** / Now the effects of Yahweh's appearance, proclaimed in verses 2–5b, narrow down to become very specific. The result of Yahweh's coming will mean the destruction of Israel and of Judah, because of their sin. And that sin is here epitomized by the sins of the capital cities of **Samaria** and of **Jerusalem**, verse 5c–f.

This is the only oracle in Micah's book concerning God's judgment on **Samaria**, probably because the northern kingdom was defeated and its inhabitants deported by Assyria in 721 BC. This oracle forms the companion piece to the announcement of the destruction of Jerusalem in 3:12, and some of the same language is used in both places ("heap of ruins," "mountain," "height").

Israel's capital city of Samaria was situated in about the middle of that kingdom, on a hill some 300 feet above deep valleys on the north, west, and south. A long, sloping ridge lay to its east. The city was first built by King Omri in the early ninth century BC, and it was the royal residence for 150 years, until it was besieged by Shalmaneser V of Assyria in 725–722 BC (2 Kgs. 17:1–6) and then captured by his successor, Sargon II, according to Assyrian annals. First Kings 16:32 reports that King Ahab built an altar and a temple for the fertility god Baal in the city, and several of the prophets give testimony to idolatrous worship there (cf. Amos 8:14; Isa. 10:10–11; Ezek. 16:46–55; 23:1–49).

**1:6–7** / Yahweh is coming, according to Micah, to destroy Samaria and Israel, and indeed, in verses 6–7, Yahweh speaks in the first person to announce that coming destruction. Once the site of Samaria was nothing but a field, and its slopes were nothing but terraces for **vineyards;** to that original state Yahweh will return Samaria. Yahweh will reduce its ornate buildings to a heap of ruins in the fields (cf. Josh. 8:28), and as the mountains "pour down" before him, verse 4, so too will he "pour down" most of Samaria's building stones into its surrounding valleys, laying bare its foundations, verse 6. He will smash her pagan **idols** to pieces, and he will burn her "harlot's hires" with **fire** (cf. "fire," v. 4), verse 7. The NIV reads **temple gifts** instead of the Hebrew text's "harlot's hires," but the latter stands in parallelism with **images,** verse 7a, and the thought is that the pagan idols have been manufactured with money secured from payment to sacred prostitutes. "Harlot's hires" is an obscure metaphor, however, and verse 7c may be an addition to explain its meaning.

The NIV has given its own interpretation of verse 7d–e. The Hebrew reads, "For from the hire of a harlot she gathers / and to the hire of a harlot they shall return." The meaning of "hire of a harlot" is now different from that of "harlot's hires" in verse 7c: Micah often gives several different meanings to the same terms.

"From the hire of a harlot she gathers" implies the image, used frequently by Hosea, of Israel as Yahweh's harlotrous or adulterous wife, and as in Hosea, "the hire of a harlot" here refers not only to fees from sacred prostitution, but to all that Israel has accumulated from its syncretistic worship, from its unjust commercial practices, and from its faithless reliance on international alliances and deals. Israel, the faithless wife, has gained its wealth and security at the expense of its loyalty to its God.

The final judgment in Yahweh's court case against Israel (see 1:2) is therefore announced: "to the hire of a harlot they shall return." The picture is of the troops of Assyria, invading the capital city and using its treasures to pay prostitutes for their services. Once again, the meaning of "hire of a harlot" has changed. But the picture is of Israel's total defeat. Yahweh comes to do the northern kingdom to death.

---

### Additional Notes §3

---

**1:5** / The Hb. reads "who" instead of **what** and thus personifies the sins of the two kingdoms.

**High place** (1:5e) is plural in the Hb. To preserve the parallelism, the LXX, Syr., and Tg. emend the word to read "sin of," but the MT is clear. Here "high places" has a different meaning than that found in v. 3d and refers to the site of the Jerusalem temple as the place of syncretistic worship.

**1:6** / **Heap:** The word is found only here, in 3:12, in the quotation from Mic. in Jer. 26:18, and in Ps. 79:1. It refers to a site of intentional destruction, as in Josh. 8:28.

## §4 The Prophet's Lament over Samaria (Micah 1:8–9)

**1:8–9** / Micah now breaks into a lament over the destruction of Samaria that he has announced. **Because of this,** because the northern kingdom will be destroyed, he must mourn Israel's fate, stripping himself of his usual clothing, walking about **barefoot,** as was the custom in grief (cf. Isa. 20:2; 2 Sam. 15:30), and crying out with howls like those of jackals at night or with screeches like those of ostriches. (The NIV improperly reads **jackal,** singular, and has **owl** instead of "ostriches.")

But why should Micah mourn the destruction of Samaria's idols and Yahweh's just punishment of its rebellion against his lordship? Is it only because Micah knows that the same fate will come also upon Judah and that the conquering armies of Assyria's Sennacherib will soon be at the gate of Jerusalem also (v. 9d)? Perhaps that is part of the answer, but the full truth is more profound than that.

The OT prophets do not rejoice over God's punishment of their sinful people, and there is no spirit of vengeance in them which makes them cry, "Aha! You got what you deserved!" To the contrary, these men of God agonize over the destruction of their sinful folk. They identify completely with their people, and they constantly intercede with Yahweh to try to turn aside the impending judgment of the covenant people (cf. Amos 7:2, 5; Jer. 7:16; 11:14; 14:11; 15:1). Jeremiah even tries, vainly, to shut up the word of judgment inside himself so he will not have to proclaim it (Jer. 20:7–9). But when Judah's punishment nevertheless must come, Jeremiah weeps bitterly (Jer. 8:22–9:1), just as Isaiah cries out, "How long, O Lord?" (Isa. 6:11) when he hears God's word of ruin, and just as Paul is filled with anguish over the unbelief of his compatriots and wishes he were cut off from Christ for the sake of his fellow Jews (Rom. 9:2–3).

Micah and the other prophets, though dedicated totally to the service of their God, know themselves to be members indissolubly of a community, which not only they love, but also God loves. They know God's judgment is worked on that community not out of vengeance but in grief (cf. Gen. 6:6; Ezek. 18:31–32; Matt. 23:37 and parallel), for love's purpose of making a new people (cf. Matt. 9:16–17; John 12:24). And so the prophets grieve with God over the necessary destruction of his people, which will rid the community of its sinful ways. The sin of Israel does not prevent the prophets from loving Israel. Indeed, it calls forth their empathy and concern and finally heartbreak. Perhaps that is a fact to remember in the midst of the bitter disputes that so often trouble the modern church.

### Additional Note §4

**1:9** / **Wound:** Following the LXX, the noun is read in the singular to accord with the singular adjective.

## §5 The Disaster Approaching Jerusalem (Micah 1:10–16)

The arrangement of the four oracles in this first chapter of Micah's book is done by a masterly hand. The first oracle (vv. 2–5b) has announced Yahweh's descent from the heavenly place because of the sin of the covenant people. The second (vv. 5c–7) has predicted the destruction and fall of the northern kingdom. The third (vv. 8–9) has portrayed the prophet lamenting over the fall of Samaria and has stated that the North's destruction spells disaster also for Judah and Jerusalem. Now this fourth oracle (vv. 10–16) takes up that latter thought and shows how it is so. Unfortunately, the text of this passage is rather badly damaged, sometimes demanding emendation, often remaining obscure in its meaning. Nevertheless, the overall portrayal of the disaster approaching Jerusalem from the west is vivid and overwhelming.

**1:10–12** / All of the eleven cities named in this passage, with the possible exception of **Gath,** are located in a quadrant in the Shephelah, the hill country of some 500 to 1,500 feet elevation that lies between the coastal plain on the west and the mountain ridge of Judah on the east. At least four of the cities were military sites fortified by King Rehoboam to protect Jerusalem from attack from the west (2 Chron. 11:5–12). Certainly all of them would lie in the path of a conqueror advancing upon Jerusalem from the Philistine plain. We do not know the precise location of some of them, and they do not seem to lie along a straight line of march, but surely any advancing enemy would send sorties into cities in the area surrounding his line of advance.

We know both from the OT and from Assyrian annals that when Sennacherib attacked Judah in 701 BC, he conquered forty-six of Judah's cities, deported over 200,000 of Judah's citizens, and exacted an impoverishing tribute from King Hezekiah (2 Kgs. 18:13–16; cf. Isa. 22:1–14). It is probably this attack that lies behind Micah 1:10–16. Here we have a vivid portrayal of Judah's settlements being plucked up one by one by a foreign conqueror. The prophet's eyes dart, as it were, first to one city and then to another. And by the use of skillful wordplays on the cities' names, Micah portrays their ruin.

The somber tone of the poem is immediately sounded by the quotation in verse 10a from David's lament in 2 Samuel 1:20a. In the latter passage, **Gath** is a Philistine city (cf. 1 Sam. 27:1–4), but its location has not been definitely established, and we do not know if it belonged to Judah in the eighth century BC. The import of verse 10a–b seems clear, however. Gath is so stunned by being overrun by foreign troops that even normal mourning rites and weeping cannot be carried out.

The inhabitants of Beth-le-aphrah, whose name the NIV has emended to **Beth Ophrah** (see the RSV), however, have heard the news from Gath and are therefore commanded to begin the lamentation practices of prostrating themselves in the **dust** and of sprinkling dust upon their heads (cf. Josh. 7:6; 1 Sam. 4:12; Job 16:15; Jer. 6:26). Indeed, their very name, ʿaprâ, which sounds very much like ʿoprâ, "dust," depicts the fate that is going to come upon them. It is as if Micah were saying, "In Dustville, roll yourselves in the dust" (Wolff, *Micah the Prophet*, p. 40.

A similar wordplay occurs in verse 11a–b. **Shaphir,** whose location is unknown, sounds like šeper, "beautiful." But far from being beautiful, its inhabitants will be deported **in nakedness and shame. Zaanan,** whose location is also unknown, is so terrified by the advance of the enemy that its troops will not even go out to fight, verse 11c–d, and their fear is captured in the name of their city, which sounds like the Hebrew word for "go out." The same passivity before the enemy is exhibited by Beth-ha-Ezel (**Beth Ezel**), verse 11e–f, whose inhabitants are so engrossed in lamentation rites and mourning that they fail to join in the battle.

Verse 12a–b, concerning **Maroth,** has often been emended, with some manuscript support, to read, "The inhabitants of Maroth *waited for* good." Considering the name of the town sounds like mārōr or mar, meaning "bitter," Micah may be creating a word play: "How can the inhabitants of Evilton hope for good?" (so Wolff). Good cannot come upon Maroth, because "*evil* has *come down* (cf. v. 3) **from the LORD**," verse 12c (RSV). Then there is added in verse 12d what is the most important thought: **to the gate of Jerusalem.** The enemy is picking off these towns one by one *and approaching Jerusalem.* That climactic thought forms the end of the first stanza in this poem and will be paralleled by an address to Jerusalem at the end of the second stanza, verse 16.

**1:13–14** / At the beginning of the second stanza, verse 13, the prophet's imperative to the important city of **Lachish** takes on an ironic tone. A large fortress city (cf. 2 Chron. 11:5–12), Lachish stood on the western edge of the Shephelah, some thirty miles southwest of Jerusalem, guarding the roads into the northern and southern hill country of Judah. Surely Lachish would attempt to halt the advancing enemy! And so Micah bids the inhabitants to harness the horses to the war chariots, using the word play of Lachish, *lakîš*, with *larekeš*, (to the) **team.** But Lachish's military preparations will be in vain, and to rely on them for security is sin in the eyes of God (cf. Isa. 30:16; 31:1; Hos. 10:13; 14:3). Indeed, it was when Israel began to try to fashion its own security apart from Yahweh that its rebellion began and its punishment became inevitable, because those who would save their own lives shall lose them.

Therefore Lachish will have to give "going away gifts" to Moresheth-gath (**Moresheth Gath**), Micah's hometown, which will fall before the enemy's advance, verse 14a–b. The word play is with *môrāšâ*, "farewell gifts," or perhaps with *me'ōrāśâ*, "betrothed," the picture being of the dowry given with a young bride who is leaving her family (Wolff, *Micah the Prophet*, p. 141). Historically, the reference is probably to an indemnity paid to the enemy upon the loss of the town.

Certainly Achzib (**Aczib**), which was northeast of Lachish and whose name sounds like *'akzāb*, "deceitful, disappointing," will be no help to Lachish, nor to the rulers of Judah, verse 14c–e, although why **kings** is in the plural here is unknown. Perhaps it is intended to refer to all of the civil authorities, or to Hezekiah and the kings following after him. The former seems to be the case, since the thought continues into the next verse.

**1:15** / A conqueror will come against **Mareshah**, verse 15a–b, another of the fortified cities to the northeast of Lachish, whose conquest will open the way into the interior of Judah. As a result, Israel's **glory**—i.e., its authorities, its wealth, its soldiers—will all have to flee to **Adullam**, where David once took refuge as a fugitive (1 Sam. 22:1–3). It is notable that the passage begins with a quote from David's lament and here alludes to his flight, bracketing the whole with tones of distress. The NIV has obscured the meaning here, however, by emending the first person, "I will again bring," to third, **he will come.** The RSV has the correct reading.

Because the reading of verse 15a is, "I will again bring a conqueror upon you," switching from the prophet's speech to Yahweh's personal address to the people, the point of the entire oracle is emphasized: The conquest of each of these Judean towns is Yahweh's work—Yahweh's "coming down" to bring judgment upon the covenant folk for their rebellion. Yahweh will use a foreign conqueror, here probably Assyria, to carry out this judgment. But behind the advance of the enemy is Yahweh's hand, stretched out in wrath against his people. No human defense can turn aside that hand, and now it reaches out even to the gates of Jerusalem.

**1:16** / In verse 16, therefore, the prophet takes up the admonition once again, speaking to Jerusalem as to a bereaved mother. Her **children,** that is, the cities just named, are being taken from her. She should therefore enter into **mourning** for them, shaving her head in the custom of one lamenting the dead (cf. Job 1:20; Isa. 22:12; Jer. 7:29; 16:6; Ezek. 7:18; Amos 8:10), and even enlarging that baldness beyond its usual width, to resemble the baldness of an eagle or **vulture.** The inhabitants of the captured cities will be exiled, deported into the foreigner's land, and Jerusalem, the supposed city of "peace," *šālôm,* will be left alone, bereft of her children and waiting for death to strike her also.

## §6 "You Shall Not Covet" (Micah 2:1–3)

The arrangement of Micah's oracles continues to show a careful logic. In chapter 1, Micah has announced that Yahweh's judgment, which will destroy Samaria, will reach also to the gate of Jerusalem (1:9). And he has portrayed the march of a foreign conqueror who captures the towns west of Jerusalem one by one and deports their populations (1:10–16). That conqueror too comes as Yahweh's instrument of judgment against Jerusalem (v. 12), and this oracle now shows why such judgment on Jerusalem is necessary.

**2:1–3** / Most commentators join this short woe oracle to the taunt song and pronouncement of judgment in 2:4–5, because both concern the Judeans' loss of their land. But the opening phrase of verse 4, "in that day," usually marks the beginning of an oracle, and while 1:10–16 reflects the situation of 701 BC, and 2:1–3 possibly comes from the same time, 2:4–5 probably refers to the fall of Jerusalem. To be sure, the whole of 2:1–5 could be directed against the inhabitants not just of Jerusalem but of the forty-six towns of Judah captured by Assyria in 701 BC. But Micah's pronouncements throughout chapter 1 have all found their climax in the fate of Jerusalem, and in my estimation, 2:1–3 and 2:4–5 have to do not with the population of Judah in general but with the inhabitants of the capital city.

The verses in 2:1–3 have the standard form of a woe oracle, which begins with the Hebrew *hôy*, **woe.** This exclamation is followed in the Hebrew by participial phrases that tell over whom the woe is pronounced (**those who . . .**). Their evil deeds are then described, and the judgment of Yahweh is announced. The form is frequently used by the prophets (cf. the whole series of woes in Isa. 5:8–25 and in Hab. 2:12–20; also Isa. 10:1–4; Jer. 22:13–19; Amos 6:1–7). A woe is not, however, simply a cry of distress. *Hôy* is pronounced in mourning over those who are dead (cf. 1 Kgs. 13:30; Jer. 22:18), and thus when Micah exclaims

"Woe" over the citizens of Jerusalem, he is saying that they are as good as dead.

Those addressed by Micah's *hôy* are those in power in the capital, who have the position and authority to fulfill their desires, verse 1. This is the energetic bunch, the Type A personalities, who can make plans and meet goals and subordinate the lives of others to their own as they fulfill their schemes.

Their schemes, moreover, involve always getting more. Not satisfied with the comfort, the power, the property, and the physical and social insulation from others that they already have, they covet the property of their neighbors, verse 2. Thereby they violate God's covenant law and the order that God has established by that law in his covenant community. "You shall not covet your neighbor's house. You shall not covet your neighbor's wife, or his manservant or maidservant, his ox or donkey, or anything that belongs to your neighbor," reads the Decalogue, (Exod. 20:17)—that law that was absolutely basic to Israel's life.

Principally these energetic Jerusalemites want land, for land was the basis for all wealth and all rights in Israel. Those who were free landholders had a place and a voice in Israelite society. Those who had no land were totally dependent on others and were debt-slaves, sharecroppers, or hired workers.

The land had been given to Israel as Yahweh's gift. It never belonged to Israel; it was Yahweh's land (Lev. 25:23). But out of love, Yahweh loaned the land to Israel to live upon, and all families of the covenant people were to share equally in the benefits of that loving loan (cf. 1 Kgs. 21, esp. v. 3). A family's land was its **inheritance** from the Lord, and the ideal was that each person would "sit under his own vine and under his own fig tree" and no one would make them afraid (4:4).

Those whom Micah addresses, however, **plot** how to increase their landholdings, probably by foreclosing on loans (cf. Isa. 5:8) or by corrupt dealings in the courts (cf. Amos 5:12). They lie awake at night **on their beds** and silently plan out their schemes for getting more (cf. Ps. 36:4). As the Bible knows so well, sin starts in the evil imagination of the thoughts of our hearts (Gen. 6:5 RSV; 8:21; Jer. 4:14; Mark 7:20–23 and parallel).

The iniquity of these schemers is therefore deliberate sin, calculated distortion of the Lord's will for this community, planned defiance of covenant law. And they wield enough power and prestige in the Jerusalem community to put their evil will into effect, verse 1.

But human will and power are not ultimate in any community, and therefore, in answer to human plans (v. 1), God has a plan (v. 3). And in judgment upon those who plan evil, God will bring evil (v. 3): The same verb and noun for **plan** and **evil** are used in both verses 1 and 3, but the NIV has obscured this correspondence by translating "evil" in verse 3 with **disaster.** The point is that, as Paul says, God is not mocked, and whatever a person sows, that will he or she also reap (Gal. 6:7–8). Human beings cannot defy God's lordly will for the community, as set forth in his commandments, and go unpunished (cf. 2 Cor. 5:10).

The content of God's judging action is announced in verse 3. Yahweh is planning to fasten evil upon "this family" (NIV: **people**) like a yoke upon their necks, and the Judeans will be unable to remove it. The NIV has very freely translated verse 3. The Hebrew reads, "Behold, I am planning for this family evil / which you shall not remove from your necks / and you will not be able to walk upright / for it will be an evil time." Judging by other passages containing the same thought (Isa. 9:4; 10:27; Jer. 27:8; 28:14; Ezek. 34:27), the evil yoke symbolizes submission to a foreign power. Micah therefore probably has submission to the empire of Assyria in mind.

Jerusalem's punishment will fit its crime. Its citizens have deprived others of their rights and security and life; they will therefore be deprived of theirs. They took away all freedom to live from their compatriots; they will therefore become captive to a conqueror's yoke that will be laid upon them by the Lord.

## §7 A Future Reversal of Fortunes (Micah 2:4–5)

**2:4–5** / While these two verses are joined in the NIV to 2:1–3, and while they are addressed to the powerful oppressors in Jerusalem, as are 2:1–3, rhetorically and historically these verses should be understood as a separate unit.

The time has changed. This brief passage looks to the postexilic time, after Jerusalem has fallen to the Babylonians and after 538 BC, when many of the Babylonian exiles have returned to the land of Palestine. In fact, this passage looks to an indefinite time, to **that day** in God's eschatological future, when God has finally saved his people and established his new community. It looks, as Isaiah puts it (2:12), to that time when "the LORD of hosts has a day / against all that is proud and lofty, / against all that is lifted up and high" (RSV).

**In that day** a **taunt** song will be sung by unknown singers, mimicking the lamentations of those powerful evildoers, mentioned in verses 1–3, who have defrauded others of their land and rights. When the Lord's day comes, the land will no longer belong to such wicked usurpers. Rather, Yahweh will take their land and assign it to "apostates." The NIV reads the latter word as **traitors,** verse 4f, giving a political connotation to the passage. But the *šôbēb* are the "rebellious," the "faithless" (cf. Jer. 49:4), the religiously incorrect.

As for those who defrauded others of their land, they will be given no land at all. Indeed, they will not even have a family member left to represent them in the **assembly** of the people when that portion of the land that is held in common is divided up by lot, verse 5. (For the custom, cf. Ps. 16:6; Amos 7:17.) The implication is that their family will no longer exist.

What this passage pictures, therefore, is God's eschatological reversal of the ways of the world, a reversal so often portrayed throughout the Bible. When God's day comes, and the kingdom of good is set up, then those who were thought to be sinners, but who rely totally on the Lord, will be justified (cf. Luke 18:9–14).

Those who were deemed religiously incorrect, but who cling to God, will be saved (cf. Luke 19:1–10). Those meek who had no power will inherit the earth (Matt. 5:5), and God will dwell with those who are humble and contrite (Isa. 57:15; cf. Zeph. 3:11–13).

> He has scattered the proud in the imagination of
>    their hearts,
> he has put down the mighty from their thrones,
>    and exalted those of low degree;
> he has filled the hungry with good things,
>    and the rich he has sent empty away. (Luke 1:51–53 RSV)

That Magnificat song of prophecy, sung by the virgin Mary, portrays accurately what God will do in that day. And it is that day toward which this passage in Micah points.

## §8 Opposition to the Prophet (Micah 2:6–11)

As the arrangement of chapter 2 now stands, this passage shows the reaction of Micah's listeners to his announcements in both 2:1–3 and 2:4–5. Those to whom he preaches take insulted exception to his words of doom directed against them; this is not an unusual reaction to the words of OT prophets (cf. 1 Kgs. 18:3–4; 19:10; Jer. 11:18–19; 20:1–2; Isa. 50:6, etc.). Persons, especially powerful persons who control others' lives, do not like to hear that their God does not approve of them, nor do they want to know that in the future God will snatch from them their power and prosperity.

**2:6–11** / As the NIV has translated verse 6, it interprets Micah's opponents to be other **prophets** who are preaching false words of weal. But in my estimation that is a misreading. Rather, Micah's adversaries here are the powerful oppressors of verses 1–3 who, despite their greedy covetousness, feel religiously secure. The text of verses 6–7 is badly damaged, but it probably should be read as follows:

"Do not preach," they preach.
  "Do not preach these things (i.e., judgment).
  Disgrace will not overtake us."
Should this [i.e., these things] be said, house of Jacob?
[The opponents are addressing their followers.]
  "Is the spirit of Yahweh impatient?
  Are these things (i.e., judgments) his doings?"
Do not his [emending **my**] words do good
  to him whose works are upright?

The prophet's opponents who utter these words are blind both to the nature of Yahweh and to the character of their own lives. Like so many in our society, they believe that God will always forgive. After all, they have it written in one of their most ancient creeds that the Lord is "the compassionate and gracious God, slow to anger, abounding in love and faithfulness, maintaining love to thousands, and forgiving wickedness, rebellion and sin" (Exod. 34:6–7; Num. 14:18; cf. Deut. 4:31; Neh. 9:17; Ps. 86:15; 103:8; 145:8; Jonah 4:2). Therefore, again like so many in our time, they doubt that such a loving, compassionate God will ever act in judgment against them.

What they have failed to notice, of course, is the last part of their ancient creed: "Yet (God) does not leave the guilty unpunished; he punishes the children and their children for the sin of the fathers to the third and fourth generation" (Exod. 34:7). But then, these prosperous oppressors in Jerusalem do not believe they are guilty. After all, their prosperity and their status are evidences of Yahweh's favor showered upon them (cf. Deut. 28:9–14; 30:9–10; Job 36:11; Ps. 25:12–13; Prov. 13:21). Thus, they count themselves **upright** and religiously secure.

**2:8–9** / Micah replies to his opponents' self-righteous words in verses 8–9 and specifies their wrongdoing. Verse 8 is damaged and unclear, but it probably should be read as in the RSV:

> But you rise against my people as an enemy;
> you strip the robe from the peaceful,
> > from those who pass by trustingly with no thought of war.

The thought is that the rich and powerful seize even the garments of the helpless, permanently confiscating their clothing as pledges on loans, which is a violation of the covenant law (Exod. 22:26; Deut. 24:12–13, 17; Amos 2:8). Or perhaps the reference is to out and out robbery of cloaks and mantels (cf. Ezek. 18:12).

Verse 9 is very clear. The powerful dispossess poor widows of their sheltering **homes** by foreclosing on loans or by simply evicting them with no cause, again a violation of the law (cf. Exod. 22:22; Mark 12:40). The women and their children are thereby left with no claim to property or rights or dignity (*hādār*) in the community. The NIV has translated *hādār* with **blessing,** which is loosely correct, but *hādār* can be connected with the ownership of land (Jer. 3:19).

**2:10–11** / Having specified their sins, Micah therefore once again pronounces judgment on the powerful oppressors who have objected to his preaching of judgment. Because the oppressors have risen up against the people as their enemy, verse 8a, therefore they must now "arise and go," verse 10a (Hebrew):

The NIV has obscured this repetition of the verb. The land cannot be their **resting place,** verse 10b.

Throughout most of the Bible, and specifically throughout the Deuteronomic History (Deuteronomy through 2 Kings), the land of Palestine is characterized as Israel's place of "rest" that Yahweh in his love will give to them (Deut. 12:9; Josh. 21:44; 1 Kgs. 8:56; cf. Heb. 3:11; ch. 4). But now, in wrath, Yahweh will take away their **resting place,** their land, and the reason is given: They have **defiled** the land with their evil deeds, verse 10c–d (cf. Lev. 18:25; Num. 35:34; Deut. 21:23)—made it unholy and "unclean," as the Hebrew text says. The land, however, belongs to Yahweh, and because these Jerusalemites have defied Yahweh, Yahweh will therefore take back the land and remove the polluters of the land from their country.

In verse 11, Micah returns to his original theme of preaching (cf. v. 6) to form the inclusio for the passage. His words are full of sarcasm. Were a prophet to come, proclaiming windy talk *(rûaḥ)* and lies (v. 11b), and promising the people nothing but careless ease, self-centeredness, and drunken dissolution, that would be a prophet of whom Micah's enemies would approve. The religion of Micah's opponents, like so much in our day, is a religion that satisfies self-indulgent needs and asks no responsibility, no righteousness, no commitment to the Lord in return. In a world ruled by Yahweh, the Lord of heaven and earth, those who walk by such shallow religiosity cannot escape Yahweh's judgment.

## §9 The Goal of Yahweh's Action (Micah 2:12–13)

The book of Micah is never content to rest with the message of one historical period or with one manifestation of Yahweh's action. (See the introduction and the comment on 1:2–5b). The preceding oracles have dealt with the fall of Samaria (1:5c–7), with the Assyrian conquest of the Judean towns to the west of Jerusalem (1:10–16), with the threatened fall of Jerusalem (2:1–3, 10), and with the postexilic reversal of the fortunes of the oppressors and the oppressed (2:4–5).

But what is the goal of this history of some two hundred years? Its goal is Yahweh's salvation of his chosen people. Yahweh's intervention, his judgment on the northern and southern kingdoms, his dispossession of the oppressing Jerusalem leaders—all have one purpose: to make a new covenant people. That is what is announced in this oracle of salvation in 2:12–13, and the announcement is couched in the terms of some of Israel's oldest traditions.

**2:12–13** / After the exiles of 721, 597, 587, and 582 BC, Israel's former population is scattered throughout the Fertile Crescent. Yahweh personally announces, in verse 12, however, that none of Israel's survivors will be lost (cf. Luke 15:3–5). Rather, like a shepherd gathering together his dispersed sheep into one fold, Yahweh will gather together all of Israel's remnant (cf. Isa. 43:5–6; Jer. 31:7–10; Ezek. 34:11–16) into one great noisy multitude. So reads the Hebrew of verse 12e.

The depiction of Yahweh as shepherd is one of the oldest images for God in the Bible (cf. Ps. 80:1). It is found repeatedly in the Psalms (23:1; 28:9; 78:52) and in the writings of the prophets (Isa. 40:11; Jer. 23:3), and it is then applied to Christ in the NT (Mark 6:34 and parallel; 14:27 and parallel; John 10:11–17; Heb. 13:20; 1 Pet. 2:25; 5:4; Rev. 7:17). While the figure embodies the thought of tenderness and care (cf. Isa. 40:11), it also serves as a royal image (cf. Ezek. 34:23). Kings in the ancient Near East were

known as the shepherds of their people (cf. Jer. 49:19), and Yahweh, who is Israel's shepherd, is at the same time also Israel's
**king,** as Micah 2:13 goes on to say. (Cf. the hymn, "The King of
Love My Shepherd Is.")

Verse 12 does not say where God's gathering will take place,
but it is clear that the Israelites will be reunited as one people
under the leadership of their shepherd-king Yahweh. The
thought is similar to Paul's, "All Israel will be saved" (Rom. 11:26).

Dispersed Israel is, however, a captive people, subject after
721 first to Assyria, then to Babylonia, and then to Persia. To be
saved by God, they must be released from their captivity (cf. Isa.
61:1). The figure of speech is therefore changed in verse 13. Once
again God takes the initiative and performs the action, but now
God is spoken of as the "wall-breaker" *(pōrēṣ),* the one who
**breaks open** the walls and gates that confine Israel to captivity
(cf. 2 Sam. 5:20; Isa. 45:2; Ps. 107:16). God is the liberator giving
Israel its freedom now as in the past, when Israel was liberated
from slavery in Egypt.

Breaking down the confining enclosure of its captivity,
God then will lead the people out into freedom, going before
them as their king. The figure of Yahweh as the **king** of Israel is
as old as the exodus (Exod. 15:18) and is found prominently in the
theology of Israel's ancient tribal federation during the time of
the Judges (Judg. 8:23; 1 Sam. 8:7). Used frequently in the Psalms
(cf. Pss. 95, 96, 98, 99), the figure is taken up also by the NT and
applied to Christ, especially in the Fourth Gospel.

Throughout Israel's history, Yahweh is said to "go before"
his people, in the pillar of cloud by day and the pillar of fire by
night (Exod. 13:21), enthroned above the ark in the time of the
wilderness wandering (Num. 10:33–36), and during Israel's battles with its enemies (cf. 2 Sam. 5:24). It is perhaps significant
therefore that the NT picks up the same terminology: "But after I
am raised up, I will go before you to Galilee" (Mark 14:28 and
parallels; 16:7 and parallel; Matt. 28:7). Our God, the king of a
gathered and freed people, goes always before us, leading us
toward final salvation in the kingdom of good.

## §10 Judgment on the Legal Butchers (Micah 3:1–4)

It would seem as if 2:12–13 has interrupted the series of judgment oracles that we find in chapters 2 and 3 and that this oracle of judgment in 3:1–4 simply continues the announcements of sins and their punishments that we have seen in 2:1–3, 4–5, and 2:8–11. As a result, many commentators have considered 2:12–13 to be a later editorial insertion unrelated to its context.

But in the sweep of Yahweh's plan in Israel's history, the book of Micah envisions that part of Yahweh's salvation of his people will include the punishment of those who have corrupted its life. The punishment that is announced in 3:4, like 2:4 with its notice of "that day," will also take place at an indefinite time in the future. It will be **then** (v. 4a) and **at that time** (v. 4c). Thus, 3:1–4 is linked in an integral fashion with 2:12–13, and the word "head(s)" in 2:13d and 3:1b joins them linguistically—a joining which the NIV has obscured by translating "heads" with **leaders** in 3:1b. The play on "head(s)" is intentional, however. Yahweh, at the head of his people, leads them into freedom and salvation, but the "heads" of Jacob lead them into death.

**3:1–4** / This oracle is addressed to those who are responsible for legal justice in Jerusalem. In the smaller towns and villages, courts met in the gates of the towns and were composed of the elders among the inhabitants, but in Jerusalem such elders probably were appointed by the crown from among family and clan leaders (cf. Deut. 16:18–20; 2 Chron. 19:4–10).

Their task was to administer *mišpāṭ*, **justice**, verse 1d, which had a broader meaning than in our use of the term. *Mišpāṭ* was not just conformity to legal norms. Rather, *mišpāṭ* was God's order for the covenant community as set forth in the traditions handed down from generation to generation. It was to reflect God's character and commands and was principally designed to restore to their proper place in the community those who had been wronged. Such "justice" was intended to rescue the endangered, and help the hurt, and secure surcease for those suffering violence. Its aim was not only to punish the wrongdoer but to give aid to the innocent. In short, *mišpāṭ* had a "saving" function, as can be seen in sentences such as, "Judge the fatherless" (Isa. 1:17, Hb.), or "He judged the cause of the poor and needy" (Jer. 22:16 RSV). This "saving" function of a judge was the prophetic ideal (cf. Amos 5:15; Isa. 11:3–5; 61:8).

Far from aiding the innocent and punishing the guilty, however, those who were appointed judges in Jerusalem were treating the people like a butcher slaughtering an animal—skinning it and then chopping up its meat to be cooked and eaten. The figure of speech is intended to convey total indifference and violence and self-serving on the part of the judges, and the figure of eating flesh is often used for oppression in the OT (Ps. 14:4; 27:2; Prov. 30:14; Zeph. 3:3).

In the Lord's indefinite time in the future, however, those who have not heeded the plight of the helpless will find themselves without help, and those who have not heard the cry of the needy will receive no answer from the Lord to their cry, verse 4. In the final reckoning of good and evil, "then" and "at that time" the Lord **will hide his face** from the evil judges, that is, God will show no mercy or favor toward them (contrast to Num. 6:25–26). And of course, if God be against us, who can be for us?

## §11 False Prophets and True Prophet (Micah 3:5–8)

**3:5–8** / In many passages in the writings of the classical prophets, we find condemnations of false prophets in Israel, who led the people astray by their preaching (see Jer. 23:9–22; Ezek. 13:1–16). Sometimes the message of such false prophets was in direct contradiction to what the true prophet was proclaiming (see 1 Kgs. 22:5–28; Jer. ch. 28; 29:9–11). Often false prophets were condemned by the classical prophets for their immorality, as is the case in this passage.

Judging from the record that we have, it was not easy for the Israelites to distinguish false prophecy from true. When the people heard two contradictory messages, how were they to judge which was actually the word of the Lord? That is still a dilemma sometimes faced by modern churchgoers. It is the morality of the false prophets that is called into question in this passage. This same issue is what our Lord had in mind when he said, "You will know them by their fruits" (Matt. 7:15–20). Micah's words are probably directed against the members of professional guilds of **prophets** in Jerusalem. It is clear that Micah does not attack the methodology of such prophets. His implication is that previously the professional prophets and seers had valid visions, and the diviners properly read the omens. Later, divination was strongly opposed in Israel (Deut. 18:10–12; Isa. 44:25; 47:12–15), but these words from God in Micah do not call its practice into question. Rather, it is its corruption that is condemned. The seers and the diviners and professional prophets have been given gifts from God, and they have misused them.

It was customary in Israel for prophets to be given gifts and fees in return for their services (1 Sam. 9:8; 1 Kgs. 14:3; 2 Kgs. 4:42; 8:8–9; cf. Luke 10:7; 1 Cor. 9:4–12; 1 Tim. 5:18). The sin of these false prophets, however, is that they are letting the size of the fee determine the content of their prophecy. To those who give them a large fee so that they can eat sumptuously, they preach only **peace** (*šālôm*), predicting that the one inquiring of them will have fullness of life and prosperity and a good future (cf. Jer. 6:14; 8:11–12; 28:8–9; Ezek. 13:10). To those who cannot pay them, they declare only hostility and evil to come, waging **war** against such inquirers by their words, verse 5.

Words were considered powerful forces in Israel; they brought about that of which they spoke. Thus, to falsely prophesy evil against a person was to subject the person to dread and fear of the most ravaging kind, and the false prophets were subjecting the poor to such injury simply out of their own greed and callousness toward their compatriots. Not a word did they say against those leaders and wealthy persons who were dispossessing and oppressing the poor (cf. 2:2, 9; 3:1–3), for the false prophets were of the same ruthless breed. And because their prophecy was untrue, they were leading astray both rich and poor alike, failing to fulfill their God-given task of guiding the people in the Lord's way toward the proper goal. They were perhaps the forerunners of every preacher who would not think of upsetting the largest contributor to the church budget, or of every institution that has named a building after a wealthy scoundrel, or of every university that has given an honorary doctor's degree to an ignorant but generous millionaire.

Because the false prophets have misused and corrupted God's gifts of revelation to them, the gifts will be taken away, and the false prophets will have no further divine illumination given to them, verses 6–7. Instead there will be only **night** and **darkness** like that after the sun has set. The images are intended to emphasize that the false prophets will be unable to see (cf. Isa. 29:18). As in the days of Samuel, the word of the Lord and visions will be rare (1 Sam. 3:1). Or as it was with Saul, the Lord will no longer speak through the **prophets** and **seers** and **diviners** (1 Sam. 28:6, 15). They will, in Amos's words, suffer a famine of the word of the Lord (Amos 8:11–12), and even should they call upon the Lord in truth, the Lord would not **answer** them (cf. 3:4; Isa. 1:15; Jer. 11:11). The God of the Bible makes himself available only to whom he will (cf. Isa. 1:15), and it is with the faithful who are humble and contrite in spirit that God chooses to dwell (cf. Isa. 57:15; Ps. 51:17).

Because the false prophets and diviners and seers will lose their gifts from God, they will be shamed before the people and will cover their lips (the NIV incorrectly reads **faces**), verse 7. To cover the upper lip was a sign of mourning in Israel (Ezek. 24:17, 22) and was a gesture required of lepers (Lev. 13:45), but here it is apparently a sign of shame because the prophets will have nothing to say.

In contrast to the false prophets who will receive nothing from God and who therefore will be powerless, Micah is **filled** with the **power** of God, like an empty container filled to the brim. (Cf. Jeremiah, who is filled with the wrath of God, Jer. 6:11, and with indignation, 15:17.) The Hebrew *wᵉʾûlām ʾānōkî,* "but I," at the beginning of verse 8 is intended to mark the strongest kind of contrast. Micah has been given power by God (cf. Eph. 3:7) to perform his prophetic function; he has been given the divine word, which in its force can be like a hammer shattering rocks (Jer. 23:29) or like a burning fire (Jer. 20:9). And the word that he has been given is a declaration of Jacob's rebellion *(pešaᶜ)* and Israel's **sin** *(ḥēṭʾ)* against the Lord. That word will measure the people's sin against the *mišpāṭ,* justice, of God (see the discussion at 3:1–4), and it will be delivered with **might,** which is the courage to stand firm against all opposition (cf. 1 Thess. 2:2).

Considering the fact that it is God's word with which Micah is filled, many commentators have suggested that verse 8b, concerning the **Spirit,** is a later addition designed to explain the meaning of **power** in 8a. That is probably correct. The Spirit, though frequently mentioned as the source of revelation for the early ninth-century nonwriting prophets, is not the fount of revelation for the classical prophets up until the time of Joel after 500 BC, when it again is prominently connected with prophecy (Joel 2:28). Most of the writing prophets have their words from the gift of the word and not from the inspiration of the Spirit, and the latter really does not play a prominent part in the OT.

Verse 8 is the closest that Micah comes to giving any account of his call to be a prophet; while brief, it has the ring of absolute certainty. Micah is filled with the power inherent in the word of the Lord, that word which cannot be turned back by any human means, but which works in human life until it is fulfilled (cf. Isa. 55:10–11).

## Additional Note §11

**3:5** / The book of Deuteronomy gives two tests by which the judgment between two contradictory messages could be made (Deut. 13:1–3; 18:21–22), and these are still good measures of true preaching and false.

## §12 The Ruin of Zion (Micah 3:9–12)

**3:9–12** / This passage now summarizes what has been said in the preceding two chapters. Once again it is addressed to the judicial officials and leaders of the Jerusalemite community, as was 3:1–4, but **rulers** has a broader meaning here in verse 9 than it had in 3:1. Here not just the judicial leaders are addressed, but all leaders of the community. If we inquire who those might be, Isa. 3:2–3 gives a list: mighty man and soldier, judge and prophet, diviner and elder, captain of fifty and man of rank, counselor and skillful magician and expert in charms—all those who in any way guided the life of the community or had authority over it.

Verse 11 repeats the indictment of the judicial **leaders** which we saw in 3:1–4. (See the comment there.) But their abhorrence of *mišpāṭ*, **justice**, is now attributed to all of Jerusalem's authorities, who abhor God's order and commandments for the community's life and who distort and corrupt every thought and action that is right, that is in accord with God's will.

The leaders of the community, Micah proclaims, build up the city at the cost of **bloodshed** and violence (NIV: **wickedness**), verse 10. We know from 2 Chron. 32:27–30 that King Hezekiah of Judah, in the time of Micah, carried on extensive building projects and had the waters of the Gihon River redirected into an aqueduct in order to furnish Jerusalem with a water supply in time of war (2 Kgs. 20:20; cf. Isa. 7:3). It may be that the reference to building Zion with blood and violence is therefore an allusion to the use of forced labor for such projects (cf. Jer. 22:13–14, 17), although "violence" can also refer to the shattering of people's hopes and security and plans (cf. Mal. 2:16). But the picture is certainly one of forceful destruction of the lives of Jerusalem's ordinary citizens.

Verse 11 repeats the indictments of the judges and **prophets** found in 3:1–4 and 3:5–8. In their greed and avarice, the judges accept bribes (cf. 7:3; Amos 5:12; Isa. 1:23; 5:23), an act specifically forbidden in the covenant law (Exod. 23:8; Deut. 16:18–20). And the prophets are similarly sinful, as has been set forth in 3:5.

Now, however, a new group is included in the indictment. The **priests teach for a price,** verse 11b. It was the responsibility of priests in Israel to teach the *tôrâ* to the populace—not just the law of Yahweh, but the whole of the sacred tradition of Yahweh's words and deeds, handed down through the centuries. From that tradition, Israel's life was given direction and meaning, and the community was knit together by a common knowledge of its God (cf. Hos. 4:1, 6). The priests in Micah's time, however, could not care less. They will teach only if they are paid.

The irony is that all of these greedy and irresponsible leaders of the Jerusalemite community nevertheless profess a pious faith in God. **They lean upon the LORD,** which means that they rely upon God (cf. Isa. 10:20; 50:10; 31:1; 2 Chron. 13:18; 14:11), they count God as their security. They believe that God is in their midst (NIV: **among us**) and that they shall therefore be protected from all harm.

From the beginning of Israel's history, God was present in the midst of the people (Isa. 12:6; Hos. 11:9; Zeph. 3:15, 17; Joel 2:27). Israel was the "visited" people, the people met by God and accompanied by God, and that visitation distinguished Israel from all other peoples on the face of the earth (Exod. 33:16).

This presence of God with this people was symbolized in Israel by the ark of the covenant, which was conceived to be the base of Yahweh's throne. At each end of the ark, there was a cherub with outspread wings, and Yahweh was invisibly enthroned above the cherubim (1 Sam. 4:4). Where the ark was, there was God, and so God's presence accompanied Israel in the wilderness (Num. 14:14), in the conquest of the land (Josh. 3:10–11; Deut. 7:21), and in subsequent warfare (1 Sam. 4:3; Deut. 23:14). When the ark was placed in the holy of holies in the temple on Zion, Yahweh therefore dwelt in the midst of his people (Exod. 25:8, 20–22; cf. Lev. 26:11). No harm could come to them as long as Yahweh was there, they thought (cf. Ps. 46:5).

The difficulty is that the leaders in Micah's time have accepted the doctrine without devoting their hearts to God (cf. Isa. 29:13); they have assumed the truth of Israel's tradition without absorbing anything of the ethic integral to it. They rely on "cheap grace," in which their religion is simply a source of security and comfort, with no thought of responsibility and obedience. Like the people in Jeremiah's time, they think that the presence of Yahweh in the temple will always shield them from harm, no matter how often they disobey God's commandments (Jer. 7:4, 8–11). Their religion has become for them a "den of robbers" (Jer. 7:11; Mark 11:17 and parallels)—a place to hide from the consequences of their evil ways.

What these pious persons forget is that Yahweh's presence in their midst can also be a consuming fire (Heb. 12:29). Yahweh cannot live with sin (Hab. 1:13a–b), and if he is among a "stiff-necked people," he will destroy them (Exod. 33:3, 5). Such, therefore, is the judgment of God in the midst of this people in the time of Micah. Because of the sin of the leaders, the fate of Samaria (1:5c–7) will also be the fate of Jerusalem, verse 12. The **temple** will be destroyed and its **mound** will become a **plowed field.** Jerusalem, with all of its buildings built "with blood," **will become a heap of rubble,** and its site will be **overgrown** by trees and **thickets.** The sin of the few will result in God's destruction of all.

The life of faith, according to the Bible, is never individualistic. While the commandments of God, for example in the Decalogue, are spoken to each individual "you" ("You shall not kill"), and while each individual is required to say "yes" in the depths of his or her heart to the call and demands of God (cf. Ezek. 18), nevertheless the individual is always placed in the context of the community, and when one suffers, all suffer, when one is honored, all rejoice together (1 Cor. 12:26). No one, according to the Scriptures, can be a person of faith all alone, and if we ask, "Am I my brother's keeper?" the Scripture's emphatic response is, "Yes!" We are responsible for one another in the community of faith, and the disobedience of a few, according to Micah 3:12, brings God's judgment on all. Jerusalem will be destroyed. That is the word of the Lord.

The sentence that is pronounced in verse 12 is recalled by the leaders of Jerusalem a century later in the time of Jeremiah (26:16–19, esp. v. 18). The announcement made by Micah has been handed down through the generations. And the truth is that Micah's words in verse 12 were not fulfilled in his time. But God's word continued to work in Israel's history, and it did not return to him void. In 587 BC, the armies of Babylonia destroyed Jerusalem with its temple, and the people mourned:

O God, the nations have invaded your inheritance;
   they have defiled your holy temple,
   they have reduced Jerusalem to rubble.
(Ps. 79:1; cf. Lam.)

---

## Additional Note §12

---

**3:10** / **Who build** is a singular participle in the Hb. but should be read in the pl.

## §13 The Future of Zion (Micah 4:1–5)

As was stated in the introduction (which see), the book of Micah represents Israel's meditation over a period of at least two centuries about its God-given role in the world of nations. In this passage, that meditation with its theological wrestling centers on the future of Jerusalem and Zion. What is the place of Zion, with its temple mount, in the history of nations?

In 3:12 we saw that God was bringing judgment on the holy city because of the sin of its leaders, and that therefore the mount of Zion would be turned into a plowed field and the city of Jerusalem into nothing but a heap of rubble. Such would be the consequences of the sinful work of human beings. But, says this passage, that will not at all be the final result of the work of God. God has further plans beyond destroying the sinful capital city.

Rather, the heap of rubble, with its plowed temple mount, will be transformed by God into the most important mountain in the world. It will become the one site of Yahweh's residence, and the one place from which God will exercise sovereign judgeship over all the nations of the world.

**4:1–5** / This passage is paralleled in Isaiah 2:2–3, with only minor variations, and both Micah and Isaiah are using traditions of long standing in Israel. In Canaanite mythology it was believed that their deities resided on a mountain in the far north. When King David of Judah brought the ark of the covenant to Jerusalem, and when Solomon finally put the ark in the holy of holies in the temple, Yahweh took up residence in that temple, enthroned above the cherubim (1 Sam. 4:4). Jerusalem had been a Canaanite, Jebusite fortress, but when David and Solomon made it their capital, much of the language of Canaanite mythology was preempted by Yahwism. Jerusalem was now the dwelling place of deity. Zion was called the mountain "in the far north" (Ps. 48:2 RSV; cf. NIV footnote). And from that mountain, Yahweh ruled over all other deities in an assembly of the gods (Ps. 82:1–2; 58:1 RSV).

Because Yahweh was present in the temple on Zion, there also existed in Israel the tradition of the invincibility of Zion and Jerusalem (cf. Ps. 46:4–7; 48:3–6; Isa. 10:27b–34; 14:32; 29:8; 30:27–33). The fate of Jerusalem and its temple was therefore closely connected with the sovereignty of God over all nations.

Whether Micah 4:1–5 originated with Isaiah or with Micah, we cannot say. Perhaps both prophets borrowed a common tradition. But certainly those who see the oracle as alien to Micah's thought are in error. It connects directly with the preceding oracle, utilizing the phrase **the mountain** of the house in verse 1 to pick up the thought of 3:12. Yahweh's functions of judging, teaching, and speaking the word are precisely those that have been corrupted by Jerusalem leaders (3:11) and will be exercised rightly by God. The original concern with the **nations,** in 1:2, once again comes to the fore. And the eschatological note of the passage, sounded by **in the last days,** verse 1a, has already been heard in 2:4 ("in that day") and 3:4 ("then"). Certainly the passage, if borrowed, has nevertheless been skillfully woven into its present position.

The oracle announces what will happen "in the latter days" (Hb.; RSV), verse 1a. As with all such introductions to eschatological announcements, the time announced is indeterminate—a time in the future that lies beyond all human possibilities of progress and goodness, but that will come in God's good time. It will be the decisive time when God intervenes to reverse the judgment on his people and to bring salvation not only to Israel but to the world. Israel will not deserve such a future, nor will the nations, but despite their sin God will bring salvation upon them in an act of free mercy.

The ruin that was Zion will become a place of pilgrimage for a multitude of peoples throughout the world, verse 1. They will urge each other to **go up to** (a pilgrimage expression) **the mountain of the LORD,** because Yahweh resides there, and it is there alone that they can hear the Lord's word spoken to them, verse 2. The Israelite custom of pilgrimage to the temple (cf. Ps. 84; 122) will be universalized.

The nations will go up to Zion because they desire to learn how to walk according to Yahweh's *tôrâ* or instruction, in accordance with God's will, verse 2. In short, the nations will come to realize that Yahweh's way alone can bring them satisfactory life, and their pilgrimage will be quite voluntary. A universal conversion to the Yahweh faith is envisioned. However, the nations will go up, not only to worship, but also to learn, in order that they may obey. Faith and life, worship and works belong together, and the nations will render both to the Lord.

In submitting themselves to the rule of Yahweh, the nations will also bring many conflicts and problems with them. Peoples fight for power and territory, for fame and wealth and resources, not only with other nations but also within their own borders among their own citizens. Wherever there is a group of more than two or three people, human conflicts arise. As a result, Yahweh will also act as **judge** over the nations' lives, rendering decisions to settle their differences, verse 3. It was the custom in Israel, when any case was too hard for the local courts of elders in the gates of towns, that the judicial case was taken to the judge or priest in Jerusalem to be decided (Deut. 17:8–11). Yahweh will now act that part from Jerusalem, deciding the **disputes** among all the peoples of the world, verse 3.

So good and just will Yahweh's decisions be that they will find ready acceptance among all the peoples, who will abandon their practice of warfare for evermore. They will turn their weapons of death into agricultural implements productive of life-giving food (cf. Ps. 46:9; 76:3; the image is reversed in Joel 3:10). Universal peace will reign throughout the earth, here concretized in the lovely portrayal of a peasant farmer sitting contentedly **under his own vine and under his own fig tree,** with nothing threatening his existence or making him **afraid** (cf. Lev. 26:6; Jer. 30:10; Ezek. 34:28; 39:26; Zeph. 3:13). God's *šālôm,* God's peace, will come upon the earthly kingdom, even as it is in heaven. The last line of verse 4 makes this picture of universal peace a certain promise for the future, because the mouth of the Lord has spoken the promise, and God always keeps his word.

The book of Micah, like all of the Bible, is utterly realistic, however, and the prophet knows that such universal peace, under God's sovereign rule, is a future, though certain, hope. Verse 5 therefore addresses the present situation in Micah's world— and in ours. At the moment, there is no universal worship and obedience of Yahweh on this planet. The nations give their allegiance to many different **gods** and goddesses. Each of the peoples of the world goes its own way and pursues its own power-struggles for prosperity and security. But knowing the promised outcome of history, Israel's faithful respond liturgically with the words of verse 5c–d: **we will walk in the name of the LORD our God for ever and ever.** God's kingdom of peace will come.

Therefore the faithful will conduct their lives in accordance with the nature of that kingdom that is coming (cf. 2 Pet. 3:11–12; 1 John 3:2–3).

In the NT, Jesus Christ replaces the temple on Zion as the one in whom God is now present and through whom God may be worshiped (John 2:19–21; cf. Mark 14:58; 15:29 and parallel; Acts 6:14). He is the one who is lifted on high, in order to draw all nations to himself (John 12:32). He has become the authority over all peoples (Matt. 28:18), and it is through him that the true word of God is spoken to guide the life of all nations. Indeed, Jesus Christ is the prince of peace, who can bring peace to all (cf. Luke 1:79; 2:14; 19:38; Eph. 2:14–17; Heb. 7:2; Matt. 10:34). At the moment, his lordship is not acknowledged by all nations. But there will come a time, in God's plan for the future, when every knee will bow and every tongue confess that Jesus Christ is Lord, to the glory of God the Father (Phil. 2:9–11). There will be a day when all peoples are united together in Christ (Eph. 1:9–10). That is God's sure promise for the future. Therefore, let us **walk together in the name of the LORD our God for ever and ever.**

## §14 God the Shepherd of Israel (Micah 4:6–8)

**4:6–8** / It is declared in Micah 4:1–5 that in the eschatological future God will rule over the nations of the world from Zion, and that Zion will become the center of the world to which all peoples will stream for worship and instruction. But what of the wounded and scattered people of Israel, who have become like sheep without a shepherd? (For the expression, cf. Num. 27:17; 1 Kgs. 22:17; 2 Chron. 18:16; Zech. 10:2; 13:7; Mark 6:34 and parallel; Matt. 26:31). Yahweh himself has "afflicted" them (RSV; NIV: **brought to grief**) because of their sin against him, verse 6.

It is almost automatic to assign this passage to the time of the Babylonian exile, after 587 BC, but there are other plausible options. Both the exile of the northern tribes to Assyria in 721 BC and the destruction wrought in Judah in 701 BC by the armies of Sennacherib would have produced a situation fitting the description of Israel here. The important point is not so much the time frame of this passage as that it is Yahweh himself who has brought such a fate upon the people.

Nevertheless, Yahweh is still the shepherd of this people, which means that Yahweh is still their king. Kings in the ancient Near East were known as the shepherds of their people (cf. 2 Sam. 5:2; Ezek. 34; 37:24; John 10:11–16; cf. 1 Pet. 2:25; 5:4). And like a good shepherd, the Lord will once more gather the **lame** and scattered "sheep" to form a saved **remnant,** over whom he will rule from Mt. Zion. The Israelites will not only be gathered; they will also be transformed from a weak and helpless scattering of people into a **strong nation,** verse 7, like the "strong nations" who will stream to Zion, 4:3. Israel will no longer be ruled over by the foreign nations; they will be ruled over by their shepherding God. The work of this powerful nation will be depicted in the oracles that follow (4:13; 5:5–6, 7–9).

The concept of a **remnant** in the OT was used by Amos to depict the pitiable remains of the people that would be left after Yahweh's judgment on them (cf. Amos 3:12; 5:3; 6:9; 9:1), but it could also be a term used to promise Yahweh's future salvation (Isa. 11:10–16; 28:5; 37:31–32), as it is here and in Micah 5:7–8; 7:18 (cf. Joel 2:32; Obad. 17; Jer. 23:3–4; 31:7; Ezek. 11:16–20). (It was this latter meaning which led the postexilic community to term itself the remnant, cf. Hag. 1:12, 14; 2:2; Ezra 9:13; Neh. 7:72.)

After punishing the sinful Israelites by wounding and scattering them, God will in time heal and gather and save the remnant of them. God will then **rule over them forever** as their eternal shepherd-king from his dwelling place on **Mt. Zion.** Very likely verse 8 was originally an independent salvation oracle, but in its present position it continues the portrayal of Israel's restoration: her Davidic king will also be restored to rule. The NIV has interpreted verse 8 to portray Jerusalem as a **watchtower** guarding a sheepfold, and the hill of Zion as a **stronghold.** The Hebrew of verse 8 reads, "And you (emphatic), tower of the flock / hill of the daughter of Zion, / to you shall be and come / the former rule, / the kingdom of the daughter of Jerusalem."

In Genesis 35:21, "Tower of the Flock" is the name of a place not far from Jerusalem, but its parallelism with "hill" (NIV: **stronghold**) indicates that it refers here to Mt. Zion, on which Jerusalem was built. A personified Jerusalem is simply being addressed here and told that the dominion that once belonged to the Davidic house will be restored to it.

Such a promise concerning the Davidic kingship is not a contradiction of Yahweh's rule over Israel, but a further affirmation of it. Precisely because Yahweh is king, he can keep his promise to David (2 Sam. 7) that there will never be lacking an heir to sit upon the throne. Yahweh is Lord over the house of David as he is Lord over all the nations.

## §15 The Necessary "Now" (Micah 4:9–10)

With this oracle there begins a three-fold series of announcements, each of which begins with **now**, which tells of Israel's present desperate situation, and which then announces God's deliverance of it (4:9–10; 4:11–13; 5:1–4). The NIV has obscured this structure by omitting the "now" at the beginning of 5:1.

In the preceding oracle of 4:6–8, Yahweh has promised the return of the remnant of the exiles to Zion, his rule over them, and the restoration of the Davidic throne. But there is a "now" in Israel's present that necessarily must take place: Yahweh must deal with its sin (see the introduction). Israel's sin must be done away before Yahweh can fulfill his purpose to be Lord over all.

**4:9–10** / The fall and destruction of Jerusalem were predicted in 3:12. This oracle in 4:9–10 now portrays life in the city shortly before it meets that fate, probably about 588 BC. Outcries of alarm are heard throughout Jerusalem, because the military foe is at the gate, verse 9. But to those outcries, the prophet responds sarcastically (cf. Jer. 8:19). Why do the people cry out? Do they not still have a **king** and **counselor**, a supposedly wise soul to guide their course? The questions are a caustic reference to the fact that the Davidic king, Jehoiachin, was carried into exile (2 Kgs. 24:11–12), and the people are left with the weak and vacillating Babylonian-appointed king, Zedekiah. (For reference to the humiliation of Jehoiachin, see 5:1.)

The prophet therefore urges greater outcry of distress and anguish, like that of a **woman** giving birth to a child, verse 10 (cf. Jer. 4:31), for like a child bursting forth from the womb, the inhabitants of Jerusalem will go forth out of the city into the surrounding fields to be gathered into camping groups for the long exile walk to Babylonia.

**There . . . there**—the repetition of the adverb in lines f and g of verse 10 is deliberate. The implication of the emphasis is, "only there." Only there in Babylonia after great humiliation and defeat, will the inhabitants of Jerusalem be delivered *(nāṣal)* and redeemed *(gāʾal)* by their God. Their old life of injustice and violence, of greed and false piety must be done away by the purging of the exile. Only then can they be returned to their land and be given a new life under their king Yahweh and their Davidic ruler. Israel must undergo its crucifixion before it can experience its resurrection to new life.

But there, then, Yahweh will **redeem** them. "To redeem," according to the Scripture, is to buy back a relative who has fallen into captivity or slavery (cf. Lev. 25:47–55). After dealing with their sin, God will redeem his chosen people once more in a repeat of their first redemption from Egypt.

---

### Additional Note §15

---

**4:10** / The NIV reads **writhe in agony.** The Hb. reads "writhe and *gōḥî*," but the meaning of the second imperative is uncertain. *Gōḥî* can have the meaning of "bring forth" or "burst forth," referring to the bursting forth of water or of an infant from the womb, and probably the word is intended to have such a meaning, consonant with the figure of the woman in labor. The exact expression, however, is obscure.

## §16 Yahweh's Final Lordship (Micah 4:11–13)

While this passage is the second in the three-fold series of **now** oracles (4:9–10; 4:11–13; 5:1–4), it differs from 4:9–10 in that it does not deal with a specific time in Israel's history, either Micah's time (ca. 701 BC) or 587 BC. Rather this is an eschatological oracle that is concerned with God's final battle for supremacy over the world. The eschatological and apocalyptic traditions of the Bible include the view that there will be one last great assault of evil, symbolized by the pagan nations, against God's lordship (Isa. 29:7–8; Ezek. 38–39; Joel 3:16–17; Zech. 14:1–5, 12–15; cf. Isa. 17:12–14; Zech. 12:1–9; Ps. 76:4–9; Rev. 16).

**4:11** / Here in verse 11, **many nations,** whose number is indeterminate and who are not named, want to defeat and defile **Zion,** the "holy" city. (For the designation, see Ps. 2:6; 46:4; 48:1.) If the nations can get rid of Zion, they can get rid of God, for Zion is the dwelling place of Yahweh and is under his protection. Sennacherib of Assyria was called "king of the world" (*ANET,* p. 288, 13–15) in a pride not unfamiliar to ancient emperors (cf. Isa. 14:13–14), and human pride has always wanted to vaunt itself above the sovereignty of God. Indeed, throughout history the efforts of the nations have been directed toward eliminating the Jews, those special people protected by God (cf. Isa. 50:8–9; 54:17). If the Jews can be done away, there is no God. Thus, here the nations set themselves to defeat and defile Zion, the **Daughter of Zion,** the protected people of the holy city.

The NIV reads, **let our eyes gloat over Zion,** verse 11d, but the Hebrew reads, "let our eyes gaze *(ḥāzāh)* upon Zion," and a sexual nuance is intended. The humiliation and defeat of Israel is often pictured in the terms of a woman stripped naked before her lovers or captors (see esp. Nah. 3:5, but also Isa. 47:3; Lam. 1:8; Ezek. 16:37; 23:29; cf. Hos. 2:3; Mic. 1:11; Rev. 3:18). If the daughter of Zion is abandoned to the lust and greed of the nations, her God will be no god.

**4:12–13** / There is, however, one king (4:4) and one Lord of all the earth (4:13), who rules over all peoples and finally determines their destiny. And that king and Lord has a **plan,** verse 12 (*ʿēṣâ;* Isa. 5:19; 19:17; 25:1; 26:10–11; cf. Jer. 29:11; 50:45), for the entire creation, to restore it to the goodness intended from the beginning. Israel is an instrument in God's work, and God works in the lives of all nations to bring his plan to its final goal. The nations think that they have gathered themselves to do away with Israel, but actually it is Yahweh who has gathered them, as a harvester would gather together the **sheaves to the threshing floor.** The supposed self-will of the nations is really the sovereign work of the Lord of all.

In the agricultural simile employed in verses 12–13, Zion is the **threshing floor,** and the threshing ox will be the inhabitants of Zion, who will tread out the grain, that is, the life of the hostile nations arrayed against it. Threshing floors were flat, hard, open surfaces on which the cut grain was spread (1 Chron. 21:20–23). The dried stalks were beaten with flails to separate the grain from the chaff, or a heavy board embedded with sharp stones or metal teeth was dragged across the grain by an ox or donkey. Or, as here in verse 13, the grain was trod out by the hoofs of the beast itself (cf. Deut. 25:4; 1 Cor. 9:9). Israel is here pictured as that beast, and therefore as the instrument of Yahweh's final judgment upon the nations. (Cf. other portrayals of Israel as an instrument of Yahweh's judgment in Isa. 41:15; Jer. 51:20–23; Zech. 12:6; Obad. 18.) The severity of the judgment is stressed by the hardness of Israel's **hoofs of bronze,** and its strength is portrayed by its **horns of iron,** horns being always a symbol of might (cf. Deut. 33:17; Num. 23:22; 1 Kgs. 22:11).

Israel, the daughter of Zion, will trample the nations—not for its own gain or glory, however. Nothing that it gains from their defeat will belong to it. Rather, following the ancient practice of *ḥērem* in the Holy War, all of the ill-gotten booty that the nations have taken from others will be devoted to the Lord. Flammable materials will be offered as a sacrifice, while gold, silver, and other metals will be used in the Lord's temple (Josh. 6:17–19; cf. Deut. 13:15–17; cf. Isa. 60:5–9; Hag. 2:6–8), and Yahweh will reign in victory as the "Adonai of all the earth." The title is used elsewhere in Joshua 3:11, 13; Psalm 97:5 (a psalm celebrating Yahweh's kingship), and Zechariah 4:14 and 6:5 (RSV). Adonai can have the meaning of **lord,** as the NIV translates it, but it also carries the connotation of "master." Having put down all foes, Yahweh Adonai will reign supreme over all the nations of the world. Such is the biblical vision of the God's future kingdom.

---

### Additional Note §16

---

**4:13** / **You will devote:** The MT of the Hb. reads "I will devote," but all of the versions emend the verb to the second person sing.

## §17 The Future Messiah (Micah 5:1–4)

In the previous chapter, 4:6–8 promised the return of a remnant to Zion, Yahweh's rule over them, and the restoration of the Davidic throne. Then there followed with 4:9 a series of three oracles, each beginning with "now," and each portraying Judah's current desperate situation and Yahweh's salvation yet to come. This passage, the third in the series, deals with the restoration of the Davidic throne in fulfillment of 2 Samuel 7:13.

**5:1** / The NIV has obscured the connection of this oracle with the two that precede it by omitting "now" at the beginning of verse 1. The word "now" is probably the only word that can be read with certainty from the Hebrew of verse 1a, however. The remainder of the line is obscure and has been variously emended (see the additional note), but the NIV reading of the line is probably as satisfactory as any. The wording is apparently a call to the inhabitants of Jerusalem to assemble their **troops** in order to turn back the attack of those who are already besieging them. In light of verse 3, which refers to exile (cf. 4:10), the Babylonian siege of Jerusalem in 588 BC is probably intended. However, the humiliation of the king mentioned in verse 1c–d probably has to do with the earlier treatment of the Davidic king, Jehoiachin, who was forced to surrender to Nebuchadnezzar of Babylonia and who was carried into exile in 597 BC (cf. 2 Kgs. 24:10–12). For the humiliating custom of striking **on the cheek,** see Job 16:10; Lam. 3:13; Matt. 26:67; and cf. Luke 22:64; John 18:22; 19:3.

The Davidic line has been humiliated, defeated, and seemingly cut off. But as in Isa. 11:1; Jer. 23:5–6; and Ezek. 34:23; 37:24–25, that is not God's planned ending for the story (cf. the optimistic notice about Jehoiachin in 2 Kgs. 25:27–30). God promised there would always be a Davidic heir to sit upon the throne, and God always keeps his promises.

**5:2** / God will bring forth a new Davidic ruler who will be set to reign over God's people, verse 2. That the new ruler will be of the Davidic line is shown by the fact that he will come from **Bethlehem Ephrathah.** David's father was Jesse, a Bethlehemite (1 Sam. 16:1, 18), and David is called "the son of an Ephrathite of Bethlehem in Judah, named Jesse" in 1 Sam. 17:12 (cf. Ruth 1:2).

**Ephrathah** could be designated a place separated from Bethlehem, as in Psalm 132:6 and Genesis 35:16, so perhaps the name referred to a specific region or district. But in Genesis 35:19 and 48:7 (cf. Ruth 4:11), it is specifically identified with Bethlehem. Thus, perhaps Ephrathah was the district immediately surrounding Bethlehem of Judea. Later it becomes so closely identified with Bethlehem that Matthew 2:6, which quotes Micah 5:2, omits "Ephrathah."

That this new Davidic ruler comes from God and not from the Jerusalem succession of Davidic kings is emphasized, however, by the statement that his tribe or clan, which designated an association of extended families, was one of the smallest in Israel, verse 2b. Similarly humble backgrounds are claimed for Saul (1 Sam. 9:21) and Gideon (Judg. 6:15). Repeatedly the Scripture emphasizes what the Apostle Paul put into words:

> God chose what is weak in the world to shame the strong, God chose what is low and despised in the world, even things that are not, to bring to nothing things that are, so that no human being might boast in the presence of God. (1 Cor. 1:27–29 RSV)

More than that, the **origins** of this ruler promised in Micah 5:2 are **from of old, from ancient times** (verse 2e–f). Two meanings may be implied. First, the origin of the coming ruler is mysterious and beyond human comprehension, because he comes from God. Second, his appearance was planned long ago in the purpose and providence of God. He is not a sudden, spontaneous answer on God's part to Israel's need for rescue. Rather, his rule has been destined from the first in God's plan for his world.

**5:3–4** / When will this Davidic ruler come forth? Verse 3 is intended to answer that question. First will come the tribulation, the punishment for Israel's sins, as previous oracles have made clear. Judah will fall and go into exile (3:9–12). Continuing the figure of the woman in travail (4:10; see the commentary there), the inhabitants of Jerusalem and Judah will go forth, as from the womb, into captivity. Some scholars have speculated that the reference in verse 3b to a woman in labor has in view a specific woman, as in Isaiah 7:14, whose birth of a child will mark the end of Judah's exile. But the meaning is the same as that found in 4:10, where the captured inhabitants of Jerusalem burst forth from the city, like a child bursting forth from the womb, to be gathered into groups for the trek to Babylonia. After the tribulation of the exile, then, the remnant of the people (cf. 4:7) will be returned to Judah, verse 3c–d, to be ruled over by God's future Davidic king or Messiah.

The word "messiah" comes from the Hebrew *māšîaḥ,* which means "anointed." Hebrew kings, along with priests, were anointed with oil for their office, and the Messiah or anointed one, in the OT, is consistently referred to as being of the house of David. When we speak of the Messiah, it is of that future Davidic, anointed ruler that we are speaking. Moreover, the nature of his rule is set forth in the royal psalms (Ps. 2, 18, 20, 21, 45, 72, 101, 110, 132, 144:1–11), which describe not a particular historical occupant of the Davidic throne but the nature of the office itself. Israel constantly looked forward to the coming of a king who would match the description given in the royal psalms, and the future ruler depicted in Micah 5:4 is consistent with that portrayal.

This future Messiah will **stand,** that is, his reign will endure (cf. Ps. 45:6; 72:5, 17; 89:36), just as the word of God is said in Isaiah 40:8 to "stand" forever. He will **shepherd** his people. "His flock" is missing in the Hebrew, but is clearly implied and so is added in most versions. Kings were always referred to in the ancient Near East as the "shepherds" of their people, and so the Messiah will shepherd his people, that is, he will provide for their necessities, guide them in the right paths (cf. Ps. 23:3), and protect them from all harm. But the Messiah will carry out his duties, not by his own strength, but by the strength given him by God (cf. Ps. 18:32–35; 20:6; 21:1; cf. Isa. 11:2), manifesting the lordship or majesty of his God over all.

Because God is Lord of the earth, the Messiah, who rules in the strength of God, will reign over a universal kingdom (Ps. 2:8; 18:43; 72:8; 89:25), and his people will live in security (Hebrew: "dwell") in everlasting fulfillment of 2 Samuel 7:10.

Luke 2:4 and John 7:42 both understand Jesus' birth in Bethlehem of Judea as a fulfillment of this prophecy, and Micah 5:2–4 is quoted from the LXX version in Matthew 2:6. Thus, the Christian church has always understood Jesus Christ to be this Messiah promised by the prophet. Certainly he is the one who rules over all in the power of God. He is the one who manifests the glory and majesty of God. He is the one whose kingdom will endure forever. And he is the one who can give his people that security which the world can neither give nor ever take away.

---

### Additional Note §17

---

**5:1** / **Marshall your troops, O city of troops:** The line has been emended and read in a variety of ways: RSV [MT 4:14]: "Now you are walled about with a wall," following Robinson's emendation of *titgēd<sup>e</sup>rî b<sup>e</sup>gādēr;* Wellhausen, followed by many: "Now you are gashing yourself with gashes," reading *hitgōdēd titgōd<sup>e</sup>dî;* some read "Now gash yourself, daughter of marauders," reading "troops" as "marauders." Gashing was a funerary practice indicating deep lamentation (Jer. 16:6; 41:5). But in Canaanite practice it was used to bring about an ecstatic trance (cf. 1 Kgs. 18:28), and it is specifically forbidden in Deut. 14:1. It is therefore doubtful that "gashing" is here the meaning.

## §18 Delivery from Future Enemies (Micah 5:5–6)

**5:5–6** / The NIV has attached the first line of verse 5 to the foregoing oracle, but in order to do so, it has had to emend the line. The Hebrew does not say, **And he will be their peace.** Rather it reads, "And this shall be peace." The line belongs with this oracle, though indeed "this" refers to the messianic figure of verses 2–4.

There has been much scholarly discussion about the proper interpretation of this brief passage and its relation to 5:2–4. The plural verbs in 5c and 6a conflict with the singular verb in 6c. The military images employed contrast with the peaceful portrait in 5:4. Thus, the questions are, Who will deliver Israel from the Assyrians, and How?

To answer the questions, we must first realize that **Assyria** in verses 5b and 6a does not refer to the historical empire of the eighth and seventh centuries BC. Rather, the word is used in the OT and here in a different sense to stand for any nation that would threaten Israel in the future (cf. Ezra 6:22; Zech. 10:10–11). Such a meaning is supported by the fact that **Nimrod** here is made the poetic parallel to "Assyria." Nimrod is mentioned in Genesis 10:8–12 (cf. 1 Chron. 1:10) as a somewhat legendary figure and "mighty warrior" who was the hero-founder of the great eastern empires that threatened Israel during much of its existence. The intention of verse 6a–b, therefore, is simply to portray any foe who would endanger Israel's life.

Verse 5a can be read, "And this (one) shall be peace," referring back to the messianic king of verses 2–4. It is clear then from verse 6c that this messianic king will be the deliverer of Israel from any future enemy. He will be the one who gives "peace" (*šālôm*), that is, prosperity and wholeness to the nation.

The passage envisions, however, that even under the universal rule of the Messiah, there may yet arise threats to that rule. The kingdom has not come in its fullness, and the Messiah and his people are still challenged by those subversive of his reign. But the messianic king will put down all such challenges, verse 6c.

When the Messiah works such deliverance and establishes peace, a military government made up of Israelite leaders will be set up over the threatening foes to keep them in check, verse 5d–6b. As in Romans 13, government is the instrument to maintain civil order by lawful force. The Messiah alone wins the victory over the assaulting foe; Israel's leaders then keep the continual threats of the foe in check.

## Additional Notes §18

**5:5** / Instead of **we will raise against him,** the verb's meaning here is "we will set over him."

**5:6** / **And the land of Nimrod with drawn sword:** The Hb. reads, "and the land of Nimrod with its gates."

## §19 Israel among the Nations (Micah 5:7–9)

We have in Micah 5:5–9 a series of three brief oracles, each beginning with the Hebrew *waw,* which describe Israel's role among the nations (5:5–6, 7, 8–9), just as before we had a threefold series of oracles, each beginning with "now" and describing Israel's present plight and future deliverance (4:9–10, 11–13; 5:1–4). Thus, 5:7 and 5:8–9 are really separate oracles, but we can treat them together here for the sake of space.

Though we have seen a passage dealing with the messianic king, in 5:2–4, Micah here is not treating the end of history or the eschatological time, as our customary discussions of the Messiah often do. Rather, the prophecy is dealing with the **remnant** of Israel living still in the midst of a threatening world. The kingdom has not yet come. Israel will be delivered and gathered, but its life will still be threatened, and this series of three oracles, 5:5–9, gives reassurance concerning that threat.

**5:7** / The beginning of 5:7 is very similar to the beginning of verse 8, and indeed, the LXX adds "among the nations" to the end of verse 7a in order to emphasize the similarity. The correspondence between the two oracles gives some indication of how the figure of the **dew** is to be interpreted in verse 7. It is not intended as the figure of a beneficial presence of Israel. (Cf. for example, 2 Sam. 17:12.) Rather, the intention is to point to the mysterious, nonhuman origin of the dew, which the Bible considers always to come from God (Judg. 6:36–40; Job 38:28. etc.). A remnant of Israel will survive the exiles of the sixth century BC. Then they will be gathered together and returned to their own country (cf. 4:6–7), once again a people in the midst of the nations. But how they got there and who delivered and gathered them will be utterly mysterious to human beings. In short, their existence and return will be solely the work of Yahweh.

**5:8–9** / The oracle in 5:8–9 then takes up Israel's defense against the nations who still want to do away with it. Just as it will control threatening enemies, according to 5:5–6 (which see), it will also be able to defeat any who lift up their hand against it. Its power will be like that of a **lion** (for the figure, cf. Gen. 49:9; Num. 24:9) in the midst of a sheepfold, fearsome and irresistible, so that all of its enemies will be destroyed. But such power will be given it by God alone. Such is the implication of the joining of verse 7 with verses 8–9. If we take the words of these prophets seriously, then perhaps they should form a warning to all of those who still in our time harbor that antisemitism which wants to get rid of the Jews.

## §20 God's Eschatological Triumph (Micah 5:10–15)

**5:10–15** / This oracle predicts God's final victory over those pagan nations that will threaten Israel's life in the future. (See the commentary on 5:5–6, 7–9.) But above all, it represents God's final triumph over those foreign peoples who will not acknowledge God's lordship. The passage is linked to verse 9b by the verb "cut off" (NIV: **destroy**) in verse 10b, a verb which is then repeated three more times in verses 11–13 in a staccato emphasizing the finality of the destruction wrought by Yahweh.

The oracle closes the section of Micah's prophecies that began with 4:6. Both 4:6 and 5:10 open with the phrase, **in that day.** The whole section, from 4:6 to 5:15, deals with Israel's life among the nations, and it is framed with a beginning (4:6–8) and ending (5:10–15) announcement of Yahweh's eschatological triumph as Lord over all peoples.

The most pressing question concerning this passage is, To whom is it addressed? **You** in verses 10–14 is singular. Does "you" therefore refer to Israel, with the foreign nations mentioned only in verse 15? Or is each one of the foreign nations being addressed here by the Lord?

Most scholars interpret verses 10–14 to refer to Israel. To the contrary, I believe they are addressed to the foreign nations. There is great emphasis in this passage on cultic sins of idolatry, but that form of trespass on the part of Israel has received only slight notice, in 1:7, in Micah's indictment of the people in chapters 1–3. Instead, the concern thus far in Micah has been with Israel's corruption of leaders, judges, priests, and prophets (2:2, 8–11; 3:2–3, 5–6, 9–11). And God's judgment on such corruption has been designed to serve as a witness to the nations of God's lordship (see the comment at 1:5). Thus 5:15 is an announcement of God's **wrath** to be poured out on those foreign **nations** who refuse to accept the import of the witness.

But the foreign nations must also be purged of their idolatry and false trusts before they can become people of the Lord, as foretold in 4:1–4. Their lives are full of false worship of their pagan gods and goddesses and of their reliance on weapons and fortresses to furnish them security. Before Yahweh can convert them all in his final, eschatological establishment of his lordship over all the earth, they must be rid of their dependence on everything but Yahweh.

Yahweh therefore announces that he will destroy their military instruments and fortified cities that they believe will give them safety. He will destroy their sorceries (NIV: **witchcraft**) and soothsayers (NIV reads a verb: **cast spells**), by which they think to manipulate their future. And he will destroy all of their idols—their images, their stone pillars (NIV: **sacred stones**), and their **Asherah poles**—to whom they look for divine guidance and protection.

Sorcery, which involved various kinds of magic and superstition, is often connected in the OT with foreign nations (Exod. 7:11; Isa. 19:3; Dan. 2:2), and Exodus 22:18 in the early book of the covenant already prescribes death for any sorceress. Deuteronomy 18:9–14 urges Israel to shun all such foreign magic as "an abomination" (RSV) to the Lord (cf. 2 Kgs. 17:17; Jer. 27:9; Mal. 3:5; Gal. 5:20; Rev. 18:23; 21:8; 22:15). And Second Isaiah is quite sure that sorcerers have no power to save their people from the judgment of God (47:9, 12).

Divination involved not the casting of spells, as the NIV has it, but the reading of omens to be found in either natural or manufactured phenomena. It sought not to control the future, as did sorcery, but rather to discern it ahead of time. While Israel had diviners (Mic. 3:7; Jer. 27:9; 29:8; Zech. 10:2), it was to rely not on them, but on its God, whose hands held the future. Diviners are included in that list of persons in Deuteronomy 18:9–14 whom Israel is to shun (cf. Ezek. 13:6).

The images, stone pillars, and Asherah poles that Micah 5:13–14 marks for God's destruction were all used in foreign and specifically Canaanite cult practices. Contrary to our usual understanding, it was not believed by the foreign peoples that such idols contained their deities. Rather such objects were considered to be transparent bearers of divine revelation. They marked the sacred spot where the deity was present, and they were transparent objects through which divine revelation was conveyed. Biblical faith, on the other hand, knows that God is not revealed through any object in the natural world, but solely through words and actions within the history and worship of Israel. Thus, Israel was to worship nothing "that is in heaven above, or that is in the earth beneath, or that is in the water under the earth" (Exod. 20:4). To the same imageless, historical faith this oracle in Micah 5:10–15 is therefore calling the foreign nations of the world. And those that will not heed Yahweh's witness in word and action will be destroyed.

God's **vengeance** in this passage, however, is not the exercise of some wrathful punishment, wrought by a rejected deity, but the exercise of lordship. As Ezekiel 20:33 has it, Yahweh declares, "surely with a mighty hand and an outstretched arm, and with wrath poured out, I will be king over you." Yahweh will be king, Lord of all the earth, sovereign ruler of every nation. And Yahweh will destroy every false trust and idolatrous worship that challenges that kingship, in order finally that all peoples may walk in his way in a kingdom where "every man will sit under his own vine and under his own fig tree, and no one will make them afraid" (Mic. 4:4). Such is the future vision toward which this oracle in 5:10–15 points.

## §21 Israel Called to Court (Micah 6:1–8)

Chapter 6 begins the third section of the prophecies of Micah, each of which opens with an imperative to "hear." The first "hear!" was a command to all the peoples of the earth (1:2), the second to the leaders of Israel (3:1). The third is now directed to the Israelite populace as a whole (6:1) and forms a command to listen to all that follows in chapters 6–7.

Scholars differ as to whether 6:1–8 is a unit or whether two separate oracles, verses 1–5 and 6–8, are involved. Certainly the two parts are very different in form. Verses 1b–5 are clearly a covenant lawsuit or *rîb*, in which Yahweh presents his complaint against his covenant people (**his people,** v. 2c, **my people,** verses 3a and 5a) before a jury made up of the **mountains** and **everlasting foundations** of the earth, verse 2a–b. (For other such covenant lawsuits in the prophetic writings, see e.g., Hos. 4:1–6; Jer. 2:4–13, and especially Isa. 41:21–29; 43:8–13; 5:20–25.) Verses 6–8, on the other hand, take the form of a torah instruction, in which the prophet sets forth Yahweh's teaching, here in answer to an inquiry made by an unknown speaker for the people. (For the form, see Isa. 1:10–17.)

The disparate forms must be regarded as two parts of one pericope, however, for two reasons. First, verse 1b–c is a command to Israel to present its case, and the representative of Israel does not speak until verse 6: The prophet would never speak in such an imperative to Yahweh! Second, the court case is not complete without the specific indictment of Israel in verse 8, which states what Israel was supposed to do and yet did not do. Thus, though the two parts of 6:1–8 are different, they belong together.

**6:1–2** / Just as the two earlier sections of the book have dealt with Yahweh's universal rule, so here the whole of creation—the heights (**mountains**) and depths (**everlasting foundations**) of nature are involved. The **foundations of the earth** are

the pillars that anchor it in the nether world of the primeval sea
(cf. 2 Sam. 22:16; Job 38:4; Ps. 104:5), and they, with the mountains, are summoned to hear, as either witnesses or jury, Yahweh's case against his covenant people, verse 2.

**6:3–5** / Beginning in verse 3, the Lord then addresses
the people directly, asking them how he has "wearied" (NIV:
**burdened**) them and demanding an answer to the question. The
verb can be read "burdened" (cf. Isa. 43:22–23), but here its meaning is "to exhaust the patience of," as in Isaiah 7:13. We do not
know Israel's specific situation when this oracle was delivered,
but it is in trouble, and its patience is exhausted, waiting for God
to deliver it.

To turn back the charge, Yahweh first of all demands of
Israel, **Answer me,** that is, say specifically how Yahweh has "wearied" Israel. Through the prophet Micah, the Lord personally
confronts Israel, one of the features found throughout the prophetic writings that make them so powerful. There is no indirect
mediation of Yahweh's voice here, no dream or vision or angel.
No, the prophets come before their people as poets of the highest
quality, and it is their word from God of direct address that is
important. It is spoken directly to the people, and it demands an
answer. Israel cannot turn aside from that word. It can not hedge
or rationalize. It is met, confronted, spoken to face to face, as it
were, and its reply is expected. "Prepare to meet your God, O
Israel!" (Amos 4:12)—that is what comes to pass when the Lord
speaks through the OT prophets.

But to answer the accusations of the Israelites in this court
case, Yahweh recounts four of the principal events in Israel's
history when the people were saved, verses 4–5. Yahweh **redeemed** them from bondage in **Egypt,** that is, Yahweh acknowledged Israel and paid a ransom price to buy back Israel his child
from slavery. Yahweh sent **Moses** to convey the covenant law to
the people, gave them **Aaron** the priest to atone for their sins
before the altar, and raised up **Miriam** as a prophetess among
them (Exod. 15:20; this is a unique emphasis on the role of
Miriam, v. 4).

Further, God foiled the attempt of **Balak** and **Baalam** to
bring the destruction of a curse upon Israel (Num. 22–24), remaining always true to the promise to Abraham (Num. 22:12;
23:8, 19–20; 24:9; Gen. 12:2; cf. Mic. 7:20). And God led Israel
safely across the Jordan from their camp in **Shittim** (Josh. 2:1; 3:1)

to their first encampment in the promised land at Gilgal (Josh. 4:19), verse 5. Yet, Israel is wearily impatient with Yahweh, believing that he is not the God who saves!

In short, Israel has forgotten. It has not remembered, and therefore it no longer knows who its God is and what God's character and will are. To **remember**, in OT parlance, is not simply to recall something, but to experience it as present event. Through past actions in Israel's history, Yahweh's character and will have been made known. And by remembering those actions, Israel can "know" God, it can experience God's presence and be assured of God's present power and desire to save it. It can know God's "saving acts" (NIV: **righteous acts**), God's *ṣidqôt*. "Righteous acts" and "saving acts" are actually identical, for God's "righteousness" which consists in the "salvation" of Israel, is the fulfillment of his covenant relation with his people. "To be righteous" in the OT is to fulfill the demands of a relationship. Thus, if Israel will "remember" God's saving deeds toward it, those deeds will become contemporary for it; it will "know" God present in its life; and it will no longer be impatiently weary, waiting for God's deliverance.

But Israel will not remember. Israel is the guilty party in this court case. Indeed, it has not only lost its faith by failing to remember; it has also violated Yahweh's covenant requirements. It is the latter which the next verses, 6–8, make clear.

**6:6–7** / An unknown speaker, representing the people, takes up the legal dialogue in verse 6 and gives a counter-argument to what Yahweh has said in verses 3–5. But the presuppositions of that counterargument are amazing. Israel still has not understood that the fault lies not with God, but with itself. And so in what is perhaps intended to be an exasperated tone, Israel's speaker asks how on earth it can make things right with this God. Its situation is apparently desperate, and it needs God's saving deliverance, so how can it appease this God and get him to come to its aid?

Should Israel offer a burnt offering, an *ʿôlâ*, in which the whole sacrificial animal was burnt and its pleasing odor (cf. Gen. 8:21) sent up by fire to God? Or perhaps God would prefer that **calves a year old** be sacrificed. Certainly they were more valuable than newborn calves (cf. Lev. 22:27).

The growing exasperation of the speaker is mirrored in the exaggerated magnificence of the suggested offering. Would

Yahweh be satisfied with **thousands of rams,** like those that Solomon is said to have sacrificed (1 Kgs. 8:63; cf. 3:4)? Or perhaps God would prefer olive **oil,** that precious substance that gave Israel food and healing and delight, poured out in immeasurable abundance. And then, the final sarcasm and disgust of the speaker is shown by the suggestion that perhaps Israel should sacrifice its **firstborn** children to this God who seems so implacable. Child sacrifice was never required in Israel (cf. Gen. 22:1–18; Exod. 34:20), it was specifically forbidden by law (Lev. 18:21; 20:2–5; Deut. 18:10), and it was condemned in the strongest terms by the prophets (Jer. 7:31; 19:5; Ezek. 16:20–21; 20:26; Isa. 57:5) as a pagan practice (cf. 2 Kgs. 3:27; 16:3; 21:6). The implication is that the Israelite speaker knows such prohibitions of child sacrifice, but is sarcastically maintaining that nothing whatsoever can please God.

**6:8** / Yahweh's answer to such blasphemy is spoken through Micah. God **has showed** Israel **what is good,** verse 8. Through all the long centuries of Israel's prophetic and cultic activity, carried by story in its oral traditions and set down in its written narratives, God's will has been shown to his people and made very clear (cf. Luke 16:31; John 5:45–47). That will is **what is good,** and it is good because it is the will of Yahweh, the Lord and redeemer of Israel's life. There is no other good outside of God, no virtue, no ideology, no civil, political or religious scheme that can qualify unless it accords with God's desire for human life. Thus, the Israelite speaker is addressed here as ʾādām, **man,** mortal, creature before the creator and subject totally to the creator's definitions of good. God has created human life on this earth, and as its creator, God alone can say what and how it should be lived.

But the Lord is a "gracious God and merciful, slow to anger, and abounding in steadfast love" (Jonah 4:2 RSV; cf. Exod. 34:6; Num. 14:18; Ps. 86:5, 15; Joel 2:13; Mic. 7:18), and so once more God spells out the "good" requirements for his impatient and exasperated people's communion with him, verse 8, telling them that this is what he is "seeking" or "looking for" (Hb. dôrēš, **require** NIV). God wants them to "do mišpāṭ," which the NIV has translated as **act justly.** The phrase can indicate the performance of justice within a court of law, and certainly that meaning is included here, in accord with Micah's earlier statements (cf. 2:2, 9; 3:1–3, 10–11). But in this generalized setting, the phrase means to set up every area of Israel's life in accord with God's will, and not according to human advantage, comfort, or desire. The "just" society is one in which God's *order* for human life is established.

The second requirement then follows naturally—"to love *ḥesed*," which the NIV translates **to love mercy.** It is possible to translate the Hebrew noun with "mercy," but *ḥesed's* meaning goes far beyond that. *Ḥesed* is "covenant love," being bound together in solidarity with both God and human beings, so that community is established between poor and rich, weak and strong, female and male, slave and free, alien and Israelite (cf. Gal. 3:28), and all care for one another in mutual respect and protection and sharing. *Ḥesed* binds people together as one in the bundle of life, so that God is not worshiped and obeyed apart from concern for one's fellow human being (cf. Matt. 5:23–24; Gal. 5:14; 6:2). That is the community solidarity that Israel is to "love"—the verb is *ʾāhab*, which is used of the deepest love of a wife for her husband or of a child for his or her parent.

The third "good" that God expects from the Israelites in his covenant relation with them is **to walk humbly with your God.** "To walk with God" means to live with God in constant communion. Here, the nature of that walk is characterized by the hiphil infinitive absolute, *haṣnēaʿ*, which is translated as the adverb "humbly" in the English. More is involved in the word's meaning than simply our thoughts of "modest," "lowly," or "self–effacing," as in Isa. 57:15 or 66:2, though certainly that meaning is included here over against Israel's exasperated blasphemy against its God. It has had the audacity to quarrel and become impatient with this Lord of its life! But the meaning of "humbly" here can also be "attentive," "paying attention to," "watching" Yahweh during their journey together. Walking humbly with God is living from God's word and not one's own, paying attention to God's will and not following one's own desires, turning one's eyes to God as a servant turns his or her eyes to the master (cf. Ps. 123:2) for guidance, approbation, and correction. It is such a humble walk with God that makes it possible to act justly and to love *ḥesed,* and thus this requirement sums up the other two. Israel is put in its place here and shown to be lacking. These are the things it should have done but has not done. It stands indicted at the bar of God and can make no further reply.

This instruction is aimed entirely at Israel in this passage, and **man** is not to be taken in a general sense to include all of humanity, as many have interpreted it. These are requirements laid upon those who stand in covenant with the Lord witnessed to in Old Testament and New. Thus, they are just as surely requirements laid upon the church of Jesus Christ, the people of the new covenant in him.

## §22 A Horror among the Nations (Micah 6:9–16)

**6:9–12** / This is a rather difficult text because of obscurities, possible displacement of some lines, and confusion of the person, gender, and number of some pronouns and verbs. Most commentators see verse 9b as a scribal gloss. Many follow the LXX suggestion and read "Hear, O tribe, and assembly of the city" for verse 9c. The same commentators then rearrange the lines, so that the relative pronoun (*ᵃšer*) at the beginning of verse 12 has as its antecedent "city" in the emended 9c. The order thus becomes: 9a, 9c, 12, 10, 11, 13–16. While accepting the suggested emendation of 9c, we shall leave the order of the lines as they stand in the MT. On the whole, the general meaning of this oracle is clear.

This passage follows immediately after 6:6–8, in which justice, community solidarity, and careful attention to Yahweh's will have been set forth as the marks of covenant faithfulness. This oracle shows that such marks are sadly lacking among the inhabitants of Jerusalem.

Those accused are the leaders of the city (v. 9c RSV), the rich (v. 12), and the commercial dealers (v. 11). But the inhabitants of Jerusalem also come in for their share of the condemnation. Wickedness rules, and Yahweh cannot abide it, verse 11 (cf. Hab. 1:13; Jer. 7:16–20; Isa. 9:12, 17, 21). When grain is measured out for sale, the **ephah**, which contained approximately three-eighths to two-thirds of a bushel, is made too small, verse 10 (cf. Amos 8:5). When silver is weighed on balance **scales**, the balance requires too much, or the waiting purse is filled with stones as well as with money, verse 11 (cf. Deut. 25:13–16; Lev. 19:35–36). This is "violence" against the well-being and status of the citizens, verse 12. The rich have become wealthy with **ill-gotten treasures** (v. 10), with lies and with deceit (v. 12).

**6:13–15** / Therefore, Yahweh's judgment has begun to come upon the city, apparently by siege or military invasion, and

most likely from the Babylonians, verse 13. As the northern
kingdom fell because of the sins of Omri (1 Kgs. 16:25–33) and of
Ahab (1 Kgs. 21), so too the southern kingdom of Judah will be
destroyed. The so-called "futility curses" in verses 14–15 are
traditional covenant curses that fall upon the perpetrator when
the covenant requirements are not met (cf. Deut. 28:30–31,
38–40; Lev. 26:26), and some forms of them are frequently used
by the prophets (cf. Hos. 4:10; 9:11–12, 16; Amos 5:11; Zeph. 1:13;
Hag. 1:6).

**6:16** / The NIV has somewhat obscured the meaning of
verse 16d–e. The Hebrew reads, "Therefore I will make you a
horror / and your inhabitants a hissing / and the shame of my
people you shall bear." The full sense of the line is clear if we
remember that God promised Abraham that Abraham's descendants would be a source of blessing for all the families of the earth
(Gen. 12:3). Micah is redacted with that promise very much in
mind (cf. the introduction and comments at 6:5 and 7:20). Instead, because of its sins and God's punishment of them, Israel
will become a source of horror and hissing among the nations
(Jer. 18:16; 19:8; 25:9, 15–18; 29:18; cf. Ps. 44:13; Jer. 51:51). The
peoples will turn away from Israel, horrified at the awful destruction that has come upon it and hissing (we would say "booing")
its manner of life, which has necessitated such calamity. Such
scornful hooting is perhaps that same reaction that the secular
world has to the church when the community that is supposed to
be the body of Christ fails to live up to its covenant with its Lord
or the degeneracy of one of its leaders is exposed.

---

### Additional Notes §22

**6:9c** / **Heed the rod and the One who appointed it:** The NIV
footnote indicates the meaning of the Hb. is uncertain. The RSV reads
*môʿēd hāʿîr* for "assembly of the city." We have no historical record of
such an assembly, however.

**6:16f.** / **You will bear the scorn of the nations:** The NIV has
emended the line. The MT reads: "And the shame of my people you
(masculine sing.) shall bear." Is that addressed to an individual leader or
king, who will share the shame that will come upon all the people? The
emendation solves the problem.

The same dilemma surrounds the whole of v. 16, however. In the MT, line a is addressed to an individual, line c (which the NIV emends) has a pl. masculine verb ("they have walked"), line d is addressed to a masculine individual, line f has a masculine sing. verb. The exact addressees escape us, and so we resort to emendations.

## §23 Jerusalem Mourns Its Sin (Micah 7:1–7)

Chapters 6 and 7 in Micah form a dialogue between God and the people, and specifically between God and Jerusalem. In the court case of 6:1–8, we saw an exasperated and impatient Israel indicted by God. In support of that indictment, the sins of Jerusalem were specified by the Lord, in 6:9–16. Now, in 7:1–7, a repentant Jerusalem recognizes its sinfulness, mourns the anarchic state of its society, and turns to its one source of hope, its Lord. Some commentators maintain that the prophet is the mourner in this passage, but it is rather Jerusalem who laments here, preparing the way for the oracles of trust and salvation that follow in the chapter.

**7:1–2** / The NIV, following the lead of many commentators, emends verse 1 with participles (**one who gathers**), but the emendation is not necessary. The MT reads, "Woe is me! / for I have become like the harvest of summer fruit, / like grapes left after the gleaning [cf. the RSV]. There is no cluster left to eat, / (no) early fruit that my soul longs for." The picture is of a personified Jerusalem after fields and vineyards have been stripped of their fruit at the harvest. There is nothing left, no good morsel to nourish and to satisfy.

That portrayal then becomes the metaphor for the condition of the city. There is no **godly** person (cf. Isa. 57:1), no **upright** citizen, no one left in all of Judah who practices covenant love (*ḥesed*) toward God or human beings, verse 2 (see the comment at 6:8). Instead, each person looks only to his or her own interest, violating the code of neighborly consideration. Rulers demand **gifts** in exchange for their favors, judges ask for **bribes**, the **powerful** act only as whim and desire dictate, verse 3. Even the best of them is like a prickly thorn in a **thorn hedge** that can wound and tear, verse 4a–b (cf. Ezek. 2:6; 28:24). As a result, the day announced by their watchman, the prophet, has come, the day of their punishment (cf. Isa. 10:3; Hos. 9:7) and **confusion**, verse 4c–d (cf. Isa. 22:5). (For prophets as **watchmen**, see Ezek. 3:17; 33:7; Hos. 9:8; cf. Isa. 56:10; Jer. 6:17.)

**7:3–6** / Verses 3 and 4 deal with the corruption of public officials. Verses 5 and 6 turn to the corruption present in the closest and most intimate relationships with neighbors, friends, wife, and family. (Cf. Jer. 9:4; Ezek. 22:7.) No one can be trusted, not even the slaves (**members**, v. 6d) in one's **household**. The bonds of community, of covenant faithfulness, are totally missing. Personified Jerusalem here admits and mourns that those relationships of *ḥesed* that are "good," according to 6:8, and that God requires of it, are totally missing from its life. The passage bears the closest relationship to the court case of 6:1–8 and especially to the requirements of 6:8. Seemingly, Jerusalem's situation is hopeless. It has nothing within its life to nourish its well-being (cf. v. 1). It has reaped only the fruit of its own faithless doing.

**7:7** / But Jerusalem has another helper beyond the society and sin of human beings. Unfettered by the people's perfidy, God reigns and is at work. And a lamenting and repenting Jerusalem finally turns around and faces God, verse 7. **But as for me,** it says, in the text's strong contrast to what has gone before, "I will look to the LORD" (RSV; NIV: **keep watch**). Jerusalem knows that, despite all, God is still its Lord (note the pronoun, **my**). It will turn from its evil ways and direct its gaze toward its God (cf. Hab. 2:1). The attitude is one of searching expectation, looking for God to act.

Then Jerusalem will wait, wait for God's action (cf. Ps. 130:5; Isa. 25:9; 40:31 RSV), patiently, confidently, without any of its former exasperation (see the comment at 6:6–7). It will wait for the God of its salvation. (The NIV incorrectly reads **God my Savior.**) It does not know when God will act on its behalf, but it trusts that God will, and its final affirmation is **My God will hear me** (cf. Ps. 4:3; Mal. 3:16). God is a listening God (cf. Jer. 8:6a) who hears when the faithful ask for help (cf. Ps. 10:17; 31:22; 55:17, etc.) and who acts to rescue them.

## Additional Notes §23

**7:3** / **Both hands are skilled in doing evil:** The MT is corrupt, reading, "For evil are their hands diligently." The NIV probably conveys the intended meaning.

**Gifts** is not in the MT and must be supplied.

**7:4** / The NIV has freely interpreted the line, which reads, "the day of your watchmen, your punishment, has come." "Your" in the line is a masculine sing. suffix, which must be emended to the feminine pl. (see the RSV).

**7:5** / **Her who lies in your embrace:** Some question whether the reference is to a "wife" or simply to a lover.

**7:6** / **Members of his own household:** This phrase usually refers to slaves. Cf. Gen. 17:23, 27; 39:14; Job 19:15.

## §24 Jerusalem's Song of Trust (Micah 7:8–10)

Ever since Hermann Gunkel of Germany in 1924 characterized Micah 7:8–20 as a prophetic liturgy, this oracle has been
treated as the opening piece of that unit. But this brief passage,
which in its tone so much resembles songs of trust found in the
Psalter (cf. Ps. 4; 11; 16; 23; 27:1–6; 52; 131), should not be interpreted apart from what has gone before in 6:1–7:7.

The setting of the court case (6:1–8) continues. Israel has
been indicted (6:1–8); its sins, specified by the sins of Jerusalem, have been set forth (6:9–16); Jerusalem has recognized
and lamented those sins (7:1–7) and turned to Yahweh as its
only possible savior (7:7). And in that turning lies Jerusalem's
hope and the certainty of its salvation (7:8–10), for whoever
comes to the Lord will not be cast out (John 6:37). "As a father
pities his children, / so the LORD pities whose who fear him"
(Ps. 103:13).

**7:8–10** / Jerusalem, in its new trust in God, can admonish its enemy not to **gloat** over its downfall (7:8), for though it
has been brought low in the present, it will in God's future once
again rise in victory over those who have defeated it and taunted
it (vv. 8, 10). The gloating of Jerusalem's enemy over its downfall
reminds the reader of the boasting and ravaging of Jerusalem
carried on by the Edomites after the city fell to the Babylonians
in 587 BC (Obad. 11–14), but that does not mean that this passage
necessarily dates from that time. Its date is unspecified and it
could as well remind the alert reader of the mocking of Jesus at
his crucifixion (Mark 15:29–32 and parallels; cf. Ps. 22:7). The
taunt of the enemy always is **Where is the LORD your God?** (Mic.
7:10; cf. Ps. 42:3, 10; 79:10; 115:2). "He trusts in God; let God
deliver him now, if he desires him" (Matt. 27:43 RSV). God is
powerless, the enemy thinks, unable to fulfill his word or to save
the elected one, whom he has professed to love (cf. Num. 14:16;
Deut. 9:28; 2 Kgs. 18:35).

What the enemy does not know is that *they* have not caused Jerusalem's downfall. *God* has caused it as the punishment for Israel's sin, and that event which the nations think is the proof of God's powerlessness is rather a testimony to God's sovereignty over all the nations. That is what Jerusalem confesses in verse 9. It has sinned, and God has exercised wrathful judgment against it. God's judgment has been entirely just (cf. Ps. 51:4). So too in the NT, those who put Jesus to death do not know that what they consider to be *their* act is rather God's act for the salvation of the world (cf. John 11:50–52; 3:16; 12:32).

According to the Scripture, however, God's judgment of the people is intended to lead to their salvation (cf. Ps. 51:7–8; Hos. 3:4–5). Jerusalem also knows that in Micah 7. And so beyond its indictment and punishment, Jerusalem looks for God's justification of it, verse 9. Its covenant with God still stands. And God will act in **righteousness** toward it, that is, God will faithfully fulfill the covenant promise to bring it out of its present darkness into a marvelous **light** in the future (cf. 1 Pet. 2:9). Then its enemies will see its salvation, and they will recognize that God has delivered his people, and they will be ashamed, verse 10 (v. 16; cf. Obad. 10).

Then what has been done to Jerusalem will be done to its enemies (cf. Lam. 1:22; Obad. 15), who will be trodden down **like mire** (or mud) **in the streets.** The latter is a traditional phrase in the OT to represent the total defeat of those who have opposed Israel and its God (cf. 2 Sam. 22:43 // Ps. 18:42). But as we shall see, the defeat of Jerusalem's enemies is also not God's last word. God works for the salvation not only of Jerusalem and Israel but also of the world (cf. 7:17).

## §25 The New Jerusalem (Micah 7:11–13)

This brief oracle promises the fulfillment of the trust and hope expressed in 7:8–10. A new Jerusalem will be built **in that day** (v. 12), in the eschatological time of God's future, and its land will be greatly enlarged. We are not told who speaks here, but we can assume that the dialogue between God and Jerusalem, which began in 6:1, continues. This is the Lord's promise to Jerusalem that a new day will dawn upon Israel. Zion's walls were razed in its destruction (cf. 2 Kgs. 25:10; Ps. 80:12; 89:40), but they will be rebuilt, establishing Zion once again as a community. In some of the prophetic promises, it is said that foreigners will rebuild the city's walls (Isa. 60:10). Other passages speak of God's work alone (Ps. 51:18; 69:35; 102:16; cf. 147:2). But certainly the reconstruction is part of God's eschatological salvation of his people (Jer. 31:38).

**7:11–13** / Verse 11b is somewhat obscure in the Hebrew, but the NIV has rendered the meaning that is commonly accepted. Implicit in the line, however, is a concept of salvation that is common to the OT. The root meaning of the verb "to save" (*yāšaᶜ*) in the Hebrew is "to make wide," "spacious," "to place in freedom." Salvation in OT thought often connotes having "broadness" or "room to live." Thus, Yahweh tells Moses that Israel is entering into a "broad land" (Exod. 3:8 RSV). David sings, "He brought me forth into a broad place" (2 Sam. 22:20), and in 2 Sam. 22:37 (RSV), "Thou didst give a wide place for my steps under me." "Thou hast given me room when I was in distress," prays the Psalmist (Ps. 4:1 RSV), or again, "thou hast set my feet in a broad place" (Ps. 31:8 RSV). And Elihu, in Job 36:16 (RSV), describes Job's former blessedness thus: "(God) also allured you out of distress into a broad place where there was no cramping." So the prophets portray Israel's future salvation in terms of having room to stretch out and to live (Isa. 54:2–3; Zech. 2:4–5), and Micah here utilizes that conception. The thought is not simply of

Israel's expanded territory, though that is included (cf. v. 14). Rather, Israel, we might say, will experience "the wideness of God's mercy," the freeing, liberating expanse of its future salvation.

In verse 12, then, Jerusalem is further promised that its dispersed people will return to it from all over the earth. The promise is similar to that given in 4:6 and is a common feature in eschatological promises (cf. Isa. 11:11–12; 27:12; 56:8; Zech. 10:8–10). The foreign nations, however, who have opposed God's work in Israel, will be destroyed and their lands made desolate, verse 13. The promise continues the thought of 7:10, but more than that, we have once again an echo of God's promise to Abraham in Genesis 12:3. (Cf. the commentary at 6:5, 16.) "I will bless those who bless you, / and whoever curses you I will curse." Finally the nations' fate, like ours, will be determined by their attitude toward the descendants of Abraham.

---

### Additional Note §25

---

**7:12** / **In that day people will come to you:** The MT reads, "he will come to you," but following the LXX, it should be emended to "they will come to you." The NIV has substituted "people" for "they."

## §26 Israel's New View of the Nations (Micah 7:14–17)

There is some question about how this passage is to be interpreted. Hillers, Mays, and Wolff all take the verses to make up a communal prayer of lament to Yahweh, like the communal laments found in Psalms 44, 74, 79, 80, and 83. As a result, "you" in line 15a is taken to refer to Yahweh, and the following lines are read as jussives: "let us see . . . ," 15b; "May the nations see . . . ," 16a; "Let them lay . . . ," 16c; "Let them lick . . . ," 17a; "Let them come trembling . . . ," 17c.

But the NIV has wisely separated verse 15 from what precedes and what follows it, to indicate the structure of a dialogue, and that is what we have here—the continuation of the dialogue between Jerusalem and its God that began in 6:1 and that has gone on through all the following oracles.

**7:14** / Verse 14 is the prayer of Jerusalem, directed by the people to their shepherd-king, Yahweh. (On the king as a shepherd of the people, see the comment at 5:4.) We do not know the historical situation of Israel that lies behind the prayer, but it is obvious from the prayer's content that the people are confined to a scrubby wasteland (**forest;** cf. Isa. 7:23–25; Mic. 3:12), without good land for flocks or farms. Their prayer, therefore, is that their shepherd once again grant them fertile pasturelands like they had in **Bashan** and **Gilead** before those territories were lost to the Assyrians in 721 BC.

**7:15** / Verse 15 is a reply to the prayer: Yahweh will once again show to the nations **wonders,** great saving events (cf. Exod. 15:11; Deut. 26:8; Neh. 9:17 RSV; Ps. 78:4, many references), like the wonder of the exodus when Israel came out from its slavery in Egypt.

**7:16–17** / Jerusalem replies in verses 16 and 17, and the important fact to note is its change in attitude toward the foreign nations. Earlier in this extended dialogue of chapters 6–7, Jerusalem looked forward to the shaming and utter defeat of its enemies, 7:10. In that verse, the nations would be shamed when they saw the restoration of the people of Israel, 7:8–9. Now, however, in 7:16, the nations will experience shame when they see the wonders that Yahweh works. To be sure, those wonders still involve the salvation of Israel, but the gaze has shifted from Israel to God. Now the nations see Yahweh at work and realize that their **power** is as nothing compared to God's. They will be overwhelmed, as if struck dumb and **deaf**, verse 16. And it is not before Israel that they will cringe in the dust (cf. trampled like mire, v. 10), making obeisance before one who has conquered them (cf. Ps. 2:11–12 RSV). Rather, it is to Yahweh that they will bow down **in fear**, that is, in awe and obedience.

Israel has begun to realize here that its salvation by God will serve a greater purpose than simply its own exaltation and the restoration of its life. Its salvation will have something to do with the salvation of all peoples, who will themselves finally turn to worship the one true God. Thus, this new response by Jerusalem/Israel prepares the way for the climax of the book in verse 20.

---

### Additional Notes §26

**7:15** / **When you came out of Egypt:** It is never said in the OT that Yahweh "came out" from Egypt, but the verb is often used of Israel's exodus. Cf. Exod. 13:3; 23:15; Ps. 114:1, etc.

**I will show them my wonders:** The MT reads "him" instead of "them" and has been emended by the NIV.

## §27 The Incomparable God of Forgiveness (Micah 7:18–20)

The dialogue between God and the people of Israel, personified in the figure of Jerusalem, that began with 6:1, now comes to an end, with Israel "lost in wonder, love, and praise." Who is a God like you? Jerusalem exclaims, verse 18a. The question is often expressed in wonder in the OT, but often too the answer is that Yahweh is incomparable because he does glorious and mighty deeds (Exod. 15:11; cf. Ps. 77:13), because he delivers from threatening death (Ps. 71:20), because he comes to the aid of the weak, poor, and needy (Ps. 35:10; 113:7), or because he is more powerful than all other gods (Ps. 89:6). Here, however, Israel exclaims that God is incomparable because God forgives sin. It is not might, nor wonders, nor succor that finally make God absolutely unique. Rather, Yahweh is qualitatively different from all other gods and human beings and things because, having great power, Yahweh also faithfully forgives humankind. With justification, Micah would say, the Christian faith has put the cross, the symbol of triumph over and forgiveness of all sin, at the center of its worship.

**7:18–20** / The three most frequently used words for sin are employed in verses 18 and 19: *ʿāwōn*, which includes the thought of guilt and crime, and which the NIV has translated with **sin** or **iniquities,** verses 18b and 19c; *pešaʿ*, which comes from political usage and means "rebellion," but which the NIV has weakly translated with **transgression,** verse 18b; and *ḥēṭʾ*, which can have the meaning of missing the mark or falling short, and which the NIV also translates with **sins,** verse 19b. Thus, the passage intends to deal with every form of sinfulness.

God **pardons** *ʿāwōn*, verse 18b; and passes over (NIV: **forgives**) *pešaʿ*, verse 18b; he treads *ʿāwōn* **underfoot,** verse 19b; and hurls *ḥēṭʾ* **into the depths of the sea,** verse 19c. By using the four verbs to describe God's treatment of sin, the message is conveyed that sin is utterly removed from God's sight—passed over of no longer any importance, or violently trampled into pieces in the dust, or sunk like a stone in the depths of the sea.

Why does God do such acts of forgiveness? Because of God's delight to show *ḥesed,* covenant faithfulness (NIV: **mercy**), verse 18e. In other words, above all else, God wants to remain faithful to his covenant with his people. The Lord loves his chosen folk, and though they have been reduced to a **remnant,** they are God's **inheritance** (v. 18c), a special people, bound to God since the days of the fathers by his choice and love of them (cf. Exod. 19:5–6; Gen. 12:1–3; 17:7). Thus, God will **not stay angry** with them forever, verse 18d, a statement which reminds us of Psalm 103:9–13. God may visit the sins of the fathers upon the third and the fourth generation, but God's steadfast, covenant love endures for thousands of generations (cf. Exod. 20:5–6). And so God will have **compassion** *(rāḥam)* upon Israel, a word used to denote the tender, unconditional love of a mother for the child of her womb *(reḥem).*

This passage does not concern Israel alone, however. The NIV and most commentators emend the possessive pronoun in verse 19c to read, "you will cast *our* iniquities into the depths of the sea." That is not what the MT text says. It reads, "their iniquities," and what the verse is saying is that not only will Israel be forgiven, but also the foreign nations who will turn to Yahweh (v. 17), will have their sins sunk like a stone in the sea. Just as Israel cannot approach its God, unless God forgives its sins, so too other peoples cannot approach and worship the Lord unless they are forgiven also. Micah looks forward to the time when Yahweh will reign as Lord over all the earth (4:2, 7; 5:4), and that reign will be made possible by Yahweh's universal forgiveness of the nations as well as of Israel. The message of the cross and resurrection of Jesus Christ encompasses that universality.

The final word of Micah, therefore, is that God will be true to the promise to Jacob and show covenant faithfulness *(ḥesed;* NIV: **mercy**) to the descendants of **Abraham,** as was promised in the days of those patriarchs. God promised Abraham that his descendants would be the means through which God would bring blessing on all the families of the earth (Gen. 12:3; 18:18; 22:18; 26:4), and that promise was renewed for both Isaac (Gen. 26:3) and Jacob (Gen. 28:14). Micah therefore foresees the time when the undeserved forgiveness and salvation of Israel will result in all peoples turning to Yahweh as their sole Lord in worship and obedience. When the nations see what God does in Israel, they too will give their allegiance to Israel's Lord. Two centuries later, Second Isaiah sang the same song (Isa. 52:13–53:12). But Micah begins the song of wonder and praise in this final word of his prophecy.

# For Further Reading

Achtemeier, E. *The Community and Message of Isaiah 56–66.* Minneapolis: Augsburg, 1982.

_____. *Jeremiah.* Knox Preaching Guides. Atlanta: John Knox, 1987.

Allen, L. C. *The Books of Joel, Obadiah, Jonah, and Micah.* Grand Rapids: Eerdmans, 1976.

Bewer, J. A. *Commentary on Joel: A Critical and Exegetical Commentary on Micah, Zephaniah, Nahum, Habbakuk, Obadiah, and Joel.* Edinburgh: T. & T. Clark, 1911.

Brettler, M. C. "The Book of Joel." *The Harper's Bible Dictionary.* Pages 495–96. San Francisco: Harper & Row, 1985.

Calvin, J. *Joel, Amos, Obadiah.* Volume 2 of *Commentaries on the Twelve Minor Prophets.* Edinburgh: Calvin Translation Society, 1846.

Childs, B. S. *Introduction to the Old Testament as Scripture.* Philadelphia: Fortress, 1979.

Driver, S. R. *The Books of Joel and Amos.* The Cambridge Bible for Schools and Colleges. Cambridge: Cambridge University Press, 1901.

Ellul, J. *The Judgment of Jonah.* Trans. G. W. Bromiley. Grand Rapids: Wm. B. Eerdmans, 1971.

Fretheim, T. E. *The Message of Jonah: A Theological Commentary.* Minneapolis: Augsburg, 1977.

Hanson, P. *The Dawn of Apocalyptic: The Historical and Sociological Roots of Jewish Apocalyptic Eschatology.* Revised edition. Philadelphia: Fortress, 1979.

Hillers, D. R. *Micah.* Hermeneia. Philadelphia: Fortress, 1984.

Limburg, J. *Jonah.* OTL. Westminster/John Knox, 1993.

Mays, J. L. *Amos.* Philadelphia: Westminster, 1969.

_____. *Hosea.* OTL. 1969. Reprint; London: SCM, 1984.

_____. *Micah.* OTL. Philadelphia: Westminster, 1976.

_____. "Words about the Words of Amos. Recent Study of the Book of Amos." *Interpretation* 13 (July 1959), pp. 259–72.

Muilenburg, J. "Book of Obadiah." *The Interpreter's Dictionary of the Bible.* Volume 3, pages 578–79. New York, Nashville: Abingdon, 1962.

Rad, G. von. *Deuteronomy.* OTL. Philadelphia: Westminster, 1966.
————. *Old Testament Theology.* 2 volumes. New York: Harper, 1962–1965.
Smith, G. A. *The Book of the Twelve Prophets.* Volume 1. Revised edition. New York: Harper & Bros., 1928.
Stade, B. "Bemerkungen über das Buch Micha." *Zeitschrift für die alttestamentliche Wissenschaft* 1 (1881), pp. 161–72.
Stuart, D. K. *Hosea–Jonah.* WBC. Waco, Texas: Word, 1987.
Thompson, J. A. "The Book of Obadiah. Introduction and Exegesis." *The Interpreter's Bible.* Volume 6, pages 857–67. Nashville: Abingdon, 1956.
Thompson, J. A. and Norman F. Langford. "The Book of Joel." *The Interpreter's Bible.* Volume 6, pages 727–60. Nashville: Abingdon, 1956.
Ward, J. M. *Hosea: A Theological Commentary.* New York: Harper & Row, 1966.
Watts, J. D. W. *The Books of Joel, Obadiah, Jonah, Nahum, Habakkuk, and Zephaniah.* The Cambridge Bible Commentary on the New English Bible. Cambridge: Cambridge University Press, 1975.
Westermann, C. *Basic Forms of Prophetic Speech.* Philadelphia: Westminster, 1967.
Wolff, H. W. *Hosea.* Trans. G. Stansell. Hermeneia. Philadelphia: Fortress, 1974.
————. *Joel and Amos.* Trans. W. Janzen, et al. Hermeneia. Philadelphia: Fortress, 1977.
————. *Micah the Prophet.* Trans. R. D. Gehrke. Philadelphia: Fortress, 1981.

# Subject Index

# Scripture Index

## OTHER ANCIENT WRITINGS